# AMPHIBIANS AND REPTILES
# OF THE GREAT LAKES REGION

GREAT LAKES ENVIRONMENT

*A Focus on Peatlands and Peat Mosses*
  Howard Crum (Warren H. Wagner, Jr., Series Editor)

*Ancient Life of the Great Lakes Basin: Precambrian to Pleistocene*
  J. Alan Holman

*Insects of the Great Lakes Region*
  Gary A. Dunn

*Butterflies of the Great Lakes Region*
  Matthew M. Douglas and Jonathan M. Douglas

*Amphibians and Reptiles of the Great Lakes Region, Revised Edition*
  James H. Harding and David A. Mifsud

*Mammals of the Great Lakes Region: 3rd Edition*
  Allen Kurta

# AMPHIBIANS AND REPTILES
## of the Great Lakes Region

### REVISED EDITION

JAMES H. HARDING

AND

DAVID A. MIFSUD

University of Michigan Press
Ann Arbor

Published in the United States of America by
The University of Michigan Press
Manufactured in China
⊗ Printed on acid-free paper

2020   2019   2018   2017      4   3   2   1

A CIP catalog record for this book is available from the British Library.

ISBN: 978-0-472-07338-2 (hardcover : alk. paper)
ISBN: 978-0-472-05338-4 (paperback : alk. paper)
ISBN: 978-0-472-12263-9 (e-book)

# PREFACE

This book is intended as a guide to the identification, distribution, and life history of the amphibians and reptiles of the Great Lakes drainage basin. Included in this area is the entire state of Michigan and portions of Ohio, Indiana, Illinois, Wisconsin, Minnesota, New York, Pennsylvania, and the province of Ontario. Emphasis is placed on the recognition and general distribution of species known to occur in this region, along with a summary of their habitats, seasonal cycles, behavior, reproduction, and interrelationships with other organisms, including humans. Notes on relative abundance, population trends, and conservation are also included. This book is intended as a reference for the nonspecialist, although the summaries of life history information should prove useful to professional herpetologists as well.

Amphibians and reptiles have historically been held in lower public esteem than their fellow vertebrates, the fishes, birds, and mammals. When asked to rank their greatest fears, many people put snakes near the top of the list. Broad public sympathy for preserving rare species of birds and mammals is rarely extended to scaly or slimy creatures. Prior to the mid-twentieth century, amphibians and reptiles were frequently assumed to be comparatively insignificant members of most North American wildlife communities, even by some biologists. Not surprisingly, these animals were often ignored or even persecuted by wildlife managers in the Great Lakes region and elsewhere. Research over the last several decades has led to a better understanding of the critical ecological roles that these animals play in nature. We now realize that preserving amphibian and reptile species and populations is an essential and worthy conservation goal. It is hoped that this volume will assist citizens and private and government resource managers in making wise decisions affecting the future of the Great Lakes herpetofauna.

# ACKNOWLEDGMENTS

In compiling the information presented in this book, an extensive and growing literature on the herpetology of the Great Lakes area was consulted. The results of ecological, distributional, and taxonomic studies on amphibians and reptiles are reported in a variety of professional print and online journals and have been summarized in various popular, semipopular, and regional publications. Published sources of information consulted during the writing of this book are listed in the "Resources" section. Major North American herpetological organizations and their publications are also listed in that section. Many colleagues familiar with the regional herpetofauna were consulted during the preparation of both the original and this revised edition of the book, and we are grateful for their assistance and advice.

Deserving special mention, the late J. Alan Holman offered constant encouragement, as well as stimulating discussions on paleoherpetology and postglacial amphibian and reptile distributions; the late James Fowler Sr. freely shared his vast field experience and knowledge of herpetological literature. Peter Wilson has offered, and continues to offer, valued companionship and critical assistance during field surveys and research forays. Many people kindly shared published and unpublished distributional or biological data and/or offered valued comments on portions of the text or range maps; these include Tom Anton, Richard Bartlett, Ellin Beltz, Tom Beauvais, the late John Behler, James Bogart, Alvin Breisch, Kevin Brewster, Bob Brodman, Ronald Brooks, William Brown, Craig Campbell, Gary Casper, Philip Cochran, the late Joseph Collins, the late Roger Conant, Justin Congdon, Francis Cook, Jeff Davis, the late Michael Ewert, Jason Folt, J. Whitfield Gibbons, James Gillingham, David Good, Carol Hall, Lisa Hallock, Dennis Herman, David Hillis, Bob Johnson, John Kaufmann, Michael Klemens, Sarabeth Klueh-Mundy, William H. "Marty" Martin, Tim Matson, Dave Mauger, the late C. J. "Jack" McCoy, Kenneth Mierzwa, the late Sherman Minton, John Moriarty, Andrew Myers, Michael Oldham, Gregory Pauly, Chris Phillips, John G. Phillips, Robert Powell, Alan Resetar, Stephen Ross, Douglas Rossman, Jeffrey Rowell, Ryne Rutherford, Al Sandilands,

Lori Sargent, Raymond Saumure, Frederick Schueler, Mark Sellers, Chris Smith, Kenneth Storey, Gordon Ultsch, Leni Wilsmann, and Sean Zera. Kraig Adler, the late Charles Cleland, S. Blair Hedges, the late J. Alan and Margaret Holman, and Ronald Richards provided information on paleontological and archaeological questions. Supplemental information on the laws and regulations of their respective states was supplied by Alvin Breisch (New York), Ned Fogle, Lori Sargent and Tom Goniea (Michigan), Bob Hay (Wisconsin), David Ross (Ohio), Clark Shiffer (Pennsylvania), and Catherine Smith (Indiana). Advice on photographing amphibians and reptiles was given by Larry West and Bill Leonard. Travis Taggart kindly provided the regional base maps. Kristine Morrissey assisted with word processing and computer problems for the first edition, while Maegan Stapleton provided indispensable help with organization and technology for the present edition. Russ Burke, Jim McGrath, and Wayne VanDevender provided specimens for photography. To all these friends and colleagues, and to any we may have inadvertently missed, please accept our heartfelt thanks for your many kindnesses. A number of people kindly provided photographic materials, and these individuals are credited adjacent to each photograph. Photographs not otherwise credited were taken by the senior author. Line art, figures 1–11, was contributed by J. Alan Holman, Gijsbert van Frankenhuyzen, and Tricia Brockman.

Scientific and common names of amphibians and reptiles used in this book are largely based on Crother 2012, with some exceptions, noted on pages 10–14.

We are grateful to the editors and staff of the University of Michigan Press for their patience and enthusiasm for this project. Harding extends a special note of appreciation to his parents for their toleration and support during a herpetologically oriented childhood and to his wife Shirley and daughters Alissa and Laura for their love, understanding, and tolerance during the preparation of this book. Mifsud would like to thank his mother Mary Mifsud, whose encouragement, love, and support will always be appreciated, and to his late grandfather Manuel Freeson, whose patience, kindness, and inquisitive nature helped the author to pursue his passion for herpetology. He would also like to thank his family and friends who have served as a source of inspiration and encouragement throughout his career

Inevitably in a book of this nature, information will become outdated or be superseded by continued research, and also as inevitably, errors of interpretation, omission, or transcription will occur. Readers are encouraged to bring any errors or new information to the attention of the authors.

# HOW TO USE THIS BOOK

This book is divided into three parts. First is a general introduction to herpetology. Here we consider the defining attributes, paleohistory, and taxonomy of amphibians and reptiles and present a classification and checklist of all Great Lakes species. Special focus is placed on the role of amphibians and reptiles in the ecosystem, their interactions with humans, and factors involved in making prudent decisions about their conservation. The climatic and vegetational history of the Great Lakes region during and since the Pleistocene epoch ("Ice Age") is discussed in an attempt to explain the present distribution of amphibians and reptiles in the area.

The second part presents an introduction to the major groups (orders) of amphibians and reptiles and a separate account of each species known to naturally occur within the Great Lakes basin. Some species have been divided into subspecies, and these are noted and described wherever this is relevant to the region. Species occurring close to the accepted boundaries of the basin, and those that have been reported therein only as isolated specimens but are not yet known to breed within the basin, are briefly described under "Marginal and Questionable Species." Each account includes one or more photographs of representative specimens and a range map showing the species' or subspecies' known Great Lakes distribution. Also included is a smaller map showing the overall North American distribution of the species concerned. Note that each species can be expected to occur only in specific habitats, which usually occupy a very small portion of the indicated range. The range maps are provided as a guide to the historical distribution of amphibian and reptile species in the Great Lakes basin and should be interpreted in conjunction with the comments under "Distribution and Status" in each account. Due to changes in habitats caused by human activities, such as agricultural development, timber harvesting, urbanization, and direct exploitation, the portion of the historical range presently occupied by each species will inevitably be smaller than that shown on these maps and in some cases drastically less for threatened or endangered species.

Each species account is divided into sections providing the following information.

**Description:** Identifying characteristics are given for adults of each species (and subspecies) and for juveniles if they differ from adults. Notable differences between the sexes are also described. The breeding calls and certain other vocalizations of frogs and toads are described. Identifying characteristics are noted for many amphibian eggs and larvae, although identification of larval amphibians can be difficult even for professional herpetologists. Watermolen (1995) has published a key to eggs and egg masses of Wisconsin amphibians, and identification keys to amphibian larvae can be found in works by Minton (2001) and Hoverman et al. (2015) for Indiana, Watermolen and Gilbertson (1996) for Wisconsin, Altig et al. (2015) for all U.S. tadpoles, and Petranka (1998) for all U.S. salamanders.

Each species' size is given as a range, usually the minimum size at sexual maturity to the maximum known size, based on published sources. All measurements are expressed in metric units, with English equivalents in parentheses. (Standard abbreviations are used.) Unless stated otherwise, sizes are expressed as total length (tip of the snout to the tail tip). Frogs and toads are measured from the snout to the vent (anal opening), which is equivalent to the total head-body length. Turtle size is the length of the carapace as measured in a straight line down the middle (not following the curve) from front to back. Because lizards frequently lose portions of their tails, the maximum head-body length (measured from snout to the vent) is included along with the total length measurements. If a species has been divided into named subspecies (see p. 8), those known to occur in the Great Lakes drainage basin are described in the species accounts.

**Confusing Species:** Characters are given to distinguish the species in question from other species that are similar in appearance.

**Distribution and Status:** The historical geographic range is described, and relative abundance and recent population trends are noted. Legal status, current at time of writing (2016), is noted for species on "official" state or provincial lists of threatened or endangered species. However, note that these terms may have very different meanings and legal implications from one state or province to another and that these listings frequently change. Persons doing field research or needing to handle amphibians or reptiles should always contact the wildlife resource agency for the state or province in question for the latest regulations and permitting rules.

Note: The term *local* is used to describe a species that tends to occur in isolated populations or special habitat types surrounded by areas that are either lacking in suitable habitat or where the species has been extirpated. A *locally common* species is one that may exist in fairly large numbers within small and/or isolated geographic areas. A species described as *uncommon and local* or *rare and local* tends to exist in low or very low numbers within very small and/or isolated geographic areas.

**Habitat and Ecology:** The preferred habitat of each species or subspecies is described, and its general behavior, feeding habits, predators, and defenses are discussed.

**Reproduction and Growth:** This section discusses breeding seasons, courtship behavior, nesting and egg laying, hatching or birth, early growth, age at maturity, and life span, if known.

**Conservation:** Here the animal's relationship with humans is discussed, with comments on economic importance, population trends, threats posed by human activities, and possible management strategies.

The third part, "Resources," includes a bibliography of books, articles, Web resources, and other important information sources on Great Lakes amphibians and reptiles, many of which were consulted during the preparation of this book. Readers wishing additional information on Great Lakes area amphibians and reptiles can consult these works and the literature cited therein. Key references that can assist in literature reviews are given at the end of the introduction for each order or suborder. Major international (North American–based) herpetological societies and a prominent regional society are noted.

A glossary of selected terms is included at the end of the book.

# CONTENTS

# Introduction to Herpetology

## Definitions and Origins

Herpetology is the branch of biology concerned with the study of amphibians and reptiles. *Herpetology* comes from the Greek word *herpeton,* meaning "something that crawls," and *logos,* meaning "word," and thus, by extension, "to study." A biologist who specializes in the study of these animals is a *herpetologist,* while the word *herpetofauna* refers to the amphibians and reptiles living in a specified geographic area. The word *herps* is sometimes used as a shortened, informal way of saying "amphibians and reptiles." Amphibians (Class Amphibia) include the frogs and toads (collectively called anurans), salamanders, and the legless, tropical caecilians. The reptiles (Class Reptilia) traditionally include the turtles and tortoises, crocodilians, lizards, snakes, and the tuatara of New Zealand. (As we will see, a good argument can be made for including birds in the Reptilia, but we will use the traditional definition for purposes of this book.) Both classes also include a large number of extinct forms known only from fossils. That these two classes of animals are grouped together in the same scientific discipline is more a product of tradition than biology. Certain amphibians and reptiles may display a superficial resemblance to one another (especially salamanders and lizards), but there are significant differences between the two groups. In their physical structure and reproductive biology, the reptiles are more similar to birds and mammals than they are to amphibians.

Amphibians and reptiles are vertebrates and, like other vertebrate groups (i.e., fishes, birds, and mammals) have backbones and an internal bony skeleton. (Some fishes, such as sharks, have a skeleton that is mostly cartilage.) Amphibians and reptiles are ectothermic, a word meaning "outside heat" that is used to denote animals that lack internal temperature regulation and depend on outside sources of heat (such as sunlight) to warm their bodies. Such animals are often called "cold-blooded" but this can be a misleading term—a turtle or lizard basking in the sun on a warm day is not "cold." Birds and mammals are endothermic (meaning "inside heat") since they can produce heat within their bodies and usually maintain a relatively constant body temperature.

Amphibians are characterized by moist skins, which may be smooth or warty but are not covered with scales, feathers, or hair. They do not have true claws on their feet. Amphibian skin contains numerous mucous glands, which secrete substances to protect the animal from desiccation. Other skin glands can produce distasteful or toxic substances to repel predators. Although most adult amphibians have lungs, much of their respiration is through the skin, and water is readily absorbed or lost through the skin as well. For this reason, the great majority of amphibian species live in moist or wet environments.

The word *amphibian* comes from Greek words that mean "double life." This refers to the fact that many amphibians lay small, unshelled eggs that are deposited and fertilized in water. These hatch into aquatic larvae that breathe with gills (fig. 1). After a variable period of time living underwater, the larvae undergo metamorphosis into air-breathing adults capable of moving about on land. There are many exceptions to this "standard" mode of reproduction. Most salamanders have a form of internal fertilization in which the male deposits a packet of sperm (the spermatophore), which the female takes into her cloaca. There the sperm is stored in special structures called spermathecae until it is needed for fertilization. Some frogs and salamanders (including our native Red-backed Salamander) lay eggs in damp places on land; larval development is completed within the egg, and their young hatch out as tiny versions of the adults. On the other hand, some salamander species are permanently aquatic and rarely or never leave the water; most of these retain external gills as breeding adults (e.g., the Mudpuppy). Some frogs are also totally aquatic, although these are mostly found in the tropical regions; a well-known example is the African Clawed Frog (*Xenopus laevis*), which has often been used as a laboratory animal for research and as an aquarium pet.

The first amphibians evolved in the late Devonian period of the Paleozoic era, about 370 million years ago. They were a pioneering group of vertebrates that had evolved adaptations allowing them to leave the water and exploit terrestrial habitats. Most paleontologists (scientists who study fossils) agree that the direct ancestors of the amphibians are to be found among the crossopterygian ("lobe-finned") fishes. The earliest true amphibians are exemplified by animals such as *Ichthyostega*, fossils of which have been found in late Devonian age rocks in Greenland. *Ichthyostega* retained a number of features found in its fish ancestors, such as the structure of the skull and teeth, a streamlined body, and a tail fin. This animal undoubtedly

Fig. 1. Larval amphibians. A. Typical larval salamander. B. Typical larval frog.
(Drawing by T. Brockman)

spent much of its time, and certainly reproduced, in water, but the robust feet, limbs, and ribs and strong interlocking backbones suggest that it was quite capable of moving about on land.

During the latter third of the Paleozoic era (about 350 to 245 million years ago), amphibian evolution produced a wide variety of adaptive forms, but most remained dependent on the water and near-shore environments for feeding and reproduction. Many were small aquatic creatures, although a diverse group generally called the *temnospondyls* included some large ones that grew to over 1.5 meters (5 feet) long and somewhat resembled chunky alligators with short legs and flattened skulls. Considerable fossil and morphological evidence suggests that all the living amphibian groups (collectively called the Lissamphibia) originated within the temnospondyls. This idea is not without controversy, however, and additional fossil discoveries will be needed to clarify the matter.

Another lineage of ancient amphibians, generally known as *anthracosaurs* (or *reptilomorphs*), produced some members that evolved improved adaptations for moving, feeding, and probably reproducing on land. Paleontologists consider it likely that one or more of the anthracosaur amphibians eventually evolved into the first reptiles. But what makes an animal a reptile?

A typical reptile is traditionally defined as an ectothermic, air-breathing vertebrate with a dry, scaly skin and clawed feet (if it has feet). Most reptiles hatch from shelled eggs that are fertilized internally and laid on land. Some

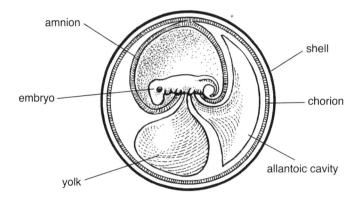

amnion

shell

embryo

chorion

allantoic cavity

yolk

Fig. 2. Diagram of Amniotic Egg

lizards and snakes do not lay eggs, but instead give birth to young that have developed within the female's body. A young reptile, whether hatched or "born alive," breathes with lungs immediately and is essentially a small version of its parents. This classical definition is based on the living reptile groups, such as turtles, lizards, snakes, and crocodiles.

At the present time, the earliest known vertebrates directly ancestral to the reptiles are described from fossils dating from the mid-Carboniferous period, about 335 million years ago. These were small, agile, lizardlike animals well adapted for terrestrial life. Their tiny sharp teeth suggest a diet of insects. Most important, they probably laid shelled *amniotic* eggs on land, a radical departure from their water-breeding amphibian ancestors. An amniotic egg has special membranes that protect the embryo and allow for respiration and waste storage (fig. 2). The amniotic membranes form a special fluid-filled sac, called the amnion, which has been likened to a private pond for the developing embryo. This feature is also found in animals in which the embryos develop in the female's body until birth, including certain lizards and snakes and nearly all living mammals. Thus, all the descendants of those first shelled-egg layers, including the living reptiles, birds, and mammals, form a natural group—the *amniotes*.

By the late Carboniferous period there were already three distinct lineages of amniotes, primarily defined by the structure of the skull and other skeletal features. The first of these, the anapsids, are characterized by a primitive skull structure; the earliest members of this "stem" group may have been ancestral to all later amniotes. The turtles and tortoises are traditionally considered to be the only living anapsids, though some biologists now question this conclusion (see below).

The second lineage, the *synapsids*, were once called "mammal-like reptiles" because they seemed to combine reptilian and mammalian characteristics. The synapsids were very successful late in the Paleozoic era but ultimately became extinct, except for one group, the advanced *therapsids*, which ultimately led to the true mammals (and thus to you!).

The third amniote lineage, the diapsids, branched into two well-defined groups—the lepidosaurs and the archosaurs. Lizards, snakes, and the tuatara (*Sphenodon*) of New Zealand are surviving lepidosaurs. The archosaurs include the pterosaurs, crocodilians, dinosaurs, and birds. Birds must be considered archosaurs since they either descended directly from dinosaurs or shared a close common ancestor with the dinosaurs and crocodilians. To further complicate matters, some biologists now think that turtles may be diapsids, and perhaps even closely related to archosaurs, based on genetics (DNA), fossils, and skeletal structure, but there remains some disagreement about this idea.

The Mesozoic era, which began about 245 million years ago, is often called the Age of Reptiles, due largely to the ecological dominance of the dinosaurs. However, all living amniote groups, including the turtles, lizards, snakes, crocodiles, birds, and mammals, had evolved by the middle of the Mesozoic, as had the "modern" amphibians (frogs, salamanders, and caecilians).

The traditional class Reptilia cannot be considered a truly "natural" taxonomic group since it does not include the birds, making the group incomplete. The word *reptile* is useful, however, when applied to living vertebrates and defined using the typical characters noted above. For purposes of this book, we will simply define a reptile as an amniote that is not a bird or mammal.

Incidentally, we can also define the class Amphibia with equal simplicity, since an amphibian is any tetrapod (four-footed vertebrate) that is not an amniote. Although the tropical caecilians are legless amphibians and sirens have only two legs, these undoubtedly descended from four-footed ancestors and thus qualify as tetrapods. (Among reptiles, legless lizards and snakes are also tetrapods thanks to their common lizard ancestry.)

## Classifying Amphibians and Reptiles

Biologists have long classified living things using a system devised by the Swedish naturalist Carolus Linnaeus in the mid-eighteenth century. Linnaeus grouped organisms into categories according to how similar or different they appeared, but today we can also incorporate information about their genetics (e.g., DNA), evolutionary relationships, and even behavior. The basic unit of classification is the **species**, but defining what we mean by the term is not a simple task. Traditionally, biologists defined a species as a genetically distinct group of organisms that, under natural conditions, breeds within, but not outside, the group (i.e., they share a common gene pool—genes being the units of heredity, containing DNA, within each organism's cells). This is called the "biological species concept." It has been thought that the evolution of new species occurs most often when a small population (or even a few individuals) becomes geographically isolated from a larger parent population. An isolated population may eventually begin to change genetically in response to new environmental conditions or "genetic drift." Eventually it changes enough that it cannot reproduce successfully with the "parent" population, even if they come back into contact. This is a new species. Reproductive incompatibility may be due to physical or behavioral differences or both.

In recent years, a new definition of *species* has been proposed that places more emphasis on the evolutionary history of each named species. Under this "evolutionary species concept," all members of a species are assumed to share specific characteristics and habits because they are the result of a single line of descent from an ancestral species. Thus, any population of amphibians or reptiles that is largely isolated from related or ancestral populations and has some uniquely evolved morphological characters would be considered to be a true species with its own separate evolutionary history and future. Rapidly changing methods for analyzing relationships among living things have led many biologists to question the utility of the Linnaean system, and new systems of classification have been proposed. But most of these systems still employ at least some elements of the Linnaean system, and this book does as well, so it will be useful to describe it here.

Under the Linnaean system, a species is assigned a unique name made up of two parts: a **genus** name and a **species** name. (The species name is often an adjective describing or modifying the genus name.) These names are either derived directly from Latin or are Latinized forms of Greek or another language. For example, in the scientific name of the Painted Turtle, *Chrysemys picta,* the genus name translates as "golden turtle" (from Greek *chrysos,* "gold," and *emys,* a freshwater turtle) while the species name is from the Latin *pictus,* meaning "painted." Note that the genus name is always capitalized, while the species name is not, and that both are either italicized or underlined in text.

In formal texts, the two-word name (genus and species) is usually followed by the name of the person who first named the species and published its description in the scientific literature; this may be followed by the date of publication. For example the Ring-necked Snake's scientific name would be written *Diadophis punctatus* (Linnaeus, 1766). In this case, the parentheses indicate that the species was placed in a different genus sometime after the original description was published.

Latin is used because it was once the universal language of science and, more important, because it offers a stable system of naming that remains the same wherever in the world it is used. One species might have several common names that change from region to region and country to country, but it has only one scientific name. For example, the Painted Turtle is locally called the mud turtle, pond turtle, or painter in different parts of its range. A French Canadian would call it *tortue peinte*, while in western Tennessee it is sometimes called the painted lady turtle. But herpetologists throughout the world recognize *Chrysemys picta* as a specific species of freshwater turtle.

While there is only one species recognized here in the genus *Chrysemys*, many genera (the plural form of *genus*) contain more than one species; thus we can define a genus as a group of very closely related species. Further, in the Linnaean system a group of closely related genera is called a **family** and a group of related families is an **order**. Continuing into still broader categories, a **class** encompasses a group of related orders, while related classes are placed in a **phylum** and, finally, a grouping of related phyla is a **kingdom**. Here is how the Common Garter Snake could be classified in the traditional Linnaean system.

KINGDOM Animalia (animals)
PHYLUM Chordata (vertebrates and some invertebrate relatives)
CLASS Reptilia (amniote vertebrates that are not birds or mammals)
ORDER Squamata (lizards and snakes)
FAMILY Colubridae ("Typical," mostly non-venomous snakes)
GENUS *Thamnophis* (striped snakes; literally, "bush snake")
SPECIES *Thamnophis sirtalis* (Common Garter Snake)

To further refine this classification system, new categories can be added, and the seven major categories are sometimes broken into subgroups. For example, the order Squamata has been defined as containing at least two **suborders**: Lacertilia (lizards) and Serpentes (snakes). But these can be used as an example of why the Linnaean system has been criticized. Recent research has shown that snakes are best considered a group of highly specialized lizards and that snakes are more closely related to some groups of lizards than to others. So using the two traditional suborders is not be the best way to categorize snakes and lizards if we take into account the evolutionary history of these animals.

Another point of contention is with the category called the **subspecies**. Wide-ranging species of reptiles and amphibians frequently exhibit regional differences in size, coloration, or other characteristics. If these differences are particularly distinct and separable by geographic area, a species may be divided into two or more subspecies. Subspecies are designated by adding a third name to the species name. *Chrysemys picta,* the Painted Turtle, has four generally recognized subspecies, of which two are found in the Great Lakes area—the Midland Painted Turtle, *Chrysemys picta marginata,* and the Western Painted Turtle, *Chrysemys picta belli.* Recently some biologists have questioned the subspecies concept, noting that the morphological (shape, color) differences and distribution patterns used to define subspecies do not always match precise genetic differences between populations. While we acknowledge this point of view, we feel that described subspecies that are easily differentiated in the field warrant recognition in a book of this nature. Only subspecies native to our area are included in the checklist and described in the species accounts.

To save space and avoid redundancy, a genus name may be abbreviated by its first letter if it is repeated one or more times in a paragraph or article. In some circumstances the species name may also be abbreviated. For example, we might list the local subspecies of the Painted Turtle as *Chrysemys picta belli* and *C. p. marginata.* Here only the first name was written in full, and in the next name the *"C. p."* clearly refers to *Chrysemys picta.* When using this shortcut, care must be taken to assure that names are written out in full if there is any chance of confusion, such as when different genus or species names begin with the same letter.

Defining what we mean by the term *species* is not always an easy task. One fascinating example is the complicated genetics of certain "mole" salamanders in the genus *Ambystoma.* Jefferson and Blue-spotted Salamanders (*Ambystoma jeffersonianum* and *A. laterale,* respectively) are distinct in appearance, but prior to the early 1950s these two species were generally combined under the former name. The confusion in identifying these species arises from the fact that many salamanders in the southern Great Lakes region that appear to be either Blue-spotted or Jefferson salamanders are really unisexual (all-female) salamanders that have intermediate morphological characters between these species. Jefferson and Blue-spotted Salamanders and their associated unisexuals are often combined within a

"Jefferson Salamander complex." The unisexual salamanders are usually **polyploids**, meaning that they carry three or more sets of chromosomes instead of the usual two. (Chromosomes are structures in the nucleus of body cells that carry hereditary information [in the form of DNA] in packets called genes. Normal individuals of vertebrate species are **diploid**, with one set of chromosomes from their father and one set from their mother.) Unisexuals are often difficult to distinguish from the females of the species that they live with in the field. Biologists can, however, identify them in the laboratory by examining blood cells (e.g., triploid hybrids have red blood cells that are almost a third larger than those of normal diploid females) or genetic material (e.g., chromosomes and DNA).

It was once thought that the triploid unisexual salamanders (with three sets of chromosomes) represented new species because they were shown to reproduce by a process known as gynogenesis (female origin). In gynogenesis, sperm from a male (Jefferson or Blue-spotted Salamander) is only used to initiate development of the embryos in the eggs, but the male's genes are not incorporated into the new generation. The resulting larvae are thus genetically the same as their mother and can be described as clones. But, rarely, the male's sperm *will* be incorporated into the egg, and the resulting larva will carry a set of the male's chromosomes. This can increase the ploidy of the larva (e.g., triploid to tetraploid) or replace a set of the female's chromosomes. Thus, over time the unisexuals end up with chromosomes that relate to their sperm-donor males. The name Tremblay's Salamander (*Ambystoma tremblayi*) was given to triploid salamanders with two sets of chromosomes from *A. laterale* and one set from *A. jeffersonianum*. Salamanders with two chromosome sets from *A. jeffersonianum* and one from *A. laterale* were given the name Silvery Salamander (*A. platineum*). All unisexual *Ambystoma* have at least one chromosome complement from *Ambystoma laterale*. A study of the mitochondrial DNA, which is only inherited and passed on through the female lineage, revealed that all unisexuals have very similar mitochondrial DNA that is very different from the mitochondrial DNA found in any of the sperm-donating species. This means that the unisexuals may not, strictly speaking, be simple hybrids of Jefferson and Blue-spotted salamanders, a concept originally thought to explain the origin of the unisexuals. Though not identical, the mitochondrial DNA most similar to that found in the unisexuals was found in a population of the Stream-side Salamander (*Ambystoma barbouri*) in Kentucky. Unisexual *Ambystoma* are not rare and are often more common than their sperm-donating species around the southern Great Lakes. In addition to Jefferson and Blue-spotted salamanders, other sperm-donating species in this complex include Small-mouthed Salamanders (*Ambystoma texanum*), Tiger Salamanders (*Ambystoma tigrinum*), and even Stream-side Salamanders. Unisexuals in the range of these other species also incorporate their chromosomes, so there are many possible chromosome combinations over the range of unisexual *Ambystoma*. They are most often triploid and incorporate chromosomes of two species, but they can be tetraploid (with four sets of chromosomes) or even pentaploid (with five sets) and include chromosomes from three or even four different bisexual species of ambystomatid salamanders. Persons trying to identify ambystomatid salamanders in the Great Lakes area should be aware that many specimens in our local populations are unisexuals that will be difficult or impossible to assign to a particular species based on external features. The habits and life history of unisexual salamanders are most similar to the sperm-donating "parent species" with which they share the most genetic material. (For more details on the "*Ambystoma* problem," see Bogart et al. 2007, and citations therein.)

Ongoing research into the genetics, physiology, behavior, and fossil history of amphibians and reptiles often leads to new and often controversial ideas about their relationships and proper classification. For example, in 2006 a group of biologists published a proposal, based largely on genetic analyses, to change long-standing scientific names of many amphibians, including some native to the Great Lakes region (Frost et al. 2006). This included splitting "old" established genera like *Rana* ("typical" frogs) and *Bufo* ("true" toads) into several new genera, leading to unfamiliar combinations such as "*Lithobates catesbeianus*" instead of *Rana catesbeiana* for the American Bullfrog. This idea was challenged by other biologists, who argued (among other things) that the older names make as much biological sense as the new ones (for example, Hillis 2007, and Pauly et al. 2009) and that maintaining stable, well-known names whenever possible was a laudable goal. However, just as many herpetologists began to use the new names and combinations, a new analysis was published that re-defined the "true frogs" and showed that the old genus *Rana* was preferable after all (Yuan et al. 2016)!

One suggestion was to use newly proposed species group names as subgenera, instead of full genera, allowing recognition of proposed new names while maintaining name stability (Smith and Chiszar 2006). We will use this method for the "true toads" pending further research on their relationships.

It is good to remember that science is an ongoing process that is always open to new data and analysis, and no classification of living things will ever be "the last word" on the subject. Every published checklist is a tentative proposal or hypothesis based on currently available data and someone's interpretation of them, always subject to change and revision. "A Classification and Checklist of Great Lakes Amphibians and Reptiles," offered below, is the authors' interpretation of relationships among these species based on information available at the time of publication. It differs in some ways from the checklist in the first edition, and we fully expect that a third edition would require additional changes.

With a few exceptions, including those noted above, we largely follow the list of "Scientific and Standard English Names for Amphibians and Reptiles of North America" (Crother et al. 2012; updated at https://ssar-herps.org/wp-content/uploads/2014/07/HC_39_7thEd.pdf) published by the Society for the Study of Amphibians and Reptiles. In species with named subspecies, if only one subspecies occurs in the Great Lakes region, it is generally listed under that name; if more than one subspecies are found in the region, only the species name is listed and subspecies are described in the species' account.

## A Classification and Checklist of Great Lakes Amphibians and Reptiles

### CLASS AMPHIBIA

**Order Caudata (Salamanders)**
**Family Proteidae (Mudpuppies and Waterdogs)**
*Necturus maculosus* . . . Mudpuppy
**Family Sirenidae (Sirens)**
*Siren intermedia nettingi* . . . Western Lesser Siren
**Family Salamandridae (Newts)**
*Notophthalmus viridescens* . . . Eastern Newt
**Family Ambystomatidae (Mole Salamanders)**
*Ambystoma maculatum* . . . Spotted Salamander
*Ambystoma laterale* . . . Blue-spotted Salamander
*Ambystoma jeffersonianum* . . . Jefferson Salamander
*Ambystoma texanum* . . . Small-mouthed Salamander
*Ambystoma opacum* . . . Marbled Salamander
*Ambystoma tigrinum* . . . Eastern Tiger Salamander
**Family Plethodontidae (Lungless Salamanders)**
*Desmognathus fuscus* . . . Northern Dusky Salamander
*Desmognathus ochrophaeus* . . . Allegheny Mountain
  Dusky Salamander

*Plethodon glutinosus* . . . Northern Slimy Salamander
*Plethodon cinereus* . . . Eastern Red-backed Salamander
*Plethodon electromorphus* . . . Northern Ravine Salamander
*Hemidactylium scutatum* . . . Four-toed Salamander
*Gyrinophilus porphyriticus porphyriticus* . . . Northern Spring
   Salamander
*Pseudotriton ruber ruber* . . . Northern Red Salamander
*Eurycea bislineata* . . . Northern Two-lined Salamander
*Eurycea cirrigera* . . . Southern Two-lined Salamander

**Order Anura (Frogs and Toads)**
   **Family Bufonidae (True Toads)**
      *Bufo (Anaxyrus) americanus americanus* . . . Eastern
         American Toad
      *Bufo (Anaxyrus) fowleri* . . . Fowler's Toad
   **Family Hylidae (Treefrogs and relatives)**
      *Acris blanchardi* . . . Blanchard's Cricket Frog
      *Hyla versicolor* . . . Eastern Gray Treefrog
      *Hyla chrysoscelis* . . . Cope's Gray Treefrog
      *Pseudacris triseriata* . . . Midland Chorus Frog
      *Pseudacris maculata* . . . Boreal Chorus Frog
      *Pseudacris crucifer* . . . Spring Peeper
   **Family Ranidae (Typical Frogs)**
      *Rana catesbeiana* . . . Bullfrog
      *Rana clamitans* . . . Green Frog
      *Rana septentrionalis* . . . Mink Frog
      *Rana sylvatica* . . . Wood Frog
      *Rana pipiens* . . . Northern Leopard Frog
      *Rana palustris* . . . Pickerel Frog

## CLASS REPTILIA

**Order Testudines (Turtles and Tortoises)**
   **Family Chelydridae (Snapping Turtles)**
      *Chelydra serpentina* . . . Snapping Turtle
   **Family Kinosternidae (Mud and Musk Turtles)**
      *Sternotherus odoratus* . . . Eastern Musk Turtle
   **Family Emydidae (Pond and Box Turtles)**
      *Clemmys guttata* . . . Spotted Turtle
      *Glyptemys insculpta* . . . Wood Turtle
      *Glyptemys muhlenbergii* . . . Bog Turtle

*Terrapene carolina* . . . Eastern Box Turtle
*Emydoidea blandingii* . . . Blanding's Turtle
*Graptemys geographica* . . . Northern Map Turtle
*Chrysemys picta* . . . Painted Turtle
*Trachemys scripta elegans* . . . Red-eared Slider

**Family Trionychidae (Softshell Turtles)**
*Apalone spinifera spinifera* . . . Eastern Spiny Softshell

**Order Squamata (Lizards, Amphisbaenians, and Snakes)**
**Suborder Lacertilia [Sauria] (Lizards)**
**Family Scincidae (Skinks)**
*Plestiodon fasciatus* . . . Five-lined Skink
*Plestiodon anthracinus anthracinus* . . . Northern Coal Skink

**Family Teiidae (Whiptails and Racerunners)**
*Aspidoscelis sexlineata viridis* . . . Prairie Racerunner

**Family Anguidae (Glass Lizards and Alligator Lizards)**
*Ophisaurus attenuatus attenuatus* . . . Western Slender Glass Lizard

**Suborder Ophidia [Serpentes] (Snakes)**
**Family Colubridae ("Typical" Snakes)**
**Subfamily Natricinae (Water and Garter Snakes)**
*Nerodia sipedon* . . . Common Water Snake
*Nerodia erythrogaster neglecta* . . . Copper-bellied Water Snake
*Regina septemvittata* . . . Queen Snake
*Clonophis kirtlandii* . . . Kirtland's Snake
*Thamnophis sirtalis* . . . Common Garter Snake
*Thamnophis butleri* . . . Butler's Garter Snake
*Thamnophis brachystoma* . . . Short-headed Garter Snake
*Thamnophis radix* . . . Plains Garter Snake
*Thamnophis sauritus septentrionalis* . . . Northern Ribbon Snake
*Thamnophis proximus proximus* . . . Orange-striped Ribbon Snake
*Storeria dekayi* . . . Dekay's Brown Snake
*Storeria occipitomaculata occipitomaculata* . . . Northern Red-bellied Snake

**Subfamily Colubrinae (Racers, Rat Snakes, and kin)**
*Opheodrys vernalis* . . . Smooth Green Snake
*Coluber constrictor* . . . North American Racer
*Pantherophis spiloides* . . . Gray (Central) Rat Snake
*Pantherophis vulpinus* . . . Western Fox Snake
*Pantherophis gloydi* . . . Eastern Fox Snake
*Lampropeltis triangulum triangulum* . . . Eastern Milk Snake

**Subfamily Dipsadinae (Rear-fanged Snakes)**

*Diadophis punctatus edwardsii* . . . Northern Ring-necked Snake
*Heterodon platirhinos* . . . Eastern Hog-nosed Snake
**Family Viperidae (Pit Vipers and Vipers)**
*Sistrurus catenatus catenatus* . . . Eastern Massasauga
*Crotalus horridus* . . . Timber Rattlesnake

## Amphibians and Reptiles in the "Age of Mammals"

By the middle of the Mesozoic era, the amphibians had been reduced from their former prominence to the three living groups, the anurans (frogs and toads), salamanders, and caecilians, possibly due to competition from the reptiles. The "Age of Reptiles" lasted for about 175 million years and ended about 65 million years ago with the extinction of all nonavian (nonbird) dinosaurs and several other groups of reptiles. The following (and present) era, the Cenozoic, has been called the "Age of Mammals." There is a growing movement to designate the period covering the last few decades or, at most, centuries of the Cenozoic up to the present, as the "Anthropocene" or "Age of Humans."

A view popular for much of the early and mid-twentieth century presumed that the supposedly superior warm-blooded mammals and birds took over the world after the dinosaurs' demise, leaving the surviving amphibians and reptiles to play only minor roles in the ecosystem. This idea is now known to be erroneous on several counts (even if we ignore the well-supported theory that birds represent a surviving lineage of dinosaurs). It is true that mammals now occupy most of the ecological niches for large terrestrial animals, but the amphibians and reptiles fill many niches for small and medium-sized animals in temperate and tropical climates. There are more described amphibian species (at this writing about 7,400) than mammal species (5,500) in existence, while reptiles (with about 10,000 species) greatly outnumber the mammals in species diversity. For the record, there are more than 10,400 bird species, while the number of fish species (about 32,900) nearly equals the total number of land-living vertebrates.

Reptiles and amphibians seem better suited for some habitats than are birds or mammals. Reptile species often outnumber their endothermic counterparts in arid desert regions, and amphibians are more diverse than mammals in humid neotropical forests. The ectotherms hold their own in temperate climates as well. For example, a study in a New Hampshire forest revealed that salamanders outnumbered the birds and mammals combined and had a biomass (living weight) 2.6 times greater than that of the birds and roughly equal to that of the resident small mammals. Over 100,000 salamanders were found in one 36-hectare test plot, of which 93 percent (95,000) were Red-backed Salamanders, a species common in the Great Lakes area as well (Burton and Likens 1975).

Being endothermic does give mammals and birds certain advantages. Compared to terrestrial ectotherms, most can remain active at lower environmental temperatures and maintain higher levels of activity over longer time periods. But these abilities come at a cost, for endotherms must take in a lot of energy (food) to produce heat (or, in hot weather, to lose heat) and to fuel the muscles and large brain needed to control their fast-paced lifestyle. (To "eat like a bird or a mouse" is to really shovel in the calories!)

In comparison, a lizard or salamander may require less than 5 percent of the food calories used by a mammal of equal size over a given time period. Ectothermic amphibians or reptiles require less energy in part because their body heat comes directly or indirectly from the sun. (In our area, amphibians are generally more active at lower temperatures than are reptiles). On a warm, sunny spring day, a frog or garter snake has all the "free" heat it needs to carry out its life processes, such as eating or breeding. If the weather turns cold and rainy for a few days, it simply stops feeding and remains inactive. A robin or rabbit under the same circumstances would soon have to leave shelter to find food.

In the Great Lakes area, most amphibians and all reptiles hibernate (i.e., become dormant) in winter, while most mammals and all resident birds remain active and continue to feed. A few completely aquatic amphibians, such the Mudpuppy, are active all winter. Some mammals sleep for extended periods during severe weather, but only a few native mammals (e.g., woodchucks, ground squirrels, and some bats) are true hibernators. Hibernation presents many hazards for an animal, including possible attacks by predators and the risks of freezing, flooding, or oxygen depletion in the hibernaculum. Mammal hibernation differs in some ways from hibernation in amphibians or reptiles, particularly in details of energy storage and metabolism. For this reason some herpetologists prefer to use the term *brumation* instead of *hibernation* when referring to winter dormancy in amphibians or reptiles; in this book the latter, more familiar term is used.

## Amphibians and Reptiles in the Ecosystem

Amphibians and reptiles are consumers that feed on living or dead plant or animal material and convert it into energy for movement, growth, and reproduction. The great majority of Great Lakes area species are carnivorous. Salamanders, frogs, and toads eat mostly invertebrates (e.g., insects, spiders, earthworms). Large frogs (especially Bullfrogs and Green Frogs) also eat smaller vertebrates such as snakes, mice, birds, and other frogs (including their own offspring). The aquatic larvae of terrestrial salamanders often feed on smaller amphibian larvae, although invertebrates make up the largest proportion of the diet of most species.

When abundant, amphibians can consume substantial quantities of favored prey organisms, perhaps serving to limit prey populations. The smaller woodland salamanders may have large populations, as noted above, with obvious impacts on their invertebrate prey. It has been estimated that an average American Toad can eat about 26 insects in one day, or over 3,200 insects per season (Pope 1947). A tiny Blanchard's Cricket Frog has been estimated to eat about 4,800 insects in one year; thus a population of 1,000 Cricket Frogs distributed around a lake could potentially consume at least 4.8 million insects annually (Johnson and Christiansen 1976).

The only herbivorous Great Lakes area amphibians are frog and toad tadpoles, most of which feed largely on algae and other aquatic plant material. However, tadpoles also consume small planktonic animals and frequently supplement their diets by scavenging the remains of larger animals. Wood Frog tadpoles, in particular, have carnivorous tendencies and often consume amphibian eggs and larvae, including those of their own species. Lesser Sirens and some salamander larvae are known to ingest plant material, but it is likely that most or all of this vegetation is swallowed accidently during the capture of small animal prey.

Most reptiles are carnivores, although many turtles are omnivorous, feeding on both plants and animals. In some species, including Box Turtles, Wood Turtles, Painted Turtles, and Sliders, the hatchlings and juveniles prefer animal food and gradually add more vegetable matter to their diets as they mature. Animal foods are higher in protein than plants and undoubtedly facilitate rapid growth in the young turtles.

A few turtle species specialize in certain foods. Blanding's Turtles and Spiny Softshells show a preference for crayfish. Map Turtles, particularly the larger females, favor mollusks such as snails and small clams, and Musk Turtles also feed heavily on mollusks. Other turtle species will accept a variety of food items, with choices influenced by opportunity and seasonal abundance. Box and Wood Turtles readily exploit strawberries, raspberries, and other fruits when available and thus, like birds, may assist in seed dispersal of food plants.

Snapping Turtles, the largest reptiles in the Great Lakes basin, feed on a variety of aquatic animals and plants. By consuming carrion, they play a part in recycling dead organisms. They will also take vertebrate prey such as fish and young ducks, which has given them a poor reputation among wildlife managers. In reality, snappers take few game fish and have a minimal effect on waterfowl populations in natural habitats. Snapping Turtles can accumulate chemical pollutants in their body tissues, a tendency that may be enhanced by the species' tolerance for polluted waters and their ability to feed at several levels of the "food chain."

Although a number of herbivorous lizard species inhabit tropical regions, Great Lakes area lizards are almost entirely carnivorous, feeding on insects and their larvae, spiders, and other small invertebrates. Large individuals of some species (e.g., Slender Glass Lizards and Five-lined Skinks) may occasionally eat small vertebrates, including smaller reptiles and their eggs.

All snakes are carnivorous throughout their lives. The larger species, such as Gray Rat Snakes, Western and Eastern Fox Snakes, Bullsnakes, Milk Snakes, and Racers, have a preference for rodents and other endothermic prey; the latter two also eat other reptiles. Eastern Hog-nosed Snakes are specialized toad eaters. Garter, ribbon, and water snakes tend to eat ectothermic vertebrates such as fish and amphibians, although many garter snakes and the secretive Brown, Red-bellied, and Kirtland's Snakes feed heavily on earthworms. The Smooth Green Snake is the only Great Lakes area snake with a primary diet of arthropods, mainly insects, insect larvae, and spiders.

In nature the consumers often become the consumed, and this is certainly true of amphibians and reptiles, which are eaten by a great variety of natural predators. Frogs are a much-favored prey item for a long list of predators, including mink, otters, foxes, raccoons, skunks, shrews, herons, bitterns, hawks, many snakes and turtles, larger frogs, and fish, especially bass and pike. Salamanders, though readily eaten by the same predators, may be less accessible since most species remain underground or beneath logs and rocks except when breeding. Frog tadpoles and salamander larvae are eaten by many of these predatory vertebrates, as well as by a number of carnivorous invertebrates, including giant water bugs, diving beetles, dragonfly nymphs, and water scorpions.

Frogs typically produce large numbers of eggs, which serves to balance the high losses to predators. For example, a female Spring Peeper might lay a thousand eggs each spring, a Green Frog perhaps 5,000 eggs, and a Bullfrog up to 20,000 eggs. It has been conservatively estimated that less than one frog egg in a hundred ultimately produces a new frog that survives to breeding size.

Clearly, a major contribution of frogs in the ecosystem is providing energy for other animals. Many salamanders (and the smaller frogs) breed in temporary ponds that lack fish and other large aquatic predators. They seem able to maintain their numbers by laying eggs by the hundreds rather than thousands, but typically over 90 percent of their eggs and larvae will still be lost to predators. There are numerous other threats to survival in addition to predation. For example, in drought years the breeding ponds can disappear before the larvae metamorphose, resulting in a total loss of new young for that season.

Amphibians do have defenses against predators. Most depend on avoidance, rapid escape, or concealment, but American and Fowler's Toads, Gray Treefrogs, Pickerel Frogs, Mink Frogs, and many adult salamanders can secrete irritating or toxic substances from skin glands. These defenses are described in more detail in the species accounts.

Reptiles also suffer high rates of predation. The buried eggs of turtles are a favorite seasonal food for many small mammals, particularly raccoons and skunks. Numerous studies show that these nest predators often destroy between 70 and 90 percent of all turtle nests at the described sites, and in certain years and locations the destruction can reach 100 percent. Hatchling turtles are bite-sized snacks for the same mammalian carnivores, as well as crows, ravens, gulls, and wading birds, and the remains of young turtles are often found in the stomachs of game fish such as pike and bass. Turtles have fewer natural predators once they mature and are notably long-lived compared to other similar-sized vertebrates. Most turtle species have potential life-spans of several decades, and Eastern Box Turtles are known for their ability to reach the century mark. It is this potentially long adult reproductive life that allows turtle populations to persist despite heavy losses of their eggs and young.

Lizards and snakes contribute to the food supply of numerous predators, particularly birds. A hawk flying off with a snake dangling from its talons or a heron spearing a water snake are routine sightings for Great Lakes area naturalists. Young snakes and lizards are vulnerable even to smaller birds such as thrushes, jays, and blackbirds. Many mammals, including raccoons, opossums, foxes, badgers, and skunks, also eat these reptiles. Shrews are significant, if often unsuspected, predators on the eggs and young of many species, and they also attack adult reptiles that are immobilized during winter dormancy.

## Amphibians, Reptiles, and People

There was a time when wildlife conservation had to be justified in economic terms. Sadly, the questions "What good is it?" and "How much is it worth?" are occasionally still heard in discussions about preserving wild species. Amphibians and reptiles do provide a number of direct benefits to the human economy, even though these values are often difficult to quantify. Many species have feeding habits that make them potentially beneficial to human interests. The vast numbers of insects eaten by amphibians and small reptiles surely includes many pest species. A toad in the garden has long been considered a symbol of good fortune, a reputation no doubt well deserved. Larval salamanders can consume significant numbers of mosquito larvae in woodland ponds. Northern Map Turtles will feed on invasive mollusk species, including zebra mussels. Bullsnakes, Western and Eastern Fox Snakes, Gray Rat Snakes, Racers, and Milk Snakes consume mice, rats, and other potential agricultural pests.

The commercial harvest of amphibians and reptiles has contributed more directly to human economic interests, although there is legitimate doubt about the long-term sustainability of this exploitation and most states and provinces now prohibit or greatly restrict this practice. Larger frogs have been harvested for edible frog legs, and great numbers of frogs, Mudpuppies, and other salamanders have been collected by biological supply companies for use in high school and college science classes. In some places, frogs and salamanders and their larvae are still collected and sometimes sold as fish bait.

Commercial trappers supplying turtle meat for human consumption usually concentrate their efforts on the two largest Great Lakes species, the Snapping Turtle and the Eastern Spiny Softshell. Substantial numbers are also taken for personal consumption. Smaller species have less value as human food but are occasionally collected and sometimes sold for this purpose. Biological supply companies have collected and sold turtles in large numbers for educational and research use, notably in Wisconsin. Certain species have been in great demand in the commercial pet trade, particularly Wood Turtles, Blanding's Turtles, Spotted Turtles, and Box Turtles; this exploitation has severely reduced or even eliminated many populations. Several species of snakes and lizards have also been collected for the biological supply and pet trade.

Of course, the intangible values of amphibians and reptiles should not be overlooked. Springtime choruses of toads and frogs are a joyful sound to many northerners seeking signs of winter's end, while basking turtles can add a feeling of tranquility to a day of fishing or canoeing. Many hikers now react with pleasure, not fear, at seeing a snake glide across the trail. Yet in the end, the conservation of amphibians and reptiles can be justified simply because they are active participants in the ecosystem and an important part of our wildlife heritage.

## Conservation of Amphibians and Reptiles

The degradation, fragmentation, and destruction of natural habitats due to human activities are undoubtedly the greatest threats to amphibian and reptile populations in the Great Lakes region. Vast areas have been converted to agricultural use, while urban and suburban developments consume more habitat each year. The draining and filling of wetlands has obvious deleterious implications for many species. Terrestrial and wetland habitats that are still available (including those "protected" in parks or wildlife areas) may be degraded by air and water pollution, bisected by roadways, or ruined by the irresponsible use of off-road vehicles.

As amphibian and reptile populations are restricted to smaller and smaller "islands" of habitat, they become increasingly vulnerable to threats such as road mortality and direct exploitation. Not surprisingly, those species with historically restricted ranges or specialized habitat requirements are the first to appear on endangered and threatened species lists. However, even some wide-ranging, so-called common species have declined, locally or regionally, in parts of the Great Lakes area. Examples of these, including the Spotted Salamander, Blanchard's Cricket Frog, Northern Leopard Frog, Common Garter Snake, and Racer, are discussed in the species accounts.

The direct exploitation of amphibians and reptiles, which was largely unregulated prior to the late twentieth century, has resulted in population declines and even localized extirpation of some species. This situation resulted both from traditional neglect of these animals by resource managers and from ignorance of their habits and populations. Government conservation agencies willing to consider their management were often faced with a lack of the basic biological data needed to guide regulatory decisions. Concerns about declining amphibian and reptile numbers have spurred new efforts to survey populations and study life cycles and habitat needs, but there is still much to be learned. Sufficient information now exists to support general recommendations on the conservation and management of amphibians and reptiles.

Many frog species are potentially very prolific and appear to have a fairly rapid turnover in their populations. But the larger species most in demand for human use, particularly the Bullfrog, may take several years to reach a size worthy of harvesting, which is also prime breeding size. Frog populations in colder climates, including the Great Lakes basin, are subject to shorter growing seasons and greater climatic stresses than those to the south. Amphibians in general are vulnerable to natural disasters, such as drought and floods, and various human-caused problems, such as industrial pollution, farm chemical and road salt runoff, and acid precipitation. The spread of emergent diseases such as ranaviruses and fungal infections (chytridiomycosis) are especially troubling and threaten populations and species of frogs and salamanders in North America and many other regions of the world (Lannoo 2005).

Many frog and salamander species congregate for breeding purposes and are especially vulnerable to exploitation at these times. Standard wildlife management tools such as minimum sizes, possession limits, and closed seasons may be useful in preserving viable populations of hunted species. Regulations on amphibians should be modified when needed to accommodate changes in habitats and populations, as they are with fish, waterfowl, and other game species.

Many turtle species have a notably low rate of recruitment of young individuals into the breeding population due to typically high egg and hatchling mortality and the long time periods needed to reach reproductive size. These factors are normally balanced by comparatively low adult mortality and long adult life-spans. Any factor that removes mature adult turtles from the population faster than they can be replaced will cause the population to decline. Research has demonstrated that most, if not all, turtle species have virtually no "harvestable surplus" of mature animals in their populations. If a primary goal of game management is to maintain stable or increasing numbers of a harvested species, then it is unlikely that turtle populations anywhere in the Great Lakes area are prolific enough to tolerate even a modest harvest by humans (see Congdon, Dunham, and van Loben Sels 1993, 1994).

It has been suggested that populations of species with wide habitat tolerances, such as Snapping Turtles, may be able to sustain a very limited, well-dispersed, and carefully regulated harvest on a "personal use" basis. However, Snapping Turtle populations in the northern parts of their range are known to have lower annual rates of recruitment and slower growth rates than those farther south, making them more likely to decline if adult animals are removed by humans (Brooks et al. 1988). It is clear that species with narrow habitat requirements and/or particularly slow growth or recruitment rates, such as Wood, Spotted, Bog, Blanding's, and Box Turtles, will inevitably experience population declines if subjected to even low levels of removal and exploitation.

Based on what is known (and not known) about amphibian and reptile populations in the Great Lakes area, it would seem reasonable to manage them conservatively, in much the same way that we manage wild birds.

The great majority of species should be protected as nongame wildlife, as are songbirds, wading birds, and birds of prey. A few species, perhaps Snapping Turtles and the larger frogs, could be carefully managed as game species, similar to waterfowl, grouse, and pheasants. The collection of small numbers of common species for classroom observation and nature study purposes could also be permitted. As has been long recognized for birds, commercial exploitation of amphibians and reptiles is incompatible with prudent conservation goals, and should be prohibited everywhere.

Within the Great Lakes basin, all states and the province of Ontario have protective laws and regulations that affect amphibians and reptiles. State and provincial wildlife regulatory agencies throughout the region are also charged with maintaining lists of rare, threatened, or endangered species, though precise categories and definitions vary. Listed species are usually given special protection and management consideration. In the species accounts we have noted the state and provincial regulatory status of each species as known at time of publication, but note that these regulatory listings are subject to frequent revision and modification. Persons wishing to study or collect any amphibian or reptile species for any reason should contact the responsible government wildlife agency in their state or province for current regulations and permit requirements.

## Effects of Glaciation on Amphibian and Reptile Distribution in the Great Lakes Region

Twenty thousand years ago there were no amphibians or reptiles in the Great Lakes basin. The Great Lakes as we know them did not exist. Several massive lobes of glacial ice, spreading south from Canada, had converged over the region, obliterating practically all life. Reaching a mile or more in height, the glaciers at one time extended as far as central Ohio, Indiana, and Illinois (fig. 3). Known to geologists as the Late Wisconsinan glaciation, this was the latest climatic assault on a region that had, during the previous 2 million years, already experienced a number of advances and retreats of glacial ice. Some scientists believe that we are now in an interglacial period and that someday glaciers may once again spread over parts of Canada and the northern United States. How the recent episode of global warming will affect natural glacial cycles is difficult to predict. However, by definition the "Ice Age" (properly called the Pleistocene epoch) began about 1.8 million years ago and ended about 11,000 years ago, by which time the ice had retreated from most of the Great Lakes area. The time period from the end of the Pleistocene to the present is called the Holocene (meaning "whole

Fig. 3. Maximum Wisconsinan glacial advance in the Great Lakes area, about 20,000 years ago. Lines represent end moraines. (Reprinted from *Quaternary Science Reviews* 11, J. A. Holman, Late Quaternary Herpetofauna of the Central Great Lakes Regions, U.S.A.: Zoogeographical and Paleoecological Implications, 345–51, Copyright 1992, with kind permission from Elsevier Science Ltd, The Boulevard, Langford Lane, Kidlington OX5 1GB, UK.)

recent") epoch—although, as previously noted, some people would say that we are now in the Anthropocene (human recent) epoch due to the significant recent impacts of humanity on the planet.

Glaciers have had a profound effect on the land and living organisms in the Great Lakes area. The Great Lakes themselves were created by glaciers scouring out ancient pre-Pleistocene river valleys. Soil, sand, boulders, and trees were picked up by the advancing glaciers and deposited hundreds of miles away. During times of glacial retreat, buried blocks of ice would become lakes and bogs, and raging meltwater flows would carve new river courses. Plant and animal species displaced by advancing glaciers survived in suitable habitats, called refugia, to the south and west, only to reinvade formerly occupied areas during times of glacial recession (interglacial periods). To understand the present distribution of amphibians and reptiles and their habitats in the Great Lakes area, it is helpful to briefly review what is known about the regional environment during and after the last glaciation.

We know very little about conditions and life in the Great Lakes region during the early and middle parts of the Pleistocene, since later glaciations tended to destroy much of the evidence of earlier ones. The latest (Wisconsinan) glacial advance began about 110,000 years ago and reached its maximum southern extent about 20,000 years ago. Prior to that time there was a warmer interglacial period called the Sangamonian, during which time amphibians, reptiles, and other organisms had undoubtedly reinhabited the proto–Great Lakes area. Fossils of giant land tortoises (*Geochelone crassicutata*) have been discovered in Sangamonian sediments of south-central Illinois and in southern Indiana, suggesting that the climate must have been even milder than today, or at least there were warmer winters, since giant tortoises cannot survive in areas with prolonged freezing temperatures. However, a fairly mild climate may have persisted in parts of the continent even at the height of the Wisconsinan glaciation. Studies of fossil amphibians and reptiles have provided much of the evidence for this idea.

During late Wisconsinan times, as converging glaciers readvanced over the Great Lakes region, conditions near the ice front were presumably quite severe. An analysis of pollen samples taken from sites that were dated by the carbon 14 method suggests that a tundralike vegetation, chiefly grasses, sedges, and scattered coniferous trees, predominated in a narrow band adjacent to the glacier. Beyond this tundra zone a mixture of different habitats existed, depending on local environmental conditions. Large areas of the eastern and central United States may have been covered with spruce forest or open savanna (mixed grassland and woodland) dominated by grasses and spruce, pine, oak, and birch trees. Open oak woodlands existed in the lower Midwest, and deciduous woodlands and swamp forests survived in lowlands and southern river valleys. But where were our Great Lakes herps during this time?

Many fossil sites dating to the late Wisconsinan contain mixes of plants and animal species that would not be found together today. The climate in the central and southern United States during the glacial maximum may have been, at least locally, rather mild, with cooler summers, warmer winters, and perhaps more precipitation than today. This equable climate allowed an unusual mixture of northern and southern species to coexist.

A late Wisconsinan fossil site in Mississippi has yielded both the extinct giant tortoise and the living Blanding's Turtle, while a site in northern Georgia has produced the remains of many amphibians and reptiles that live there today, as well as giant tortoises and an assortment of species that do not presently occur in the area. Warm-adapted Southern Toads (*Bufo [Anaxyrus] terrestris*) and Florida Red-bellied Turtles (*Pseudemys nelsoni*) were then living alongside such cold-adapted Great Lakes species as the Wood Turtle and a Fox Snake. The strange Pleistocene climate allowed our northern herps to survive well south of their modern ranges, while southern species were able to move north. Similarly, intermixes of eastern and western species are known from the present Great Plains area, which is thought to have been at least partially forested during much of the Wisconsinan glaciation. (For further discussion on Pleistocene climatic equability, see Wright and Porter 1983; and Holman 1995a.)

Responding to warmer temperatures and perhaps less precipitation, the Wisconsinan glaciers began a slow, vacillating retreat about 18,000 years ago. As the ice receded, plants and animals began to disperse back into the Great Lakes area. By 15,000 years before present (BP) there was already a fairly diverse herpetofauna in south-central Indiana, including several species of frogs, turtles, and snakes found in the area today. Between 12,000 and 11,000 BP, with glacial ice still covering portions of northern lower Michigan, Leopard and Green Frogs, American Toads, and Painted Turtles were sharing southeastern Michigan habitats with mastodonts, mammoths, and giant beavers. Spruce woodlands gave way to pine forests, and then to deciduous hardwood forests, and vast new areas of marsh and bog habitats became accessible.

By 9,500 BP the Great Lakes region was nearly ice free, but it took several thousand more years for the climate, vegetation, and herpetofauna to take on a modern aspect. The levels of the Great Lakes fluctuated considerably during the glacial retreat, as drainages changed in response to melting rates and the rebounding of land newly free of its ice burden. During times of low lake levels, amphibians and reptiles were able to disperse over dry land to places that are now offshore islands; this probably explains why many Great Lakes islands have a surprisingly diverse herpetofauna. The climate during the early and middle Holocene was highly variable; the earliest Holocene appears to have been warmer and more moist than today. This so-called hypsithermal period, or *climatic optimum*, allowed southern species to disperse rapidly northward. Presumably relict Great Lakes populations of certain "southern" species, such as the Western Lesser Siren, Marbled Salamander, and Copper-bellied Water Snake, may be remnants of a northern dispersal during this warm period.

A time of reduced precipitation and increased warmth, sometimes called the xerothermic period, is thought to have occurred in the Midwest from about 7,000 to 5,000 years ago. This allowed prairie-type vegetation (grasses and associated herbaceous plants) to spread eastward at the expense of forest in the lower Great Lakes region. This so-called *prairie peninsula* at one point extended well into Illinois, Indiana, and southern Michigan, and probably (at least on a spotty basis) to Pennsylvania and points east.

Relict prairie and savanna habitats still exist in Indiana, Ohio, southwestern Michigan, and southern Ontario, and much more existed at the time Europeans first entered the region. Fire, whether caused by lightning or set by humans, may have promoted the spread of prairie habitat or at least helped to maintain it. A number of reptile species have modern ranges that strongly suggest that they followed the prairie peninsula into the Great Lakes area (Schmidt 1938; Smith 1957). For example, the Ornate Box Turtle (*Terrapene ornata*), Prairie Racerunner, Western Slender Glass Lizard, and Plains Garter Snake are characteristic grassland reptiles of the west-central United States with range extensions or relict populations in or near this area. Kirtland's Snake exists today almost entirely within the presumed prairie peninsula, while the Eastern Massasauga Rattlesnake, an inhabitant of marshes, bogs, and wet prairie, may fit the pattern as well.

Woodland species would have been displaced by the spread of drier grassland habitats during the xerothermic period. The absence of the Wood Turtle in southern Michigan and Ohio and the scarcity of Eastern Box Turtles in northeastern Ohio may be the result of forest decline in the early Holocene. The Northern Ring-necked Snake is another woodland reptile conspicuously absent from the prairie peninsula. However, an alternate explanation rooted in the absence of fossil evidence is that these species failed to invade (or reinvade) these areas postglacially.

The effects of Pleistocene glaciation and the resulting faunal displacements and dispersals in the Great Lakes area are reflected in the distribution of many native amphibians and reptiles. In addition, the changing glacial and interglacial climates may have contributed to the development of new species and subspecies.

The Eastern Gray Treefrog (*Hyla versicolor*) is one species that may owe its existence to Pleistocene climatic disruption. This species is practically identical in outward appearance to Cope's Gray Treefrog (*Hyla chrysoscelis*), but the two species can be distinguished by their spring mating calls. The male *H. chrysoscelis* typically gives a fast, rather high-pitched trill, with a sound pulse rate of about thirty-eight to seventy pulses per second (as measured by a sonograph, an audio analyzing device). At like temperatures, the male *H. versicolor* has a slower, more musical trilled call with a pulse rate of about fifteen to twenty-nine pulses per second. The two species can be most readily identified when they are calling at the same time, allowing a direct comparison. A laboratory test may also be used to distinguish the species. *Hyla versicolor*, a genetic tetraploid, has red blood cells that are considerably larger and fewer in number than those of the diploid *H. chrysoscelis,* its probable ancestor. It has been suggested that *Hyla chrysoscelis* was split into at least two populations during a glacial advance and that these underwent genetic changes during this separation. *Hyla versicolor* was probably produced as glaciers receded and the now slightly different populations came back into contact.

The Painted Turtle is a wide-ranging species consisting of (in our view) four intergrading subspecies, two of which are found in the Great Lakes area. It appears likely that a single ancestral species was split into several populations during one or more glacial advance. These isolated populations would have begun the evolutionary transition toward becoming new species but were presumably not separated long enough to complete the transformation. Once the ice retreated and the populations again came into contact, they were still genetically similar enough to interbreed freely and produce fertile offspring.

Butler's Garter Snake and the Short-headed Garter Snake are closely related species that may have evolved due to shifting habitats and isolation during glacial times. It has been suggested that the common ancestor of these two snakes evolved from the Plains Garter Snake in the eastern part of its range, perhaps early in the Pleistocene. This ancestral population was possibly split again during a later glaciation, with the ancestral Butler's Garter Snake population forced south of the ice front below the proto–Great Lakes and the ancestral Short-headed Garter Snake population isolated on the unglaciated Allegheny Plateau in Pennsylvania.

In another example, two forms of the Fox Snake have been described in the Great Lakes region, one (*Pantherophis vulpinus*) largely west and north of Lake Michigan and another (*P. gloydi*) along the Lake Huron and Lake Erie shorelines, with a large unoccupied area in between. Some biologists, noting the complete geographic and reproductive isolation of the two populations, as well as differences in color pattern and habitat preference, have recognized these two forms as separate species, the Western Fox Snake and the Eastern Fox Snake, a view retained here. It was thought that these two disjunct populations may have been the result of snakes reinvading the area postglacially from separate refugia. However, a recent genetic study found that the separation of a previously continuous xerothermic population may have occurred much more recently as a result of habitat changes in the last few thousand years (Row et al. 2011). Another recent study (Crother et al. 2011) failed to find a significant genetic difference between the two Great Lakes populations but instead found a notable genetic split at the Mississippi River, so fox snake history and taxonomy remains unsettled.

It is interesting to note that despite the drastic climatic changes of the last two million years, the North American herpetofauna appears to have been quite taxonomically stable compared to mammals and birds (Holman 1995b, 2012). During the late Pleistocene and early Holocene, at least nineteen genera of birds and forty-six genera of mammals became extinct in North America, but only one reptile genus (the giant tortoise, *Geochelone*) disappeared. Eastern North America lost its mammoths, mastodonts, horses, ground sloths, saber-toothed cats, short-faced bears, and many other mammals but apparently no frogs, salamanders, aquatic turtles, lizards, or snakes. Amphibians and reptiles may have benefited from their relatively small body size, an ectothermic metabolism (and the ability to hibernate), and more flexible and prolific reproductive habits. It is also likely that they were less intensively or less effectively exploited by early human hunters than were the larger mammals.

## Environments for Great Lakes Amphibians and Reptiles

The suitability of a particular area as a habitat for amphibians and reptiles is closely related to the types of vegetation growing there, which in turn is dependent on a combination of factors, including seasonal temperatures, precipitation, soil, drainage, and the contours of the land. Figure 4 illustrates the primary vegetation types that are thought to have existed in the Great Lakes basin prior to European settlement. The actual plant communities growing in any particular place within a mapped vegetational region will depend on local conditions. It should be kept in mind that these mapped vegetation categories are based largely on dominant forest tree species. Relatively few Great Lakes amphibians and reptiles are true forest animals per se; many species occupy ecotones (edge habitats) between dense woodlands and open grasslands, and many others live in wetlands or open-water habitats.

It is obvious that human activities have drastically altered natural plant communities. Agricultural fields, orchards, roads, and cities now occupy vast areas of former forests and wetlands, and plant species introduced from Europe and elsewhere often crowd out native species. Even in existing natural areas the mix of trees, shrubs, and herbaceous plants may be quite different from that which greeted the first European settlers, due in part to accidental or intentional introductions of nonnative species.

The Great Lakes region is a transition zone between the boreal coniferous forests north of Lake Superior, the mixed-hardwood forests to the south,

Fig. 4. Map of major pre-settlement plant communities in the Great Lakes basin. (From Kurta, 1995)

and the drier prairie and savanna to the west. A glance at the range maps in the species accounts will reveal that many amphibian and reptile species reach their distributional limits in the region and that the number of species increases from north to south. These trends are largely related to seasonal temperatures, though precipitation may be a limiting factor on the western edge of the drainage basin.

Large bodies of water such as the Great Lakes have a moderating effect on both winter and summer temperatures. The number of frost-free days each year ranges from as few as one hundred in northern Minnesota and Wisconsin to two hundred or more along the southern shores of Lake Michigan. This factor is undoubtedly reflected in the ranges of several "southern" species that reach their northern limits along Great Lakes shorelines; examples include the Marbled Salamander, Fowler's Toad, Spotted Turtle, and Eastern Box Turtle. Winter survival of terrestrial amphibians and reptiles is also enhanced by the greater snow depths along the lakeshores (particularly the leeward sides), which offer increased insulation and thus reduce penetration and duration of ground frost.

Some hardy amphibian and reptile species can survive in a variety of habitat types and may occupy a very broad geographic range. The Northern Spring Peeper, American Toad, Painted Turtle, and Common Garter Snake are examples of adaptable, often abundant species found throughout the Great Lakes region. Many other species have more specialized habitat requirements and are associated with specific aquatic or terrestrial plant communities.

The major vegetation regions (and the special habitats they encompass) are summarized below, along with notes on some of the characteristic species of amphibians and reptiles that are found within them. The species mentioned as "typical" for certain plant associations are not necessarily restricted to those regions, nor are they necessarily found throughout the region. Many aquatic species are associated with wetland and open-water habitats that are represented in several vegetation regions.

True **boreal (coniferous) forest** is found in the Great Lakes basin north of Lake Superior, but it grades into the northern transitional forest in a broad band from the western edge of Lake Superior to the Maine coast. The dominant boreal forest trees are the balsam fir and white spruce, along with varying mixtures of paper birch, aspen, poplar, maple, white pine, white cedar, and eastern hemlock. Long, cold winters and short, cool summers contribute to a sparse herpetofauna. Wood Frogs, Blue-spotted Salamanders, and Red-backed Salamanders are found in the moister forests, while Mink Frogs and Northern Leopard Frogs inhabit pond and lake edges.

The **northern transitional (mixed) forest** is the most variable forest type in the Great Lakes and extends from Minnesota and northern Wisconsin across the Upper and northern Lower Peninsulas of Michigan, through central Ontario to upper New England. Sugar maple is the most characteristic tree species where soils are moderately moist, along with hemlock, beech, and yellow birch. Stands of oak and pine trees are common where soils are dry and sandy. As noted above, this forest type blends with the fir-spruce forest in the northern parts of the region. Typical species of the mixed-hardwood forest include the Spotted Salamander, Eastern Gray Treefrog, Northern Red-bellied Snake, and Northern Ring-necked Snake. The Eastern Hog-nosed Snake and Smooth Green Snake inhabit open oak-pine woods and associated grassy clearings and edges, while Wood Turtles occur in the vicinity of streams and rivers within mixed forest habitats.

The **deciduous forests** of the southern Great Lakes are also quite variable, depending on soil moisture levels and elevation. Here the climate is milder, with ample precipitation. Forests of sugar maple and American beech occupy the moist lowland sites with rich soils, while oak-hickory forests may dominate in slightly higher, drier areas. Spotted, Blue-spotted, Jefferson, Red-backed, and Dusky Salamanders; Gray Rat Snakes; and Eastern Box Turtles are characteristic species of deciduous woodlands.

The true **prairie,** dominated by grasses and herbaceous flowering plants, approaches the Great Lakes drainage basin in northern Illinois and southern Wisconsin. As previously noted, prairie habitats also extend (at least in relict form) into Indiana, Ohio, and southern Michigan and Ontario. This eastern prairie peninsula exists (or existed) largely in the form of a mixture of tallgrass prairie and oak-hickory woodland, with elevation and moisture levels determining the local vegetative type. Oak savannas are grasslands with scattered clumps of trees (especially the bur oak). Other grassland habitats occur where the soil is dry and sandy, for example, in the dune areas along the southern Great Lakes shoreline. Most of the original prairie is now under cultivation. Characteristic grassland and savanna herps include the Eastern Tiger Salamander, Plains Leopard Frog, Ornate Box Turtle, Prairie Racerunner, Western Slender Glass Lizard, Plains Garter Snake, and Bullsnake.

**Aquatic communities** offer habitats to many amphibians and reptiles. Large, permanent bodies of water (inland lakes and rivers) are home to Mudpuppies, Bullfrogs, Northern Map Turtles, Eastern Spiny Softshell Turtles, Snapping Turtles, and Northern Water Snakes. Few species enter open Great Lakes waters, but Mudpuppies and Snapping Turtles inhabit the shallower bays, and the peripheral marshes and weedy inlets support Bullfrogs, Green Frogs, Northern Leopard Frogs, Blanding's Turtles, Painted Turtles, Northern Water Snakes, and Northern Ribbon Snakes. These same species also occur in or around inland marshes, ponds, and weedy lakes.

Some amphibians and reptiles depend on unique aquatic habitats. Temporary (vernal) ponds in both woodlands and open grassland are important breeding places for many species of anurans and salamanders. The lack of fish and other aquatic predators in these sites may compensate for the risk of premature drying and loss of larvae in drought years. Spring-fed bog ponds, fens, and flooded sedge meadows are preferred habitats for Pickerel Frogs and Spotted and Bog Turtles. Small ponds and seepages fringed with moss are breeding sites for the Four-toed Salamander, while woodland brooks and springs are utilized by the Northern Red, Two-lined, Spring, and Dusky salamanders. Permanent streams with rocky bottoms and overhanging shrubbery are favored by Queen Snakes.

Adaptable species with broad habitat tolerances are usually the most successful species in human-altered environments. For example, Painted and Snapping Turtles can be common in moderately polluted rivers and lakes in urban areas. Tiger Salamanders, Eastern Newts, Spring Peepers, Gray Tree Frogs, American Toads, and Green Frogs often breed in farm stock ponds and ornamental pools in suburban gardens. Common, Butler's, and Short-headed Garter Snakes and Brown Snakes may be found in suburban yards and vacant urban lots and parks, while these and Red-bellied Snakes, Eastern Milk Snakes, Western Fox Snakes, and Racers will inhabit abandoned or fallow farm fields, grassy-edged hedgerows, and lightly grazed pastures. Kirtland's Snake is another species known to inhabit vacant city lots and moist pastures, but it is now scarce or absent in many places where it was once common.

## Observing and Studying Great Lakes Amphibians and Reptiles

"Herp-watching" is not yet as popular a hobby as bird-watching, but amphibians and reptiles offer similar opportunities for "nonconsumptive" outdoor recreation. Finding and observing amphibians and reptiles is much like "birding," for you must learn the habits of the creatures you seek and be in the right place at the right time. Relevant habitat and behavioral information is noted for each species in the second part of this book. What follows are some general notes on discovering amphibians and reptiles in the wild. For readers interested in more systematic studies or surveys of Great Lakes amphibians and reptiles, the publications by Heyer et al. (1994) and Mifsud (2014) offer useful information on commonly used techniques.

The majority of salamanders spend most of their lives underground or hidden beneath forest debris or in aquatic vegetation. Woodland species may sometimes be discovered by carefully turning (and then replacing) logs and rocks, but the surest way to find them is to venture out in early spring and investigate potential breeding ponds or streams. For many of the "mole" salamanders in the genus *Ambystoma,* this can be the only reliable way to observe them. Breeding activity is greatest at night, often during rainy weather. When wading after dark, take a good flashlight or head lamp and be alert for deep spots and underwater debris. Respect the habitat and the animals—get only as close as is necessary for observation, and avoid disturbing breeding salamanders or their egg masses. While it is unwise to go out alone at night, large groups of people will inevitably cause damage to fragile habitats. A deep footprint in the mud at the edge of a pond can be a significant obstacle to a migrating salamander.

Frogs and toads are usually easier to locate and observe than the secretive salamanders. Like birds, breeding anurans vocally announce their presence with characteristic calls. With practice, breeding calls can be used to identify a frog or toad species and estimate the size of its population. Learning to identify frog and toad vocalizations is not difficult, and recorded calls are commercially available or free on the Internet to help the beginner (for example, http://www.umesc.usgs.gov/terrestrial/amphibians/armi/frog_calls.html). Frog-breeding activity tends to be greatest on warm, damp evenings; the calling males can often be spotted with a flashlight. After the breeding season, some anurans stay close to breeding areas, while others disperse to new habitats. Green Frogs, Mink Frogs, and Bullfrogs tend to remain in or near ponds and lakes, while Northern Leopard Frogs often move into surrounding fields and uplands. Toads, Wood Frogs, Gray Treefrogs, and Spring Peepers prefer moist woodlands but sometimes wander into fields and yards.

Amphibians should be handled only when necessary for positive identification or study, and captured specimens should be released as quickly as possible where they were found. Smaller individuals and species are quite delicate and sensitive to the heating and drying effects of human hands. Never handle an amphibian if your hands have insect repellent, sunscreen, or other chemical substances on them, as these can be harmful or fatal to the specimen. The skin secretions of Great Lakes amphibians are not generally harmful to humans who handle them, but it is wise to avoid getting secretions in your mouth or eyes and to wash your hands after handling any animal.

Aquatic turtles are most easily observed and identified as they bask on logs and along shorelines. They are usually wary and ready to dive into the water at any disturbance, but a careful approach and a good pair of binoculars will allow ample opportunities to see important field marks and behavior. Lizards and snakes can be encountered by walking slowly and carefully through likely habitats or by examining likely hiding places. If you carefully turn over logs, flat rocks, boards, or other debris, small secretive species may be revealed. (Use special caution in areas where venomous snakes are found.) Always respect the habitat—return cover objects to their original positions and leave critical habitats such as rotting logs and rock formations intact and undisturbed if they cannot be explored without their destruction.

Reptiles are more tolerant of handling than amphibians, but it is always a good idea to observe them from a distance to avoid disrupting their normal behavior. Specimens that are captured should be released where they were found. **Only well-trained people, doing legitimate research or conservation work, should ever approach or handle venomous snakes.** Remember that even nonvenomous reptiles may bite if they feel threatened. Avoid the temptation to take herps home as pets or vacation souvenirs. All amphibians and reptiles have special environmental and nutritional needs that are often difficult to meet in captivity, and most children (and their parents) soon tire of the day-to-day maintenance. Amphibians and reptiles have no need for play and are not suitable pets for small children, who often view live animals as animated toys. Remember that all states and provinces have regulations that protect certain species from capture or disturbance.

Many scientific and educational benefits can be derived from studies or exhibition of captive amphibians and reptiles, and many useful books and online resources on the care, husbandry, and breeding of these animals are now available. Many regional herpetological societies offer captive care information to their members and the public. Captive-breeding programs for rare or endangered species can be important conservation tools when integrated into well-planned and officially sanctioned restoration efforts. But studies of amphibians and reptiles in their natural habitats are often more enlightening and valuable. Each year thousands of amateur ornithologists derive much enjoyment from seeking, observing, and photographing birds in the wild, and much useful scientific information is often gathered at the same time. Amateur herpetologists, on the other hand, have been largely concerned with the keeping and breeding of captive amphibians and reptiles. Refocusing some of the interest and enthusiasm of "herp hobbyists" toward the observation and study of wild amphibians and reptiles would add an important recreational dimension to herpetology that would benefit both science and conservation. State-sponsored "Herp Atlases" (e.g., Michigan [www.MIHerpAtlas.org] and Wisconsin [http://www4.uwm.edu/fieldstation/herpetology/atlas.html]) and other Web-based programs (see: https://www.herpmapper.org/) offer opportunities for both amateur and professional herpetologists to document their observations and contribute to our knowledge of amphibian and reptile populations. Resources like these, in conjunction with museum collections, serve as critical data repositories allowing future generations to better understand historic and current species distributions and document species declines or expansions.

## Venomous Snakes and Snakebite

Of the twenty-two species of snakes found in the Great Lakes region, only two are potentially dangerous to humans. The Timber Rattlesnake is extremely rare and possibly extirpated from the region, while the Eastern Massasauga Rattlesnake can be locally common in the proper habitat.

There are no venomous species reported from Michigan's Upper Peninsula, the northern third of Wisconsin, or north of Lake Superior.

Both rattlesnake species tend to avoid confrontation with potential predators, including humans, if given the chance. Rattlesnake venom probably evolved as an aid in capturing food rather than as a defensive weapon. It is produced in modified salivary glands and delivered by hollow fangs mounted at the front of the mouth. Bites from rattlesnakes are very rare in the Great Lakes area, and many of those that do occur are provoked by attempts to handle, prod, or kill the snakes. It bears repeating that rattlesnakes should be approached and handled only by trained persons involved in legitimate research.

There is no reason to let a fear of these snakes interfere with enjoyment of the outdoors. The great majority of people that hunt, fish, camp, or hike in the Great Lakes region will never encounter a venomous snake. Anyone planning activities in or near natural habitats should familiarize themselves with the snake species of the area, including harmless species that could be mistaken for venomous ones. Wear protective clothing, such as sturdy, high-topped footwear and long, loose pant legs and sleeves, when hiking off cleared trails. (However, staying on established trails is not only safer but helps to preserve vegetation and habitats.) A little common sense goes a long way, and the very small chance of accidental snakebite is reduced even further by simply watching where you put your feet and hands.

Should a venomous snakebite occur in our region, most experts now recommend that the victim be kept calm and transported as quickly as possible to a hospital or other emergency medical facility. Traditional first-aid measures, such as cutting and sucking the bite wound and use of tight tourniquets, have fallen into disfavor, as these can lead to severe complications. The use of antivenin serum, administered by a medical professional, is the accepted way to treat snake envenomation, although in cases of mild envenomation or allergy to antivenin serum, a physician might opt for symptomatic treatment and observation. Because of the rarity of snakebite in our area, many physicians will not have firsthand experience with its treatment, but information should be available from poison control centers located in major cities.

In all snakebite cases it is critical that the snake be properly identified, since treating a bite from a nonvenomous snake as though it were a venomous bite would expose the patient to needless risk and worry. If doubt exists, photographing the snake with a camera or cell phone is a good idea; in rare cases it may reasonable to kill the snake for later identification, providing it can be done safely and without undue delay. Rattlesnake bites typically produce pain and swelling, sometimes accompanied by faintness and nausea. Marks left by the two enlarged fangs are usually visible, although occasionally only one fang will penetrate. It has been estimated that perhaps a quarter of all bites from venomous snakes are "dry" (that is, no venom is injected). A bite from a nonvenomous snake will show scratches or pinpoint wounds (from the numerous tiny recurved teeth), and often bleeds freely. It can be treated as one would any scratch or skin puncture, taking care to avoid infection. Seek professional medical advice if any doubt exists as to the severity of the wound.

# AMPHIBIANS (CLASS AMPHIBIA)

# Salamanders

ORDER CAUDATA

There are 676 species of salamanders known worldwide to date, grouped into 66 genera. A large majority of these are native to the Western Hemisphere, and the eastern (especially Appalachian) and far western (Pacific coastal) regions of the United States appear to be centers of salamander evolution and diversity. Salamanders are tailed amphibians that generally have four legs of roughly equal size, though sirens have only two legs. Their lack of scales and claws and a preference for cool, moist surroundings distinguishes them from the scaled, warmth-loving lizards, with which they are often confused. Most species have a characteristic number of vertical creases (costal grooves) on their bodies between the front and hind legs that may be helpful in identification (fig. 5).

A majority of Great Lakes salamanders are largely terrestrial as adults but lay eggs in or near water and have aquatic larvae. Species in the genus *Plethodon* live and reproduce entirely on land. Some species, including the Mudpuppy and Lesser Siren, are permanently aquatic and retain external gills throughout their lives. Under certain conditions, some species of salamanders that are normally terrestrial when sexually mature can remain in the water and reproduce in a gilled "larvalike" state; this condition is called *neoteny*. Neotenic populations of the Tiger Salamander have been found in the Upper and northern Lower Peninsulas of Michigan; Eastern Newts sometimes display neoteny as well.

Most salamanders have a unique method of internal egg fertilization. During or after courtship (which may be simple or elaborate, and occur on land or in water, depending on the species) the male salamander deposits one or more *spermatophores*, which are cylindrical or cone-shaped globs of

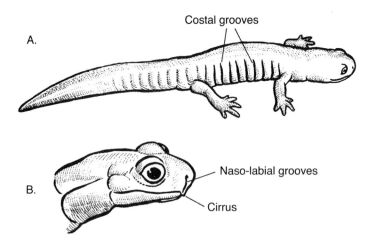

Fig. 5. Salamander characteristics. A. Typical salamander showing costal grooves. B. Head of plethodontid salamander showing nasolabial groove and cirrus. (Drawing by G. van Frankenhuyzen)

gelatinous (jellylike) material capped with sperm. The female then crawls over the spermatophore and takes up the sperm through her vent, where it is stored in the cloaca until the eggs are laid. The period of sperm storage may range from a few hours to a year or more, again depending on the species. This fertilization method differs greatly from the external fertilization of most frogs and toads. A few salamanders, such as the Hellbender (*Cryptobranchus alleganiensis*) and, probably, the Lesser Siren, also have external fertilization.

Selected references for salamanders: Bartlett and Bartlett 2006; Bishop 1941, 1943;; Duellman and Trueb 1986; Green et al. 2013; Petranka 1998; Pfingsten and Downs 1989; Powell, Conant, and Collins 2016; and Stebbins and Cohen 1995.

# Mudpuppies

## FAMILY PROTEIDAE

The family Proteidae includes two genera of permanently aquatic, neotenic salamanders. Inhabiting lakes and streams of eastern North America are at least five species of "mudpuppies" and "waterdogs" in the genus *Necturus.* Only one species is found in the Great Lakes area. The only other member of the family is the blind, cave-dwelling Olm (*Proteus anguinus*) of the European Adriatic coast.

## Mudpuppy (*Necturus maculosus*)

**Description:** The Mudpuppy is a large aquatic salamander with bushy reddish gills behind its head. The gills are larger and bushier in warm, oxygen-poor water and smaller in cooler waters with a higher oxygen content. The Mudpuppy's body, sides, and tail are brown or grayish-brown with scattered bluish-black spots or blotches. Dark pigment tends to increase in older specimens, and some may appear almost black. The head is broad and flattened, and the eyes are small; an irregular dark stripe runs through each eye. The belly is usually pale gray or yellow, often with dark spots. The tail is vertically flattened, and there are four toes on each foot. Mudpuppies have slimy skins and are difficult to hold in the hand. Adult length: 20 to 48.6 cm (8 to 19.1 in).

The sexes are similar, but the male Mudpuppy's vent has wrinkled margins and appears swollen during the breeding season; behind the vent is a curved groove with two backward-pointing papillae. In contrast, the female has a simple slitlike vent.

Larval Mudpuppies are generally black with a yellowish or cream-colored stripe running down each side from nose to tail.

**Confusing Species:** Larvae of the "mole" salamanders (genus *Ambystoma)* have five toes on each hind foot; Mudpuppies have four toes. The Western Lesser Siren has external gills but is eel-like and lacks hind legs.

**Distribution and Status:** Mudpuppies range from New England, New York, and southern Quebec west through the Ohio Valley to southeastern Manitoba and south along the Mississippi Valley to Missouri, Tennessee, and northern Alabama. They are found throughout most of the Great Lakes region but appear to be absent along much of the western shore of Lake Superior and in the boreal forest region north of the lake.

Mudpuppies can be locally abundant but have declined or even disappeared from many places where they were once common. They are considered threatened in Illinois and are a species of concern in Indiana and Michigan.

**Habitat and Ecology:** Mudpuppies inhabit permanent waters, including rivers, reservoirs, inland lakes, and Great Lakes bays and shallows. In clear waters they tend to be nocturnal, remaining hidden beneath rocks and other objects during the day. They can be active both night and day in shallow inlets and coves with thick aquatic vegetation. Mudpuppies are primarily bottom-walkers but can swim with a fishlike motion, their legs folded against the body. They tend to move into shallower waters in spring and fall but seek deeper water in winter and summer and have been recorded at depths of nearly 30 m (100 ft) in Lake Michigan. Young Mudpuppies usually occupy habitats separate from those of the adults.

Mudpuppies are active throughout the year and are often caught on baited hooks in winter by people ice fishing. They feed mostly at night and eat a wide variety of aquatic animal life, including crayfish and other

Mudpuppy, lateral
view (Photo: Richard
D. Bartlett)

Mudpuppy, head and
gills (Photo: David A.
Mifsud)

crustaceans, insect larvae, worms, mollusks, fish eggs, small fish, and other
amphibians (including smaller Mudpuppies). Carrion is readily consumed
and is probably located by a well-developed sense of smell. Mudpuppies are
often caught in traps baited with dead fish.

Enemies of the Mudpuppy include fish, water snakes, herons, and
humans. These salamanders (and many other aquatic amphibians) have sense
organs in the skin, equivalent to the lateral-line system in fish, which can
detect motion and pressure changes in the surrounding water. These epidermal sensors probably help Mudpuppies avoid predators and locate prey.

**Reproduction and Growth:** Mudpuppies often form aggregations in shallow
water in the fall (late September through November), when the normally
solitary males join the females in their shelters beneath submerged rocks
and wood. Occasional mating may occur through the winter into April.
During courtship, the male may swim or crawl under, around, and over
the female. Eventually, the male deposits spermatophores, which are gelat-

inous, sperm-capped globs about 1 cm (0.4 in) high. The female picks up a spermatophore with her vent, and stores the sperm in her cloaca until spring. Egg laying usually occurs in late May or June. Female Mudpuppies typically locate or excavate a nest cavity under a rock, log, board, or other flat object, in water from about 10 cm to 3 m (4 in to 10 ft) deep. In rivers and streams, the opening of the nest tends to face downstream. From 18 to over 140 eggs are attached to the roof of the cavity, where they hang suspended on gelatinous stalks. Egg laying may extend over several days, and the female usually remains with her eggs at least until hatching. Incubation takes from one to two months, with most larvae hatching in July and August. Warmer water temperatures can speed up the process.

At hatching the larvae range from 2 to 2.5 cm (0.8 to 1 in) long. They grow rapidly, more than doubling their length by the end of their first year. Maturity is reached in four to six years, at a length of about 20 cm (8 in). Mudpuppies may live twenty years or more.

**Conservation:** Mudpuppies are often persecuted due to their odd appearance, slimy skins, and undeserved reputation as a menace to game fish. Ice fishers who catch Mudpuppies on their lines frequently throw the hapless creatures out on the ice to die, in the mistaken belief that the salamanders are worthless or even dangerous. The Mudpuppy is harmless to humans and an important contributor to the aquatic ecosystem. While they may occasionally eat fish eggs or small fish, there is no evidence that these salamanders significantly reduce natural game fish populations. Mudpuppies will consume the invasive Round Goby (*Neogobius melanostomus*), which may benefit impacted local fisheries.

Mudpuppy numbers have reportedly fallen in parts of the Great Lakes region, including southern Lake Erie, Saginaw Bay, and many inland lakes and rivers in Wisconsin, Michigan, Indiana, and Ohio, but information on populations and trends is lacking for most areas. Mass die-offs have been reported in Lake Erie and other places, sometimes associated with algae blooms or attributed to botulism outbreaks. Severe storms can wash numbers of Mudpuppies onto the shore where they desiccate and perish. In some places these salamanders have been harvested in large numbers for the biological supply trade, with collectors often targeting breeding aggregations. Since Mudpuppies accomplish most of their respiration through their skin and exposed gills, they will predictably be vulnerable to various pollutants and changes in water quality. They are highly sensitive to chemicals used in Great Lakes lamprey control programs, and Mudpuppy populations in treated streams can be reduced or even extirpated.

# Sirens

## FAMILY SIRENIDAE

The Sirenidae is a North American family of aquatic, eel-like salamanders consisting of four mostly southern species. All have external gills and lack hind feet. Two species of tiny Dwarf Sirens (*Pseudobranchus*) are restricted to Florida, Georgia, and South Carolina, while the Greater Siren (*Siren lacertina*), of Florida and the lower Atlantic coastal plain, is one of the largest salamanders, with a record length of over 3 ft (97.8 cm). The range of the Lesser Siren (*Siren intermedia*) is centered in the deep South but extends up the Mississippi, Ohio, and Wabash drainages into Illinois and Indiana, barely reaching the Great Lakes basin.

## Western Lesser Siren (*Siren intermedia nettingi*)

**Description:** Western Lesser Sirens are aquatic salamanders with bushy reddish gills, elongate, eel-like bodies, and vertically flattened tails. The front legs are tiny, with four toes on each foot, and there are no hind legs. The head is wider than the neck, the snout is rounded, and the eyes are small. Sirens are dark gray, brown, or olive in color, usually with scattered dark spots or flecks, though some specimens may appear almost black. There may be a light stripe on the upper lip. The belly is grayish, often with light spotting. Sirens, like Mudpuppies, have very slimy skin and are difficult to hold. Adult length: 18 to 50 cm (7 to 19.7 in).

The sexes are similar, though males may be larger than females in some populations. Very young larvae may have variable red, orange, or yellow markings on the head, neck, and feet, a yellowish stripe down each side of the body, and a dorsal tail fin (though occasional larvae are uniformly dark and unmarked).

**Confusing Species:** Mudpuppies also have bushy external gills, but they are not eel-like and have four legs (sirens have only front legs).

**Distribution and Status:** The Western Lesser Siren ranges from eastern Texas and the lower Mississippi Valley north to central and eastern Illinois and the Wabash and Kankakee drainages of Indiana. There are records for Porter County, Indiana, and single sites in Allegan and Van Buren Counties in southwestern Michigan. Based on the lack of recent records, the species can be considered extremely rare, and may even be extirpated, within the Great Lakes basin. Other subspecies occur in the southeastern states, from the Carolinas and Florida to Alabama, and in southern Texas.

**Habitat and Ecology:** Western Lesser Sirens are found in ponds, ditches, backwater sloughs, sluggish streams, and shallow lake inlets. Habitats with muddy bottoms and an abundance of aquatic plants are preferred.

They are largely nocturnal, remaining hidden in clumps of thick vegetation or beneath submerged debris during daylight hours. Sirens are well adapted for an aquatic existence but can move overland on occasion, and they can colonize artificial ponds unconnected to natural habitats. They are able to survive drought and the drying of their habitat by retreating into crayfish tunnels or by burrowing into the mud. If the surrounding mud begins to dry, a Siren can conserve water by producing a protective cocoon, which covers its body except for the mouth. The cocoon is probably derived from skin gland secretions (mucus) and layers of epidermal skin.

Sirens eat a wide variety of invertebrate prey, including small crusta-

Western Lesser Siren
(Photo: Richard D.
Bartlett)

Western Lesser Siren,
eating earthworm
(Photo: Richard D.
Bartlett)

ceans, insect larvae, snails, and worms. Although their eyes are small and their vision is often obscured by mud and vegetation, an acute sense of smell assists them in finding food. Quantities of algae and other aquatic plants have been found in their stomachs, but this material is probably swallowed accidently when these salamanders feed on small animals in thick vegetation.

Few salamanders are known to make noises of any kind, but Lesser Sirens reportedly make a variety of hisses, squeaks, whistles, and other sounds. A Siren may "yelp" if seized by a predator or taken in hand and can produce clicking sounds if approached by another siren.

**Reproduction and Growth:** Courtship has not been observed in this species, although fertilization is presumably external since there are no sperm storage areas in the female's cloaca and males lack the cloacal glands needed for producing spermatophores. The eggs are laid in spring in small depressions in the bottom mud or in thick vegetation and in some cases may be attended by the female. The number of eggs produced in a season is highly variable, ranging from about two hundred to five hundred or more, although individual clutches may contain fewer than a dozen. The eggs adhere to each other as well as surrounding vegetation. The larvae hatch after an incubation period of six to nine weeks at a length of about 1.15 cm (0.45 in). Western Lesser Sirens reach maturity in about two to three years after hatching and may live for twenty years or more.

**Conservation:** Western Lesser Sirens are harmless to humans and human interests. They are at the periphery of their range in the Great Lakes region and were perhaps never well established north of the Kankakee River in Indiana.

It has been suggested that the Michigan populations could have been introduced by humans, but it seems at least as likely that the species dispersed there naturally from Indiana, perhaps during a postglacial warm period known as the hypsithermal. Sirens are secretive and inconspicuous, and it is possible that undetected populations still exist in the lower Lake Michigan drainage basin. Unconfirmed accounts have placed them as far north as Muskegon County, Michigan, and additional surveys are warranted. It is noteworthy that both disjunct Michigan populations were reportedly discovered when rotenone, a pesticide used to kill fish, was applied to the shallow inlets of two lakes for fish management purposes. While the use of rotenone revealed the presence of Western Lesser Sirens, it presumably could have eliminated them as well.

# Newts

## FAMILY SALAMANDRIDAE

The family Salamandridae presently includes 114 species in 23 genera found in Europe, northern Africa, Asia, and North America. Of the 2 North American genera, *Taricha* contains 4 species restricted to the Pacific coast region, while *Notophthalmus*, with 3 species, occurs in the eastern United States and Canada. The Eastern Newt, *Notophthalmus viridescens*, is the Great Lakes representative.

Newts lack the costal grooves and slimy skins that are typical of most other salamanders. Their rather rough-appearing skins are well supplied with poison glands, which help discourage predators. Some species can be deadly if swallowed. Reproduction in the Salamandridae involves internal fertilization with spermatophores, but the family shows diverse breeding strategies.

Most species have aquatic larvae, but the female Alpine Salamander (*Salamandra atra*) retains the developing larvae in her body and gives birth to fully formed baby newts. Several species have aquatic adults, eggs, and larvae, with an intervening terrestrial juvenile stage. The Eastern Newt follows this pattern.

## Eastern Newt (*Notophthalmus viridescens*)

**Description:** The Eastern Newt is unique among Great Lakes salamanders in that the gilled aquatic larvae usually metamorphose into a nonbreeding terrestrial stage called an eft. After a variable time on land, the eft undergoes another metamorphosis as it changes into an aquatic breeding adult.

The aquatic adults are olive, greenish-brown, or reddish-brown above, with small black dots scattered over the back and tail. Depending on the subspecies, there may be a row of red spots along each side, and sometimes the spots are bordered with black. There is usually a dark stripe through the eye. The throat and belly are yellow, with scattered tiny black dots.

The dull-looking skin is soft to the touch but not slimy. Neoteny can occur in some populations, in which the breeding adults will retain at least remnants of external gills. Adult length: 6.4 to 14 cm (2.5 to 5.5 in). Males in breeding condition develop very high, rounded tail fins, which extend to a point above the front of the hind legs. The females have straight tail fins, which extend only to a point above the back of the hind legs. In addition, the hind legs of males are thicker than those of the females and develop rough, black ridges on the inner thighs and black nubbins on the toe tips during the breeding season.

Terrestrial efts are usually red, orange, or reddish-brown above and light yellow on the belly. In populations in which adults are typically red spotted, the spots are visible on the eft as well. Efts have a rough, bumpy-textured skin that feels dry to the touch. Their tails are round in cross section, unlike the flattened tails of adults. Efts that are in the process of changing to the aquatic form are darker and may appear intermediate in skin texture and body shape as well as color. Complicating the picture is the fact that adult newts that leave drying ponds to hibernate or aestivate will darken in color, lose the tail fin, and regain a rougher skin texture, and thus they can be confused with transforming efts. Efts are smaller than the adults, ranging in length from 3.5 to 8.6 cm (1.4 to 3.4 in).

Larval Eastern Newts are typically grayish- or olive-brown with black speckling, one or two rows of light yellowish spots on each side and a black stripe running through the eye. When viewed from above, the head narrows toward the nose, appearing wedge-shaped . Larvae have tail fins that extend well up the back.

Eastern Newt, aquatic adult (Photo: Richard D. Bartlett)

Eastern Newt, eft stage

Note: Four subspecies of the Eastern Newt have been described, of which two are found in the Great Lakes region. Red-spotted Newts (*Notophthalmus viridescens viridescens*) usually have two rows of black-bordered red or orange spots on the back as both efts and adults. In the slightly smaller Central Newt (*Notophthalmus virisdescens louisianensis*), the red spots either lack the black borders or are entirely absent.

**Confusing Species:** All other potentially confusing salamanders have costal grooves and smooth skins.

**Distribution and Status:** Eastern Newts are found throughout most of southeastern Canada and the eastern United States west to the edge of the Great Plains. They appear to be absent from the "prairie peninsula" in Illinois, Indiana, and Ohio. Newts occur throughout the Great Lakes region, with the Red-spotted Newt occupying the eastern part (Lake Erie and Lake Ontario drainages) and the Central Newt the western part (Lake Michigan and southern Lake Superior drainages). There is a broad zone of intergradation across Michigan's Lower Peninsula and into Indiana; specimens from this area often display coloration intermediate between the two subspecies. Population densities of Eastern Newts in the Great Lakes basin appear to be generally lower than those typically observed east and south of the region. Newts can be locally common in good habitat but decline or disappear where ponds are drained or polluted or when the surrounding area is deforested.

**Habitat and Ecology:** Small, permanent ponds with ample aquatic plant life are preferred habitats for adult Eastern Newts, although they also occur in temporary ponds, in the shallows of large lakes, and in river sloughs and backwaters. The terrestrial efts are usually found in wooded areas near the breeding ponds, taking refuge under rotting logs, boards, and other natural and unnatural objects. They tolerate drier habitats than other woodland salamanders do but are most active on the surface during and after rain.

Adult Eastern Newts may remain active all year in the deeper ponds, while those in shallow waters that become dry in summer or freeze solid in winter are able to aestivate or hibernate on land, becoming darker and regaining an eftlike skin texture. In some areas, newts join other woodland salamanders in the late winter and early spring migration back to the breeding ponds. Once in the water, the characteristics of the aquatic form (e.g., skin texture, color, and tail fins) redevelop.

Adult Eastern Newts eat many types of small aquatic invertebrates, including crustaceans (e.g., fairy shrimp, cladocerans, and copepods), insect larvae (e.g., mosquito and midge larvae), and mollusks (e.g., fingernail clams and snails). They will readily consume the eggs and larvae of other amphibians when available. Newt larvae feed largely on small invertebrates, including mosquito larvae. The land-living efts eat insects, worms, snails, and other small animals of the leaf litter.

All life stages of the Eastern Newt have toxic skin secretions that can discourage certain predators. Adults are seemingly distasteful to some predatory fish. The terrestrial eft appears to have the greatest concentration of poison glands, and it is believed that the eft's bright red or orange color may serve to warn potential enemies that it is distasteful or even dangerous to eat. When attacked by a bird or small mammal, an eft may arch its back, raise its head and tail, and become immobile. This stiff posture, called the Unken reflex, occurs in a number of amphibians and may serve as a warning, as well as eliminating movement that could stimulate the predator to attack.

**Reproduction and Growth:** Courtship in Eastern Newts can occur both in late fall and in spring, but eggs are laid only in spring. Courtship behavior can be quite complex and usually begins with the male nudging the female's cloaca and displaying by twitching and undulating his body. She may repeatedly swim away, only to be approached again by the persistent male. The male will eventually crawl over the female and move forward until he can clasp her at the neck or just behind her front feet using his hind feet. While in this embrace, called amplexus, the male uses a rippling movement of the end of his tail to "fan" the female, probably to spread stimulating secretions from his cloaca toward her head. He may also rub the side of his head on her snout, again to spread glandular secretions. The female may also raise her own tail and produce the fanning motion. Amplexus can last for several minutes or hours, after which the male releases the female and crawls forward, often with tail still raised and with continued body undulations. The female then follows while nudging the male's tail and cloaca, stimulating him to deposit a spermatophore. The female may then pick up the sperm packet at the tip of the spermatophore with her cloaca, although the male may deposit several more spermatophores before sperm transfer is complete.

Most egg laying occurs in April and May. Females deposit from a few dozen to three hundred or more eggs over a period of several days or weeks, usually attaching them singly (rarely in small clusters) to plants or other objects. The incubation period lasts from two to five weeks, depending on water temperature; at hatching the tiny larvae measure about 0.7 to 0.9 cm (0.3 to 0.4 in) long. The larvae grow quickly, and in late summer they leave the water, transforming into efts. An eft can remain on land for two to seven years before undergoing a second metamorphosis into an aquatic breeding adult. In some populations, particularly in the western part of the Great Lakes area, newts may skip the terrestrial eft stage and metamorphose directly into adults. They can live for ten or more years.

**Conservation:** Eastern Newts are harmless to humans and human interests, and their habit of feeding on mosquito larvae and pupae is certainly a desirable trait. This species has been collected for the commercial pet and biological supply trade, although data on the volume or effect of this collection in the Great Lakes region is lacking. Sale of wild-caught salamanders is now prohibited in most states and provinces of our region. Using Eastern Newts as fish bait is ill-advised for several reasons, including the fact that many fish are repelled by this amphibian's skin secretions. Eastern Newts have declined or disappeared in many areas where habitats have been destroyed or degraded. Populations at the northern periphery of their range might be expected to be more sensitive to disturbance than those farther south or east, where densities are often initially higher. Newts are best conserved by protecting or creating fish-free ponds that are close to woodland habitats.

# Mole Salamanders

FAMILY AMBYSTOMATIDAE

Members of the family Ambystomatidae are medium to fairly large salamanders with prominent costal grooves, robust limbs and bodies, and broad heads. The common family name "mole" salamander comes from the habit of usually staying underground or beneath objects except when breeding. Fertilization is internal via spermatophores, and eggs hatch into typical aquatic gilled larvae that transform into terrestrial adults, although neoteny can occur in some species. There are presently thirty-two species in the genus *Ambystoma*, with six of these occurring in the Great Lakes region. Species identification can be confounded by the presence of unisexual polyploid individuals and populations; this problem is discussed in the "Introduction" (pages 8–10) and the pertinent species accounts.

## Spotted Salamander (*Ambystoma maculatum*)

**Description:** These are fairly stout salamanders with broad heads and rounded snouts. They are black, dark gray, or dark brown above, with two irregular rows of rounded yellow spots running from the back of the head onto the tail. Spots may also be present on the legs and snout; often the head spots are bright orange. Occasional specimens have whitish or tan spots or (rarely) may lack spots altogether. The normally unspotted sides and belly are gray or purplish-gray. Costal grooves: 11–13. Adult length: 10.8 to 24.8 cm (4.3 to 9.8 in).

The sexes are quite similar, but male Spotted Salamanders generally have slimmer bodies than the females, and the area around the male's vent is greatly swollen during the breeding season.

The older larvae (greater than 4 cm in length) are usually greenish-gray to brown above with small yellowish spots or flecks along the side. Their tail fins are often grayish, mottled with light yellow. Newly transformed Spotted Salamanders tend to be dark gray or brown with scattered greenish-yellow flecks or patches and dull yellow or tan bellies. The characteristic rounded spots can develop fairly quickly, usually by the time the young salamanders are around 6 cm (2.4 in) long.

**Confusing Species:** The larger Tiger Salamander has irregularly shaped spots or blotches that extend onto the sides and belly. Newly transformed Blue-spotted Salamanders may have yellow spotting on the sides and belly; in Spotted Salamanders the spots are usually restricted to the upper surfaces.

**Distribution and Status:** Spotted Salamanders occur throughout most of the eastern and south-central United States and southeastern Canada, with the exception of Florida and portions of the Atlantic coastal plain. They have been recorded in all parts of the Great Lakes region except the western shore of Lake Superior.

This species can be locally abundant where mature forested habitat remains intact, but quickly disappears when woodlands are cleared or disturbed by cutting or grazing.

**Habitat and Ecology:** Moist closed-canopy deciduous or mixed woodlands are the preferred habitats for Spotted Salamanders. They usually avoid swamp forests subject to flooding and are uncommon or absent in disturbed forests that have been recently grazed, burned, or harvested for timber. Temporary or semipermanent ponds, either within or adjacent to the woods, are critical habitat elements for this species.

Spotted Salamander,
adult

Spotted Salamander,
recent metamorph

Spotted Salamanders are rarely seen after the spring breeding season. They spend much of their time in burrows underground and have been recorded at a depth of 1.3 m (4.3 ft). They are occasionally found under or within rotting logs, leaf litter, and other moist places. These salamanders probably do not dig their own burrows but use or modify tunnels dug by other animals, such as rodents or large earthworms, or follow cracks and root systems. Hibernation occurs on land, usually close to the breeding ponds but sometimes up to 800 m (2,600 ft) away.

Adult Spotted Salamanders eat worms, snails, slugs, insects, millipedes, spiders, and other invertebrates. The larvae feed on small aquatic invertebrates such as crustaceans (especially copepods and cladocerans), insect larvae, and mollusks, as well as tiny fish and the larvae of other amphibians (including newt larvae). In turn, Spotted Salamander eggs and larvae are eaten by aquatic insects (e.g., diving beetles, giant water bugs, caddisfly larvae, and dragonfly nymphs), fish, Eastern Newts, and the larvae of other *Ambystoma* salamanders, particularly Tiger and Marbled Salamanders. Both the adults and larvae fall prey to snakes, turtles, herons, and raccoons.

Spotted Salamanders have granular ("poison") glands that produce secretions capable of repelling some predators. When confronted with a predator, a Spotted Salamander may extend its forelegs and lower its head or raise and lash its tail, depending on the direction of the attack. This behavior presumably presents the predator with the greatest concentrations of poison glands, which are located behind the eyes and on the tail. These secretions may be irritating to humans if rubbed into the eyes or mucous membranes.

**Reproduction and Growth:** In the Great Lakes area, Spotted Salamanders usually migrate to their breeding ponds from late March to mid-April, depending on local weather conditions. Migration is stimulated by the thawing of the ground and high humidity and often begins on a relatively warm night with heavy rain. Individual salamanders do not always breed every year but tend to return to the same pond each time they breed, probably the pond in which they hatched. Spotted Salamanders often arrive in the ponds a few days later than Blue-spotted or Jefferson Salamanders or their hybrids, perhaps because the latter species overwinter closer to the ponds and thus have a shorter distance to travel. Spotted Salamanders appear to use established routes when traveling to and away from the breeding ponds, even entering and leaving the pond at about the same point each time.

Once in the breeding pond, the males (which often arrive a day or two ahead of the females) congregate in groups and begin moving in circles, swinging their heads back and forth and nudging other salamanders in the sides and vent region with their snouts. When females approach the courting area, the activity increases, as males frantically mill about, trying to identify potential mates. From time to time each salamander will swim rapidly to the surface to get a breath of air and then sink back to the bottom to continue courtship; the frenzied courting and air gulping can cause a noticeable disturbance on the water's surface.

Upon contacting a female, the courting male may continue nudging her vent, as well as walking under her lower jaw ("chin") and rubbing his own chin on her back and tail. The female also joins in the nudging and chin lifting, and the two may continue circling in this odd "dance" for some time. Eventually, the male crawls under the female's chin and then moves away, undulating his body and tail. If the female follows, he will place his vent against the pond bottom or a twig and deposit a spermatophore. As the female moves from side to side, her vent may contact the spermatophore, at which time she can take the sperm into her cloaca. The male may return to nudging and chin rubbing and deposit additional spermatophores. In crowded situations, a female can be courted by several males at the same time and will pick up sperm from any spermatophore that she encounters. In addition, if a male happens upon another male's spermatophore, he often covers it with one of his own.

Eggs are laid from one to several days after courtship and sperm transfer. Each female can lay from 50 to over 250 eggs, in one large globular gelatinous mass or divided into several smaller clusters, attached to sticks or vegetation. Fresh egg masses expand to a diameter of 4 to 10 cm (1.5 to 4 in) and are quite dense in consistency, often retaining their shape even if lifted from the water. The stiffness of the surrounding mass offers the eggs extra protection against some predators.

Spotted Salamander egg masses can be transparent or an opaque milky color, which obscures the eggs. Additionally, many masses take on a greenish color due to the growth of a harmless and probably symbiotic species of algae (*Oophila amblystomatis*) within the egg membranes. The algae reportedly provide the developing salamander embryos with additional oxygen while presumably benefiting from the carbon dioxide given off by the embryos.

The eggs hatch in twenty to sixty days, with shorter incubation periods occurring at higher water temperatures. The newly hatched larvae average about 1.3 cm (0.5 in) in length. They metamorphose in late summer at lengths of 4.0 to 7.5 cm (1.6 to 3 in). Larvae living in drying ponds can hasten their development but will transform at a smaller size than those completing development in more stable aquatic environments. The minimum larval period appears to be about sixty days, while occasional larvae living in cold, permanent waters may not metamorphose until the spring of the following year. Larval mortality is typically very high; often fewer than 10 percent of larvae survive to metamorphosis. Male Spotted Salamanders can probably breed when two or three years old, females when three to five years old. Approximately equal numbers of males and females transform, but males usually outnumber females in breeding aggregations. Annual adult survivorship appears to be quite high, with 80 percent or more of adults often returning to breeding ponds from one year to the next. Spotted Salamanders may live for more than twenty years.

**Conservation:** The future of the Spotted Salamander is tied to the continued presence of relatively undisturbed woodlands and associated temporary and semipermanent fishless ponds. Any human activity that opens the forest canopy, such as selective logging, can lower humidity and create conditions unsuitable to their survival. The construction of roads running between wooded uplands and lowland breeding sites can lead to mass mortality of migrating salamanders.

Spotted Salamanders have been exploited for the biological supply and pet trades, with the animals usually trapped or seined while they are concentrated in breeding ponds. Persistent exploitation during this vulnerable part of their yearly cycle can reduce or eliminate local populations, particularly if collecting pressure is focused on a few scarce breeding sites. Acid precipitation may also be a threat to Spotted Salamanders, although the sensitivity of their eggs and larvae to the effects of pond acidification reportedly varies among populations.

## Blue-spotted Salamander (*Ambystoma laterale*)

**Description:** This is a black or grayish-black salamander with blue spots and flecks on the sides, limbs, belly, and tail, occasionally extending onto the back. The color of the belly may be either black or slightly lighter than the upper surfaces, but the vent area is usually black. Costal grooves: 12–14. Adult length: 7.6 to 14 cm (3 to 5.5 in).

The sexes are similar, though males average slightly smaller than females and have relatively longer, more flattened tails. During the breeding season the males have swollen vents.

The larvae vary in appearance, but older individuals (those with all four legs present) tend to be dark brown, olive, or gray above with dark mottling on the tail fins. Some may have dull yellow dorsal blotches and/or a yellowish stripe down each side of the back. The belly is usually unmarked and lighter than the back.

This species is involved in the unisexual "Jefferson Salamander complex" of polyploid *Ambystoma*. Blue-spotted/Jefferson Salamander combinations are most common, but specimens involving Small-mouthed and Tiger Salamanders can occur, especially in the Lake Erie drainage area. The polyploids are usually intermediate in form and color between the two parent species but will look more like the species from which they received the most inherited genetic material. It is usually difficult or impossible to confirm the identity or parental origin of a polyploid *Ambystoma* without laboratory analysis.

**Confusing Species:** The Jefferson Salamander is larger and is brown or gray, not black, on the back and paler on the belly, with gray color around the vent. Bluish flecking, if present, is confined to the sides and limbs. The Jefferson also has longer limbs and toes and a relatively longer, broader snout.

The Small-mouthed Salamander has a very short snout, with a slightly protruding lower jaw, and its markings are usually grayish, not blue. The Slimy Salamander has white markings on the back and a groove between each nostril and the lip. The dark phase of the Red-backed Salamander has a much narrower body, tiny legs, and small black and white spots on the belly.

**Distribution and Status:** The Blue-spotted Salamander is a cold-tolerant species occurring from northern New Jersey and New England north through Quebec to Labrador and west through southern Ontario and the Great Lakes basin to southeastern Manitoba, Minnesota, and Wisconsin. Populations of unisexual polyploid *Ambystoma* that appear to be combinations of Blue-spotted and Jefferson Salamanders occur in portions of the southern part of this range, from Nova Scotia west through southern Michigan and adjacent Ohio and Indiana to northern Wisconsin. Unisexuals representing combinations with the Blue-spotted and Small-mouthed Salamanders occur largely in or near the western Lake Erie basin.

Blue-spotted Salamanders can be quite common in woodlands with the required breeding ponds. They seem to be more tolerant of human habitat disturbance than is the Spotted Salamander, persisting in fragmented and cutover woods long after the latter species has disappeared. "Pure" (non-polyploid) populations are scarce at the southern edge of the range. This species is listed as endangered in Ohio and Pennsylvania and of special concern in Indiana and New York.

**Habitat and Ecology:** These salamanders inhabit both deciduous and coniferous forests, from moist bottomlands to dry uplands. They are perhaps most abundant in moist woodlands with sandy soils but turn up in a variety of places, including open fields and suburban backyards. The presence of vernal ponds that retain water into midsummer is an essential element of their habitat.

Blue-spotted Salamanders spend much of their time hidden beneath logs, rocks, and leaf litter and will use or enlarge the burrows of other small woodland animals. Unlike other *Ambystoma* species, however, they are often found aboveground throughout the warmer months and may move about in the open during rain showers.

These salamanders eat many types of small invertebrates, including earthworms, spiders, snails, slugs, centipedes, and various insects and their larvae. Adults in and around breeding ponds in spring will reportedly eat aquatic insect larvae and nymphs. The larvae feed on aquatic invertebrates, particularly cladocerans (water fleas), copepods, and insects. Where abundant, larval *Ambystoma* may be significant predators on mosquito larvae.

The skin of this species contains granular ("poison") glands that produce a whitish, noxious substance. These glands are especially concentrated on the upper surface of the tail. If gently prodded by a curious human, a Blue-spotted Salamander may raise and undulate its tail; poking or grasping the animal's body can lead to a lashing of the tail accompanied by greater production of the noxious secretions. The head may be tucked beneath the tail for protection. Presumably these defensive behaviors would also be elicited by the probing nose of a hungry shrew or raccoon.

**Reproduction and Growth:** Migration of Blue-spotted Salamanders to their breeding ponds occurs in late March or early April, often spurred by warm evening rains, though warming temperatures and rapid snowmelt may be enough to trigger movement. This species generally arrives at the ponds a day to several days before the other spring-breeding *Ambystoma* salamanders.

Courtship can involve an often brief phase in which the male nuzzles and nudges the female with his snout. He then crawls above the female, grasps her behind the front legs with his own front legs, and begins rubbing his chin on her head and snout. The pair may stay in this position for several hours, occasionally rising to the surface for air and then sinking slowly

Blue-Spotted
Salamander, adult

Blue-Spotted
Salamander, new
metamorph

to the bottom. If approached by a rival male, a clasped male will attempt to carry his mate away with vigorous swimming motions of his tail. Eventually, after much thrashing and chin rubbing, the male releases the female and moves forward, depositing a spermatophore in front of her. She may then move over the spermatophore and take the sperm into her cloaca. The male often deposits several spermatophores during one mating sequence and can produce from about ten to forty or more during a breeding session, many of which are not used by the courted female. Polyploid unisexual salamanders, which are entirely female, will sometimes "steal" sperm by picking up these "excess" spermatophores.

Female Blue-spotted Salamanders normally lay their eggs within two days of mating, attaching the rather flimsy gelatinous egg masses to sticks, rocks, leaves, and other submerged objects. There are from one to a dozen or so eggs per cluster, with the total egg complement per female ranging from 35 to over 500, probably averaging about 225. The larvae hatch after three to five weeks (depending on water temperature) at a length of 0.8 to 1.2 cm (0.3 to 0.5 in).

In late summer, the larvae metamorphose into land-dwelling salamanders at a total length of about 5.5 to 7.5 cm (2.2 to 3 in). If a breeding pond begins to dry up prematurely, the larvae can transform earlier but at a smaller size than usual. Newly transformed Blue-spotted Salamanders may have yellowish instead of bluish spotting on the sides and tail but usually attain the adult coloration over a period of several weeks. These salamanders mature in about two years.

**Conservation:** Blue-spotted Salamanders and their unisexual kin require wooded habitats adjacent to fishless ponds and other still, shallow waters. They are fairly tolerant of selective logging and low-density residential development as long as the critical parts of the habitat remain intact. Local populations of this species are threatened by clear-cutting of woodlands and the building of roads between breeding ponds and terrestrial habitats.

## Jefferson Salamander (*Ambystoma jeffersonianum*)

**Description:** This salamander is dark brown, brownish-gray, or slate gray above, with a paler belly and a grayish vent region. Many specimens have light bluish flecks scattered along the sides and tail, sometimes extending onto the back. This flecking is most conspicuous in younger salamanders and may virtually disappear in older adults. Compared to other *Ambystoma species,* Jefferson Salamanders have relatively long, wide snouts and long toes. Costal grooves: 12–14. Adult length: 10.7 to 21 cm (4.2 to 8.3 in).

Breeding males have swollen vents, and their tails are relatively longer and more compressed and bladelike than those of females; they also appear more slender than egg-carrying females. Both sexes reportedly become darker and less conspicuously marked after the breeding season. Newly hatched larvae are usually yellowish-green with darker blotches on the back and a tail fin, which is mostly uncolored except toward the tip. Older larvae are mottled greenish-gray above, sometimes with small yellowish spots along the sides, and have a pale, mostly unmarked belly.

The Jefferson Salamander and the Blue-spotted Salamander contribute their genes to populations of all-female polyploid salamanders throughout the central and southern Great Lakes basin. These unisexual specimens may appear more like one or the other of the parent species, depending on which species contributed the majority of its inherited genetic material.

**Confusing Species:** A Blue-spotted Salamander is smaller and darker (usually black) with conspicuous bluish spots on the sides; its vent area is usually black. Small-mouthed Salamanders have very short snouts, short toes, and grayish markings. The Slimy Salamander has white markings and a groove running from each nostril to the lip.

**Distribution and Status:** Jefferson Salamanders are found from western New England, New York, and Pennsylvania west to southern Indiana and northern Kentucky. The "hybrid zone" with the Blue-spotted Salamander extends from the Maritime Provinces west through the southern and central Great Lakes region to Indiana and Wisconsin. Within the Great Lakes region, pure populations of Jefferson Salamanders are most likely to occur in the drainages south of Lake Erie and Lake Ontario, and in southwestern Ontario west of Lake Ontario (they are considered to be endangered in Ontario). They can be locally common in a suitable habitat.

**Habitat and Ecology:** Jefferson Salamanders prefer relatively undisturbed deciduous woodlands. They are most common in moist, well-drained upland forests and usually avoid lowland areas prone to flooding. Like other *Ambystoma,* this species breeds in ponds within or adjacent to their woodland habitats. Ideal breeding ponds are fishless but must hold water at least into midsummer. They frequently share habitat and breeding sites with the Spotted Salamander and Wood Frog.

For much of the year these salamanders remain hidden underground or beneath or within rotting logs or leaf litter. They often use or modify the burrows of other small woodland animals. Most Jefferson Salamanders spend the summer-winter period within 400 m (0.25 mi) of their breeding ponds, although a few specimens may travel up to 1,600 m (1 mi). Surface activity and migration occur at night or occasionally on overcast rainy days.

Adult Jefferson Salamanders are known to eat insects and snails and probably take an assortment of small invertebrates. The larvae consume aquatic invertebrates, as well as smaller siblings and Spotted Salamander larvae.

Like their relatives, this species has skin glands that produce noxious secretions; these are particularly concentrated on the upper base of the tail. Defensive behaviors include tail waving and lashing, and tucking the head under the tail. Skin secretions of these salamanders may cause irritation if rubbed into eyes or mucous membranes.

**Reproduction and Growth:** Jefferson Salamanders migrate to breeding ponds in late winter or very early spring, often while snow still covers much of the ground and ice has barely begun to retreat from the pond edges. A day or two of rain or rapid snowmelt appears to trigger the movement. If cold weather returns, the migrating salamanders take cover and wait for more favorable conditions; thus the salamanders may arrive at the ponds in "waves" over a period of several days or weeks. The first contingent of males usually precedes the arrival of the first females, and Jefferson Salamanders are often well into breeding before Spotted Salamanders arrive at shared breeding sites.

Courtship behavior of this species closely resembles that of the Blue-spotted Salamander. The male grasps the female behind her front legs with his own forelimbs and rubs her head with his snout and chin. The pair may remain clasped together for several hours. Eventually the male releases the female and crawls ahead of her while wriggling his body and waving his tail. If she follows and nudges his tail and vent, he will deposit a spermatophore on a leaf or twig on the pond bottom. The female may move over the spermatophore and pick up the sperm, or perhaps the whole spermatophore, with her cloaca. The last part of the sequence is often repeated when necessary, and the male can release additional spermatophores, up to a dozen or more, during a courtship sequence.

The females deposit their eggs in small, elongate gelatinous clusters attached to underwater sticks and vegetation. Anchoring the eggs below the surface assures their survival if the pond should refreeze during a cold

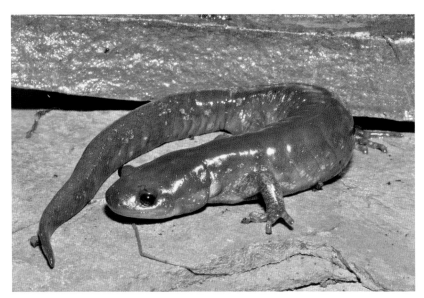

Jefferson's Salamander
(Photo: Richard D.
Bartlett)

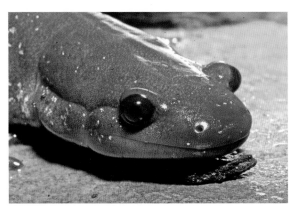

Jefferson's Salamander
(Photo: Richard D.
Bartlett)

period. The number of eggs per mass varies from 1 to 60 (usually 20 to 30), and the total number of eggs produced per female ranges from 100 to about 280. Egg masses often appear green due to the invasion of certain algae into the egg membranes.

The length of incubation varies with the water temperature. Eggs removed to a warm (21°C) indoor tank can hatch in about two weeks, but under natural conditions up to forty-five days may be required. Newly hatched larvae range in length from 1.0 to 1.4 cm (0.4 to 0.55 in). Hatching success can be quite high, but the survival rate of larvae is normally very low (often less than 1 percent), due mostly to predation. Surviving larvae transform into terrestrial salamanders in two to three months, with metamorphosis occurring sooner, and at a smaller size, if the breeding pond begins to dry prematurely. In a dry summer, however, many larvae will die if the ponds dry too quickly. New metamorphs are from 4.8 to 7.5 cm (1.9 to 2.9 in) long. They can breed in two to three years, and individual Jefferson Salamanders may live for six years or longer.

**Conservation:** This species can persist as long as relatively undisturbed woodland habitats adjacent to suitable, fishless breeding ponds are preserved. The construction of roads between terrestrial winter habitats and breeding sites can have disastrous consequences, as large numbers of salamanders are often destroyed during the brief spring migration.

## Small-mouthed Salamander (*Ambystoma texanum*)

**Description:** As its name implies, this species has a relatively small head and a very short, blunt snout. The head often looks somewhat swollen behind the eyes. When viewed from the side, the lower jaw barely protrudes beyond the upper jaw. The dorsal coloration varies from light gray to brownish-gray or black. Most specimens have an irregular pattern of grayish or whitish blotches and flecks on the upper surfaces, becoming heaviest on the sides and extending onto the otherwise dark belly. Small-mouthed Salamanders in their breeding ponds may appear paler and have more conspicuous light markings than those found on land after the breeding season. Costal grooves: 14–16. Adult length: 11 to 17.8 cm (4.3 to 7 in).

Male Small-mouthed Salamanders have swollen vents during the breeding season and tend to be smaller than females but with longer and more compressed tails.

Newly hatched larvae are dark brown or olive green with light bars or crossbands on the back. Larger larvae may still show crossbands and have a light stripe down each side of the back, but those nearing metamorphosis often have the light markings obscured by dark pigment.

Small-mouthed Salamanders are included in the "Jefferson Salamander complex" of all-female polyploids, as mentioned in the Introduction, and specimens that appear close to this species or a combination of this and other *Ambystoma*, are likely unisexuals, particularly in the region south and west of Lake Erie. Individual salamanders possessing genetic material from the Small-mouthed, Blue-spotted, and Tiger Salamander are known from Kelleys Island in southern Lake Erie.

**Confusing Species:** Both Blue-spotted and Jefferson Salamanders have longer snouts and bluish markings on the sides. Marbled Salamanders have a bold pattern of whitish bands on a black background. The Slimy Salamander and the dark phase of the Red-backed Salamander both have a groove running from each nostril to the lip.

**Distribution and Status:** This species is found from northeastern Ohio west to Missouri and eastern Nebraska and south through western Kentucky and Tennessee to the Gulf Coast. Within the Great Lakes basin it occurs in northern Ohio, northeastern Indiana, southeastern Michigan, and on several of the islands in southern Lake Erie.

These salamanders are common in many parts of the wider range, and they are reported to be fairly tolerant of human environmental disturbance, persisting even in some agricultural and suburban areas. Small-mouthed Salamanders are extremely rare and considered an endangered species in Michigan, where they reach the northern limit of their range. Ontario also lists this species as endangered, due to a declining population on Pelee Island in Lake Erie.

**Habitat and Ecology:** Small-mouthed Salamanders are most abundant in lowland floodplain woods, but they also occur in areas where the forest cover has been fragmented or largely removed and seem quite at home in open habitats such as prairie and farmland. Shallow bodies of water are required for breeding purposes, and they often share woodland vernal ponds with other *Ambystoma*. However, Small-mouthed Salamanders also breed in runoff ponds, floodings, river backwaters, and roadside ditches, where there is less competition from forest-dependent species.

In spring, when not in the breeding ponds, these salamanders remain hidden beneath rotting logs, rocks, or leaf litter. Later, during the warm summer months and over the winter, they are largely underground, using the burrows dug by crayfish and small mammals. Evening rain showers may stimulate them to wander above ground, perhaps seeking food or alternative cover.

Earthworms, insects, and slugs are favored foods of adult Small-mouthed Salamanders, while the larvae eat a variety of small aquatic invertebrates and occasionally smaller larvae of their own and other salamander species. The larvae are, in turn, eaten by crayfish, predaceous aquatic insects, birds, and snakes, while adults are consumed by garter and water snakes and other vertebrate predators.

This species, like other *Ambystoma*, has concentrations of granular ("poison") glands on the upper surface of the tail. Secretions of these glands are probably toxic or at least repellent to some predators. When confronted with a potential enemy, a salamander will raise and undulate its tail, while curling the head underneath the tail. At times the tail may be lashed at the attacker, and if grasped by a limb the salamander may roll toward the attacker. Some Small-mouthed Salamanders may also use a defensive posture (the Unken reflex) in which the body is curled up with head and tail arched upward and limbs held tightly to the side. It is thought that the attack response of some sight-oriented predators may be inhibited when the prey becomes stiff and motionless.

**Reproduction and Growth:** Small-mouthed Salamanders often migrate to their breeding ponds very early in the year, seemingly at the first hint of springlike weather. A couple of days of rain in late winter may stimulate movement, frequently while ice still covers portions of the ponds. This salamander typically remains closer to the aquatic breeding sites in summer and winter than related species do and thus may not have as far to travel for reproduction.

Courtship behavior in the Small-mouthed Salamander is quite similar to that of the Spotted Salamander. They may gather in courting groups with males bumping and nudging the females and each other. Now and then a male will move off and deposit several spermatophores on sticks or leaves or the bottom substrate, often in the presence of one or more females. They will also cover the spermatophores of other males with their own. Females

Small-mouthed Salamander, note defensive secretions on tail

Small-mouthed Salamander, note short snout

walk over the spermatophores and take up the sperm into their cloacas; each female may receive sperm from several different males. Courting male Small-mouthed Salamanders occasionally clasp the females behind the front legs, as occurs in Blue-spotted and Jefferson Salamanders, but clasping (amplexus) appears to be the rare exception rather than the rule in this species.

Each female can produce from about 300 to 700 eggs annually; these can be deposited singly or (more often) in small, rather loose gelatinous masses containing 3 to 30 eggs each. The masses are attached to sticks, leaves, or plant stems. Hatching may occur in three to eight weeks, with the incubation period dependent on water temperature. Newly hatched larvae are about 1 cm (0.4 in) in length. They grow quickly and transform into terrestrial salamanders in two to four months, when about 5 cm (2 in) long, and probably reach breeding size in the second year after metamorphosis.

**Conservation:** Small-mouthed Salamanders remain common in portions of their range, due no doubt to their wide habitat tolerances. On the other hand, the clearing of forested land for agriculture or timber harvest has certainly reduced their numbers. Particularly on the northern edge of their range, where they are generally rare and most vulnerable to extirpation, critical management would include the preservation of woodlands with known populations, along with maintenance of adjacent shallow, fish-free ponds that hold water into midsummer. Northern populations may be impacted by competitive interbreeding with unisexual polyploids.

## Marbled Salamander (*Ambystoma opacum*)

**Description:** The Marbled Salamander is a stout, thick-bodied salamander with white or gray markings on a black to dark-brown-black background color. The light markings usually occur as bands across the head and back; sometimes these merge into an irregular stripe along each side of the back and neck. The tail is banded with black and white, and the belly may be black or brownish-black, occasionally with some light speckling. Costal grooves: 11–13. Adult length: 8.5 to 12.7 cm (3.4 to 5 in).

In males the light dorsal markings are pure white, while in females they are gray. The male's vent appears more swollen than the female's. Both of these sexual characters are more pronounced during the breeding season. The larvae are usually brown or gray-brown with light spots or blotches on the sides and tail fins. Newly transformed juveniles are brown or black with scattered light markings, which are often quite dense on the head and more diffuse on the back and tail. These markings may start out yellowish and become bluish to silvery white during the first few days out of water. The crossbanded pattern of the adult develops gradually over a period of several weeks or months.

**Confusing Species:** These stocky and boldly marked salamanders are unlikely to be confused with other species in the Great Lakes area. Small-mouthed Salamanders are slimmer, with light markings scattered along their sides that are not arranged in crossbands. Spotted Salamanders have rounded yellow spots that do not merge on the sides. Tiger Salamanders are much larger, with irregular yellowish or brownish spots and blotches.

**Distribution and Status:** Marbled Salamanders are found from southern New England to northern Florida, west to eastern Texas and north to southern Indiana and Ohio. Disjunct populations occur in northern Ohio (including Kelleys Island in western Lake Erie) and in northern Indiana and southern Michigan along the southern edge of the Lake Michigan basin. These latter localities may host relict populations, indicating a formerly wider northern distribution, perhaps during a warm postglacial period.

This species is fairly common, even locally abundant, in some parts of its range but is generally rare in the Great Lakes region. It is considered an endangered species in Michigan, where it is at the northern limit of its distribution, and a species of special concern in New York.

**Habitat and Ecology:** Marbled Salamanders are most common in moist lowland forests but also occupy drier wooded ridges and rocky hillsides. They spend most of their time hidden beneath logs, rocks, and leaf litter or below ground level in tunnels dug by small mammals and are rarely seen outside the fall breeding season. This species is quite tolerant of dry conditions but will move into deeper burrows to avoid the summer heat.

Adult Marbled Salamanders eat small invertebrates such as worms, slugs, snails, and various insects and their larvae. Their larvae feed on zooplankton, crustaceans, insects (immature and adult stages), and the eggs and larvae of other amphibians. By breeding in fall, this species gives its larvae a head start on spring-breeding salamanders, which often share the same ponds. Thus, Marbled Salamander larvae have usually grown considerably by the time the larvae of other species, such as Spotted Salamanders and Eastern Newts, are just beginning to hatch and so can easily feed on them.

Like other *Ambystoma*, this species has granular ("poison") glands in its skin that are particularly concentrated on the upper surface of the tail. If threatened, a specimen will raise its tail and lash it at the potential enemy. This not only exposes the predator to the noxious skin secretions but may attract its attention to a less vital portion of the salamander's body. These defenses have been shown to work against shrews, which are potentially important predators in the forest floor environment.

**Reproduction and Growth:** Marbled Salamanders court, mate, and deposit eggs on land in the fall, unlike other eastern *Ambystoma* that breed in water in the spring. From late September through October the adults migrate at night to the edges of woodland vernal ponds, which typically have receded or dried up during the summer. Here they hide beneath logs, leaves, fallen bark, or leaf litter.

Courtship behavior is much like that described for the Spotted Salamander, except that it takes place on land. Marbled Salamanders reportedly will drown if submerged in water. The males engage in much head butting and nudging of other salamanders, and a male may use his tail to block the retreat of another individual. If a female is encountered, the male tries to thrust his snout under her vent, stimulating her to nudge the male's vent. This behavior often results in the courting pair moving in circles and has been likened by human observers to a waltz. Eventually the male moves forward and deposits a spermatophore; the female can then move over the spermatophore and take the sperm packet into her cloaca.

The female lays from 50 to more than 200 eggs in a small cavity beneath leaf mold, moss, fallen bark, a rotted log, or other cover. The nest location is generally at the edge or bottom of a dry pond bed that will refill during fall or winter rains. The eggs may adhere together in a loose cluster but are not surrounded by an enclosing gelatinous mass. They soon pick up soil particles and blend with their surroundings. The female often curls around her eggs until the nest is flooded, probably helping to keep them moist and offering protection from fungal invasion and small predators. Two or more females sometimes deposit their eggs in communal nests.

The time from egg laying to hatching is extremely variable, depending

Marbled Salamander, adult

Marbled Salamander, larva (Photo: Wayne VanDevender)

on temperature and water levels, but is minimally about two weeks. The developing eggs tolerate rather cool temperatures but are destroyed by freezing. Normally the larvae emerge soon after the nest is inundated; if rains are delayed, they can survive in the egg for several weeks or even months. At hatching the larvae range from about 1.4 to 1.9 cm (0.5 to 0.7 in) in length. Larval growth rates depend on water temperatures and food supply. Metamorphosis usually occurs in late spring or early summer, when the larvae are from 4.5 to 7.5 cm (1.8 to 3 in) long. Losses of eggs, larvae, and juvenile salamanders to predators and other hazards (such as drying and freezing) are often extremely high; survivors can reproduce in their third or fourth year and potentially live at least nine years.

**Conservation:** The unique fall breeding habits of Marbled Salamanders can give their larvae a competitive advantage over spring-breeding amphibians, as noted above. However, this advantage will be lost in most years over much of the Great Lakes region, where small woodland ponds typically freeze completely during long, cold winters, leading to the total loss of eggs or larvae. This factor may, at least in part, explain the general scarcity and spotty distribution of the species in the Great Lakes basin. An effort should be made to protect known Marbled Salamander localities, but it seems unlikely that populations of this salamander will be able to expand in the region without significant climatic warming and the availability of large contiguous tracts of suitable habitat. Scientists studying the predicted effects of "climate change" might well focus some attention on the fate of this species in the Great Lakes basin.

## Eastern Tiger Salamander (*Ambystoma tigrinum*)

**Description:** Eastern Tiger Salamanders are robust animals with irregular yellow, olive-brown, or tan blotches and spots on a black, gray, or brown background color. The head is large, with a broad, rounded snout. The eyes are small and often have gold irises. The belly is usually yellowish or olive-yellow with invading dark pigment, but in some specimens it may appear gray with yellowish spots or streaks. This is the largest terrestrial salamander of the Great Lakes region. Costal grooves: 12–13. Adult length: 17 to 33 cm (6.7 to 13 in).

Males have proportionally longer, more compressed tails and longer, thicker hind legs than do females. During the breeding season the male's vent area is greatly swollen.

Newly hatched larvae are usually yellowish-green or olive with darker blotches along the back, a light stripe along each side, and whitish bellies. The older larvae often retain the light stripe on the sides and the light belly, but some develop numerous black dots on the upper surfaces, while others become darker, with light mottling on the tail and fins. All have pointed toes and broad, flattish, rounded heads. In some populations a cannibalistic form of the Tiger Salamander larvae may appear, possibly in response to crowded conditions or limited food resources. Compared to normal larvae, these individuals have larger heads, more flattened snouts, and longer teeth and feed largely on other salamander larvae, including those of their own species. In addition, neotenic populations of Tiger Salamanders occur in some places; gilled adults have been reported in both the Upper and northern Lower Peninsulas of Michigan.

Newly transformed specimens tend to be grayish or greenish-brown in color, with a dull mottling of lighter pigment. Within a few weeks a scattering of widely separated yellow or tan spots appears, which gradually merge over time into the blotched pattern of the adult.

**Confusing Species:** Spotted Salamanders have rounded yellow spots in two irregular rows (not randomly distributed spots, streaks, or blotches) and grayish bellies. The large size of the Tiger Salamander will distinguish it from most other *Ambystoma*.

**Distribution and Status:** The Eastern Tiger Salamander occurs in numerous isolated populations from central New York and Long Island south along the coastal plain to the eastern Gulf of Mexico and eastern Texas. A more contiguous center of occurrence includes the western Ohio River valley from western Tennessee and Kentucky north through the southern Great Lakes basin and west to Minnesota, Iowa, and Missouri. The species is absent from the Appalachian Highlands and the lower Mississippi Delta. In our region the species is found in northern Ohio, Indiana, and Michigan's Lower Peninsula to northern Illinois and eastern Wisconsin. A disjunct (perhaps introduced) population occurs in Alger County in Michigan's Upper Peninsula.

A number of introduced populations have become established outside the natural range of the species, probably due to the use of salamander larvae as fish bait. Unisexual polyploid salamanders possessing genetic material (DNA) from *Ambystoma tigrinum* are occasionally found in the southern Great Lakes area; these hybrids may be very difficult to identify based on external features.

This species varies greatly in abundance within its Great Lakes range. Large populations can occur where ideal breeding habitat is available, but elsewhere the species may be uncommon or rare, especially toward the northern and eastern periphery of the range. It is listed as endangered in New York and possibly extirpated in Ontario.

**Habitat and Ecology:** Eastern Tiger Salamanders are less dependent on forested habitats than most other *Ambystoma*. They live in woodlands but also in more open habitats such as marshes, grasslands, farmlands, and suburbs. The primary requirement is access to permanent and semipermanent (preferably fishless) ponds for breeding, including farm ponds, gravel pits, floodings, and ornamental backyard ponds.

Adult Tiger Salamanders live underground for most of the year and are quite capable of digging their own burrows, in contrast to related species that usually use the burrows of other animals. They have been found over 60 cm (2 ft) below the surface. This burrowing habit allows them to escape the temperature extremes on the surface and may explain the wide habitat tolerances of the species. There are two major periods of surface activity—the late winter/early spring migration to breeding ponds, and a second, less directional movement in early fall. These nocturnal movements are often stimulated by rainfall and result in these creatures turning up in basements, window wells, garages, and swimming pools. Many are killed while trying to cross roads.

The usual food of this salamander includes worms, snails, insects, and slugs. Captive specimens have eaten smaller salamanders, frogs, newborn mice, and baby snakes, and it is likely that similar items are also eaten in the wild when the opportunity presents itself. Tiger Salamander larvae begin feeding on small crustaceans (e.g., ostracods and copepods) and insect larvae but soon grow large enough to eat tadpoles, smaller salamander larvae, and even small fish.

Tiger Salamander eggs and smaller larvae are consumed by various aquatic insects and their larvae, including dragonfly nymphs, caddisfly larvae, and diving beetles, as well as by newts and larger salamander larvae.

Tiger Salamander, old
adult

Tiger Salamander,
recent metamorph

Older larvae are readily taken by wading birds, water snakes, and fish; this
species may be eliminated from breeding ponds when game fish are introduced. Terrestrial adults and juveniles are eaten by snakes, larger birds, and
mammalian predators. Their habit of remaining underground much of the
time probably contributes, at times, to a fairly high adult survivorship.

Like other *Ambystoma*, Tiger Salamanders have granular ("poison")
glands concentrated on the upper surface of the tail, and they can raise and
lash their tails if prodded or otherwise threatened. This may discourage
some predators. However, many specimens fail to display any defensive
behavior when exposed except for trying to walk away or wriggle out of a
restraining hand.

**Reproduction and Growth:** Migration to the breeding ponds occurs in late winter or early spring, usually during a (relatively) warm night rain that results in a thawing of the ground surface. Males often arrive several days before the females, with the first to appear probably having overwintered nearer the breeding site. During the nocturnal courtship, a male uses his snout to nudge and butt other salamanders, which are sometimes lifted off the pond bottom in the process. Upon contacting a female, a male may literally shove her along with his snout, apparently to move her away from other males.

Eventually the male will walk under the female's chin, leading her forward, and she may follow, nudging his tail and vent area. This latter behavior stimulates the male to deposit a spermatophore. The female may wriggle the posterior part of her body until her vent contacts the spermatophore, allowing her to take sperm into her cloaca. The pair maintains contact as they move forward, with the female continuing to nudge the male's vent, and the latter producing additional spermatophores. There is much breeding competition in this species. Males will purposefully interfere with courting pairs and frequently cover the spermatophores of other males with their own.

Females lay their eggs at night, normally from twenty-four to forty-eight hours after courtship and insemination. The egg masses are attached to twigs, grass stems, or leaf litter, usually near the pond bottom. The masses can be globular or elongate in shape and contain from 1 to over 100 eggs. Larger masses may resemble those of the Spotted Salamander, but the jelly mass of the Tiger Salamander is less firm than the Spotted's and tends to fall apart if lifted from the water. Each female produces from 100 to over 5,000 eggs in a season.

Embryonic development may require from two to six weeks or more, depending on water temperature. Newly hatched larvae are 1.3 to 1.7 cm (0.5 to 0.7 in) long. The time from hatching to metamorphosis is quite variable and depends on the relative quality and permanence of the breeding site. In shallow ponds that dry out early in summer, larvae can transform in less than three months, at a length of about 7 cm (2.8 in). This is exceptional, however, and in more permanent ponds the larvae may not transform until they are four to six months old, at lengths of 8.5 to 15 cm (3.4 to 6 in). Some larvae may overwinter in the water and transform the following year, nearly reaching adult size in the meantime. Larger metamorphs are probably able to breed the spring following transformation.

The many hazards of pond life can result in high mortality between egg deposition and metamorphosis, and often only a tiny fraction of eggs laid results in new salamanders entering the breeding population. Adults can potentially live long lives, however, and some captives have survived for more than twenty years.

**Conservation:** Eastern Tiger Salamanders are generally harmless to human interests. They are efficient predators in their aquatic and subterranean habitats, and their prey undoubtedly includes some insect pests. The larvae are sometimes considered undesirable in fish hatcheries. Large larvae will feed on very small fish, but their main effect might be to act as competitors with the fish. As the fish grow larger they can turn the tables and feed on the salamander larvae. In some places larval *Ambystoma*, mostly *A. tigrinum*, are captured, usually with seine nets, and sold for fish bait. Thousands of migrating Tiger Salamanders are killed on roads each year. The draining or polluting of ponds and other wetlands and the introduction of game fish into formerly fishless bodies of water are detrimental to this species. On the other hand, the construction of stock ponds and ornamental garden pools can provide new breeding sites, provided they are not stocked with predatory fish.

# Lungless Salamanders

## FAMILY PLETHODONTIDAE

With about 450 species in 26 genera presently recognized, this is the largest salamander family in the world. There are three centers of abundance for this family, in the eastern (Appalachian) and Pacific coastal regions in North America and in Central America. Two species occur in southern Europe. It is likely that the ancestral plethodontids evolved in stream habitats, probably in what is now the eastern United States. All members of this group lack lungs (hence the common family name); they "breathe" through their skins and membranes in the mouth and throat. Air-filled lungs might have been detrimental to aquatic, bottom-crawling animals, and their permeable skins were quite sufficient for oxygen absorption. Some lungless salamanders still live in or near streams and have aquatic gilled larvae, but others are fully adapted for a terrestrial life, laying their eggs on land and skipping the free-swimming larval stage.

Most lungless salamanders are rather small, narrow-bodied animals of moist woodlands. A defining characteristic of the group is a groove in the skin running between each nostril and the upper lip (see fig. 5B, page 38). Called nasolabial grooves, they are thought to enhance the salamander's sense of smell by funneling odors to the nostrils and to play a part in finding prey and identifying potential mates. In some species the grooves extend downward below the upper lip in projections called cirri; these tend to be larger on males during the breeding season. In very small species or individuals, a hand magnifying lens may be needed to see the nasolabial grooves. Many species will drop portions of their tails if attacked or roughly handled; although the tail will regrow, the new portion will usually be shorter and a different color than the original.

## Northern Dusky Salamander (*Desmognathus fuscus*)

**Description:** This relatively stout little salamander has hind legs that are larger than the front legs and (usually) a light stripe that angles from the eye to the back of the jawline. The dorsal coloration is highly variable, but many specimens have a broad yellowish-gray, tan, or reddish-brown stripe running from head to tail, often spotted with a darker color and bordered on each side with an irregular dark brown or black stripe. Juvenile specimens have a series of paired light (reddish or yellowish) spots along the back, while older adults may darken and lose any trace of a dorsal pattern. The belly may be whitish, cream, or gray, often mottled with darker gray. The tail is flattened toward the tip and has a narrow ridge (keel) along the upper edge. Costal grooves: 14. Adult length: 7 to 14.2 cm (2.8 to 5.6 in).

Males tend to be longer than females, and their heads are broader and more swollen behind the eyes. During the breeding season the male's vent area becomes swollen, and there are tiny fingerlike projections (papillae) at the cloacal opening that are lacking in the female. The male also has a rounded lobe on the tip of the lower jaw (chin) called the mental gland.

The larvae, about 1.6 cm (0.6 in) long at hatching, have well-developed limbs and small, whitish gills. They are grayish or brownish above and usually have paired light spots running down the back and tail that are often separated by a light mid-dorsal stripe. The belly is white or gray.

**Confusing Species:** The Northern Dusky Salamander is very similar to the Allegheny Mountain Salamander, but the latter species has a rounded, unkeeled tail, and a dorsal stripe (when visible) that is often edged with black pigment. All other small Great Lakes area salamanders lack the light line from the eye to the back of the jaw and have hind legs about the same size as the front legs.

**Distribution and Status:** The Northern Dusky Salamander is found from southern New Brunswick and Quebec south through New England to the western Carolinas and west to Ohio, southern Indiana, and Tennessee. In the Great Lakes region, they occur south of Lake Erie and Lake Ontario (including the Niagara River gorge area in Ontario). A small breeding population in Tuscola County, Michigan, was possibly introduced.

This is a common to abundant species in many parts of its range, wherever there is suitable habitat. They are generally less common in formerly glaciated areas with low relief. Ontario lists the species as endangered.

**Habitat and Ecology:** Northern Dusky Salamanders inhabit the edges of rocky streams, hillside springs, and seepage areas, usually in wooded or partly wooded terrain. They spend most of their time hidden beneath flat rocks, logs, and other objects, particularly those that are adjacent to or partially submerged in the water. If disturbed, they may enter the water and hide beneath rocks and other debris. They can remain active all winter in springs or seepages where moving water prevents freezing of the substrate.

These salamanders eat a variety of small invertebrates, including earthworms, slugs, snails, crustaceans, spiders, mites, and various insects. Feeding may take place on land or in water. The larvae eat aquatic crustaceans and insect larvae.

Numerous predators will eat Northern Dusky Salamanders, including raccoons, skunks, shrews, birds, snakes, and larger salamanders such as Northern Spring and Northern Red Salamanders. Dusky Salamanders appear to lack defensive skin secretions but are able to move quickly when disturbed and jump surprisingly well. They have slippery skins, are difficult to grasp, and may even try to bite an attacker. Like many lungless salamanders, this species can lose its tail when physically attacked; the wriggling tail may distract the predator's attention away from the escaping salamander. The tail is later regenerated.

**Reproduction and Growth:** Courtship and mating occur on land in both spring and fall. A courting male approaches a prospective mate with a tail-wagging display and rotational movements of his front limbs; he then nudges and prods the female with his snout. These behaviors presumably help to identify and stimulate his prospective mate. The male may forcefully press his chin (i.e., mental gland) on the female's back while arching

Northern Dusky
Salamander (Tuscola
County, Michigan,
population)

Northern Dusky
Salamander, head,
nasolabial groove
visible

the forward part of his body upward, then straighten his back with a sudden snap. Eventually he moves under the female's head until she can straddle his tail, with her chin contacting the base of his tail (which is supplied with secretory glands that presumably facilitate courtship). The pair may move about in this position for some time. The male then produces a spermatophore that the female can pick up with her vent, taking the sperm packet into her cloaca. The spermatophore may occasionally be deposited directly on the female's cloacal opening.

The female deposits her eggs in summer, in one or two compact clusters hidden in a cavity beneath a rock or log or under mats of rotting leaves or moss. The nest site is normally adjacent to a stream or spring, but eggs may also be attached beneath submerged rocks. The eggs, which number from eleven to around forty, are attended and defended by the female until hatching, which occurs in about forty-six to eighty days. The well-developed larvae may stay with the female for several days before moving to the water and can survive on land for considerable periods if required, as long as they remain moist. Larvae generally spend from seven to twelve months in the water, usually transforming the following spring or summer at a length of about 2.8 to 4.4 cm (1.1 to 1.7 in). Young males reach maturity in two to three years, while females require three to five years before producing their first eggs.

**Conservation:** These salamanders are most common in shaded streamside habitats and are threatened by forestry practices that remove tree cover and thus increase water temperature and decrease humidity. Pollution of streams by agricultural runoff, mining waste, or siltation also threatens their survival.

## Allegheny Mountain Dusky Salamander
(*Desmognathus ochrophaeus*)

**Description:** This slender little salamander has hind legs that are larger (stouter) than the front legs, and a slanting light line between each eye and the back of the jaw. Most specimens have a broad, light dorsal stripe from head to tail tip that varies from yellow or orange to tan, olive, or gray. This stripe is often bordered by darker pigment, which fades to mottled gray or brown on the lower sides; there may be a row of dark (sometimes V-shaped) spots within the stripe. The belly is usually an unpatterned brown or gray. Older males may darken and lose the characteristic color pattern. The tail is about half the animal's length and is rounded in cross section. Costal grooves: usually 14. Adult length: 7 to 11.2 cm (2.8 to 4.4 in).

Males differ from females in having a conspicuous mental gland, visible from below as a blunt lobe on the tip of the chin, and a more sinuous ("zigzag") mouth line when viewed from the side. They also tend to be slightly larger than females. As noted above, old males frequently lose the dorsal stripe and become dark brown or black on the back and tail.

The newly hatched larvae are usually yellowish, with two rows of small light spots on the rear of the back and a light spot on the snout and behind each eye. In older larvae the spotting becomes less conspicuous, and the dark-bordered dorsal stripe characteristic of the adult begins to appear.

**Confusing Species:** This species is most often confused with the Northern Dusky Salamander, which is a somewhat stouter animal with a tail that is keeled along the upper edge. The edge of the dorsal stripe in the Northern Dusky tends to be more irregular and often lacks a continuous dark border. Hybridization between these two species is suspected in the area south of Lake Erie, possibly confounding identification. Northern Two-lined and Red-backed Salamanders may superficially resemble the Allegheny Mountain Dusky Salamander, but both lack the slanting light line between the eye and back of the jaw and have hind legs about the same size as the front legs.

**Distribution and Status:** Allegheny Mountain Dusky Salamanders range from extreme southern Quebec and northern New York (northern Adirondacks) south through the Allegheny and Appalachian highlands to western Virginia and portions of the Cumberland Plateau in eastern Kentucky and northern Tennessee. They were recently recorded from the Niagara River gorge in Ontario (where they are considered endangered) and occur in the eastern Great Lakes area south of Lake Ontario and Lake Erie to the northeastern corner of Ohio. These salamanders can be common in suitable habitats.

**Habitat and Ecology:** This species is usually found under logs, pieces of bark, leaf litter, flat rocks, and other shelter in cool, moist woodlands, usually close to springs, seepage areas, and small streams. They are more terrestrial than the Northern Dusky Salamander, however, and will move up the sides of ravines well away from water. Most activities occur within small, temporary home ranges of perhaps a square meter (ten square feet) or so in size. In winter they seek sites with flowing water, where they may stay active as long as the substrate remains unfrozen.

Allegheny Mountain Dusky Salamanders are nocturnal foragers, with most feeding reportedly occurring soon after sunset when their invertebrate prey is most active. When food resources are limited, these salamanders may aggressively defend small feeding territories (such as the space beneath a rock or other cover object) against their own and other salamander species. Favored food items include small insects and insect larvae, earthworms, spiders, mites, and millipedes. The larval salamanders presumably eat small aquatic invertebrates.

These salamanders are eaten by small mammals (shrews, raccoons, possums, etc.), birds, snakes, and larger salamanders. They apparently lack effective defensive skin secretions but are quick moving and slippery, and their strong hind legs allow them to jump away from danger (an unexpected maneuver for a salamander). They will also bite at snakes when seized, another surprising defense for such a small creature. Their tails break off easily, and the twitching of the lost tail may distract a predator, giving the salamander time to escape.

**Reproduction and Growth:** Mating may occur in both spring and fall. Courtship behavior closely resembles that of the Northern Dusky Salamander and other plethodontids and involves the male nudging and rubbing the female with his snout and chin, followed by the female straddling the male's tail as they move forward. Spermatophore deposition follows; after the sperm packet is taken into the female's cloaca, sperm can be stored for several months until needed for fertilization of the eggs.

Females deposit from eight to thirty-seven eggs in grapelike clusters attached to the underside of a rock, log cavity, or other shelter, usually in a seepage area or near a stream or spring. The eggs are usually laid from late spring through midsummer, but egg laying can occur in late winter and early spring in some populations. The females stay with their eggs until they hatch, usually spending most of the incubation time coiled around the egg mass. The larvae hatch in about seven to ten weeks (generally from late summer through early fall) at a length of 1.4 to 1.8 cm (0.5 to 0.7 in). They possess gills and a low tail fin, but have well-developed legs and soon move to the water. Growth rate is influenced by food availability and water temperature, and transformation to the terrestrial form can occur in as few as three weeks to as many as ten months after hatching, at an average length

Allegheny Mountain
Dusky Salamander
(Photo: Richard D.
Bartlett)

Allegheny Mountain
Dusky Salamander
(Photo: Richard D.
Bartlett)

of about 1.8 cm (0.7 in). Males become sexually mature by their third year, while females may not reproduce until their fourth year after hatching. This species has lived more than twenty years in captivity.

**Conservation:** This species is dependent on the existence of shady woodlands with cool flowing waters such as small streams and springs. Clear-cutting of trees, and thus removal of the leaf canopy, can harm this species by raising ground and stream temperatures and lowering humidity.

## Northern Slimy Salamander (*Plethodon glutinosus*)

**Description:** This is a medium-sized black or blue-black salamander with a variable number of scattered white spots or flecks on the back, sides, legs, and tail. The head is widest behind the eyes, and the snout in front of the eyes is broadly rounded and quite short. The tail is round in cross section and makes up a half or more of the salamander's total length. The belly, throat, and underside of the tail are blackish or gray, usually slightly lighter than the back. True to their name, Slimy Salamanders secrete a whitish sticky slime from their skin glands when handled. This material adheres like glue and is hard to remove from the hands once it dries.

Costal grooves: 15–17. Adult length: 10.5 to 20.6 cm (4.1 to 8.1 in). On average, males are slightly longer than females and have a conspicuous mental gland that looks like a circular swelling on the animal's chin. There is no free-swimming larval stage. The young are colored like the adults but have proportionally shorter tails.

**Confusing Species:** The Blue-spotted, Jefferson, and other "mole" salamanders do not have a groove between the nostril and mouth (nasolabial groove). The Northern Ravine Salamander and dark phase of the Red-backed Salamander are smaller and thinner, with more costal grooves, and their light markings are diffuse and less distinct.

Northern Slimy
Salamander (Photo:
Richard D. Bartlett)

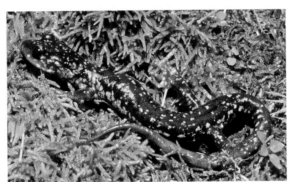

Northern Slimy
Salamander (Photo:
Richard D. Bartlett)

**Distribution and Status:** The Northern Slimy Salamander ranges from southern New Hampshire and central New York west to southern Illinois and south to northern Georgia and Alabama. In the Great Lakes region it is found south of Lakes Ontario and Erie; a few records exist for northwestern Indiana, including Indiana Dunes State Park and Starke County. This salamander is one of a complex of species that are closely related and in some cases almost indistinguishable except by means of laboratory analysis of their genetic material or knowledge of their geographic origin. These relatives extend the range of the "slimy salamander complex" south through the Atlantic coastal plain to central Florida and west to Missouri, Oklahoma, and Texas.

This species can be common in suitable habitats.

**Habitat and Ecology:** Moist shaded hillsides and ravines in mature hardwood forests are the preferred habitat for Slimy Salamanders. They appear to avoid cutover areas and bottomland forests prone to flooding. Most specimens are found in rotting logs or stumps or beneath rocks, bark, and leaf litter. They often forage on the surface on warm, rainy nights. In dry or cold weather they may descend deep underground, probably by following animal burrows, root systems, or crevices in rocky outcrops.

These salamanders eat small invertebrates such as insects (ants, beetles, termites, etc.) and insect larvae, centipedes, millipedes, pill bugs, spiders, slugs, snails, and earthworms. The diet of any particular salamander is probably influenced largely by which prey species are most available. The slimy skin secretions provide a defense against many potential predators. While the secretions reportedly are irritating if rubbed in the eyes, their adhesive properties may be the most effective predator deterrent. A snake attempting to grab a Slimy Salamander can find its mouth "gummed up" by these secretions and may forget the intended meal as it tries to wipe off the slime.

**Reproduction and Growth:** Mating occurs mostly in fall, more rarely in spring. During courtship, the male nudges and rubs the female with his snout and mental gland. Eventually he will move beneath the female's head while undulating his tail. The female then presses her chin on the base of his tail, and the two move forward with the female straddling the male's tail. At some point the male stops, moves his tail to one side, and deposits a spermatophore. They then move forward until the female can take the sperm packet into her cloaca.

Females appear to reproduce every other year in northern populations. From ten to thirty-eight eggs are laid in late spring or summer in an underground burrow, in a cavity under a rock, or within a rotting log. The eggs, which are suspended in a loose cluster from the side or upper surface of the nest cavity, are attended by the female. Incubation requires two to three months, with hatching occurring in late summer or fall. The young, which range in length from about 2 to 3 cm (0.8 to 1.2 in), may have gills upon emergence from the egg, but these are absorbed in a few days. They can breed when four or five years old and can potentially live for twenty years or more.

**Conservation:** Northern Slimy Salamanders require moist wooded habitats with ample shelter in the form of rotting logs or rocky outcrops. Forestry practices that remove the leaf canopy or eliminate natural ground debris can reduce or eliminate populations of this species.

# Eastern Red-backed Salamander (*Plethodon cinereus*)

**Description:** These are small, thin-bodied salamanders with tiny legs and rounded tails. There are two common color phases. The "red-backed" phase has a red, orange-red, or brownish-red stripe from the back of the head to the middle of the tail; this stripe is bordered on the sides by dark gray or black. The "lead-backed" phase lacks the red stripe and is entirely dark, with a faint pattern of light spots and flecks on the head, back, and sides.

Some individuals will appear to be intermediate between these two phases. In both the belly is mottled with gray and white in what is often described as a "salt and pepper" pattern. A rare erythristic color morph is almost entirely reddish or reddish-orange above, with black spots on the distal part of the tail and a light belly. (The relative distribution of these color phases is discussed under "Distribution and Status.") Costal grooves: 17–22 (usually 18 or 19). Adult length: 5.8 to 12.7 cm (2.3 to 5 in).

The male Red-backed Salamander is, on average, slightly smaller than the female and has a rounded mental gland under the chin and a snout that looks slightly swollen around the nasolabial grooves. The cloacal area is often lighter in color in males than in females.

There is no aquatic larval stage; the young lose any remnant gill buds within a few days of hatching and are colored like the adults.

**Confusing Species:** All "mole" salamanders (*Ambystoma*) are heavier bodied than Red-backed Salamanders and lack nasolabial grooves. Among other plethodontids, the Northern Ravine Salamander is similar to a lead-back-phase Red-backed Salamander, but it has a more uniformly dark gray belly. (Hybrids that appear intermediate between the Red-backed and the Northern Ravine Salamander do occur; see comment in the latter species' account.) The Northern Two-lined Salamander has a yellowish back stripe bordered by black side stripes and a yellow belly. The Four-toed Salamander has a white belly with bold black spots, a constriction at the base of the tail, and only four toes (instead of five) on the hind foot.

**Distribution and Status:** The Eastern Red-backed Salamander ranges from Nova Scotia and southern Quebec south to North Carolina, and north through Ohio and Indiana to Minnesota and the Lake Superior basin. They are generally more abundant north of the Wisconsinan glacial boundary and are the most common woodland salamander throughout most of the Great Lakes region.

The proportion of the two primary color phases in Great Lakes populations of the Eastern Red-backed Salamander is highly variable. Both phases occur together throughout most of the area. In general, the striped red-back phase tends to be proportionally more common at higher altitudes and latitudes, while the unstriped lead-backs become more abundant in lowland habitats in the southern part of the basin. The red-back phase does constitute an increasingly higher proportion of the population as one goes from south to north in the Great Lakes region, with the lead-back uncommon or absent in much of Wisconsin, Minnesota, and Michigan's Upper Peninsula.

The erythristic "red" phase of this salamander is rare or absent over most of the species' range but may make up from 15 to 20 percent of the population in northeastern Ohio (Lake Erie drainage), western New England, and southeastern New Brunswick.

**Habitat and Ecology:** Eastern Red-backed Salamanders occur in deciduous, coniferous, and mixed woodlands. Areas prone to frequent flooding or with dry, sandy soils are avoided, but otherwise a wide range of forest conditions are tolerated. They are most often encountered under logs, fallen bark, leaf litter, and rocks. Primarily nocturnal, they frequently forage on the surface on rainy nights and may even climb into shrubs and up tree trunks—a surprising feat considering their tiny, weak-looking legs.

These salamanders require a humid environment and spend much of their time below the surface, moving deeper in hot, dry weather, as well

Red-backed
Salamander, red-
backed morph

Red-backed
Salamanders, red-
backed and lead-
backed morphs

as in winter, following root systems, animal tunnels, and natural crevices. Numbers of overwintering individuals may congregate in preferred sites and can remain active and even feed if temperatures are suitable. Many may die during cold winters when snow cover is insufficient to insulate the ground and frost penetration is deep.

Individual Red-backed Salamanders tend to occupy fairly restricted temporary home ranges and may defend a territory against their own and other salamander species, using threat displays and a biting attack. Territories are marked with cloacal and mental gland secretions and fecal pellets. Territorial defense probably occurs most often when food resources are scarce, since at times numbers of individuals can be found sharing the same log or other cover.

This species will eat a variety of small invertebrate animals, including insects and their larvae (e.g., ants, beetles, and springtails), spiders, mites, pill bugs, centipedes, snails, slugs, and earthworms. They are in turn eaten by various mammals, birds, snakes, and larger salamanders.

Red-backed Salamanders have several defenses against predators. When first uncovered they often remain still, but if touched they can use a combined "swimming-running" motion to move rapidly into the leaf litter. They are also able to jump, using the tail for propulsion. If seized by a predator, they writhe violently and can detach a portion of their tail, which continues to wriggle; this movement may distract the predator's attention long enough to allow the salamander to escape. A new tail is later regrown. This species has sticky skin secretions that may be distasteful or annoying to some mammalian predators such as shrews, though many birds and snakes appear to be undeterred. Some birds, such as robins and blue jays, reportedly avoid eating the erythristic (red) phase of the Red-backed Salamander, and it has been suggested that this morph is a mimic of the red eft (terrestrial form of the Eastern Newt), a species with toxic skin secretions.

**Reproduction and Growth:** Male Eastern Red-backed Salamanders seek females in the fall (October through December), but mating activity can continue through the winter into early spring in some places. Courtship is similar to that of other *Plethodon,* with the male rubbing his head and chin (with its mental gland secretions) on the female's snout. It is also thought that mating secretions may also be introduced directly into the female's bloodstream when the male scratches her skin with his teeth. Eventually the pair walks forward with the female straddling the male's tail and her head pressed against the base of the tail. Deposition of a spermatophore by the male and retrieval of the sperm packet by the female occur soon after.

Females probably breed only every other year, perhaps due to the great amount of energy required to produce and yolk the eggs. The nest may be underground or within a cavity in a rotting log or stump. From three to seventeen eggs are laid in early summer in a grapelike cluster that is usually suspended from the top of the cavity by a gelatinous stalk, though sometimes it simply rests on the cavity floor. The female stays with her eggs, probably using skin secretions to keep them moist and free of mold. She aggressively defends her eggs against invertebrate predators, and even larger foes such as other salamanders, and may move her eggs if the nest is disturbed.

The young salamanders hatch in one to two months (usually in August or September) at a length of about 2 cm (0.8 in). They often remain with their mother for several days or weeks, at least until their remnant gill buds are absorbed. They may grow to maturity in two years, with females probably producing their first eggs at the beginning of their third year. Natural longevity is unknown, but adults in captivity have lived for more than five years.

**Conservation:** The Eastern Red-backed Salamander may be the most abundant vertebrate in many eastern North American woodlands. Population densities of about 500 to 9,000 salamanders per hectare (200 to 3,600 per acre) have been estimated for sites in Michigan, with variation between sites probably related to soil moisture and habitat structure. Estimates for sites in other states tend to fall between these extremes. Many studies have looked only at salamanders on the surface, though a portion of the population will be below ground during much of the year. Thus many published population studies may have underestimated the numbers of salamanders. In a study in a New Hampshire forest, salamanders (of which the Red-backed constituted 93.5 percent) outnumbered the birds and mammals combined, and their biomass (living weight) was more than 2.5 times the biomass of all breeding birds and equaled the biomass of small mammals in the woodland. (For further discussion, see Burton and Likens 1975.)

This species plays an important ecological role in Great Lakes area forests. They "process and recycle" vast numbers of invertebrate prey and contribute to the food supply of numerous predators. It follows that the loss of these salamanders could have significant consequences for the forest environment. Red-backed Salamanders are a tolerant species that can persist in human-modified woodlands as long as critical habitat components (e.g., fallen logs, leaf litter, or humid underground retreats) are conserved. It is important to consider the welfare of this and related species in any forest management plan.

# Northern Ravine Salamander (*Plethodon electromorphus*)

**Description:** The Northern Ravine Salamander, like its relative the Red-backed Salamander, is often described as a "worm with legs." These are elongate, thin-bodied creatures with tiny legs. The upper parts are dark brown, gray, or black with scattered whitish or bronzy speckles. The belly is dark gray, finely flecked with lighter gray; the chin may be more mottled and paler than the belly. Costal grooves: 19–22 (usually 20 or 21). Adult length: 7.5 to 14.4 cm (3 to 5.6 in).

Males are slightly smaller than females on average and have a conspicuous mental gland on the chin. As in other *Plethodon*, there is no aquatic larva in this species; larval development is completed within the egg, and hatchlings resemble their parents.

**Confusing Species:** The nasolabial grooves and elongate body shape distinguish this salamander from small *Ambystoma* species. The Northern Ravine Salamander is very similar to the unstriped "lead-back" phase of the Eastern Red-backed Salamander. However, the Ravine usually has a more uniformly dark gray belly, while the Red-backed has a lighter, more mottled ("salt and pepper") belly. Hybridization between these two species has been reported in northeastern Ohio; hybrids may be difficult to discriminate from "pure" specimens based on external morphology (Lehtinen et al. 2016).

**Distribution and Status:** This species occurs from western Pennsylvania and West Virginia west through Ohio to southeastern Indiana. It enters the Great Lakes (southern Lake Erie) basin in north-central Ohio, particularly in Erie, Huron, and Lorain Counties. Northern Ravine Salamanders can be common in proper habitats but rarely attain the population densities seen in the closely related Eastern Red-backed Salamander.

Northern Ravine
Salamander

Northern Ravine
Salamander (Photo:
Richard D. Bartlett)

**Habitat and Ecology:** This salamander's common name comes from its preference for inhabiting the slopes of woodland ravines and valleys. They are usually found hiding beneath flat rocks rather than logs or bark. In the heat of summer they move well below the surface, sometimes to depths of over a meter (3.3 ft).

The diet of the Northern Ravine Salamander consists of small insects, especially ants and beetles, as well as pill bugs, earthworms, spiders, and snails. Their enemies and defenses are presumably similar to those described for the Eastern Red-backed Salamander.

**Reproduction and Growth:** Information on the reproductive habits of this species is limited, but its breeding cycle appears to be very similar to that of the Red-backed Salamander, with courtship and mating occurring from fall through early spring. The females, which probably breed biennially, lay clutches of about four to twelve eggs in late spring or early summer under rocks or in underground cavities. New hatchlings have been found in late August. They may grow to maturity in about two years.

**Conservation:** Northern Ravine Salamanders seem to be more specialized than other Great Lakes area *Plethodon,* with a decided preference for rocky, wooded habitats with fairly steep gradients, including talus slopes. Within these habitats they are undoubtedly important members of the woodland floor community. Removal of forest cover, with associated changes in temperature and humidity levels, are the primary human-induced threat to local populations.

## Four-toed Salamander *(Hemidactylium scutatum)*

**Description:** This is a very small, slender reddish-brown or grayish-brown salamander with only four toes on each hind foot. The long tail is constricted (narrows) where it joins the body. The sides are often grayish and speckled with black and light bluish flecks (particularly in males). The belly is white or bluish-white with small black spots. Costal grooves: 13–14. Adult size: 5 to 10.2 cm (2 to 4 in).

Male Four-toed Salamanders are smaller than females, on average, and have relatively longer tails. When viewed from above, the male's snout is somewhat squared off (due to the swollen area around the nasolabial grooves); the female's snout looks more rounded. In addition, the male has an overhanging upper lip and an enlarged mental gland on the chin (the latter most prominent during the breeding season).

Soon after hatching, the aquatic larva is tinged with yellow, orange, and green on the head, and numerous black spots often merge to form a Y-shaped mark on the back of the head and a dark band behind each eye. (This dark eye band is often prominent in older larvae and newly transformed individuals as well.) The upper tail fin extends well up the back, nearly to the head. Hatchlings usually have all four legs, though the toes may not be fully developed.

**Confusing Species:** The combination of four-toed hind feet, pure white belly with black spots, and tail constriction will quickly separate this species from the several other small salamander species that might be found in the same habitat.

**Distribution and Status:** Four-toed Salamanders are found from southern Maine west through New York and southeastern Ontario to eastern Minnesota and south to northern Georgia and Alabama. A number of scattered, isolated populations occur from northern Illinois south to Louisiana and northern Florida and in Nova Scotia. They are found throughout much of the Great Lakes region, but are absent from the area north of Lake Superior and are apparently also lacking along the southwestern shore of Lake Michigan. It is likely that the species once had a more continuous range, but dramatic climatic fluctuations, particularly over the last two million years, may have led to range contraction and fragmentation.

This salamander is a habitat specialist (see below), and it is generally uncommon to rare and localized over much of the region. It is considered a threatened species in Illinois and a species of concern in Indiana and Ohio.

**Habitat and Ecology:** Adult Four-toed Salamanders inhabit moist deciduous, coniferous, or mixed woodlands, usually in the vicinity of spring-fed creeks, sphagnum seepages, bogs, or boggy ponds. Males and nonbreeding females are sometimes found with other salamander species under logs and other forest debris. In winter they hibernate in rotting logs, beneath leaf litter, or below ground in burrows or decaying root systems, and numbers may congregate in a suitable site.

The food of this salamander consists of small arthropods and other invertebrates, including various insects and their larvae (e.g., beetles, ants, springtails, and flies), spiders, snails, and earthworms. When disturbed by a potential predator, a Four-toed Salamander will often curl its body and tuck its head under its tail. The tail may be raised, exposing the bright white underside, perhaps to distract the predator's attention from the head and body. If threatened, the salamander can voluntarily detach its tail, which separates readily at the constriction near its base. The lost tail continues to twitch, perhaps distracting the predator long enough to allow the salamander to escape. A new tail begins to regenerate soon after.

**Reproduction and Growth:** Courtship and mating reportedly take place in late summer and fall in this species. Mating behavior is reportedly very similar to that of the Eastern Red-backed Salamander and other small plethodontids, with the male rubbing his snout, chin (mental gland), and sides on the female's snout, followed by a "tail-straddling walk" with the female pressing her chin on the base of the male's tail prior to spermatophore deposition.

Females migrate to breeding sites from late March through May, seeking fish-free woodland ponds, springs, or creeks where mosses, rotting logs, leaf litter, or clumps of grass or sedges are hanging over or at least adjacent to the water's edge. Sphagnum moss over shallow, permanent or semipermanent water appears to be a favored nest site when available. Within a small cavity the female turns upside down and deposits fifteen to sixty-four eggs, which adhere to each other and the surrounding material. She may remain in her nest throughout much of the incubation period, eating spoiled eggs and perhaps using her skin secretions to retard fungus growth and predation. Attended eggs have been found to have a greater chance of hatching than those that are left unguarded. Frequently two or more females will lay their eggs in a communal nest, but only one female at a time will attend the eggs.

In one to two months the larvae hatch and wriggle or drop into the water. About 1.1 to 1.4 cm (0.4 to 0.6 in) long at hatching, the larvae grow quickly and metamorphose into the terrestrial form in three to eight weeks, at a length of 1.6 to 2.4 cm (0.6 to 1 in). They reach sexual maturity in their second or third year. The potential longevity of this species is unknown, but one captive specimen lived for nearly nine years.

Four-toed Salamander

Four-toed Salamander

**Conservation:** The spotty distribution of the Four-toed Salamander within the Great Lakes region and elsewhere is undoubtedly related to the scarcity of suitable breeding habitat. Populations are often restricted to isolated colonies, and opportunities for dispersal into new habitats may be limited or nonexistent. Such species are much more vulnerable to the effects of human activities than are those with wider habitat tolerances. Identifying and preserving known habitats of this salamander will have the added advantage of simultaneously preserving other rare and specialized species of animals and plants.

# Northern Spring Salamander (*Gyrinophilus porphyriticus porphyriticus*)

**Description:** This is a fairly large and robust salamander with a vertically flattened and keeled tail. The dorsal coloration varies from pinkish or salmon to yellowish-brown mottled or clouded with darker pigment on the back. Newly transformed specimens are often a bright salmon-red but tend to darken as they age. The lower sides and belly may be plain pinkish or yellowish, but scattered dark spots often appear on the belly, throat, and lower jaws of older adults. On the snout, a light line (often bordered with gray or black) runs between each eye and nostril, then down the nasolabial groove to the lip. Costal grooves: 17–19. Adult length: 12 to 23.2 cm (4.7 to 9.1 in).

Male and female Northern Spring Salamanders are very similar in external appearance. From fall through early spring, adult females may have yellowish-white eggs visible through the belly skin. Adult males have glandular papillae on the inner surface of the cloaca, while the cloacal wall of the female is smooth.

Larval Northern Spring Salamanders are usually yellow to yellowish-white in color with a brownish, netlike mottling on the upper surfaces of the head and back. The tail may also be mottled, and the gills are reddish. The head is rather elongated, and the eyes are small.

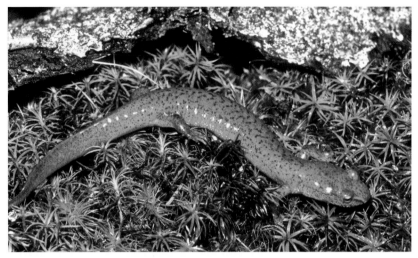

Northern Spring
Salamander, young
adult

Northern Spring
Salamander, larva
(Photo: Richard D.
Bartlett)

**Confusing Species:** All "mole" salamanders (*Ambystoma*) lack a nasolabial groove between nostril and lip. The eft stage of the Red-spotted Newt
may be reddish, but efts have dull, nonslimy skins and lack costal grooves.
Northern Red Salamanders have more rounded heads and do not have a
light line bordering the nasolabial groove between eye and nostril.

**Distribution and Status:** Northern Spring Salamanders range from southern
Maine and Quebec west to Ohio and south to northern Georgia and Ala-
bama. Within the Great Lakes basin they occur in Pennsylvania and New
York in the region south of Lake Ontario and along the eastern shore of Lake
Erie. There is an old record (from 1877) in the Niagara area of Ontario, but
we are not aware of recent records for the province.

This species can be common in suitable habitat but is generally uncommon and local in the Great Lakes drainage basin. This is probably due to the scarcity of habitats in formerly glaciated areas with low relief; in Ohio the species is largely absent from formerly glaciated terrain but is fairly common south of the glacial boundary on the Allegheny Plateau.

**Habitat and Ecology:** Northern Spring Salamanders live in or near cool, well-oxygenated streams, seepages, and springs, usually in shady wooded terrain or caves. The adults can be found in the water or on land, in small stream bank cavities or beneath rocks or logs, although they may forage in the open on rainy nights. They sometimes move considerable distances away from breeding habitats by following underground springs. In winter these salamanders may remain beneath rocks and other debris in the streambed or in seepage areas or burrows in unfrozen, saturated soil near the water's edge.

Since their habitat rarely if ever freezes, they may feed actively all winter. Feeding occurs both on land and in water. Insects, crustaceans, spiders, snails, worms, and various other terrestrial and aquatic invertebrates are included in the Spring Salamander's diet. In addition, they frequently eat other salamanders and their larvae, including Two-lined and Dusky Salamanders and smaller individuals of their own species.

These salamanders are undoubtedly eaten by a number of predators, but they are agile and have very slippery skins, making them difficult to grasp. When attacked, they will often coil their bodies and lash their tails. This species appears to have slightly noxious skin secretions but may gain additional protection from a resemblance (particularly when young) to the more toxic red eft stage of the Eastern Newt and the moderately toxic Northern Red Salamander.

**Reproduction and Growth:** Mating probably occurs from fall through spring. Courtship is similar to that of other plethodontid salamanders, with the male rubbing his head on the female's body and a "tail-straddling" walk prior to spermatophore deposition. Females lay their eggs in summer (June through August) beneath stones or flat rocks in cool, flowing water. A female will turn upside down and attach from 16 to 160 eggs to the underside of the rock, with larger females laying larger clutches. Each egg, along with its gelatinous coverings, has a diameter of about 0.9 cm (0.4 in).

The eggs hatch in late summer or fall, into larvae that range from 1.8 to 2.6 cm (0.7 to 1.0 in) in length. The aquatic larval stage may last for three or four years. They metamorphose at a total length of about 8 to 12 cm (3.1 to 4.7 in) and become sexually mature a year or two later. A captive specimen lived for more than eighteen years, but potential longevity in the wild is unknown.

**Conservation:** Northern Spring Salamanders require clear, cool waters free of predatory fish. Their relatively large size compared to other lungless salamanders (with less oxygen-absorbing surface area compared to body mass) suggests that they would be very sensitive to changes in dissolved oxygen levels. Forestry practices or other human activities that result in stream warming or siltation would adversely affect this species. In addition, being larger and feeding on other salamanders would place the Spring Salamander at a higher trophic level (i.e., higher on the "food chain") than many related species. Thus, they might be expected to be less abundant, to reproduce more slowly, and perhaps to be more sensitive to environmental stresses than their smaller relatives.

## Northern Red Salamander (*Pseudotriton ruber ruber*)

**Description:** Northern Red Salamanders, when young, are among our most brightly colored amphibians. The head, back, and tail are coral red to reddish-orange, grading to light salmon-red on the lower sides and belly. Small black spots and dashes overlay the ground color from the nose to at least the first half of the tail; the lower jaw usually has some dark spotting, which may continue onto the belly. In older adults, the dark dorsal spots begin to spread and fuse, and the ground color darkens to dull orangish-brown or purplish-brown. The iris of the eye is yellow. This is a rather stout-bodied salamander with short, thick legs and a short, rounded snout. The base of the tail is rounded in cross section, but the last third of the tail is vertically flattened. Costal grooves: 16–17. Adult length: 10 to 18.1 cm (3.9 to 7.4 in).

Male Northern Red Salamanders are slightly smaller than females, on average, but the sexes are very similar in appearance. In gravid females, the yellowish yolks of the eggs may be visible through the belly skin. Typical larvae are light brown to purplish-brown on the upper surfaces grading to a lighter, whitish to yellowish color on the belly. The back, sides, and tail may have evenly scattered black dots or streaks. Older larvae approaching metamorphosis often take on the brighter red or orange color that is normal for newly transformed juveniles. Compared to the larvae of the Northern Spring Salamander, larval Northern Red Salamanders have more uniform and distinct dark spotting; shorter, more rounded snouts; and larger eyes.

**Confusing Species:** Young Northern Red Salamanders are quite distinctive, but older adults can be confused with the Northern Spring Salamander. The latter species usually has a light line, bordered by black or gray, between eye and nostril and a longer, less rounded snout.

**Distribution and Status:** The range of the Northern Red Salamander extends from southern New York, Pennsylvania, and eastern and southern Ohio to southern Indiana, Kentucky, and Tennessee, through the western Carolinas to Alabama and northern Georgia. Small and isolated populations are reported in northern and central New York. Other subspecies extend the species' range to Mississippi and the Florida panhandle. This salamander enters the Great Lakes region primarily in northeastern Ohio, where they are locally common at specific sites with suitable habitat. It is listed as endangered in Indiana, but is not known in the Great Lakes portion of that state.

**Habitat and Ecology:** Northern Red Salamanders live in or near cold, clear springs, seepages, and small streams, usually in deciduous or mixed forest, but sometimes in open meadows and on hillsides. The adults are mostly aquatic in fall and winter, becoming more terrestrial in spring and summer. Largely nocturnal, they may move and forage on the surface on damp or rainy nights but otherwise remain hidden in burrows or beneath rocks, logs, or other shelter, sometimes in the company of other salamander species. In

Northern Red
Salamander, young
adult

Northern Red
Salamander, new
metamorph (Photo:
Richard D. Bartlett)

winter they appear to move into the deeper springs where temperatures can remain quite constant.

Adult Northern Red Salamanders eat insects, worms, snails, slugs, centipedes, and various other invertebrates, as well as smaller salamanders. The larvae feed on crustaceans and aquatic insect larvae and probably other salamander larvae.

Defensive behaviors in this species include curling the body, hiding the head beneath an upraised or undulating tail, and slapping the tail at the disturbing object. These maneuvers present the potential enemy with whitish skin secretions that are noxious and repellent. This salamander's bright reddish skin color may advertise its distastefulness to predators, as is true for the red eft stage of the Eastern Newt.

**Reproduction and Growth:** Pairing and spermatophore transfer probably can occur from late spring through fall. Courtship behavior (as observed in the laboratory) is similar to that of other plethodontids, with the male rubbing his snout on the female's head and chin, then moving beneath her chin. The female places her chin on the base of the male's undulating tail, and the two move forward. After arching his tail to one side, the male deposits a spermatophore and attempts to lead the female over it.

This species is unusual in that egg laying occurs in late fall and early winter. A female will attach from thirty to eighty eggs to the underside of a rock in a cold spring or stream and probably stays with the eggs till they hatch. Sometimes two or more females will share a communal nest site. The incubation period lasts a minimum of eight to ten weeks, and newly hatched larvae are 1.3 to 2.3 cm (0.5 to 0.9 in) long. They may spend between two and four years as aquatic larvae before transforming into terrestrial juveniles at lengths of 8 to 10 cm (3.1 to 3.9 in). They mature within the year following metamorphosis and potentially can live for twenty years or more.

**Conservation:** Northern Red Salamanders require clear, cold springs or spring-fed streams free of predatory fish and surrounded by terrestrial cover in the form of rocks, logs, or leaf litter. Declines in many local populations have been reported, perhaps due to deforestation, pollution, and other forms of habitat degradation. Comments on conservation of the related Northern Spring Salamander may be equally pertinent to this species.

## Northern Two-lined Salamander (*Eurycea bislineata*) and Southern Two-lined Salamander (*Eurycea cirrigera*)

**Description:** These are very small, slender salamanders with tiny legs and a vertically compressed tail. They have a broad yellow, greenish-yellow, or tan stripe running from head to tail, bordered on each side by a narrow black stripe that may break up into dashes toward the end of the tail. The light dorsal stripe often has a medial row of dark spots or flecks. The sides may be yellowish or mottled with dark pigment, and the belly is yellow. Costal grooves: 14–16. Adult length: 6.4 to 12.1 cm (2.5 to 4.8 in).

Males have a prominent mental gland on the chin, whitish glands on the lower eyelid, and (in some populations) downward projections of the nasolabial grooves, called cirri, particularly during the breeding season (October through May). In the spring, the eggs of gravid females may be visible through the belly skin. Young larvae typically have a yellowish ground color with grayish or brownish spots and flecks on the head and back and an irregular dark stripe down each upper side. Each of these stripes usually encloses a series of six to nine light spots. The short gills are light reddish-brown (larvae of Dusky Salamanders usually have whitish gills). Older larvae often retain the hatchling color pattern but may develop a second row of light spots on each side.

**Confusing Species:** Both species of Dusky Salamanders have hind legs that are noticeably larger than the front legs and a light line from the eye to the back of the mouth. Long-tailed Salamanders have vertical dark markings along the sides of the tail and 13 to 14 costal grooves. The Eastern Red-backed Salamander has a mottled "salt and pepper" belly and 17 to 22 costal grooves.

**Distribution and Status:** The Northern Two-lined Salamander is found from southern Quebec and New Brunswick south through New England to northern Virginia and west to northeastern Ohio. In the Great Lakes basin this salamander occurs in Ohio, Pennsylvania, and New York, south and east of Lake Erie and Lake Ontario, and in Ontario east of Georgian Bay. The very similar Southern Two-lined Salamander (*Eurycea cirrigera*), until recently considered a subspecies of *E. bislineata*, occurs in eastern Illinois, Indiana, and southern Ohio, south to eastern Louisiana and the Gulf Coast and east to coastal Georgia and the Carolinas. This species usually has only 14 costal grooves but is otherwise defined largely on the basis of genetic differences rather than external characters. An isolated (and perhaps introduced) population of Two-lined Salamanders in Tuscola County, Michigan, has been identified genetically as *E. cirrigera*. An additional isolated population of Two-lined Salamanders (presumably *E. cirrigera*) is known from the Kankakee River drainage in northeastern Illinois.

Where habitat remains intact, these are often the most common streamside salamanders throughout their ranges.

**Habitat and Ecology:** Two-lined Salamanders live in the vicinity of flowing water where there is sufficient cover in the form of rocks, logs, or mats of fallen leaves, both in woodlands and in more open habitats. Most often discovered by turning over rocks along stream banks, they may also occur several meters from the nearest water. They often forage on the surface on

Great Lakes range of Northern Two-lined Salamander

rainy nights. In winter these salamanders may burrow deep under leaf litter or remain active in saturated soil, seepage areas, or springs and streams where temperatures remain above freezing.

Adults feed on small invertebrates, including insects (beetles, mayflies, springtails, etc.), spiders, pill bugs, centipedes, earthworms, and snails. The larvae eat aquatic insects such as the larvae of caddisflies, stoneflies, midges, mosquitoes, and beetles, as well as copepods and other crustaceans; older larvae may occasionally eat smaller amphibian larvae. These little salamanders have numerous predators, including various birds, mammals, and snakes, as well as larger salamanders such as Northern Spring, Red, and Dusky Salamanders. However, Two-lined Salamanders are active animals that often escape using rapid undulations of the body and tail, and they can jump by curving and then suddenly straightening their bodies. Like many related species, they can also drop a part of their tail when seized; the separated tail continues to wriggle, perhaps distracting the predator while the salamander escapes.

**Reproduction and Growth:** Courtship and spermatophore transfer take place from fall through early spring. Courtship behavior is reportedly very similar to that of the Red-backed Salamander and most other small plethodontids. A male will poke and nudge a prospective mate and often curls the

Northern Two-lined
Salamander (Photo:
Richard D. Bartlett)

Northern Two-lined
Salamander (Photo:
Richard D. Bartlett)

front of his body around the female's head. It is thought that by scratching the female's skin with specialized teeth, stimulating secretions from his mental gland may enter her bloodstream. Eventually the two move forward together in a "tail-straddling" walk, with the female's chin pressed against the glandular area at the base of the male's tail. Spermatophore deposition soon follows.

Females lay their eggs in spring or early summer, most often in April or May. By turning upside down, a female attaches from fifteen to more than

Great Lakes range of Southern Two-lined Salamander

one hundred eggs, in a single layer, to the underside of a rock beneath the flowing water of a spring or stream. Each egg hangs from the "roof" of the cavity suspended by a short stalk. The female usually attends her nest for at least a portion of the incubation period. Two or more females may lay their eggs at the same site, but normally only one female is in attendance at a time.

The larvae hatch out in about thirty to sixty days at a length of 1.2 to 1.4 cm (0.5 to 0.6 in). They usually spend two (occasionally three) years as aquatic larvae before transforming into semiterrestrial juveniles. Sexual maturity may be attained the first fall after metamorphosis but may take two to three years in some places.

**Conservation:** Northern and Southern Two-lined Salamanders seem to tolerate a wider range of habitat situations than related streamside species do. They reportedly suffer significant predation losses during their terrestrial movements and presumably have a fairly high annual population turnover. Along with other small salamanders, Two-lined Salamanders are sometimes collected by people for use as fish bait. Such exploitation, if sustained, could significantly reduce or eliminate an affected local population, particularly if collection methods disrupt the habitat.

Southern Two-lined Salamander (Photo: Richard D. Bartlett)

Southern Two-lined Salamander, larva, Tuscola County, Michigan population

# Frogs and Toads

## (ORDER ANURA)

Frogs and toads, collectively called anurans, are short-bodied, tailless amphibians with enlarged hind limbs adapted for jumping or swimming. With over 6,500 anuran species, grouped into 435 genera, recognized worldwide, this order must be considered one of the most successful vertebrate groups. In general, warty-skinned, short-legged, hopping anurans are called toads, while smoother-skinned, long-legged, leaping anurans are called frogs, although there are no widely accepted definitions for these terms. Two Great Lakes anurans are commonly called toads, both members of the family Bufonidae or "true toads." Important identifying characters of the order are shown in figure 6.

The reproductive habits of Great Lakes anurans follow a pattern typical of most north-temperate species. Males move to aquatic breeding sites in spring and use species-specific calls (the "advertisement" call) to attract

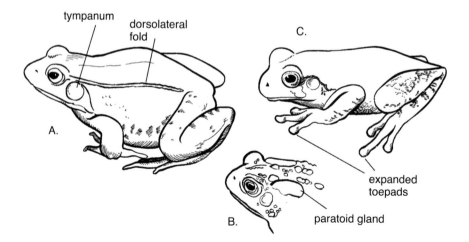

Fig. 6. Anuran characteristics. A. Typical frog (*Rana*). B. Toad (*Bufo/ Anaxyrus*). C. Treefrog (*Hyla*). (Drawing by G. van Frankenhuyzen)

females and (in some species) to warn other males away from their territories. Either the male or the female may play the larger role in choosing a mate, depending on species. Using his front feet, the male clasps the female from above in an embrace called amplexus. In this position the male fertilizes the eggs externally as they are deposited by the female. Depending on the species, the eggs may be laid singly, in submerged loose or globular masses, spreading surface masses, or (in toads) in long strings. The aquatic larva, commonly called a tadpole or polliwog, has a short oval body and a long compressed tail with an upper (dorsal) and lower (ventral) fin. The gills of new hatchlings are external but soon are enclosed by the opercular fold. During respiration, water taken in through the mouth passes over the gills and exits through an opening, called the spiracle, on the left side of the body. Tadpoles feed largely by filtering minute plants (algae), bacteria, and other organic material from the water or bottom debris. Their beaklike mouths, rimmed with keratinous denticles (toothlike structures), are used for scraping attached algae from rocks, plants, and substrate. Many species are at least partly carnivorous and may eat the eggs and larvae of other amphibians or even their own siblings. During metamorphosis, the hind legs become visible near the vent, while the front legs develop within the opercular (gill) chamber and are not visible until just before transformation. Numerous other internal and external changes must occur before the fishlike herbivorous larva becomes a semiterrestrial carnivorous tetrapod, including drastic modifications of the mouth parts and digestive tract.

Many anurans from subtropical and tropical regions display unique reproductive strategies that differ significantly from the "typical" life cycle summarized above. As with salamanders, some species have direct development (i.e., they lack a free-swimming larva and hatch directly into an immature "adult" form), but none of these is native to the Great Lakes area.

Unlike the largely silent salamanders, all native frogs and toads possess distinctive voices that facilitate field identification and population surveys. The spring "advertisement" calls of males are most familiar and are described in the species accounts. Other types of vocalizations include distress and warning calls, territorial announcements, and a "release" call that is given by a male or nonreceptive female frog or toad when it is mistakenly grasped by another male.

Selected general references for anurans: Altig et al. 2015; Bartlett and Bartlett 2006; Dodd 2013; Duellman and Trueb 1986; Powell et al. 2016; Stebbins and Cohen 1995; and Wright and Wright 1949.

# True Toads

## FAMILY BUFONIDAE

Most "true" toads are terrestrial or burrowing anurans with relatively thick, warty skin and short legs. As of this writing there are about 590 species in 49 genera distributed throughout most of the world's temperate and tropical regions. Bufonids have toothless jaws, and most have prominent enlarged parotoid glands behind the eyes. The classification of North American toads is controversial; here we include a newly proposed, though disputed, genus name (*Anaxyrus*) as a subgenus under the traditional genus *Bufo* for the two species that inhabit the Great Lakes region.

### Eastern American Toad (*Bufo [Anaxyrus] americanus americanus*)

**Description:** This is a typical "true toad," with a short, stocky body; warty skin; and relatively short hind legs. Unlike frogs, they walk or hop rather than making long leaps. This species is highly variable in color, ranging from tan, brown, or reddish-brown to gray or olive. They have some color changing ability, and the same animal may slowly darken or lighten depending on its immediate environment. Most specimens display dark, rounded spots on the back, each of which encircles one or two warts. The large parotoid glands behind the eyes are oval or kidney shaped, and there are enlarged warts on the tibia (lower part of the hind leg, below the knee). A light line may run down the middle of the back. The throat and belly are whitish or yellowish with black or gray spotting, particularly on the "chest" area. Adult length: 5.1 to 11.1 cm (2 to 4.4 in).

Note: American Toads living on some islands in the Great Lakes reach considerably larger sizes than those on the mainland. Snout to vent lengths of up to 15.5 cm (6.1 in) have been reported. It is not yet known if the greater size of island toads is due to genetic differences, greater longevity, or other factors. Despite this uncertainty, some herpetologists have given the name *Bufo americanus "alani"* to the giant toads of northern Lake Michigan islands.

Male American Toads are generally smaller than females and have darkened, enlarged "thumbs" on the forefeet. The male's vocal sac is visible as a grayish flap of skin on the throat, especially during the breeding season.

The tadpoles are blackish, with plump bodies and thin, rounded tails. The tiny black tadpoles often collected by children from suburban ponds are usually this species.

Voice: A prolonged, high-pitched musical trill that may last for more than thirty seconds.

**Confusing Species:** Fowler's Toads usually have three or more warts within each of the larger spots on their backs and lack enlarged warts on the tibia. In addition, Fowler's usually have unmarked whitish undersides, though some individuals may have one or a few dark spots on the chest. Their short, nasal breeding call is quite unlike the long, musical trill of the American Toad. These two toad species occasionally interbreed. The hybrid offspring may show a blending of traits or they can resemble one of the parent species, but their advertisement calls are usually intermediate between the two.

**Distribution and Status:** The Eastern American Toad ranges from Labrador and central Quebec west to James Bay and southeastern Manitoba, south to Kansas and Mississippi, and east to Virginia and New England. It is found throughout the Great Lakes region. A smaller subspecies, the Dwarf American Toad (*Bufo [Anaxyrus] a. charlesmithi*), occurs from southern Indiana to Oklahoma and northeastern Texas.

American toads are a generally common and tolerant species, but recent local population declines have been reported in portions of the Great Lakes region.

**Habitat and Ecology:** American Toads tolerate a wide variety of habitats, including open woodlands and woods edges, prairies, meadows, marshes, suburban yards and parks, and agricultural areas. Toads are most active on rainy or humid evenings. When not foraging, they usually remain buried in moist soil or leaf litter or beneath logs or rocks. When digging, they "back in" using their hind feet as shovels. During winter and prolonged dry periods they burrow deeply into the soil and remain dormant until conditions improve.

Long valued as a friend of the gardener and farmer, American Toads eat many types of insects and insect larvae, as well as spiders, centipedes, millipedes, snails, slugs, and earthworms. The type of food chosen depends largely on what is most available. It is common for these amphibians to gather under yard lights and streetlights on warm nights to consume insects attracted there. Toads use a quick flick of their sticky tongues to capture prey and will use their front feet to push larger prey items into their toothless mouths.

American Toads have a number of behavioral and chemical defenses against predators. Encounters with predators are undoubtedly reduced by their cryptic coloration and burrowing habit. When approached by a potential enemy, a toad may lower its nose and hunch its body forward. This makes the toad appear larger and also presents the attacker with the poison-producing parotoid glands. The whitish parotoid secretions contain steroidal chemicals that can affect heart function and blood pressure and can cause illness or death in small mammals that chew or consume a toad. A seized toad will expel urine and may puff up by inflating its lungs, perhaps making itself more difficult to swallow. Despite these defenses, certain predators regularly eat toads, including the Common Garter and Eastern Hognose Snakes, hawks, herons, and some waterfowl. Raccoons feed on toads by eating them from the belly side and avoiding the glands on the head and back. Humans can handle toads safely but should avoid getting toad skin secretions into the eyes or mouth, as these can be irritating. Handling toads does not cause warts.

**Reproduction and Growth:** Eastern American Toads prefer to breed in shallow, temporary waters with sparse to moderate amounts of emergent and

American Toad

American Toad,
tadpole (Photo: Wayne
VanDevender)

submergent vegetation. Typical sites include flooded fields, ditches, stock and ornamental ponds, open marshes, and backwaters of slow-moving streams. They will also use the shallows of larger lakes if other sites are lacking. First movement to breeding sites is often triggered by humid or rainy conditions combined with warm evening temperatures, typically in mid- to late April in the southern part of the basin and late May in the north. Males arrive a few days before the females, and most breeding occurs within a period of about ten to fourteen days. If interrupted by cold weather, breeding activity may be resumed after temperatures moderate and can (rarely) extend into June or July.

Male American Toads usually call while sitting upright in shallow water or on land at the water's edge. During the prolonged call, the large grayish vocal sac is fully inflated. A male will attempt to clasp any passing toad; if the intended mate is a male, it gives a special chirping "release" call while vibrating its body to inform the first toad of its mistake. Once a receptive female is amplexed, the pair often moves to another part of the pond, perhaps to avoid attempts by other males to "cut in." Female toads sometimes drown when clasped by two or more competing males.

During amplexus, the female lays from 2,000 to more than 20,000 eggs, which emerge in two gelatinous strings. The egg strings may be twined among submerged branches or vegetation or simply left in loops on the bottom. Hatching occurs in two to fourteen days, depending on water temperature. The black tadpoles form schools during the day (often congregating preferentially with siblings) and move about together in the shallows, seeking warmth and food. They eat algae, diatoms, and other planktonic organisms, soft vegetation, and carrion. Although toad tadpoles appear to be repellent to some predators, they are readily eaten by many fish, diving beetles, and other aquatic insects.

The tadpoles grow quickly and transform in six to ten weeks into tiny toadlets about 0.8 to 1.3 cm (0.3 to 0.5 in) long. At the time of metamorphosis young toadlets may swarm by the hundreds near breeding ponds, but few will survive the two to three years required to reach sexual maturity. These toads can survive for more than ten years in the wild, and potentially much longer; a captive specimen of a related species lived for thirty-six years.

**Conservation:** American Toads are adaptable animals, and populations often persist in urban parks, suburban gardens, and farming areas. Local declines in this species can result from the loss or degradation of breeding sites. Use of certain pesticides can also pose a threat, though more research is needed to determine levels of sensitivity to various chemical formulations. Another significant local threat is vandalistic destruction during the breeding season. Calling and amplexed toads in shallow waters are extremely vulnerable to wanton killing; sadly, such vandalism is often perpetrated by unsupervised children not sensitized to wildlife values.

## Fowler's Toad (*Bufo [Anaxyrus] fowleri*)

**Description:** This species resembles the Eastern American Toad in general appearance. Background color varies from tan or brown to olive green or gray, and there is usually a light stripe down the middle of the back. Most specimens have a number of dark spots or blotches on the back, with each large spot enclosing three or more warts. There are no enlarged warts on the tibia (lower leg). The throat and belly are white or dull yellow, sometimes with a dark spot or a few small spots on the chest. Adult length: 5 to 9.5 cm (2 to 3.7 in).

Male Fowler's Toads are smaller in average size than females and have thickened, dark thumbs and a grayish throat (vocal sac). The blackish tadpoles are very similar to those of the American Toad.

Voice: A rather mournful, low-pitched nasal bleat ("waaaaa") lasting from two to seven seconds. The call can be heard from a considerable distance away.

**Confusing Species:** American Toads typically have only one or two warts in each dark spot on the back and have enlarged warts on the tibia. They also have heavier dark spotting on the throat and chest. The breeding call of the American Toad, a prolonged musical trill, is very unlike the harsh nasal bleat of the Fowler's Toad. Populations of American and Fowler's Toads tend to be separated by differences in habitat preference and timing of breeding activity. There are many places where both species occur, however, and breeding periods can overlap, leading to opportunities for interbreeding. The call and appearance of hybrid specimens may be intermediate between the two species, thus confounding attempts to identify them.

**Distribution and Status:** Fowler's Toad ranges from New England south to Virginia and the central Gulf Coast, west to western Texas, Arkansas, Missouri, and Illinois and north to western Michigan, Ohio, and southern Ontario. In the Great Lakes region it most often occurs along the southern and eastern shore of Lake Michigan and the Lake Erie shoreline. This toad was formerly considered an eastern subspecies of Woodhouse's Toad (*Bufo [Anaxyrus] woodhousii*); Sullivan, Malmos, and Given (1996) offer reasons for considering Fowler's Toad a full species. Though generally less abundant than the American Toad in the Great Lakes region, Fowler's Toads can be locally common in proper habitats. This species' distribution along the shores of Lake Michigan and Lake Erie suggests that it is less cold hardy than the American Toad since the lakes tend to moderate local temperatures compared to inland areas. It is considered endangered in Ontario.

**Habitat and Ecology:** Open woodlands, sand prairies, meadows, and beaches are typical habitats for Fowler's Toads, though they also occur in suburban and agricultural areas. They are closely associated with sandy soils, particularly along lakeshores and river valleys. This is a characteristic species of dune habitats in northwestern Indiana and western lower Michigan. Fowler's Toads seem to be more tolerant of warm temperatures than American

Toads and are often active during the day, though in hot weather activity peaks during twilight and early evening. Conversely, they are less active under cold conditions and enter dormancy earlier in fall and emerge later in spring than do most other native anurans.

Fowler's Toads eat insects and other small terrestrial invertebrates. They are reportedly less likely to eat earthworms than the American Toad, though this may be related to their more diurnal feeding habits. The potential predators and defensive behaviors of Fowler's Toads are much the same as those described for the American Toad. This species reportedly will "feign death" (i.e., become immobilized) if roughly handled; presumably this behavior has some defensive value.

**Reproduction and Growth:** Breeding sites for this species are usually warm, shallow waters that are fairly open and include woodland and farm ponds, lake edges, stream backwaters, marshes, sloughs, and natural pools between dunes or along beaches. Migration to these sites and calling by males may begin as early as late April or early May, but the peak of breeding activity typically occurs in late May and June, well after the height of breeding activity in the American Toad.

From 7,000 to 10,000 eggs are laid in long gelatinous strings that closely resemble those of the American Toad. Close examination, especially with the aid of a magnifying lens, will allow eggs of the two species to be differentiated; the eggs of the American Toad are enclosed in a double-layered

Fowler's toad, dorsal
view

Fowler's toad, front
view

tube and are separated by partitions, whereas the eggs of Fowler's Toads are enclosed in a single tubular membrane and are not separated by partitions. The eggs hatch in two to seven days, and the tadpoles may metamorphose into tiny (1 to 1.4 cm, 0.4 to 0.6 in) toadlets thirty to forty days later. Since incubation and growth are hastened by warmer temperatures, tadpoles of the late-breeding Fowler's Toad may transform at about the same time as those of the earlier-breeding American Toad. Fowler's Toads may grow to sexual maturity in one growing season, though slower-growing individuals may require two or even three years. A captive specimen is known to have lived for four years, but normal life expectancy is unknown.

**Conservation:** Preservation of known breeding sites is critical to the existence of Fowler's Toads in their limited range within the Great Lakes basin, but terrestrial habitats also need protection. Intensive recreational use of beach and dune habitats, particularly by off-road vehicles, is detrimental to this species. Agricultural chemicals have also been blamed for the decline or disappearance of this toad in some places. Fowler's Toads are considered an endangered species in Canada.

# Treefrogs and Relatives

## FAMILY HYLIDAE

The treefrogs and their kin form a large family (about 950 species in 50 genera) found throughout North and South America, as well as parts of Europe, Central Asia, and Australia. These are mostly small to medium-sized frogs, many of which have expanded sticky toe pads, giving them the ability to climb trees and shrubs, though some species lack enlarged toe pads and are entirely terrestrial (fig. 6C, page 114).

## Blanchard's Cricket Frog (*Acris blanchardi*)

**Description:** This is a very small, warty-skinned frog with long hind limbs and fully webbed hind toes. The toe tips are not obviously expanded. The snout is bluntly pointed, and there are usually two light bars extending from the corner and edge of the jaw to the eye. The upper surfaces can be brown, tan, olive, or gray, sometimes with scattered green, reddish, or black blotches or spots and a broad light stripe down the back. A dark triangle, pointed backward, is usually visible between the eyes. Other markings often visible include a dark stripe from the shoulder to the groin, another dark stripe on the inner side of each thigh, and dark bars across the upper legs. Some Great Lakes specimens, particularly older individuals, can be dark gray or brown, without distinct markings. The belly is white or cream colored. Adult length: 1.6 to 3.8 cm (0.6 to 1.5 in). Male Blanchard's Cricket Frogs have a slightly thickened pad on the inner part of the thumb and a yellowish, gray-mottled vocal sac; these features are most prominent during the breeding season.

The elongate tadpoles are usually olive to brownish, speckled with black and gold. The upper and lower tail fins are rather narrow, and the tail often has a conspicuous black tip.

Voice: A series of metallic clicks, similar to the sound made when two pebbles are tapped together. The call, which may last for over thirty seconds, usually starts slowly, then increases in tempo, sometimes ending in an irregular rattle.

**Confusing Species:** The Chorus Frogs have a whitish stripe along the upper lip and lengthwise brownish stripes on the sides and back; their toes are only slightly webbed. Spring Peepers have smoother skin and, usually, a roughly X-shaped marking on the back.

**Distribution and Status:** Blanchard's Cricket Frog ranges from Ohio, lower Michigan, and southern Ontario (including Pelee Island) west through Indiana, Illinois, and Wisconsin to southeastern South Dakota, south through Texas and northern Mexico in the west to Arkansas and Louisiana. This species was formerly considered a subspecies of *Acris crepitans,* an arrangement still preferred by some biologists, which would extend the species' range to the Gulf Coast and Florida panhandle north to southeastern New York.

This formerly common frog has experienced notable population declines since the early 1970s throughout the upper Midwest and the Great Lakes basin and is now largely restricted to small localized colonies in our area. It is listed as endangered in Wisconsin, Pennsylvania, and New York, threatened in Michigan, a species of special concern in Indiana, and possibly extirpated in Ontario.

Blanchard's Cricket
Frog, adult

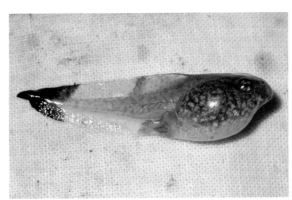

Blanchard's Cricket
Frog, tadpole

**Habitat and Ecology:** These frogs usually inhabit the more open edges of permanent ponds, bogs, lakes, abandoned gravel pits, and slow-moving streams or rivers. Where aquatic vegetation is abundant, the frogs are often seen on floating algae mats and water lily leaves; sparsely vegetated mud flats and muddy or sandy shorelines are also favored habitats. Cricket Frogs are generally diurnal during cool weather but are active throughout the day and night in the warmer months, particularly in the breeding season. Winter is spent beneath shoreline debris or burrowed into wet soil near water. Although they may emerge from hibernation as early as March or April,

Cricket Frogs prefer warmer temperatures than most hylid species and do not breed until late in spring or early summer.

Blanchard's Cricket Frogs eat a wide variety of small terrestrial and aquatic insects and other invertebrates and appear to consume whatever food items of the proper size are most available in the habitat. They will feed on the shore, at the water's surface, or while submerged, both during the day and at night.

These little frogs are eaten by snakes, birds, and larger frogs. They attempt to evade enemies by leaping erratically on the shore or jumping into the water and hiding beneath vegetation or bottom debris. Vertical leaps of over 90 cm (35 in) and horizontal leaps of nearly 1.2 m (4 ft) have been reported.

**Reproduction and Growth:** In the Great Lakes area, Blanchard's Cricket Frogs usually breed from mid- to late May through early July. Warm, humid, rainy weather seems to stimulate breeding activity. Males give their clicking call both night and day from the edges of ponds, streams, and sloughs; calling sometimes will continue into late summer. Amplexus and egg laying occur in warm shallows close to the calling sites.

From 200 to 400 eggs are laid singly or in small clusters; they may float at the surface or adhere to submerged twigs or plants and hatch within a few days. The tadpoles tend to be solitary bottom dwellers. Metamorphosis occurs in five to ten weeks, from mid-July through early September. The new froglets range from 1.0 to 1.5 cm (0.4 to 0.6 in) in length but grow quickly, and some may reach sexual maturity and breed the following year. Captive Cricket Frogs have lived for more than five years, but few wild individuals are likely to survive longer than one or two breeding seasons.

**Conservation:** Blanchard's Cricket Frog declined drastically in the northern portions of its range during the late 1970s and 1980s. Many formerly healthy populations in Michigan and Wisconsin are now greatly reduced or extirpated, and the species is considered to be nearly or totally extirpated from known sites in Ontario (including Point Pelee and Pelee Island). Population declines are reported for northern Illinois and Indiana as well, though the species remains common in the southern and western parts of its range. Reasons for these declines are unclear, but suggestions for further study include contamination of wetlands and waterways by pesticides or other pollutants, vegetational succession, climatic fluctuations, drought, and competition from other frog species. It will be important to monitor existing populations of Cricket Frogs throughout their range and to identify and preserve known habitats.

## Midland Chorus Frog (*Pseudacris triseriata*) and Boreal Chorus Frog (*Pseudacris maculata*)

**Description:** These little frogs have a distinctive white or cream-colored stripe along the upper lip, bordered above by a dark brown stripe running through the eye from nostril to groin. There are usually three additional dark stripes running down the back. The background color ranges from brown, reddish, or tan to gray or olive, while the belly is cream or white, sometimes with dark spots on the throat and chest. The skin is moist and slightly bumpy, and the toes end in slightly expanded pads. Adult length: 1.9 to 3.9 cm (0.75 to 1.5 in).

The sexes are similar; males are slightly smaller on average and have a yellowish vocal sac, which (when the frog is not calling) can be seen as a loose, dark flap of skin on the chin and throat, particularly in the breeding season.

The tadpoles have plump, rounded bodies that are gray or brown above, sometimes mottled with brassy color in older specimens. The tail fins are clear, with dark flecks. The intestinal coil shows through the bronzy belly skin. Maximum length prior to metamorphosis is about 3 cm (1.2 in).

Note: Two species of chorus frogs are presently recognized in the Great Lakes basin. The description above applies to the Midland Chorus Frog (*Pseudacris triseriata*), *formerly called the Western Chorus Frog*, which has the widest range in the basin. The Boreal Chorus Frog (*Pseudacris maculata*), occurs in the western portion of our area, in Minnesota, Wisconsin, and the western edge of Michigan's Upper Peninsula but also apparently in portions of east-central Ontario. This species is very similar to the Midland Chorus Frog but has shorter hind legs (it tends to hop instead of leap), and the three back stripes are frequently broken into rows of spots.

Voice: A short, rising, scratchy "cree-ee-ee-ee-eek." The call has often been likened to the sound made by strumming the small teeth of a stiff pocket comb, from middle to end, with a fingernail. How close this simulation comes to approximating the actual call depends on both the quality of the comb and the extent of one's imagination.

**Confusing Species:** The Spring Peeper lacks a distinct white upper lip line and usually has an X-shaped marking instead of lengthwise striping on the back. Blanchard's Cricket Frog is wartier and also lacks the white lip stripe and dark back stripes. Small metamorph Wood Frogs lack the back stripes and have dorsolateral folds (a ridge of skin down each side of the back).

Great Lakes range of Midland Chorus Frog

**Distribution and Status:** The Midland Chorus Frog ranges from western New York west through lower Michigan and extreme southern Ontario and south through Ohio and Indiana to southern Illinois and western Kentucky. They appear to be absent or are underreported in east-central Ontario; anecdotal reports for the central and eastern portions of Michigan's Upper Peninsula appear to be as yet unconfirmed. The Boreal Chorus Frog occurs in the western and northern Lake Superior basin; its broad range extends from James Bay in northern Ontario west to the Northwest Territories and eastern British Columbia and south to New Mexico and eastern Arizona. A genetic study suggests that chorus frogs in parts of east-central Ontario and Quebec may also be this species (Moriarty Lemmon et al. 2007). The ecological and breeding notes below pertain to both species.

Chorus Frogs can be common to locally abundant, but recent population declines have been noted, particularly in suburban and agricultural areas.

**Habitat and Ecology:** This is generally a frog of marshes, meadows, swales, and other open habitats, though they also occur in damp woods and wooded swamps. They tend to remain near their breeding sites year-round, spending most of their time hidden beneath logs, rocks, and leaf litter or in loose soil or animal burrows; they hibernate in these places as well. They occasionally move about on the surface on warm, rainy nights. Chorus Frogs are poor climbers but occasionally ascend clumps of grass or other small plants, perhaps in search of food.

Midland Chorus Frog, adult

Boreal Chorus Frog, tadpole (Photo: Bill Leonard)

These frogs consume a variety of small invertebrates, including beetles, ants, flies, moths, caterpillars, leaf hoppers, and spiders. The newly trans-formed froglets feed on tiny prey such as mites, midges, and springtails. The tadpoles are largely herbivorous, mostly feeding on algae.

Garter and ribbon snakes are known to eat Chorus Frogs; these little frogs are undoubtedly bite-sized morsels for many birds, small mammals, and larger frogs as well. Their primary defense seems to be concealment, and they are rarely seen in the open except during the early spring breeding season. Even then these little frogs are difficult to see amid the dead grasses and reeds

Great Lakes range of Boreal Chorus Frog

in their breeding sites; any disturbance will cause them to cease calling and dive to the pond bottom, where they hide in the mud or bottom debris.

**Reproduction and Growth:** Chorus Frogs often begin calling when patches of snow still cover the ground and ice has barely receded from the edges of the shallow ponds, ditches, and flooded swales that are this species' favored breeding sites. Calling may extend from early March into late May, but most egg laying seems to occur in April, at least in the southern Great Lakes basin. Early breeding choruses are often heard on clear, sunny days, but as water and air temperatures warm, calling is mostly confined to evenings or cloudy, rainy days. Individual males sometimes call in late summer and fall, perhaps in response to the shorter length of the day or hormonal changes, but the females are not ready to breed at that time.

During amplexus the female lays from 500 to 1,500 eggs in several loose, gelatinous clusters attached to submerged grasses or sticks. Each cluster contains from 20 to 300 eggs. The rate of development in both the eggs and the larvae depends on water temperature. Hatching generally occurs in three to fourteen days, probably depending on water temperature, and the tadpoles transform into tiny (0.8 to 1.2 cm, 0.3 to 0.5 in) froglets from forty to ninety days later. They can grow to maturity and breed in less than a year.

This species and others that breed in shallow, temporary bodies of water

Boreal Chorus Frog, adult (Photo: Richard D. Bartlett)

may avoid losing eggs and tadpoles to certain predators, such as fish, that require more permanent waters. There is a trade-off, however, since in drought years most or all of these temporary ponds may dry up before metamorphosis can take place, leading to reproductive failure for the season.

**Conservation:** This frog appears to be quite tolerant of human activities, considering its presence in many agricultural and suburban areas. Local declines in Chorus Frog numbers have been reported but remain poorly studied; natural factors affecting populations (such as drought and other climatic variations) must be separated from those caused by humans. Many of the shallow breeding sites used by Chorus Frogs are filled by means of surface runoff and are thus vulnerable to contamination by pesticides, fertilizers, and other pollutants, some of which may affect this frog's eggs and larvae.

## Spring Peeper (*Pseudacris crucifer*)

**Description:** A Spring Peeper is a small brown, tan, or gray frog with slightly expanded pads on its toe tips. Dark slanting stripes on the back usually merge to form an X-shaped marking, but the X may be incomplete or have spurs or side bars. A narrow, roughly V-shaped line is usually visible between the eyes, and a dark stripe often runs from the nostril through the eye to the tympanum, sometimes extending down the side. The upper surfaces of the legs have crossbars, and the undersides of the hind legs and groin may be yellowish or pinkish. The belly is white, yellowish, or cream colored. This frog has some color-changing ability and can darken or lighten in response to its mood or surroundings. Adult length: 2 to 3.7 cm (0.8 to 1.5 in). Male Spring Peepers are slightly smaller and darker, on average, than females. During the breeding season the male's vocal sac is visible as a mottled brownish or greenish area of loose skin on the throat.

Tadpoles, which grow to about 3 cm (1.2 in) long prior to transformation, are brown or green with metallic gold flecks on the upper surface. The belly is lighter and iridescent, and the tail fins may be clear or orange tinted, with black or purplish blotches at the outer edges.

Voice: An emphatic, high-pitched, rising "peep!" given about once per second, with the single large vocal sac fully inflated. A male Peeper may also give a lower-pitched trilled whistle, usually when another male has

Spring Peeper

Spring Peeper, male
calling

moved too close to its calling site. This trilled call is sometimes mistaken
for that of the Chorus Frog.

**Confusing Species:** Chorus Frogs have a light upper lip line and lengthwise
stripes (instead of an X-shaped marking) on the back. Cricket Frogs are wartier and have a dark stripe on the inner thigh.

**Distribution and Status:** Spring Peepers are found throughout most of eastern North America, from Nova Scotia west to eastern Manitoba, south to Texas, and east to New England, the Carolinas, and northern Florida.

Spring Peepers are generally common throughout the Great Lakes basin and persist even in many suburban and agricultural areas.

**Habitat and Ecology:** Spring Peepers use temporary and permanent ponds, marshes, floodings, and ditches for breeding. After the breeding season they disperse into woodlands, old fields, and shrubby areas, where they are occasionally seen hopping through leaf litter or climbing on grass clumps, herbaceous plants, and shrubs, especially during rainy weather. Peepers overwinter shallowly beneath logs, bark, and fallen leaves and can survive subfreezing temperatures by producing a glucose-based "antifreeze," which causes ice to form in the extracellular spaces rather than in the body cells.

Peepers eat small arthropods such as spiders, mites, ticks, pill bugs, ants, beetles, springtails, and caterpillars. The tadpoles feed largely on algae and other soft or decaying plant material.

Water bugs, diving beetles, spiders, and dragonfly nymphs are known to capture tadpoles and adult Spring Peepers. Fish, larger frogs, snakes, and many birds will eat these frogs without hesitation. Spring Peepers are secretive and cryptically colored, and their habit of breeding in cool temporary waters in early spring undoubtedly reduces contact with many potential predators.

**Reproduction and Growth:** Spring Peepers may begin calling from breeding ponds in late March or early April and are the earliest calling frogs in some areas. (In other places Chorus Frogs, which hibernate nearer the water, precede them by a few days.) Calling is particularly intense on warm, damp nights, though some individuals will call during the day, especially if stimulated by high humidity or rainfall. Males may call from the water's edge, while partially submerged, or from elevated perches such as emergent shrubs or grass clumps. (Some male Peepers, called " satellite males," do not call but instead remain near a calling male and attempt to intercept females attracted to the latter's call.)

Although choruses can be heard well into May or even June, most actual breeding seems to occur in April, at least in the southern and central Great Lakes basin. Male Spring Peepers are often heard calling briefly in late summer or fall, usually at some distance from the spring breeding sites.

Females may favor males with louder, faster calls; these are usually the older, larger males. The female approaches and contacts her chosen mate; amplexus soon follows. The eggs, which number from 750 to 1,300 per female, are laid singly or in small clusters, usually distributed in irregular rows attached to twigs or aquatic vegetation. The tadpoles hatch in four to fifteen days, perhaps dependent on temperature, and transform into tiny (about 1.3 cm, 0.5 in) froglets from forty-five to ninety days later. Most Spring Peepers are able to breed the spring following their metamorphosis, at a length of about 2 cm (0.8 in). Their maximum life span is unknown, but a Peeper that reached its third breeding season would be fortunate indeed.

**Conservation:** Breeding choruses of Spring Peepers are still a welcome and familiar sign of winter's end throughout the Great Lakes region. While the species remains widespread and locally abundant, many populations of this frog have been reduced or eliminated by the draining of small wetlands and the conversion of their habitat to urban or agricultural use. Although many states and local governments have instituted regulations to protect wetlands, the need to conserve adjacent upland habitats and small temporary wetlands has received little attention by resource managers and politicians. If these critical areas are lost to development, even "common" species like the Spring Peeper will inevitably disappear along with their habitats.

## Eastern Gray Treefrog (*Hyla versicolor*) *and* Cope's Gray Treefrog (*Hyla chrysoscelis*)

**Description:** Both species of Gray Treefrogs have moist, warty skins and large adhesive pads on the tips of the toes. They have considerable color-changing ability, with the same frog varying from light gray to brown to pale green or any color in between. (The change from one color to another may take an hour or more and is thought to be influenced by environmental factors such as temperature and humidity.) One or more irregular dark blotches, sometimes outlined in black, may be visible on the back. A dark stripe or band often slants from the back of the eye to the front leg, and most specimens have a squarish white spot beneath each eye. The belly is white, and the underside of the hind legs and groin is bright yellow or orange. Adult length: 3 to 6 cm (1.2 to 2.4 in).

Male Gray Treefrogs are, on average, slightly smaller than females and can be recognized by the loose, grayish skin covering the chin and throat area (vocal sac).

The tadpoles are greenish or yellowish above, with gold flecks or streaks, and whitish below. The rather high-arched tail fins are often blotched or tinged with red or orange, sometimes with black spots at the outer edges.

Great Lakes range of Gray Treefrogs (species combined)

Newly transformed juveniles are usually bright green, without extensive dark markings on the back.

Note: Of the two species of "Gray Treefrogs" that occur in our area, the Eastern Gray Treefrog (*Hyla versicolor*) is a genetic tetraploid, while Cope's Gray Treefrog (*Hyla chrysoscelis*) is a genetic diploid. They are practically identical in habits and outward appearance, though Cope's Gray Treefrog tends to be slightly smaller and smoother skinned than its relative and is more often entirely green when calling in spring. These differences are inconsistent, however, and unreliable for field identification. The two species are best distinguished by differences in the male advertisement calls (see below), and by laboratory tests that examine blood cells or chromosomes. The ecological and behavioral notes below pertain to both species.

Voice: The Eastern Gray Treefrog gives a loud, musical trill lasting from one-half to three seconds. At the same air temperature, the call of Cope's Gray Treefrog is a faster, harsher, more nasal trill. When both species are calling at the same time, the calls are readily distinguished, but care must be taken when identifying treefrogs in a single species chorus, since temperature can affect the duration and pulse rate of the call. (For further details on the possible origins of this species complex, see "Effects of Glaciation on Amphibian and Reptile Distribution in the Great Lakes Region" in the Introduction, page 26.)

Eastern Gray Treefrog

Eastern Gray Treefrog,
tadpole

Eastern Gray Treefrog

**Confusing Species:** Gray Treefrogs are unlikely to be confused with other Great Lakes frogs. The much smaller Northern Spring Peeper has smaller toe pads and lacks yellow coloring under the hind legs. When listening to spring choruses of unseen anurans, note that the trill of the American Toad is considerably longer in duration (six to thirty seconds) than that of the treefrog, while the trilled "warning call" of the Spring Peeper is almost always preceded or followed by a series of the typical short "peep" calls.

**Distribution and Status:** Gray Treefrogs range from New Brunswick and Maine west to southern Manitoba and south across most of the eastern United States to Texas, the Gulf of Mexico, and the south Atlantic states, excluding most of peninsular Florida. Within this range, the Eastern Gray Treefrog is generally most common in the north and northeast, while Cope's Gray Treefrog is widespread in the western and southern portions, but there are numerous areas of overlap, including the western Great Lakes region. Additional studies are needed to better define the comparative distribution of these frogs. *Hyla versicolor* is the more common treefrog from the eastern Great Lakes through lower Michigan, while both species may share the same breeding ponds in Wisconsin and a few scattered localities in both northern and southern Michigan. Gray Treefrogs remain common throughout most of the Great Lakes area.

**Habitat and Ecology:** Gray Treefrogs are found in deciduous or mixed forests, farm woodlots, swamps, old fields, and well-planted suburban yards—almost anywhere that suitable breeding ponds are adjacent to trees or shrubs. Largely nocturnal, they may forage in low shrubbery or climb to heights of 9 m (30 ft) or more above the ground. Mucus produced on the large toe pads enhances surface tension, allowing the frogs to adhere to smooth surfaces. On warm nights these frogs are often seen on windows or near yard lights or streetlights, feeding on moths and other insects attracted to the light. In winter, treefrogs hibernate on land under logs, leaf litter, or loose house siding or in hollow trees. They tolerate subfreezing temperatures by producing large amounts of glycerol in their blood and body tissues, which acts as a natural "antifreeze" that prevents ice from forming in the body cells. Experiments have shown that Gray Treefrogs can survive temperatures as low as -6°C (21°F) for several days, when over 40 percent of their body fluids may be frozen.

Insects and their larvae form the bulk of the adult Gray Treefrog's diet, along with spiders, mites, harvestmen, and snails. The tadpoles consume

Cope's Gray Treefrog
(left), Eastern Gray
Treefrog (right)

Cope's Gray Treefrog

algae and other vegetable matter, either by filter feeding at the surface or by rasping food off plants or the bottom substrate.

Gray Treefrogs are readily eaten by larger frogs, many snakes, birds, and small mammals, but their arboreal habits, cryptic coloration, and inactivity during daylight hours undoubtedly reduce their visibility to potential predators. Their skin secretions are moderately noxious, but little is known about how effective these are as a deterrence to enemies. They are most vulnerable to predators at or near breeding ponds in spring. Giant water bugs have been seen attacking these frogs in the water. Green Frogs and Bullfrogs sometimes locate and eat breeding male Gray Treefrogs by orienting to their calls.

**Reproduction and Growth:** Temporary ponds, swamps, floodings, and the shallower edges of permanent lakes and sloughs are used by breeding Gray Treefrogs, and these sites may be surrounded by forest or in unshaded, open situations. Although the frogs may emerge from winter dormancy quite early in spring, breeding choruses are rarely heard before late April or early May, usually after evening air temperatures remain at 15°C (60°F) or higher. Breeding may extend into late June or early July, particularly if interrupted by periods of cool weather. Calling is generally most intense between dusk and midnight, though loud choruses can sometimes be heard at midday on warm, overcast days.

Male Gray Treefrogs call from the water's edge, from clumps of emergent vegetation, or from overhanging branches, though it appears that unobscured horizontal perches over the water are preferred. A special prolonged call is used to warn away rivals, and calling territories may be aggressively defended. Noncalling "satellite" males often hide near a calling male, waiting for an opportunity to take over the latter's perch when he leaves. Males will remain at the ponds for several weeks, while females visit the site only briefly, to mate and deposit eggs. At the end of the breeding season, males often continue to call for some time as they gradually retreat from the pond and move into nearby trees and shrubs. Individual males may call briefly during late summer or fall, especially on rainy days, but this generally occurs well away from breeding ponds and is not associated with reproduction.

Females reportedly choose males with the longest and most frequently repeated calls. A male being approached by a female often gives a distinctive "courtship call," which is longer and more emphatic than the advertisement call. During a sometimes prolonged period of amplexus, the female deposits from 1,000 to 2,000 eggs, divided into small loose clusters of 10 to 40, which are usually attached to plants or other objects near the water's surface. The tadpoles hatch in three to seven days, depending on water temperature, and metamorphose into tiny (1.5 cm, 0.6 in) green treefroglets in about six to eight weeks. They reach maturity after their second winter. Their potential life-span is unknown, but captive specimens have survived for more than seven years.

**Conservation:** Gray Treefrogs remain common throughout much of the Great Lakes basin and often persist in the presence of agricultural activity and low-density residential development provided suitable breeding ponds are available. Most people seem to enjoy having these frogs around their homes. The drainage or degradation of small ponds, marshes, and other wetlands can eliminate treefrog populations in a short time. The introduction of game fish into formerly fishless ponds is also detrimental to treefrog reproduction. Pesticide applications on trees and shrubs or near wetlands inhabited by treefrogs could be harmful to these animals, but research is needed to assess the direct and indirect effects of different chemicals and formulations, including the presumed reduction in insect prey.

# Typical Frogs

## FAMILY RANIDAE

Anurans in the family Ranidae are often called typical or "true" frogs, largely because the members of this family in the United States and Canada are what many people would consider "normal" frogs, that is, mostly medium- to large-sized leaping frogs with long legs; generally smooth, moist skin; and rather low-pitched "croaking" calls. The family has undergone considerable taxonomic revision in recent years (see comments in Introduction); presently it includes about 378 species in 14 genera and is found on every major continent in the world with the obvious exception of Antarctica. An important identifying characteristic is the presence or absence of a ridge of skin along both sides of the back, starting above the tympanum (eardrum). Called the dorsolateral fold, this feature is found on all Great Lakes ranids except the Bullfrog and many Mink Frogs (Fig. 6A, page 114).

## Bullfrog (*Rana catesbeiana*)

**Description:** The largest frog species in North America may be green, yellow-green, olive, or brown, sometimes with brownish spots or blotches on the back and dark bands on the upper legs. Dorsolateral folds are lacking, but there is a ridge of skin beginning at the eye and curving behind the tympanum to the shoulder. The dorsal skin of young Bullfrogs is smooth but becomes bumpier as they get larger. The belly is white or cream colored, often mottled with gray. The toes of the hind feet are fully webbed except for the tip of the fourth (longest) toe. Adult body length: 9.5 to 20.3 cm (3.7 to 8 in).

In male Bullfrogs the tympanum is much larger than the diameter of the eye, and the throat is yellow. The female's tympanum is roughly the same size as the eye, and its throat is usually whitish. Males are, on average, more uniformly colored and smaller than females. Bullfrog tadpoles are green, olive, or brownish above, often with dark spotting that extends onto the upper tail fin. (Green Frog tadpoles are similar but usually have dark spotting on both the upper and lower tail fins.) The belly is white to yellowish-white. They may reach a length of over 15 cm (6 in) during an extended larval period, which may last two years or more.

Voice: The advertisement call is a very low-pitched, resonating "brr-rr-rrum." The challenge call, given when a male detects an intruding male, is a one- or two-noted call, described as a "squawk" or "hiccup." Other, nonreproductive calls are described below.

**Confusing Species:** Green Frogs have distinct dorsolateral folds extending at least partway down the back, and their adult size is smaller. The smaller, darker Mink Frog of the far north may lack dorsolateral folds but has rounded spots or lengthwise blotches on the upper surface of the hind legs and a musky, minklike odor when handled.

**Distribution and Status:** The natural range of the Bullfrog extends from Nova Scotia to southern Florida, west to Wisconsin and southern South Dakota, and south through Oklahoma and Texas to the western Gulf of Mexico. Due to numerous accidental and intentional introductions, this species is now well established throughout much of the western United States, southwestern British Columbia, Hawaii, and elsewhere.

Bullfrogs occur throughout most of the Great Lakes region, though they are less common to the north and are absent from the northern Lake Superior basin. Their occurrence in Michigan's Upper Peninsula is spotty and widely scattered.

This species can be locally common in ideal habitats, although it has recently declined in or even disappeared from some areas of former abundance.

**Habitat and Ecology:** Almost any still, permanent body of water may be home to this species, including river backwaters, sloughs, lakes, farm ponds, impoundments, marshes, and shallow Great Lakes bays. Places with abundant submerged and emergent vegetation are preferred. Temporary waters are rarely used, except as resting places for dispersing juvenile frogs. Both tadpoles and adult frogs usually bury themselves in the bottom mud during hibernation, which may last from mid-October until April or May. Adult frogs often cease activity earlier in fall and emerge later in spring than the tadpoles or juvenile frogs. These warmth-loving frogs remain generally inactive until water temperatures approach about 15°C (60°F).

Bullfrogs will eat nearly any animal they can capture and swallow, including vertebrates such as fish, amphibians (including juvenile and larval Bullfrogs), snakes, small turtles, young waterfowl and other birds, and small mammals. They are known to locate (and eat) smaller frogs by orienting to their breeding calls. However, much of the Bullfrog's diet is made up of aquatic and terrestrial invertebrates such as dragonflies, beetles and other insects, spiders, snails, and crayfish. Food may be captured either above or below the water's surface. The tadpoles feed mostly on algae and other aquatic plants, though they will scavenge in the bottom debris and consume decaying animal matter.

Despite being formidable predators, Bullfrogs (and their larvae) are eaten by a host of fellow carnivores, including fish, larger frogs, snakes, turtles, herons, raccoons, otters, and mink. Due to their large size, Bullfrogs are hunted by humans for their legs. Most hunting takes place at night, since these frogs tend to "freeze" in a bright flashlight beam. They are wary during the day, leaping into the water at any disturbance, often giving a single "yelp" (which can actually sound more like a "burp"!) as they jump. When seized by a predator, they can emit a piercing scream or wail that presumably might startle an attacker long enough to allow the frog to escape. Bullfrog tadpoles are reportedly distasteful to some fish; in any case the species successfully reproduces in waters where fish are abundant.

**Reproduction and Growth:** Breeding activity rarely begins before mid-May, usually peaks in June, and often continues well into July. Males call most vigorously on warm nights, but some continue calling during the day. A

Bull Frog, adult male

Bull Frog, new
metamorph

male may call while partly submerged or perched on a log or floating vegetation. The larger males defend roughly circular calling territories about 2 to 5 m (6 to 18 ft) in diameter, with the largest males taking the most desirable breeding sites. A territorial male uses a one- or two-note challenge call to warn an intruding male; if the warning is not heeded, a direct conflict that resembles a shoving or wrestling match may result. More often than not, the resident male succeeds in driving the intruder from his territory.

A female Bullfrog appears to choose a mate according to the suitability of its territory as an egg-laying site, although some pairs will move away from the calling area before eggs are laid. During amplexus the female deposits from 5,000 to over 20,000 eggs in a very thin floating mass that may be up to 1 m (3.3 ft) in diameter. Individual eggs are tiny, only 0.12 to 0.17 cm (0.05 to 0.07 in) in diameter. Hatching occurs in three to six days. Some of the tadpoles will transform into froglets during their second summer, but many others will overwinter a second time and metamorphose in July or August of their third summer. Young Bullfrogs generally reach breeding size in two to four years, when they are 10 to 12 cm (4 to 4.7 in) in body length. One Bullfrog lived for more than fifteen years in a zoological park.

**Conservation:** Local declines in Bullfrog populations have been attributed to habitat degradation and loss, water pollution, pesticide contamination, and overharvesting. Lakeside residential developments often lead to removal of shoreline and submerged vegetation, and heavy recreational use of these waters disrupts Bullfrog reproductive activities. More information is needed on the sensitivity of this species to the various pesticides that are used in or near lakes and wetlands. Bullfrogs have been heavily collected for the restaurant and biological supply trades. It is unlikely that this species can tolerate intensive exploitation for commercial or even personal use, due to the extended time period needed for its development and maturation and comparatively slow population replacement rates. Bullfrogs are considered game animals by most state and provincial resource agencies, and their harvest is controlled by closed seasons and "bag" limits throughout the Great Lakes area.

Ironically, while native Bullfrog populations have declined in many places in the East, introduced populations on the West Coast and elsewhere seem to be thriving and are reportedly having a serious negative impact on numbers of native frog species.

## Green Frog (*Rana clamitans*)

**Description:** A Green Frog may be green, yellowish-green, olive, brown, or any combination of these colors; occasional aberrant individuals are blue. The upper lip area is green or yellow. Many have dark spotting on the back and sides, and the hind legs have dark crossbands. A ridge of skin (the dorsolateral fold) extends from each eye to about one-half to two-thirds of the way down the back; a spur of this ridge curves behind the tympanum. The belly is white, sometimes mottled with gray. Adult length: 6 to 10.8 cm (2.4 to 4.2 in).

In mature males the throat is bright yellow, and the tympanum is much larger than the eye. The female has a white, light yellow, or cream-colored throat, often mottled with gray or black, and a tympanum about the same size as the eye.

The plump, long-tailed tadpoles are olive to brownish-green above, with varying amounts of dark flecking extending over the back and upper and lower tail fins. (In the very similar Bullfrog tadpole, dark spots are usually smaller and restricted to the upper half of the tail fin.) The belly is iridescent white or cream, often mottled with gray, and the intestinal coil is not visible through the skin.

Voice: The male's advertisement call is a brief "clung!" (often compared to plucking a loose banjo string), which may be given singly or several times in succession. A low growl is sometimes heard just prior to or during territorial battles.

**Confusing Species:** Bullfrogs are similar but larger and lack dorsolateral folds on the back. Green Frogs are often heavily marked with dark pigment like Mink Frogs, particularly where the two species' ranges overlap, and they may (rarely) lack dorsolateral folds. A form of mimicry may be occurring; Mink Frogs have protective musky skin secretions and a characteristic odor, which Green Frogs lack. The possibility of hybridization between these species should also be investigated. Green Frogs have dark crossbands on the hind legs, while Mink Frogs generally have rounded spots or lengthwise stripes.

**Distribution and Status:** Green Frogs range across eastern North America from Maine, Quebec, and the Canadian Maritime Provinces west through the Great Lakes region to western Ontario, south through Oklahoma and eastern Texas and east to northern Florida and the Atlantic seaboard. There are presumably introduced populations in Washington and southern British Columbia. This is one of the more abundant frogs in the Great Lakes region; it is certainly a conspicuous shoreline species around many permanent water habitats.

**Habitat and Ecology:** Ponds, lakes, swamps, sloughs, impoundments, and slow streams are all inhabited by Green Frogs. They seem to be more tolerant of open, sparsely vegetated sites than the larger Bullfrog. Shallow, temporary waters are generally avoided, at least by the adults. Green Frogs spend most of their time around the water's edge but may take advantage of warm, rainy nights to disperse overland to new habitats. At these times, large numbers of mostly juvenile frogs can be seen crossing roads and yards, often taking up a brief residence in small ponds, ditches, and puddles. Green Frogs overwinter in the water, shallowly buried beneath bottom mud or debris. Dormancy typically lasts from early November to early April, but frogs inhabiting ice-free waters (such as creeks or spring-fed ponds) may be active and bask on sunny days even in midwinter.

Green Frogs are largely "sit and wait" predators, taking any prey of appropriate size that comes within reach. They consume a variety of aquatic and terrestrial insects and other invertebrates, including beetles, flies, butterflies, caterpillars, grasshoppers, spiders, millipedes, slugs, snails, and crayfish. Large individuals also eat smaller frogs, snakes, and hatchling turtles. The tadpoles feed on whatever ingestible organic material is most available, largely algae (e.g., diatoms), along with other planktonic organisms and decaying animal and plant debris.

These common frogs contribute to the food supply of many other animals. Their eggs are eaten by leeches, aquatic insects, and Painted Turtles. The tadpoles also fall prey to predaceous insects, as well as fishes, turtles, snakes, and herons. After metamorphosis, Green Frogs are eaten by larger frogs, turtles, snakes, wading birds, raccoons, otters, mink, and occasionally humans. This species appears to lack repellent skin secretions and is generally palatable to predators. However, they are wary and agile; when disturbed they leap into the water, often simultaneously giving a loud squeaking cry, and then bury themselves in the bottom mud or hide under submerged objects.

Green Frog, normal male (right), blue variant (left)

Green Frog, juvenile female

**Reproduction and Growth:** Males usually begin calling in early to mid-May and may continue to call throughout the prolonged breeding season, sometimes into August. The area around a calling site is defended against other males. When an intruder is detected, the normally single-noted advertisement call may be repeated rapidly several times. If the challenger does not retreat, an emphatic squawklike version of the advertisement call may be given as the defender advances. Usually the intruder retreats; if not, a "wrestling match" may occur, accompanied by low growling sounds.

Unlike the persistent males, a female will spend only a brief time at the breeding site, apparently seeking a mate with a desirable territory for egg laying. She approaches and turns her back to the chosen male; he will initiate amplexus when contacted by the female. Egg laying normally occurs at night, often during rainy weather. The thin, floating egg mass is usually attached to emergent or surface vegetation and contains from 1,000 to 5,000 eggs. Hatching occurs in three to five days. Tadpoles that hatch early in the season may transform into froglets late in their first summer, but those hatching later will overwinter as larvae and transform during the following summer. The newly metamorphosed froglets average about 3 cm (1.2 in) long but can double their length the first year, reaching maturity the following summer. Maximum size is reached in four to five years. The potential life-span is unknown, but zoo specimens have lived at least ten years.

**Conservation:** Green Frogs are occasionally harvested by people seeking "frog legs," though relatively few specimens reach a size worthy of such attention. This species remains widespread and reasonably common throughout most of the Great Lakes region, but populations should be monitored and studied nevertheless. It is as important to understand the success of common species as it is to study species that are rare and declining. Should Green Frogs ever suffer a sustained decline, we would certainly have cause for concern.

## Mink Frog (*Rana septentrionalis*)

**Description:** Mink Frogs are named for the musky odor produced by the skin when they are handled, which is said to resemble the smell of a mink—or rotting onions. The back and sides are green, olive, or brown, moderately to heavily marked with darker spots and/or irregular blotches and reticulations. The upper surfaces of the hind legs have rounded spots or lengthwise bars or stripes, and the upper "lip" area is green. Dorsolateral folds tend to be poorly developed or even absent but are occasionally prominent. Undersides are whitish, often grading to pale yellow on the sides and chin, or sometimes entirely yellow. Adult length: 4.8 to 7.6 cm (1.8 to 3 in).

In male Mink Frogs the tympanum is larger than the eye, and the throat is often bright yellow. Females have a tympanum that is smaller or the same size as the eye, and their throats are white or pale yellow. The tadpoles may reach 10 cm (nearly 4 in) in length prior to metamorphosis. The dorsal coloration is green, olive, or brown, often with a scattering of small, dark spots or heavy mottling that may extend onto the tail. The tail is long, with a pointed tip, and the fins may be edged with pinkish-buff spots. The belly is yellowish and opaque.

Voice: The advertisement call of the male Mink Frog is a series of rather soft, low-pitched croaks ("tok . . . tok, tok, tok, tok . . ."), which has been likened to the sound of distant hammering.

**Confusing Species:** Young Bullfrogs tend to be green with only a scattering of small spots. Green Frogs are often heavily marked with dark pigment where their range overlaps that of the Mink Frog, and confusion between the two is common. Only Mink Frogs have a musky odor when handled, and they have dark spots or lengthwise stripes on the hind legs, while Green Frogs have dark crossbands. Additionally, the hind-foot webbing of the Mink Frog reaches the tip of the fifth (outer) toe and the last joint of the fourth toe, while the webbing in the Green Frog fails to reach the tip of the fifth toe and rarely passes the second joint of the fourth toe. Possible mimicry and/or hybridization between these two species is possible and in need of study.

**Distribution and Status:** This northern species ranges from central Quebec and Labrador south to Maine and northern New York, west to southeastern Manitoba and northern Minnesota. In the Great Lakes basin they occur from eastern Lake Ontario to Georgian Bay and the northeastern shore of Lake Huron, then west through the Lake Superior basin and south through Michigan's Upper Peninsula to the northern shore of Lake Michigan. Anecdotal reports from Michigan's Lower Peninsula are unverified to date, and there are no records for the southern two-thirds of Wisconsin.

Mink Frogs can be locally common in suitable habitats, but local declines have been reported, and their rangewide status is in need of review.

**Habitat and Ecology:** Cool, permanent waters with ample emergent and floating vegetation are the preferred habitat of these frogs. Favored sites include sluggish streams, boggy lake inlets, beaver impoundments, and spring-fed ponds, particularly where lily pads, spatterdocks, or clumps of pickerelweed are abundant. They rarely leave the immediate vicinity of water, although juveniles may disperse to new habitats during periods of heavy rainfall. Mink Frogs hibernate underwater in the bottom mud, often entering dormancy by late September and remaining inactive until well into May.

The Mink Frog's diet reflects its preferred habitat, being made up largely of aquatic insects and other invertebrates. Most feeding occurs at the water's surface or on lily pads and includes whirligig and diving beetles, water boatmen, water striders, stoneflies, mayflies, blackflies, dragonflies, damselflies, spiders, and snails. Terrestrial insects that fall in or fly over the water are readily taken. The tadpoles largely eat soft plant material such as algae.

This frog's musky skin secretions are presumably distasteful to some predators, but giant water bugs, herons, raccoons, and large Green Frogs will eat both adults and tadpoles. Leeches often parasitize them as well. Mink Frogs are wary, and any disturbance will send them skimming over the lily pads and the water's surface before diving to the bottom, where they conceal themselves in the mud and may remain there for some time.

**Reproduction and Growth:** The breeding season of this "north woods" frog may extend from late May into early August, depending on the local climate; in the Great Lakes area most egg deposition occurs in June and July. The males may call day or night, either singly or in a group chorus. During amplexus, from 500 to 4,000 eggs are laid in brownish, globular clusters from 7.5 to 15 cm (3 to 6 in) in diameter attached to water lily stems or other submerged vegetation. The egg mass may be over 1 m (3.3 ft) below the surface and often sinks to the bottom prior to hatching. Cold, well-oxygenated water is needed for proper development of the embryos, which may explain this frog's northerly range. The tadpoles spend about a year (sometimes two) as larvae before transforming into froglets measuring from 3 to 4 cm (1.2 to 1.6 in) in length. Male Mink Frogs become sexually mature in a year or less, but the slightly larger females may need a second year to reach breeding size. The average and maximum life-spans are unknown.

Mink Frog, adult

Mink Frog (left) and
Green Frog (right)

**Conservation:** These cold-adapted frogs would seem to have ample available habitat within their restricted northern range. It is possible that Mink Frogs were more abundant and widespread during cooler glacial and postglacial periods and that their range contracted as the climate warmed. Anecdotal reports suggest that some Mink Frog populations may be declining, while Green Frogs appear to be maintaining their numbers or even increasing at the same sites. Mink Frogs are somewhat more specialized than the larger and more ubiquitous Green Frogs, and studies that focus on interactions between these species could provide useful information for evolutionary biologists and conservation planners.

## Wood Frog (*Rana sylvatica*)

**Description:** This is a brown frog with a dark "mask" extending from the eye through the tympanum to the shoulder, a dark stripe from eye to snout, and a white line along the upper lip. The dorsal color actually varies from grayish-brown to bronze, reddish-brown, or tan. (Males in cold breeding ponds are often very dark, with an inconspicuous mask.) There may be black spots along the prominent dorsolateral folds and on the sides and dark bands across the hind legs. The belly is white, sometimes mottled with gray; some specimens have a yellowish tinge on the sides or in the groin area. Wood Frogs from the northern parts of the region often have a light stripe down the middle of the back and, occasionally, light lengthwise stripes on the hind legs as well. Adult length: 3.5 to 8.3 cm (1.4 to 3.3 in).

In male Wood Frogs the edges of the webbing between the hind toes is straight or curved outward. During the breeding season, males are usually darker than females, their thumbs are thickened with an inner pad, and the paired vocal sacs may be visible as skin folds between the end of the jaw and the shoulder. Females have the edge of the webbing between the hind toes curved inward, and they tend to be larger and lighter in color than their mates.

The tadpole, which can reach a length of up to 4.8 cm (1.8 in), is plump bodied, with a short, high tail fin. The body is brown or olive, often speckled with black and gold; the tail is lighter, sometimes with black spotting. The belly is iridescent whitish to pinkish or bronze, with the intestinal coil usually visible through the skin.

Voice: The male's advertisement call is a series of clucklike croaks, and a chorus may sound like quacking ducks when heard from a short distance. A chirplike "release" call is given by the male when he is accidently clasped by another male Wood Frog in the breeding pond.

**Confusing Species:** Chorus frogs also have a brown masklike facial stripe and light upper lip, but they are much smaller, lack dorsolateral folds, and have slightly expanded toe pads.

**Distribution and Status:** Wood Frogs range farther north than any other North American amphibian, occurring from Labrador and northern Quebec south to Georgia, then north through the entire Great Lakes region, Minnesota, northeastern North Dakota, and across Canada to the edge of the permafrost in the Yukon and northern Alaska. Isolated populations are found in Alabama, Arkansas, Missouri, Wyoming, and Colorado. These relict populations are likely evidence that Wood Frogs occupied a more southerly and westerly range during Pleistocene glacial events.

This is a common species in suitable habitats throughout most of the region.

**Habitat and Ecology:** Wood Frogs prefer moist wooded habitats (including deciduous, coniferous, and mixed forests), and the adults are rarely found in water except during the short breeding season. They will cross open areas to reach a suitable breeding pond, but otherwise normally remain under the tree canopy. These frogs usually hibernate on land beneath loose soil, leaf litter, or decaying logs. They can survive intermittent periods of subfreezing temperatures in winter by producing large amounts of glucose, which acts as a natural "antifreeze," causing ice to form in the extracellular spaces rather than within the body cells. A dormant Wood Frog at a subfreezing temperature may seem solidly frozen; more than half of its body water may be ice, and breathing and heartbeat cease. Once temperatures warm sufficiently, however, the frog can recover rather quickly, and it can go from frozen to fully functional in about one day.

Wood Frogs eat mostly terrestrial invertebrates such as beetles, crickets, caterpillars, spiders, earthworms, slugs, and snails. Juveniles include a somewhat higher percentage of aquatic invertebrates in their diets. The tadpoles typically consume algae, diatoms, and decaying plant and animal matter, but at times they can be quite carnivorous, feeding on the eggs and larvae of other amphibians.

Wood Frog eggs are consumed by leeches, aquatic insects and their larvae, and Eastern Newts, while the tadpoles fall prey to predaceous diving beetles, water bugs, and the larvae of *Ambystoma* salamanders. Tadpoles approaching metamorphosis develop poison glands that repel some insect predators. In most years the worst danger to tadpoles is the threat of their ponds drying up before they can transform. Numerous predators will eat Wood Frogs, including larger frogs; garter, ribbon, and water snakes; herons; raccoons; skunks; and mink. Their skin secretions are reportedly repellent to shrews. Wood Frogs are most vulnerable when gathered in their early spring breeding choruses, but cool temperatures at that time would limit the activity of reptilian predators. When disturbed on land, they will often make a series of erratic leaps and then freeze, sometimes seeming to disappear amid the vegetation and leaf litter. When seized, a Wood Frog can give a piercing cry, perhaps to temporarily startle its attacker and allowing it to escape.

**Reproduction and Growth:** Vernal ponds, floodings, wooded swamps, and quiet stream backwaters are all used by Wood Frogs during their rather short six- to fourteen-day breeding season. Males move rapidly to these sites during the first warm days of early spring (late March to early April), often while patches of snow still persist in the woods and ice remains on the shady edges of ponds and swamps. Their frantic clucking, along with the white flashes of their paired vocal sacs, soon attracts the females. The males outnumber the females at any one time and will attempt to clasp anything that remotely resembles another Wood Frog; other males give a chirplike release call when grabbed, while egg-laden females remain silent.

Once in amplexus, a pair usually moves to a deeper part of the pond before the female deposits from 500 to more than 3,000 eggs in one to several rounded gelatinous masses, usually attached to plant stems or twigs near the surface. The gelatinous egg cluster is clear to grayish when first laid but later may turn green from algae growth. Often many pairs of frogs will lay their eggs in one place in the pond, and several advantages to this communal nesting within a brief "explosive" breeding cycle have been suggested. Large numbers of dark egg masses absorb heat more efficiently than a lone mass, and temperatures in the center of communal egg aggregations can be warmer than the surrounding water. Synchronizing egg laying may also reduce the chances of larval cannibalism, and the sudden bounty of eggs could glut predators, assuring that some will survive to hatch. It is also

Wood Frog

Wood Frog in red
phase

possible that moisture retention is enhanced in communal masses, giving some protection to the embryos if water levels fall during rainless periods.

The incubation period is temperature dependent, ranging from as few as four days to as long as four weeks. The tadpoles grow quickly and are normally ready to transform in six to fifteen weeks. The juvenile froglets, which range from 1 to 2 cm (0.4 to 0.8 in) in length, can often be seen in large numbers around the edges of the ponds from late May through early July, but they soon disperse into the surrounding woods. Males can reach breeding size in one to two years, females in two to three years.

**Conservation:** Wood Frogs appear to be holding their own wherever woodlands enclosing or adjacent to suitable breeding ponds persist. They disappear when forest cover is removed or breeding sites are drained or filled. Large numbers of migrating adults can be killed by automobiles when roads are built between terrestrial habitats and breeding sites, and their eggs are reportedly sensitive to runoff of road salt. Studies on the sensitivity of this frog's eggs and larvae to the effects of acid precipitation show that their shallow breeding ponds can experience rapid changes in acidity due to melting snows and rainfall. Tolerance appears to vary regionally, with acid-exposed populations showing better tolerance to acidity than unexposed populations.

## Northern Leopard Frog (*Rana pipiens*)

**Description:** Northern Leopard Frogs are green, greenish-brown, or brown above, with a variable number of rounded dark spots scattered over the back and sides. The spots may have whitish or yellowish borders. There is usually a dark spot over each eye and on the snout; the legs are also spotted or barred. A white line extends from the nose to the shoulder above the upper lip, and the dorsolateral folds are light colored and conspicuous. The belly is white to pale greenish-white and sometimes faintly yellowish in the groin area. Adult length: 5 to 11.1 cm (2 to 4.4 in).

Male Leopard Frogs have enlarged thumbs and are usually smaller than the females, which also appear fatter when swollen with eggs in spring. There is no difference in the size of the tympanum between sexes. During calling, the male's paired vocal sacs inflate over his shoulders. The tadpole, which reaches a maximum length of 8.4 cm (3.3 in), is green, olive, or brown above, often with a light speckling of yellow and/or black. The otherwise light-colored tail may also be weakly spotted with black. The belly is an iridescent white or cream color, with the intestinal coil visible.

Voice: The male's advertisement call sounds much like a low, rumbling snore punctuated with hoarse clucks and croaks. Both males and nonreceptive females may give a vibrating chuckle (the "release" call) if accidently clasped by a male. When seized by a predator, a Leopard Frog can give a loud, pitiful scream.

**Confusing Species:** The Pickerel Frog has spots that are more angular and arranged in two rows between the dorsolateral folds, and it has bright yellow or orange color on the groin and undersurfaces of the hind legs.

Note: The range of the Plains Leopard Frog (*Rana blairi*) approaches the lower Lake Michigan basin in Cook and Will counties in northeastern Illinois. This species differs from the Northern Leopard Frog in having dorsolateral folds that are "broken" over the hind legs, with the distal portions displaced toward the middle of the back. It is a brown frog with a light spot on the tympanum and dark dorsal spots that often lack distinct light borders (see account under "Marginal and Questionable Species," page 362).

**Distribution and Status:** Northern Leopard Frogs are found over a broad area from Labrador and Quebec west to southern British Columbia, then south through the Rocky Mountain region to Nevada, Arizona, and New Mexico, with numerous disjunct populations in Washington and California. In the eastern United States it occurs in much of New England, west through the entire Great Lakes basin and the northern Great Plains, and south to northern Kentucky, West Virginia, and Pennsylvania. Related species in the "leopard frog complex" occur throughout the southeastern United States and the prairie and desert regions of the central and southwestern states and northern Mexico.

Northern Leopard Frogs were generally abundant in most of the Great Lakes basin until the late 1960s and 1970s, when they suffered a notable population decline. They remain uncommon or rare in some places but have seemingly recovered in others, and they can be locally abundant when conditions are favorable.

**Habitat and Ecology:** Northern Leopard Frogs are typically found in open habitats, including marshes, bogs, lake and stream edges, sedge meadows, hayfields, and suburban lawns. They usually overwinter in permanent waters (larger ponds, lakes, and streams), where they may sit on the bottom or under the edges of rocks or logs or conceal themselves beneath a light layer of silt. In early spring these frogs seek shallower water for breeding, sometimes migrating to temporary ponds, stream backwaters, or marsh pools over 1 km (0.6 mi) from the hibernation site. In summer they often disperse well away from the water into meadows and other grassy places, more rarely into open woodlands. They tolerate dry conditions by absorbing moisture from dew or damp soil through their skin. In the fall they migrate back to their "home" waters prior to hibernation.

Leopard Frogs feed on terrestrial invertebrates such as insects and insect larvae, spiders, slugs, snails, and earthworms. Larger adults will also eat small vertebrates such as Spring Peepers and Chorus Frogs. Considering the frequent movement of this frog into gardens and agricultural fields, its feeding habits are undoubtedly beneficial to human interests.

The tadpoles consume algae, diatoms, and minute animal life, either filtered from the water and bottom debris or gleaned from plants and other surfaces.

A host of predators eat Leopard Frogs; a partial list would include giant water bugs, fish (e.g., bass and pike), Green Frogs and Bullfrogs, garter and water snakes, hawks, waterfowl, herons, raccoons, foxes, mink, and otters. In some places humans capture large numbers of this species for research and classroom study and even for food (i.e., "frog legs"). Leeches, newts, and turtles consume Leopard Frog eggs, while the tadpoles are eaten by diving beetles, water bugs, and most of the vertebrates mentioned above. Newly metamorphosed froglets are especially vulnerable; mortality may exceed 95 percent in the first months after transformation.

These frogs escape enemies by leaping into the water and burying themselves in the bottom mud or (when on land) by taking several erratic jumps and then obscuring themselves beneath the vegetation; their green or brown coloration often blends with their surroundings. They do not appear to have skin secretions effective in deterring predators. Some Leopard Frogs (especially certain populations in Wisconsin and northern Michigan) display the more squarish dorsal spots that are a characteristic of Pickerel Frogs, which may share the same habitats. Because Pickerel Frogs have skin secretions repellent to some predators, this may represent a case of evolving mimicry. Leopard Frogs that more closely resembled their noxious relatives could presumably have a survival advantage over normally patterned frogs. However,

Northern Leopard Frog, green (left) and brown (right) color phases

Northern Leopard Frog, juvenile

hybridization between Leopard and Pickerel Frogs has also been reported and offers an alternative explanation for this phenomenon.

**Reproduction and Growth:** Males move to breeding sites in early spring and begin giving their snorelike calls while sprawled on or just below the surface in shallow water. The peak of breeding in the Great Lakes area is usually in April, though the season may extend into May in northern parts of the region. Calling and amplexus occur most often in the evening, occasionally during the day.

An amplexed pair will often move to an area where other pairs have already deposited eggs before leaving their own complement. A female lays from 300 to 6,000 eggs in one or more globular or flattened oval masses, usually attached to submerged twigs or stems but sometimes floating near the surface. Each egg is black above and white below. As with Wood Frogs, communal egg laying in this species may aid in heat absorption or act as a defense against excessive losses to egg predators. Hatching occurs in four to twenty days, depending on water temperature, and the tadpoles are ready to transform in two to three months. The 2 to 3 cm (0.8 to 1.2 in) froglets will grow to maturity in one to three years (depending on individual growth rates) and may live up to nine years, though few will be lucky enough to attain such longevity.

**Conservation:** The Northern Leopard Frog was probably the most abundant (and certainly the most conspicuous) anuran in the Great Lakes region prior to the late 1960s, but since that time naturalists and biologists have reported population declines over much of the species' range. Many explanations have been offered for this phenomenon. The intensive and often poorly regulated harvest of Northern Leopard Frogs for the biological supply and fish bait trades is known to have reduced local populations. Fragmentation and loss of wetland and adjacent upland habitats are undoubtedly important factors that affect the species rangewide. Road mortality can be significant during pre- and postbreeding migrations.

The widespread use of persistent pesticides in the mid-twentieth century is also a suspected cause of Leopard Frog decline. Experimental evidence indicates that this species may be more sensitive to the effects of certain pesticides in use at that time (e.g., DDT and other chlorinated hydrocarbons) than certain other native ranid species, but additional research would be needed to clarify this problem. They are also intolerant of acidification of breeding waters; a pH of 4.8 suppresses egg development. Massive seasonal die-offs of these frogs have been attributed to disease or winter freezing and oxygen deprivation. Dead Leopard Frogs often have a reddish flushing of the underparts ("redleg"), a symptom caused by various bacteria, particularly *Aeromonas hydrophila*. Such infections are thought to be related to physiological stress.

Where habitat is available, Northern Leopard Frogs have the reproductive potential to recover from population declines, and in some places the species has rebounded from earlier lows. It seems probable that numbers of these frogs have naturally varied from year to year, depending on environmental (especially climatic) factors. However, Leopard Frogs remain scarce or absent in many locations where they were formerly common, and continued monitoring of their populations and habitats is important.

## Pickerel Frog *(Rana palustris)*

**Description:** The Pickerel Frog is a medium-sized spotted frog with a light line along the upper lip. Though similar in appearance to the Northern Leopard Frog, it has more angular (squarish) brown spots, often outlined in black and arranged in two irregular rows between the light-colored dorsolateral folds. In a rare variation, these dorsal spots may merge into lengthwise stripes. The background color is light brown, tan, gray, or olive, sometimes with a bronze or yellowish-green cast. Bright yellow, orange, or gold color is present on the groin and undersides of the hind legs, contrasting with a whitish belly and throat. Adult length: 4.4 to 8.7 cm (1.7 to 3.4 in). Males tend to be slightly smaller than females and have enlarged thumbs (with inner pads) during the breeding season. Pickerel Frog tadpoles reach a total length of 5 to 7.6 cm (2 to 3 in) prior to metamorphosis. They are green, grayish-brown, or brown above, often with scattered black and yellow spots, and iridescent white or cream bellies. Their tail fins are heavily pigmented with dark spots or blotches (in contrast to the lighter, more faintly spotted tail fins of larval Northern Leopard Frogs).

Voice: The male's advertisement call is a low-pitched, snore-like croak, similar to the Leopard Frog's call but shorter and weaker, with less carrying power.

**Confusing Species:** Northern Leopard Frogs have light-bordered, rounded or oval spots on the back and lack bright orange or yellow color on the groin and undersides of the hind legs. Occasional Leopard Frogs appear to "mimic" the Pickerel Frog spot pattern and may have a faint yellowish color in the groin area, making identification difficult. In the Plains Leopard Frog, the dorsolateral folds are broken and offset above the hind legs.

**Distribution and Status:** Pickerel Frogs range from Nova Scotia and southern Quebec south to the Carolinas and northern Georgia and west to Minnesota and the northern Mississippi Valley to eastern Oklahoma and Texas. The species is rare or absent in parts of Ohio, Indiana, and Illinois formerly dominated by prairie habitat. This frog has been recorded throughout most of the eastern and central Great Lakes basin; it is generally uncommon to rare across the region but can be locally common in ideal habitats.

**Habitat and Ecology:** This frog can be found in or near bogs, fens, ponds, streams, springs, sloughs, and lake coves. Cool, clear waters are preferred;

conversely, polluted or stagnant water is avoided. Favored habitats include grassy stream banks and places where streams or cold springs flow into bogs, marshes, or weedy ponds. They are active both day and night in spring, though they become more nocturnal in the heat of summer. In winter Pickerel Frogs hibernate in soft mud or beneath submerged logs or rocks on stream bottoms or in the deeper parts of ponds and bogs. Those occupying streams, springs, or spring-fed ponds may remain active all winter, though they probably do not feed during the coldest months. Most emerge from hibernation in April and move to shallow, quiet water for breeding. Afterward these frogs may move into nearby meadows and open woods for the summer but seem less inclined than Northern Leopard Frogs to wander far from water.

Pickerel Frogs eat insects, spiders, and other invertebrates and will take either terrestrial or aquatic prey species, depending on availability. Tadpoles are largely herbivorous, consuming mostly algae and other soft plant material but also scavenging dead animal matter in the bottom mud.

Pickerel Frogs produce skin secretions that are at least distasteful, and possibly toxic, to many potential predators. A distinctive odor has also been described in this frog—though this alleged trait has not been readily apparent in numerous specimens handled by the senior author. Literature accounts describing the reactions of various predators to Pickerel Frogs are largely anecdotal and sometimes conflicting. Most garter, ribbon, and water snakes appear to avoid eating them, though several instances of snake pre-

Pickerel Frog

Pickerel Frog, new
metamorph

dation are known. Other frog species kept in close confinement with Pickerel Frogs may die, but Bullfrogs and Green Frogs apparently eat them without consequence. Dogs are said to be repelled by these frogs, while mink
are known to eat them. The name Pickerel Frog has been attributed to the
popularity of this species as a bait for pickerel, which suggests that its skin
toxins are ineffective in repelling at least some predatory fish . . . or that
people were using the wrong bait!

**Reproduction and Growth:** The majority of breeding takes place in April, though the season can be delayed by cold weather until well into May, particularly in the north. Most breeding takes place when water temperatures are between 10° and 20°C (50° to 68°F). Males may congregate in large choruses at preferred sites, and their low snorelike calls may seem to merge into a continuous drone. A male can call while floating at the surface or while submerged.

During a period of amplexus that may extend over several days, a female will deposit from 800 to 3,000 eggs in one to several globular clusters attached to submerged twigs or grasses. Freshly laid eggs are brown above and yellow below, with the egg mass having a light brownish appearance. The tadpoles hatch in seven to twenty-one days, with higher temperatures shortening the incubation period. Metamorphosis generally occurs in sixty to ninety days, with the newly transformed froglets measuring from 2 to 3 cm (0.8 to 1.2 in) in length. They can reach sexual maturity during the second spring after hatching.

**Conservation:** Pickerel Frogs are somewhat specialized in their preference for cool, clear waters and intolerance of pollution. Human activities have certainly reduced or degraded many formerly occupied habitats. It is unclear whether the Pickerel Frog has suffered a population decline similar to that noted for its look-alike relative, the Northern Leopard Frog. Although it is generally rare and local over most of the Great Lakes area, this species persists in numbers equal to or greater than those of the Leopard Frog in other parts of its range (e.g., the northeastern United States and New England).

# REPTILES (CLASS REPTILIA)

# Turtles

ORDER TESTUDINES

About 317 species of turtles and tortoises exist worldwide, arranged within 96 genera and 15 families. While greatly outnumbered by lizards and snakes in numbers of species, turtles have a comparable diversity at the family level and have been an ecologically successful group of reptiles since the early Mesozoic era. The probable reason for this long success, and the defining character of the group, is the shell, which has retained its basic form since the late Triassic period, about 225 million years ago.

The top part of the shell, the *carapace*, is formed from flattened, expanded ribs, fused together with dermal bones and vertebrae. The lower shell, or *plastron*, is derived, in part, from bones of the shoulder girdle and abdominal ribs. The plastron and carapace are connected at each side by a *bridge* of bone or cartilage. Overlying the bony layer of the shell are broad, flat, horny scales, called *scutes* (fig. 7). These shell elements are reduced in some species, apparently an adaptation to increase mobility at the expense of protective armor. In the fast-swimming soft-shelled turtles much of the bony portion of the shell has been lost and leathery skin covers the shell's surface. In snapping and musk turtles, the plastron is reduced to a cross-shaped structure, perhaps facilitating their bottom-walking habits. The well-armored box and Blanding's Turtles have evolved a flexible hinge across the plastron, allowing the two plastral lobes to move upward to better protect the withdrawn head, limbs, and tail.

All living turtles are toothless, but their sharp-edged horny jaws are quite capable of grabbing and slicing food items—and sometimes their enemies. Some native species, such as the Eastern Musk, Blanding's, Northern Map, and Spiny Softshell Turtles, are largely carnivorous, while others,

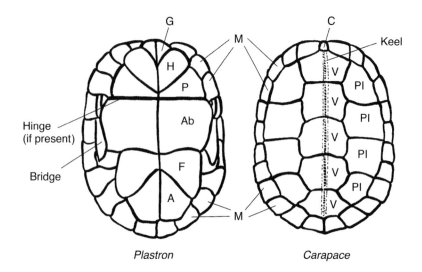

Plastron                    Carapace

Fig. 7. Standardized names for the scutes of a typical turtle's shell: **Plastron** (left)—
A= anal, Ab= abdominal, F= femoral, G= gular, H= humeral, M= marginal, P=
pectoral; **Carapace** (right)— C= cervical (nuchal of some authors), M= marginal, PL=
pleural (costal of some authors), V= vertebral. (Drawing by G. van Frankenhuyzen)

including the Wood, Eastern Box, and Painted Turtles are omnivorous, with
plant products forming a considerable part of their diet. Some turtle species
are almost totally herbivorous (e.g., cooters in the genus *Pseudemys*, most
true tortoises, and certain marine species), but none of these occurs naturally in the Great Lakes region.

Turtles reproduce with internal fertilization and shelled eggs. After engaging in courtship behavior that varies in complexity from species to species,
the male will mount the female's carapace and attempt to bring his vent into
contact with that of his mate; the penis is then inserted into the cloacal opening to effect fertilization. Females of some species, including Spotted, Eastern
Box, Blanding's, and Snapping Turtles, may store sperm and produce fertile
eggs for two to four years after mating. Again depending on the species, turtle
eggs are either round or elliptical in shape and have shells that are either rigid
and rather brittle or flexible and easily dented. Eggs of Snapping and Blanding's Turtles often have rigid shells when first laid, but they soon become
flexible as water is absorbed and incubation progresses.

Females of almost all turtle species deposit their eggs in an underground
nest excavated with their hind feet. Some species will moisten the nest site
with water stored in accessory bladders located around the cloaca. After

the eggs are laid, the nest cavity is carefully refilled and then abandoned. A female turtle never sees her eggs and offers no protection or care to her nest or offspring. Predation on turtle nests is typically very high; losses routinely exceed 70 percent and can approach 100 percent of all nests in some places, depending on predator numbers and the availability of nesting sites. Raccoons are the major nest raiders in the region, although shrews, skunks, mink, foxes, coyotes, and bears also relish turtle eggs. In the Great Lakes area, most nesting occurs from late May through early July. Incubation generally requires from two to three months, with hatchlings emerging in August or September. Hatching turtles have a pointed caruncle ("egg tooth") on the snout to assist in breaking or slicing the eggshell. Hatchlings of some species, such as Painted and Northern Map Turtles, can resist freezing and overwinter in the nest, delaying emergence from the ground until spring. In many turtle species the sex of the hatchling is determined by the temperature of the egg at a critical period during incubation. The most common pattern is for males to result from cooler egg temperatures and females from warmer temperatures. A narrow "pivotal" temperature range, which varies between species and even populations within species, results in a roughly equal sex ratio. For example, in Painted, Northern Map, Blanding's, Eastern Box, and Spotted Turtles, eggs incubated at 25°C (77°F) will produce nearly all male hatchlings, whereas those kept at 30°C (86°F) will produce mostly females. Pivotal temperatures in the Painted Turtle were found to vary from 27.5° to 29°C (81.5° to 84.2°F) across its range. Snapping and Eastern Musk Turtles follow a similar pattern, but in these species females are also produced at still lower temperatures, close to the coolest temperature at which the egg can successfully develop (about 21.5°C or 71°F). In a few species, including the Spiny Softshell and perhaps the Wood Turtle, sex is not affected by incubation temperatures but is genetically determined as in birds and mammals. The ecological consequences of temperature-dependent sex determination are still under study. The variability of temperatures within nests and between sunny and shaded nest sites presumably allows for sufficient numbers of each sex to be produced, particularly over a number of years (Ewert, Jackson, and Nelson 1994).

Note: Any shelled reptile can be properly called a turtle. In North America, the word *turtle* is used for all marine, freshwater, and semiterrestrial members of the order, while the word *tortoise* is applied only to members of the exclusively terrestrial family Testudinidae, none of which is native to the Great Lakes region. The word *terrapin* (of American Indian origin) is restricted to the species *Malaclemys terrapin*, of the brackish coastal marshes of the Atlantic and Gulf states, while outside North America it is sometimes applied more broadly to semiaquatic turtles. In Great Britain and Australia, marine species are called *turtles,* while *tortoise* may be used for both freshwater and terrestrial species.

Selected general references: Carr 1952; Congdon, Dunham, and van Loben Sels 1993, 1994; Ernst and Lovich 2009; Harless and Morlock 1979; Klemens 2000; Moll and Moll 2004; and Powell, Conant, and Collins 2016.

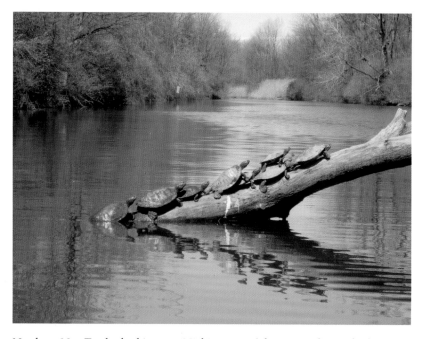

Northern Map Turtles basking on a Michigan river (Photo: David A. Mifsud)

# Snapping Turtles

## FAMILY CHELYDRIDAE

These are large aquatic turtles with long tails, reduced plastra, and quick, sharp jaws used for defense. There are four species in two genera. The Alligator Snapping Turtle (*Macrochelys temminckii*), the largest freshwater turtle in North America, reaches a length of 80 cm (31.5 in). Its range centers on the lower Mississippi drainage system, extending from Iowa in the north to eastern Texas and the Florida panhandle in the south. It is threatened by overharvesting in much of this area.

A proposal to split the Alligator Snapping Turtle into three species has been published; see Thomas et al. (2014). The smaller and more widespread Snapping Turtle (*Chelydra serpentina*) is described below; two additional, poorly known species of *Chelydra* occur in Central and northern South America.

## Snapping Turtle (*Chelydra serpentina*)

**Description:** The "snapper" has a broad brown, black, or olive carapace, which is often obscured with mud or algae. The rear edge of the carapace is strongly serrated; the four rearmost marginal scutes are sharply pointed. Young specimens have three lengthwise keels (ridges) on the carapace, but the shells of older adults may be nearly smooth. The yellow, tan, or gray plastron is small and cross-shaped, leaving much skin exposed around the muscular legs. The feet are webbed and bear heavy, curved claws. The head is large, with a short, pointed snout and sharp jaws with a hooked upper beak. The jaws are sometimes marked with dark streaks. There are two barbels on the chin, and the skin on the long neck is warty and often covered with blunt tubercles. Skin color on the upper surfaces of the head, neck, and legs is usually dark brown, gray, or olive, grading to lighter shades of dull yellow below. There may be one or two light yellowish stripes slanting back from the eye and a few yellow spots elsewhere on the neck and legs. Three rows of upright triangular scales run down the very long, thick tail, with the middle row being larger and more conspicuous. This is the largest Great Lakes turtle. Adult carapace length: 20.3 to 50.3 cm (8 to 19.8 in).

Note: Snapping Turtle size is often expressed as total mass (i.e., weight). An average female snapper nearing sexual maturity will have a 20.3 cm (8 in) carapace and weigh about 2 to 2.5 kg (4.4 to 5.5 lbs). By the time its carapace is 30 cm (12 in) long, it may weigh around 6.4 kg (14 lbs), and if it survives to a shell length of 35 cm (13.7 in), it might tip the scales at around 10 kg (22 lbs). One Minnesota snapper had a carapace 49.5 cm (19.5 in) long and weighed 30.4 kg (67 lbs); the record weight for a wild-caught specimen is 34 kg (75 lbs), while the record for a fattened captive is 39 kg (86 lbs). Of course, the weight of any individual turtle can vary according to the season and its nutritional state.

The sexes are similar and sometimes difficult to distinguish based on external characters. In males the precloacal tail length (measured from the end of the plastron to the vent) is proportionally longer than in females. When the tail is extended, the male's vent is usually beyond the rear edge of the carapace, while the female's vent is usually beneath the edge of the carapace. Male snappers grow larger than females; most specimens weighing more than 10 kg (22 lbs) will be males.

Hatchlings are black or dark brown, often with white spots below the edge of the carapace and on the plastron, with a carapace length of 2.5 to 3.8 cm (1 to 1.5 in). Their tails are usually longer than their shells.

Snapping Turtle,
juvenile

Snapping Turtle,
adult female nesting
(eggs exposed by
photographer)

Snapping Turtle,
juvenile plastron (note
musk droplets at base
of bridge)

**Confusing Species:** The combination of large head, muscular legs, long spike-topped tail, tiny plastron, and belligerent attitude should distinguish the Snapping Turtle from all other Great Lakes turtles. The much smaller Eastern Musk Turtle also has a relatively small plastron and a feisty disposition, but its tail is short and its carapace is highly domed.

**Distribution and Status:** Snapping Turtles range from Nova Scotia west to southern Alberta, south to New Mexico and east to the Atlantic and Gulf coasts and peninsular Florida. This encompasses nearly all of the United States east of the Rocky Mountains and includes the entire Great Lakes region except the area north of Lake Superior.

This species is generally common throughout most of the Great Lakes basin except where local populations have been depleted by overharvesting.

**Habitat and Ecology:** Snapping Turtles inhabit most permanent bodies of water in the region, including shallow, weedy inlets and bays in the Great Lakes themselves. Quiet, mud-bottomed ponds, lakes, sloughs, and slow streams with dense aquatic vegetation support the largest populations. This species appears to be quite tolerant of polluted waters. Daylight hours are usually spent in shallow water, buried in mud, in weed beds, or hidden under logs or other cover. Although capable of swimming, they more often walk along the bottom. They are less inclined to bask in the open than other turtles but occasionally haul out on logs, stumps, or sloping banks on cool sunny days; more often they warm themselves by floating near the surface.

In the warmer months Snapping Turtles often restrict their activities to the morning and early evening or may even become nocturnal. Despite strong aquatic tendencies, they will travel overland when necessary and are sometimes found considerable distances from water. The colder months are spent hibernating in shallow water, where they may simply sit on the bottom or dig into bottom mud or under submerged debris or overhanging banks. They may congregate in numbers in preferred sites, which tend to be the less stagnant, better-oxygenated portions of the water body when available. Snapping Turtles are generally dormant from mid-October until early April in the Great Lakes region, but they are sometimes seen moving about under the ice in winter.

Snapping Turtles often remain within a specific home range for a number of years. Reported home ranges of adults range from about 0.25 hectares (0.6 acres) to nearly 9 hectares (22 acres), but the turtles may regularly use only a small portion of the calculated home range. There are many published accounts of vicious fights between male Snapping Turtles, and it is possible that some males will aggressively defend portions of their home range against other males, at least during the breeding season.

These turtles eat both plant and animal food and also scavenge dead animals that are not too decayed. A complete dietary list would undoubtedly include many of the invertebrate and smaller vertebrate animals that share the turtle's habitat, along with a variety of aquatic plants. Snappers will stalk potential prey by creeping slowly forward with head lowered and partly withdrawn. When in range, the prey is seized with a rapid extension of the head and neck; smaller prey items may literally be sucked in, since the turtle strikes open-mouthed, causing a rush of water (and often much debris and vegetation) into its throat. Small Snapping Turtles will actively pursue prey, but large adults tend to employ a sit-and-wait strategy. The forefeet and claws are used to tear larger prey into bite size pieces, and food is swallowed underwater.

Snapping Turtle eggs and young suffer very high losses to predators. Nest losses typically range from 60 to 100 percent, depending on local conditions, with raccoons being the primary egg predators in the Great Lakes area, followed in frequency by skunks, foxes, and mink. Hatchlings and juveniles are eaten by these mammals, as well as by large fish (e.g., bass and pike), Bullfrogs and Green Frogs, Northern Water Snakes, crows, ravens, gulls, and herons. Adult snappers have few enemies except for humans and their automobiles. A number of adult specimens in Ontario were reportedly killed by otters during winter dormancy. Many Snapping Turtles are parasitized by leeches (*Placobdella* sp.). When on land, a Snapping Turtle normally turns to face a potential enemy and, if closely approached, strikes quickly with its sharp jaws. The long neck allows a striking distance about as great as its shell length, and the jaws can cause severe lacerations to unprotected skin. The safest way to handle a large snapper is by grabbing the base of its tail, keeping the head pointed away from your body. However, lifting a large turtle off the ground with this method will likely injure its tail vertebrae (and perhaps lead to spinal cord injury), and it is best to avoid handling them whenever possible. When disturbed underwater, snappers prefer to flee or conceal themselves in the mud and rarely bite unless restrained. Biting is a less effective defense for hatchlings and small juveniles, but they can secrete a foul-smelling musky fluid from glands along the lower edge of the carapace and bridge, which may repel some predators.

**Reproduction and Growth:** Mating can occur at any time during the active season but is most frequent in spring and fall. A courting pair will sometimes face each other and sway their heads back and forth in a horizontal arc. Often the male simply mounts the female's carapace after a brief chase and grasps the edge of her shell with his claws. While mounted the male will extend his neck and press the female's snout with his own, or grip her neck skin with his jaws, usually without causing serious injury. His tail is eventually extended beneath the female's, bringing the cloacal openings into contact and allowing copulation.

Nesting generally occurs from late May through early July; in most years nesting activity peaks in early to mid-June. Females may travel a kilometer (0.62 mi) or more from the water to find a suitable nest location, often starting and abandoning several holes before completing a nest. Open, sunny locations with moist but well-drained sand or soil are preferred, but they will nest in gravel beds, road edges, and lawns if better sites are not available. Using her hind feet, the female snapper scoops out a narrow-necked, flask-shaped cavity and deposits from 10 to more than 100 (usually 25 to 50) eggs. She then refills the cavity and returns to the water. Larger females tend to lay more and larger eggs. The eggs are spherical and range from 2.5 to 3.5 cm (1 to 1.4 in) in diameter. Freshly laid eggs usually have rigid shells, but after a few days they absorb water and the shells become flexible. Females probably produce only one clutch in a season in the Great Lakes area and may not nest every year.

Under normal conditions Snapping Turtle eggs hatch in sixty-five to ninety-five days. While cooler, damper conditions tend to lengthen the incubation period, warmer, drier conditions will shorten it. Incubation temperature also influences the sex of the hatchlings in this species. The newly hatched turtles remain in the nest for several days while they absorb their sacs of leftover yolk, and then may dig to the surface and emerge almost simultaneously or over a period of hours or days. They generally head for the nearest body of water. Hatchlings from later nests sometimes attempt to overwinter in the nest, but during colder winters and in northern parts of the range many of these young freeze to death. Newly emerged hatchlings are vulnerable not only to predation but also to desiccation (if they cannot find water) and drowning (if the water is too deep or lacks supportive vegetation).

Growth is rapid in young snappers but slows as they mature and may practically cease in older adults. In the southern Great Lakes basin a female Snapping Turtle will reach sexual maturity in eleven to sixteen years, at a carapace length of about 20.3 cm (8 in). Farther north they mature in about seventeen to twenty years at a slightly larger size. A female's first nesting is more related to reaching a minimum size than reaching a minimum age. The maximum age attained in the wild is unknown, but published estimates suggest potential ages of forty to fifty years; a zoo captive lived more than thirty-eight years.

**Conservation:** Snappers are often blamed for reducing populations of game fish and waterfowl. Studies in natural lakes, marshes, and streams show that the quantities of game fish eaten by Snapping Turtles are generally insignificant and of no concern to sport fish management. Mammalian nest predators and large game fish typically take a far greater toll on waterfowl reproduction than do turtles. Being opportunistic feeders, Snapping Turtles can be a problem in fish hatcheries and enclosed, intensively managed waterfowl-breeding areas; their removal might be justified in these situations.

Snapping Turtles are important members of lake and stream communities in the region. Their eggs and young provide a considerable food resource for an assortment of predators, while the adults play an important role as both predator and scavenger. Snappers are large enough to be harvested as human food, although they are of minor economic importance. Commercial trapping can lead to severe local declines in turtle numbers, and it is unlikely that Snapping Turtles can be commercially harvested on a truly sustainable basis since their population stability is dependent on the relative longevity of breeding adults. Research on a stable population in southern Michigan revealed that annual survivorship of adult females ranged from 88 to 97 percent, while juvenile survivorship averaged about 77 percent. Almost any increase in the loss of mature turtles (such as by trapping) would predictably cause the population to decline. Additionally, there is no evidence that removing mature turtles from a population results in increased reproductive success for those remaining. Recovery of a depleted population would take many years, even if further exploitation is halted (see Congdon, Dunham, and van Loben Sels 1994). In response to recent population studies, most states and provinces have banned commercial exploitation of Snapping Turtles and carefully regulate personal harvest.

Snapping Turtles can store environmental contaminants in their body fat, livers, muscle tissues, and eggs. Specimens taken from polluted waters have been shown to carry high concentrations of organochlorine pollutants such as polychlorinated biphenyls (PCBs). Thus, the harvest and consumption of turtles from certain Great Lakes waters might be inadvisable from a human health as well as a conservation standpoint.

# Musk and Mud Turtles

## FAMILY KINOSTERNIDAE

The majority of kinosternids are small, bottom-walking turtles of shallow waters. About twenty-five species range from southern Canada to Argentina, with the greatest diversity in Mexico and Central America. The musk turtles (*Sternotherus*) have very small plastra (bottom shells) with a single hinge and varying amounts of skin showing between the plastral scutes. Mud turtles (*Kinosternon*) have larger, more solid plastra with two transverse hinges. All members of the family can secrete a musky-smelling substance from glands at the edge of the carapace and bridge, presumably to repel predators. Only one species occurs in the Great Lakes basin.

## Eastern Musk Turtle (*Sternotherus odoratus*)

**Description:** This is a small turtle with a rather narrow, domed carapace, and a large head with a pointed snout. The brown, gray, or black carapace is sometimes streaked or spotted with darker pigment and is smooth (but often algae-covered) in adults and keeled in juveniles. The yellowish or brownish plastron is small and somewhat cross-shaped and usually has areas of smooth skin between the scutes, especially toward the center. The front part of the plastron is flexible and can move upward, but this flexure offers little additional protection to the turtle's soft parts. Two yellow stripes extend from the nose, above and below the eye, and along the side of the head and neck; these stripes often fade in older specimens. There are two or more pointed barbels on the chin and throat. Adult carapace length: 7.5 to 13.7 cm (3 to 5.4 in).

The sexes are similar in size. The male has wide areas of skin between the plastral scutes, a longer, thicker tail with a stiff blunt spine at its tip, and two patches of rough scales on the inner side of each hind leg. The female has less skin between the plastral scutes and a very short tail. The tiny hatchling Eastern Musk Turtle has a carapace length of 1.9 to 2.5 cm (0.7 to 1 in). The rough black carapace has white spots on the outer edge of the marginal scutes. The central keel is prominent, and two lateral keels may also be evident. The yellow head stripes are usually well defined.

**Confusing Species:** The Eastern Musk Turtle's small plastron and willingness to bite in self-defense sometimes leads to its being mistaken for a young Snapping Turtle; the snapper, however, has a very long tail topped with a row of large, upright scales. Mud turtles (*Kinosternon*), which are probably absent from the Great Lakes basin, have a relatively larger plastron with two hinges.

**Distribution and Status:** This species occurs from southern Maine and southeastern Ontario south through peninsular Florida, west to central Texas and north to southern Wisconsin. They are generally absent from higher elevations. In the Great Lakes region they range from the Lake Ontario and Lake Erie drainages north to Georgian Bay and west across the lower half of Michigan's Lower Peninsula to the southern drainages of Lake Michigan.

Eastern Musk Turtles are locally common in the lower Great Lakes area. Some populations have declined or disappeared in recent years, particularly where lake edges have been altered by residential development. They are a species of special concern in Ontario.

**Habitat and Ecology:** These little turtles inhabit a wide variety of permanent waters, including ponds, lakes, marshes, sloughs, and rivers. In the Great Lakes area they seem to be most common in clear lakes or ponds with marl, sand, or gravel bottoms and a moderate growth of aquatic plants. Eastern Musk Turtles are highly aquatic and rarely wander far from water. If kept dry they lose body water faster than other native turtles. Although they occasionally climb out on rocks, branches, or logs to sun themselves, most basking is done while partially submerged in shallow water. During the warmer months these turtles are most active in early morning and evening; in hot weather they may be largely nocturnal. They are often seen walking along the bottom in weedy shallows but will use deeper waters to escape summer heat or predators. Eastern Musk Turtles usually enter hibernation when water temperatures drop below 10°C (50°F). They burrow into bottom mud or beneath logs, overhanging banks, or muskrat houses. This dormant period generally lasts from mid-October to mid-April in the region.

Eastern Musk Turtles eat a variety of small animals, including worms, leeches, aquatic insects, snails, crayfish, small fish, and tadpoles. Carrion, such as dead fish, is also eaten if it is not overly decayed. Live, healthy game fish are rarely, if ever, taken. They also consume aquatic plants, including algae, rooted plants, and seeds. A hungry Eastern Musk Turtle will creep slowly along the bottom, probing with its snout into the mud, clumps of algae or other plants, and under the edges of submerged branches and other debris. Large food items are held in the jaws and torn into smaller pieces with the front claws.

Musk Turtle eggs are eaten by many predators, including crows, rodents, raccoons, and skunks, and nest mortality in a given area often exceeds 80 percent. The hatchlings and juveniles are prey for predatory fish such as bass and pickerel, large frogs, water snakes, and herons. Raccoons, otters, mink, and Bald Eagles will eat both juveniles and adults. Muskrats will attack dormant turtles in winter. Older turtles often show signs of injury from previous encounters with predators. When disturbed or handled, Eastern Musk Turtles may attempt to bite or at least threaten with mouth open. They can secrete a musky smelling substance from glands located at the edge of the bridge and carapace, which may repel some predators. For this reason the species is sometimes informally called "stinkpot."

**Reproduction and Growth:** Mating occurs underwater, usually in April or May, though breeding activity may resume in fall. A courting male will chase the female while nudging or biting her head and carapace edges. A receptive female will eventually slow down enough to be caught, allowing the male to crawl over her and cling to her carapace with the claws of all

Eastern Musk Turtle,
adult

Eastern Musk Turtle,
hatchling

four feet. The scaly patches on the inner side of the male's hind legs may be employed to hold the female's tail, while his tail is curled around the female's, with the stiff, spinelike tip contacting her cloaca, thus bringing the vents together and facilitating copulation.

Nesting usually occurs between late May and early July. Female Eastern Musk Turtles may dig a typical nest cavity in sand or soil with the hind feet, but just as often the eggs are deposited in shallow excavations beneath logs, clumps of vegetation, or shoreline debris or in the tops of rotting stumps or muskrat houses. Sometimes the eggs are not even completely covered. Eastern Musk Turtles farther south may lay two or more clutches per year, but a single clutch appears to be the norm in the Great Lakes area. From one to thirteen eggs (but usually three to five) are laid at one time. Sometimes more than one female will use a nesting site, leading to exaggerated estimates of clutch size. The eggs are elliptical, range from 2.3 to 3.1 cm (0.9 to 1.2 in) in length, and have rigid, brittle shells that give the embryos added protection against drying out—a useful adaptation considering this turtle's rather casual approach to nest construction.

Incubation can require between sixty and ninety days, depending on incubation temperature. Incubation temperatures also determine the sex of the hatchlings. Young Eastern Musk Turtles grow rapidly, but growth slows as they approach sexual maturity; older adults may practically stop growing. Males are able to reproduce in their third or fourth year, but females may require four to eleven years to mature, depending on growth rate. Counting growth rings (annuli) visible on the scutes of the carapace or plastron may give a reasonable estimate of age up to about ten years, after which wear and a slowing growth rate make the method unreliable. Eastern Musk Turtles have reached a known age of at least twenty-eight years in the wild and more than fifty-four years in a zoo.

**Conservation:** Dietary studies confirm that these inconspicuous little turtles do no harm to game fish populations and are generally harmless to human interests. Eastern Musk Turtles are frequently caught by people fishing with live bait and are sometimes killed for being a nuisance or in the mistaken belief that they consume game fish. This practice is unfortunate and can deplete local populations. One of the most serious threats to the Eastern Musk Turtle is residential shoreline development, which often results in removal or poisoning of aquatic vegetation from shallow waters (to improve swimming and boating) and the loss of suitable terrestrial nesting sites.

# Pond and Box Turtles

## FAMILY EMYDIDAE

This is the largest and most diverse turtle family in North America; nearly fifty species are distributed over temperate to tropical parts of the Americas, with two species extending the range into Europe, western Asia, and northern Africa. Emydids range in size from the little 10 cm (4 in) Bog Turtle (described below) to the larger cooters (*Pseudemys*) and tropical sliders (*Trachemys*), which may reach carapace lengths of 40 cm (15.75 in). Most are aquatic to semiaquatic pond, lake, or river dwellers with fairly strong shells and at least partially webbed feet; a few, like the American box turtles (genus *Terrapene*), are largely terrestrial.

## Spotted Turtle (*Clemmys guttata*)

**Description:** This very small turtle is named for the rounded yellow spots scattered over the smooth, unkeeled black or brownish-black carapace. These spots are highly variable in number; an occasional specimen will have no carapace spots, while in others the original spots may fade or darken with age. There are nearly always at least a few spots on top of the mostly black head and one or more irregular orange or yellow blotches on each side of the head. The outer surfaces of the legs are black, usually with a few yellow spots, while the lower surfaces of the legs, neck, and other "soft parts" are often orangish or pinkish, mottled with black. The hingeless plastron is usually yellow or orange with a black blotch covering the outer portion of each scute; sometimes the black color may cover most or all of the plastron, particularly in older males. Adult carapace length: 9 to 13.6 cm (3.5 to 5.4 in).

The sexes are quite distinct in form and coloration. Males typically have a slightly compressed and elongate carapace and a concave (centrally depressed) plastron. The vent is beyond the edge of the carapace when the tail is fully extended. The male's eyes are brown, and the chin (lower jaw) is tan, brown, or black. The female's carapace is comparatively broader and higher, the plastron is flat or slightly convex, and the tail is thinner, with the vent beneath the carapace edge with the tail extended. The female has orange eyes and a yellowish or orange chin. The hatchlings average about 2.9 cm (1.14 in) carapace length and are nearly circular in outline. They are colored above like the adults, but usually with just one spot per carapace scute. The plastron is yellowish-orange, with a central dark blotch. Carapace scute annuli (growth rings) are more conspicuous in juvenile Spotted Turtles than in adults.

**Confusing Species:** The Bog Turtle lacks round yellow spots on the carapace and head. (Even Spotted Turtles lacking carapace spots will have a few spots on the head.) Some Blanding's Turtles may have yellow spotting on a dark head and carapace, but the spots are smaller and more numerous, and the entire chin, throat, and lower neck are solid yellow. Most Blanding's Turtles have a functional plastral hinge (allowing at least partial closure of the shell), which is lacking in the Spotted Turtle.

**Distribution and Status:** The Spotted Turtle's range is discontinuous and quite fragmented, but there two primary areas of occurrence. One extends from southern Maine south through the entire Atlantic seaboard to northern Florida. The other centers on the Great Lakes region, from eastern Ontario and north-central New York to Georgian Bay and the eastern and southern Lake Michigan basin in Michigan, Indiana, and Illinois. There are (or, in

Spotted Turtle, adult female

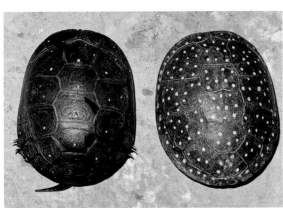

Spotted Turtle, carapace pattern variation

Spotted Turtle, female plastron

some cases, were) isolated populations in southeastern Quebec, northern Vermont, the western Carolinas, southern Ohio, and central Illinois.

Spotted Turtles are generally rare and local throughout their Great Lakes range and largely occur in isolated colonies surrounded by unsuitable or unoccupied habitats. They are considered endangered in Illinois, Indiana, and Ontario, threatened in Michigan and Ohio, and of special concern in New York.

**Habitat and Ecology:** These turtles are found in shallow ponds, wet meadows, tamarack swamps, bogs, fens, marsh channels, sphagnum seepages, and slow streams. Common qualities of occupied habitats include clear, shallow water with a mud or muck bottom and ample aquatic and emergent vegetation. Spotted Turtles tolerate cool water temperatures and resume activity earlier in the year than most other turtle species. On cool, sunny spring days they may bask on logs, muskrat houses, and grass or sedge hummocks. They are inactive at night. Spotted Turtles often wander on land and may turn up in temporary ponds; males appear to travel longer distances, particularly in spring, perhaps to increase mating opportunities. Spotted turtles are difficult to find in summer, due to reduced movement and lack of basking activity, along with the seasonal proliferation of wetland vegetation. Some individuals become dormant (aestivate) during hot weather, especially if their habitat begins to dry out; at this time they may enter muskrat burrows or dig into the mud or under submerged root systems. Others will leave the water and burrow into soil or leaf litter. They typically overwinter by hibernating in shallow water from about mid-October to late March. Spotted Turtles tend to remain within small home ranges of about 0.5 to 3.5 hectares (1.2 to 8.6 acres), however the total area of suitable habitat available for many local populations often falls within this range.

Spotted Turtles are omnivorous but with a decided preference for animal food. They will also eat carrion. Favored prey include worms, mollusks, small crayfish, spiders, adult and larval insects, and tadpoles. Vegetable foods include algae, tender plant leaves, and water lily seeds. Feeding occurs almost entirely underwater, although food may be captured on land and taken to the water for swallowing.

Spotted Turtle eggs are often eaten by mammals such as raccoons and skunks, and the juvenile and adult turtles are also vulnerable to these and other predators. Spotted Turtles that become dormant in active muskrat burrows risk attack by the opportunistic rodents. Many living turtles bear the scars of past predatory encounters, and it is common to find specimens that are missing parts of limbs or the tail. When frightened while in or adjacent to water, they dive to the bottom and bury themselves in the mud or beneath vegetation. They are most at risk during their terrestrial wanderings. These shy turtles rarely bite when threatened, and their only direct defense is to withdraw into their shells—a largely ineffective tactic when confronted with a persistent raccoon or other narrow-snouted predator.

**Reproduction and Growth:** Spotted Turtles begin breeding almost as soon as they emerge from winter dormancy in March or April; mating may also occur in fall prior to hibernation. Mating activity has been recorded at a body (cloacal) temperature as low as 5°C (46°F). Male Spotted Turtles often fight with each other at this time, presumably due to sexual rivalry, though battles are not always in the immediate vicinity of a female. Combatants will bite aggressively and often attempt to mount or overturn their competitors; eventually the victor will drive its rival from the immediate area. Courtship typically involves the male chasing the female while biting at her legs, tail, and carapace edges. A successful male will climb over the female's shell and bite at her head and neck while clasping the edges of her carapace with his claws. He then slides backward or to one side of her carapace and curls his tail under hers, allowing the vents to come into contact. Copulation usually occurs in shallow water and may last from fifteen minutes to over an hour.

Nesting usually occurs in early to mid-June in the Great Lakes area. The female will leave the water in the early evening and seek a sunny, open spot with sandy or loamy soil that is moist but well drained. If such places are scarce, they may also nest in grassy sites, clumps of sphagnum moss, or the tops of grass or sedge hummocks. The female digs a flask-shaped nest cavity with her hind feet and deposits from two to seven elliptical, flexible-shelled eggs; the cavity is then refilled, and the nest site is abandoned. Each egg is from 3 to 3.4 cm (1.2 to 1.3 in) long. Occasionally a female will lay a second, smaller clutch a few days or weeks after the first, with a reported maximum total production of fourteen eggs per year.

The incubation period ranges from forty-five to eighty-three days, with warmer temperatures increasing the development rate. Nest temperatures also influence the sex of the offspring. Eggs experimentally incubated between 22.5° and 27°C (72.5° to 80.6°F) produced from 70 to 92 percent male hatchlings, while those kept at 30°C (86°F) produced only females. Most young Spotted Turtles emerge from the nest in August or September. Overwintering in the nest has been reported, but its frequency in the Great Lakes area is unknown. A young Spotted Turtle can grow rapidly, and a hatchling may nearly double its size in the first year. Growth slows considerably after the young turtle reaches sexual maturity at the age of 7 to 14 years. Northern turtles generally grow more slowly and mature later than those in the southern parts of the range. A wild individual had a known age of 26 years, and a captive specimen survived for 42 years. However, an Ontario study suggests a theoretical longevity of 110 years for female Spotted Turtles and 65 years for males (Litzgus 2006).

**Conservation:** The boggy habitats preferred by Spotted Turtles were probably quite widespread in the southern Great Lakes basin until the early twentieth century, but most have now been drained and converted to agricultural and other human uses. In this region Spotted Turtles survive mostly in small isolated colonies in remnant wetlands, many of which are threatened by development and pollution. Preserving viable populations of the species will require identifying and then protecting the core wetland habitats, along with adjacent upland nesting sites and dispersal routes between colonies.

Unfortunately, Spotted Turtles are not secure even where their habitat is protected. These turtles are highly valued in the commercial pet trade due to their small size and bright coloration, and illicit collectors have reduced or eliminated many populations throughout the species' range. This turtle has been given legal protection in all states and provinces of the Great Lakes region where it occurs; however, total rangewide protection is fully warranted and will be necessary to eliminate commercial exploitation. Additional threats to this species include road mortality, large predator populations (particularly raccoons), and vandalistic shooting.

## Wood Turtle (*Glyptemys insculpta*)

**Description:** The Wood Turtle's scientific name means "sculptured turtle," and its rough brown or grayish-brown carapace does look as though it was carved from wood. There is usually a low central keel, and the carapace scutes have well-defined growth lines (annuli) crossed by raylike ridges (fig. 8). Some specimens also have a pattern of radiating yellow and black lines on the vertebral and pleural scutes. The rear carapace margin over the tail is shallowly serrated. The plastron is yellow with a black blotch at the rear outer corner of each scute and has a V-shaped notch at the tail. The head and upper surfaces of the neck, legs, and tail are black; the large outer scales of the front legs are black or brown, sometimes edged or speckled with yellow. The lower surfaces of the neck, legs, tail, and other "soft parts" are variable in color. Yellow or yellowish-orange predominates in the Great Lakes area,

Fig. 8. Wood Turtles have prominent growth rings (annuli) on their scutes that can be used to estimate a turtle's minimum age. This specimen would probably be at least 12 to 13 years old. (Drawing by G. van Frankenhuyzen)

while a brighter orange is seen mostly in the central and eastern part of the range, and specimens from the eastern and northeastern edge of the range may display a rusty-red to salmon-red color. Adult carapace length: 16 to 25 cm (6.3 to 9.8 in).

Mature males and females are easily distinguished. Males have comparatively higher, often narrower shells; larger, wider heads; and more robust limbs and feet, with thicker claws. The male's tail is longer and thicker than the female's; with the tail extended, the vent is well beyond the rear edge of the carapace. The male's plastron is concave (depressed in the center). In comparison, the female's carapace is broader and less domed, and the rear marginals are more outwardly flaring. The tail is narrower, and (with tail extended) the vent is at or beneath the rear edge of the carapace. The female's head and limbs are less massive, the claws are thinner, and the plastron is flat or slightly convex. Immature males may be mistaken for females when these criteria are applied to specimens with carapace lengths of less than about 16 cm (6.3 in), since female characters are essentially juvenile characters.

Hatchlings are a uniform gray, tan, or brown color and have nearly circular carapaces and long, thin tails. They range from 2.8 to 3.8 cm (1.1 to 1.5 in) in carapace length. The typical color pattern described above is gradually acquired during the first full year of growth.

**Confusing Species:** Blanding's Turtles are also yellow under the neck and legs and have a similar plastral pattern, but they have a notched upper jaw, a hinged plastron, and an unkeeled, domelike carapace. The Bog Turtle does not exceed a carapace length of 11.5 cm (4.5 in) and usually has a large orange or yellowish-orange blotch on each side of its head.

**Distribution and Status:** Wood Turtles are found from Nova Scotia west through southern Quebec and Ontario to eastern Minnesota and northern Iowa, and south through New England, New York, and Pennsylvania to western Maryland and northern Virginia. Within the Great Lakes basin the species occurs from the western end of Lake Superior through northern Wisconsin and the western and central Upper and northern Lower Peninsulas of Michigan. It is also recorded from a small area east of Whitefish Bay and from Georgian Bay to the western end of Lake Ontario and portions of northwestern New York.

Within its Great Lakes range the Wood Turtle is generally uncommon to rare, and in recent years many local populations have been greatly reduced or extirpated by human activities. This species remains locally common only in a few places where the habitat is intact and human disturbance is minimal. It is legally protected rangewide and listed as endangered in Ontario and a (protected) species of special concern in Michigan, Wisconsin, and New York.

**Habitat and Ecology:** Wood Turtles are most common in or near sandy bottomed streams or rivers, although they also occur in streams with partially

Wood Turtle, older
juvenile

Wood Turtle, female
plastron

rocky, gravelly, or silty beds. They are largely aquatic and sometimes gregarious from fall through late spring but are generally more solitary and terrestrial during the summer months, wandering through woodlands, alder thickets, swamps, wet meadows, and fields within or near the floodplain. Some Wood Turtles, particularly males, stay in or near the water throughout the year, and those found on land are usually within 150 m (500 ft) of moving water. Juveniles tend not to wander as far from water as the adults. Wood Turtles generally remain within rather restricted home ranges of about 1 to 5 hectares (2.5 to 12.4 acres), though some individuals will move considerably greater distances using a stream or river as a dispersal route.

These animals have modest homing ability, and can return to a home range if displaced up to 2 km (1.24 mi).

Wood Turtles are diurnal and fond of basking, whether on logs over water or in sunny places on land; in hot weather they return to water or bury themselves in soil or plant debris. Hibernation (typically early October through mid April) nearly always occurs under moving water. A dormant Wood Turtle may rest unburied on the stream bottom or wedge itself under a submerged log, rock, or an overhanging bank. They sometimes congregate during winter dormancy, a habit not clearly related to a lack of suitable hibernation sites.

Wood Turtles are able to feed both underwater and on land. They are opportunistic omnivores, consuming various leaves (including violet, strawberry, dandelion, and willow), berries (strawberry, raspberry, blackberry), algae, fungi, insects (both aquatic and terrestrial), slugs, snails, and earthworms. They will also scavenge recently dead animals. Wood Turtles sometimes use an unusual and unique method of procuring earthworms—the worm-hunting turtle will "thump" the ground by pushing down with alternating movements of the front feet to lift and then drop the front of the plastron. The resulting vibrations cause the worms to surface, where they are seized by the turtle. Wood Turtles use a similar "thumping" behavior during courtship and during aggressive encounters with other Wood Turtles, but it is unclear whether the use of the behavior for feeding is instinctive or fortuitously learned by a few individuals. "Worm thumping" has been observed in turtles from several geographic portions of the range but is apparently used by only a small percentage of turtles from any one population.

Nest mortality typically exceeds 80 percent; the raccoon is usually the most abundant and efficient nest predator, but in some areas skunks, mink, otters, foxes, coyotes, and ravens destroy many eggs. Hatchling and juvenile turtles are eaten by these same enemies, as well as by feral cats and dogs, large fish, and frogs. Adult Wood Turtles are better protected against attacks, but raccoons are able to kill them, and the turtles often sustain serious injuries during nonfatal encounters. Wood Turtles rarely bite in self-defense, and withdrawal into the shell is their only recourse when attacked. The lack of a plastral hinge leaves them especially vulnerable to narrow-snouted predators during their terrestrial wanderings. In many populations, a high percentage of adult turtles examined will be missing one or more limbs or the tail and often have healed cracks and puncture wounds in the shell. Porcupines sometimes gnaw on the shells of living and dead turtles, presumably for the mineral content. Wood Turtles are often host to leeches (*Placobdella* sp.) during their aquatic periods.

**Reproduction and Growth:** Although they do not specifically defend territories, Wood Turtles will chase and attack other individuals of the same or the opposite sex and are known to form dominance hierarchies in the wild. Dominant males (most often the larger, older animals) appear to have better success at mating and fertilizing eggs than do subordinate males. Mating nearly always occurs in shallow water, usually on a sloping stream bank, and is more frequent in spring and fall when these turtles are most aquatic. A courting pair of Wood Turtles may perform a mating "dance" in which the two face each other and swing their heads back and forth. More frequently the male simply pursues and mounts the female by clinging to the edges of her carapace with his claws. He often bites at her head and legs and may rock from side to side or bang his plastron against the female's carapace by extending and then relaxing his forelegs (presumably to discourage her from trying to escape his attentions). Copulation may last for several hours. Successful fertilization reportedly occurs in only a small fraction of mating attempts.

Female Wood Turtles lay one clutch of three to eighteen (usually five to thirteen) eggs in late May or June, though not all will reproduce annually. Most females nest in the evening; preferred nest sites are open and unshaded (having little or no vegetation cover), with moist sand or sandy soil, and sufficiently elevated above the water that flooding is unlikely. She may make several exploratory attempts at digging with her front and/or hind feet before settling on one spot, but the nest cavity itself is dug only with the hind feet. The elliptical, flexible-shelled eggs range in length from 2.7 to 4.2 cm (1.1 to 1.7 in). Incubation requires from forty-seven to sixty-nine days, with most hatchlings emerging in late August or early September. Nest temperature will affect the rate of embryonic development but may not influence the sex of the hatchlings in this species.

Young Wood Turtles attain sexual maturity in twelve to twenty years in the wild. Attainment of maturity generally takes longer in northern populations due to the shorter season of activity and resultant slower growth. A count of scute annuli will usually give a reasonable estimate of age in juvenile and subadult specimens; annuli counts will tend to underestimate true age in mature specimens, as growth slows, or even stops, after about age twenty to twenty-five. In a Michigan study, a majority of reproductive adults were in their third and fourth decade of life. A captive specimen lived fifty-eight years, and, based on shell wear patterns, it is thought that wild individuals may occasionally survive to age seventy or longer.

**Conservation:** Wood Turtle numbers have declined significantly over much of their Great Lakes range, including areas where suitable habitats remain.

There is no doubt that in some places they have suffered from habitat fragmentation and surface water pollution. The building of roads close to rivers and streams has led to the untimely deaths of many turtles.

Certain fisheries management practices, such as sand bank stabilization and the digging of sand traps in streams, can eliminate nesting sites and reduce preferred turtle habitat. On the other hand, human activities that open up dense, unbroken floodplain forest near streams can potentially create new feeding, basking, and nesting areas. Wood Turtle populations can persist despite modest levels of riparian development and use, such as timber harvest, light grazing, low-intensity agriculture, and recreational activities such as fishing and canoeing, provided the turtles themselves (along with critical nesting sites) are left undisturbed. Unfortunately, this last provision is rarely assured.

In the past Wood Turtles have been exploited for human food and by biological supply companies for use in teaching and experimentation. More recently the species has been in great demand in the pet trade. The tendency for Wood Turtles to congregate in shallow streams in winter and their linear habitats in general make them extremely vulnerable to mass collecting, and commercial collectors have seriously depleted or eliminated many local populations. The species is legally protected by all states and provinces in Great Lakes region (and, to varying degrees, over all of its range elsewhere), but poaching will likely continue as a threat as long as demand remains high. Incidental collecting by canoeists and hikers and the shooting of basking turtles by vandals are additional drains on their numbers.

Wood Turtle populations are characterized by high nest and hatchling mortality and delayed sexual maturity, balanced by a long expected adult reproductive life. Turtle species with these characteristics depend on a very high annual survivorship of adults, and a surprisingly high survival rate for immature animals, to maintain a stable or growing population. Any factor that increases mortality beyond normal low levels will inevitably lead to a population decline and possible extirpation or extinction.


## Bog Turtle (*Glyptemys muhlenbergii*)

**Description:** This very small turtle has a brown or black, somewhat domed carapace with a low central keel. A light central blotch or a radiating pattern of light lines may occur on each of the large carapace scutes. The plastron is also brown or black, often with contrasting yellowish blotches, particularly toward the center or the front edge. Scutes on both the carapace and plastron are usually sculptured with circular ridges (annuli), but in older specimens the shell may be worn nearly smooth. A conspicuous, irregularly shaped orange, yellowish, or reddish blotch is usually present on each side of the head and neck. In some specimens the blotches may meet on top of the neck to form a continuous band, while in old adults the blotches may fade or darken. Otherwise the head, neck, limbs, and tail are mostly dark brown, frequently mottled with red, orange, or yellow. Adult carapace length: 7.9 to 11.5 cm (3.1 to 4.5 in). An adult male Bog Turtle has a concave plastron and a long, thick tail. With tail extended, the male's vent is beyond the rear edge of the carapace. The female has a flat plastron and a thinner tail. With tail extended, the female's vent is at or beneath the rear edge of the carapace. The male's carapace is usually flatter and less domed than the female's. Hatchling Bog Turtles are colored like the adults but have rounder carapaces and proportionally longer tails and measure from 2.3 to 3.4 cm (0.9 to 1.3 in) in carapace length.

**Confusing Species:** The Spotted Turtle has rounded yellow or orange spots on the head and neck and usually on the smooth, black carapace as well. Wood Turtles lack the bright orange blotches on the sides of the head, have a yellowish plastron with large black blotches, and quickly grow to exceed the size of the largest Bog Turtle.

**Distribution and Status:** The Bog Turtle exists in small, isolated colonies within a highly fragmented range, the largest portion of which extends from eastern New York and western Massachusetts south through New Jersey and southeastern Pennsylvania to Maryland. Another portion, at generally higher elevations, extends from southern Virginia through western North Carolina and eastern Tennessee to northeastern Georgia. Bog Turtles also occur (or recently occurred) in northwestern Pennsylvania and enter the Great Lakes drainage basin in north-central New York, south of Lake Ontario. They have disappeared from several known sites in the basin, where their continued existence is precarious at best. This species is extremely rare and localized in distribution throughout its range. It is listed as endangered in Pennsylvania and New York (see further notes under "Conservation" below).

**Habitat and Ecology:** Bog Turtles occur in saturated wetlands such as sphagnum bogs, fens, wet meadows, alder swamps, and sedge marshes. Open habitats with slowly flowing, mud or silt-bottomed streams, springs, rivulets, or surface seepages are preferred, while densely shaded sites are avoided.

Bog Turtles spend much time basking in the sun in spring and on cooler summer days but may aestivate in burrows or under vegetation during periods of hot weather or drought. They often move about by following rivulets or tunneling through sphagnum moss or other vegetation; they also utilize the tunnel systems of muskrats, voles, and bog lemmings. When not basking, active Bog Turtles are usually in shallow water. Home ranges reported for these turtles are quite small, ranging from about 0.1 to 2 hectares (0.2 to 5 acres); however, the total area of suitable habitat in many Bog Turtle colonies often does not exceed this range. Males appear to range slightly farther, on average, than females. In winter Bog Turtles generally burrow into the mud beneath moving water, such as in marsh rivulets, rodent burrows or runways, or under sedge clumps, moss, or roots. Dormancy typically lasts from late September or early October through late March or early April.

Bog Turtles can eat on land or underwater. They feed mostly on invertebrates such as insects, snails, slugs, crayfish, and earthworms but will opportunistically scavenge carrion and capture small vertebrates such as tadpoles and frogs. Some plant material is also eaten, including berries, pondweed (*Potamogeton* sp.), watercress, and the seeds of pondweed and sedge (*Carex* sp.). These little turtles are attacked and sometimes eaten by raccoons, skunks, foxes, dogs, mink, and even shrews. These same predators will also consume Bog Turtle eggs. In some populations, a significant percentage of adults will have injuries from past predatory attempts, including shell fractures or missing limbs or tails. The use of muskrat tunnels by

Bog Turtle, adult

Bog Turtle, old adult

these turtles may lead to occasional attacks from the opportunistic rodents. Bog Turtles blend into their surroundings well and spend much of their time in concealed situations. When surprised while basking, a Bog Turtle will usually dive into the water and quickly burrow into the mud or vegetation, but some individuals remain motionless, perhaps to avoid attracting attention.

**Reproduction and Growth:** Male Bog Turtles often show aggression toward one another, including open-mouthed threats, shoving, and biting. It is unclear whether these encounters involve the formation of dominance hierarchies, or if they represent defense of territory or competition for mates.

Mating occurs from late April through early June and can take place either in water or on dry land. Courtship begins with the male approaching and sometimes circling the female while nudging or "smelling" her tail region, perhaps seeking cues for species and sexual recognition. He then bites at her head and legs in an attempt to keep her from escaping, and eventually mounts her carapace and holds on with his claws. In some cases the male will thump the female's carapace with his plastron, a behavior also seen in the related Wood Turtle. The male may continue to nip at the female's head during copulation, which normally lasts about twenty minutes.

Nesting is in late May, June, and early July. When seeking a place to nest, the female moves from the wetter parts of the habitat to a higher, drier area. Typical nest sites include the tops of sedge or grass tussocks, mounds of decaying moss or other vegetation, muskrat houses, or elevated road or railroad beds. The nest cavity is dug with the hind feet, and one to six eggs are deposited, arranged in the nest, and then covered. A female may tamp the top of the nest with her plastron before leaving the site.

The eggs are white and elliptical and average about 3 cm (1.2 in) in length. Incubation requires from forty-five to sixty-five days, with most hatchlings emerging in August and September at a carapace length averaging about 2.6 cm (1 in). As with most turtle species, growth is quite rapid in the early years but slows markedly after maturity is attained. Bog Turtles can reach breeding size in five to ten years and can live for thirty years or more; a zoo specimen reached a minimum age of forty years.

**Conservation:** The boggy, saturated wetlands preferred by Bog Turtles were probably quite widespread after the retreat of continental glaciers and were not an uncommon habitat type even up to historical times. Range fragmentation in this species may have begun long before the arrival of European settlers in eastern North America, due to natural changes in climate and vegetation. Human activities have greatly accelerated the loss of suitable habitat over the last century, since bogs and sedge meadows are prime targets for drainage and filling; these turtles quickly disappear along with their habitats.

Natural wetland succession resulting in the invasion of open areas by trees and shrubs is also detrimental to the sun-loving Bog Turtles. At one time they were usually able to shift their home ranges into new habitat as required, but now, with wetlands hemmed in by human development, such succession can result in local extinction of the turtles. The trapping of beavers and the suppression of fire in the northeast have also hastened the succession of open wetlands into shaded swamps and woodlands. Light grazing by domestic livestock, especially horses, may benefit Bog Turtles by suppressing the spread of shade-producing plants. Another potential threat is the invasion of wetlands by introduced plants such as purple loosestrife (*Lythrum salicaria*), which may displace native plant communities favored by the turtles.

Identifying, protecting, and managing critical habitats are key elements in conserving Bog Turtle populations. Unfortunately, even setting aside dedicated reserves is not enough. Bog Turtles bring high prices in the "underground" (illegal) pet trade, due to their rarity and small size. Unscrupulous collectors have been known to remove whole populations, sometimes invading protected wildlife reserves and sifting through entire bogs to do so. This species is afforded legal protection throughout its range and is given the highest level of protection from international trade; it is listed as "threatened" under the US Endangered Species Act, and is on appendix I of the CITES Treaty (Convention on International Trade in Endangered Species of Wild Fauna and Flora). Unfortunately, enforcement is difficult and poaching is likely to continue as long as the potential profits from illegal collecting remain high.

## Eastern Box Turtle (*Terrapene carolina*)

**Description:** This is a small land turtle with a domed ("helmet-shaped") carapace and a hinged plastron. The carapace has a slight keel along the midline, and the scutes usually have prominent annuli, though shells of older individuals may be worn quite smooth. The carapace coloration is variable but is usually brown or black with a radiating pattern of yellowish or orange spots, blotches, or lines in each scute. In some specimens the lighter color may cover much of the shell, so that they appear to be yellow animals with dark markings. The plastron, which nearly fills the opening under the carapace, has a distinct flexible hinge between the pectoral and abdominal scutes, allowing total closure of the two plastral lobes. Plastron coloration can be a solid black, brown, tan, or yellow or any combination of these colors arrayed in blotches or streaks. The upper jaw forms a short, hooklike beak. Skin color on head, neck, and legs is as variable as the shell color, being typically brown with some yellow, orange, or white spots or streaks. In some turtles (usually males) the lighter colors may predominate. The tail is very short. Adult carapace length: 11.8 to 19.8 cm (4.6 to 7.8 in); few adults ever exceed a carapace length of 16 cm (6.3 in).

Males usually have red eyes (irises), and their carapace margins are more flared at the rear. The rear lobe of the male's plastron is concave, the hind claws are thick and quite curved, and the tail is slightly longer and thicker than the female's, with the vent at or beyond the end of the carapace with tail fully extended. Females usually have brown or yellowish-brown eyes and less flared rear marginal scutes. The female's plastron is flat to slightly convex (occasionally very slightly concave), the hind claws are comparatively thin and less curved, and the tail is short, with the vent beneath the rear edge of the carapace.

Hatchling Eastern Box Turtles have flatter, more circular carapaces that are brown or grayish-brown with a light spot in the center of each scute and a prominent central keel. The plastral hinge is nonfunctional. Carapace length at hatching ranges from 2.6 to 3.1 cm (1 to 1.2 in).

**Confusing Species:** Blanding's Turtle also has a plastral hinge, but its elongated carapace is smooth and unkeeled in the adult, its upper jaw is notched (rather than hooked) at the front, and its throat and lower neck are usually bright yellow. The sometimes terrestrial Wood Turtle has a broader, less domed carapace, and its plastron lacks a hinge. The Ornate Box Turtle, found in prairie habitats in Wisconsin, Illinois, and Indiana (see "Marginal and Questionable Species" page 365), has a dorsally flattened, usually unkeeled carapace and a less variable color pattern on the shell consisting of radiating yellow lines on a dark background on both carapace and plastron.

Eastern Box Turtle, adult male

Eastern Box Turtle, female nesting

Eastern Box Turtle, plastron closed, showing hinge

**Distribution and Status:** The Eastern Box Turtle ranges from southern Maine south to northern Florida, and west to Tennessee and southern Illinois, and north through Indiana, southern Michigan, and southern and western Pennsylvania. In the Great Lakes area it has been found from Grand Traverse County, Michigan, south along the Lake Michigan shore to northern Indiana and east through southern Michigan and northwestern Ohio; it also occurs in Erie County, Pennsylvania and adjacent New York. The apparent scarcity or absence of Box Turtles in a band from east-central Indiana to northeastern Ohio has been attributed to forest regression during the warm, dry postglacial xerothermic period; subsequent deforestation due to intensive cultivation undoubtedly eliminated the remaining habitat, perhaps discouraging the turtle from recolonizing the area. Archaeological records indicate that Box Turtles were probably present in the Lake Ontario drainage basin of western New York, and in adjacent southern Ontario, within the last thousand years but had practically disappeared by about 1700. Their extinction in this area has been linked to overexploitation and habitat modification by American Indians, who collected the turtles for food and ceremonial purposes (for a discussion, see Adler 1970). Box Turtles are sometimes found in places outside of their recognized range or where they were thought to be extirpated. Recent examples include a possibly viable population reported near Cleveland, Ohio, and several records in southern Ontario (including in Point Pelee National Park). These and other presumed out-of-range records are often attributed to the intentional or accidental release of pet turtles. However, given this animal's potential longevity, the possibility that some of these occurrences represent the last vestiges of former natural populations should not be discounted without sufficient evidence to the contrary.

Eastern Box Turtles are now an uncommon to rare and steadily declining species in the region but were historically quite common and widespread in the woodlands of the eastern Lake Michigan and western Lake Erie basins; they can remain locally common in intact habitats that are not bisected by busy roads. They are considered a (protected) species of special concern in Michigan, Indiana, Ohio, and New York.

**Habitat and Ecology:** Eastern Box Turtles favor deciduous or mixed woodlands, especially those with sandy soils, but also utilize adjacent thickets, old fields, pastures, vegetated dunes, marshes, and bog edges. Access to water (e.g., small ponds, seepages, springs, bogs, or slow streams) is an important factor, as is the availability of unshaded nesting sites. Moist, open hardwood forest and forest/old field edges with some relief, such as ravines or modest slopes, tend to support higher turtle densities than drier forests in flat terrain or frequently inundated floodplain woods. These turtles are diurnal and most active in spring and fall; during the summer they may have a brief activity period in the morning, or following moderate to heavy rain showers, but otherwise spend much time buried in leaf litter, shallow burrows, or under the edges of brush piles or rotting logs. During hot weather Box Turtles are often found soaking around the edges of ponds or small streams, or even paddling in open water. They are rather inefficient swimmers, tending to float on the surface with poor directional control, but individual turtles may temporarily adopt aquatic habits and can become fairly proficient at swimming and bottom walking.

At the onset of cool weather in the fall these turtles dig into the soil, typically going deeper as temperatures decline. While some eventually burrow as far as 60 cm (24 in) into the ground, other hibernating Box Turtles successfully overwinter in far shallower burrows, sometimes with the tops of their carapaces still visible below the leaf litter. They are able to tolerate subfreezing body temperatures, with over half of their body water frozen, for periods of several days. Some Box Turtles die, however, when early spring thaws stimulate early emergence, only to be followed by a return to severe cold. Most emerge from dormancy in mid- to late-April, when warmer weather is more reliable. Occasionally, a Box Turtle will overwinter completely submerged in a pond or stream.

Eastern Box Turtles frequently spend many years, or even their entire lives, within small home ranges of about 1.5 to 16 hectares (3.7 to 40 acres). Home ranges of several turtles may overlap. Although "nip and tuck" battles between males may take place on occasion, there is no clear evidence of territorial defense. Brief trips beyond the normal home range for nesting or mating may occur, and these turtles have modest homing abilities. Adult specimens have successfully returned to their home range when displaced 1 km (0.6 mi) or so away, probably using the sun for orientation. Homing success falls as displacement distances increase. Some Box Turtles, mostly males, appear to be habitual transients, and their movements through the home ranges of other turtles may be important in maintaining genetic diversity within and between populations.

Eastern Box Turtles consume a wide variety of plant and animal foods, including earthworms, snails, slugs, insects, mushrooms, various leafy greens, and fruits. They often remain within patches of ripening raspberries or blackberries until every reachable berry is consumed. Box Turtles act as seed dispersal agents for many forest plants and may be particularly important to reproduction and dispersal of the mayapple (*Podophyllum peltatum*); seed germination for this species was found to be much enhanced after passing through a turtle's digestive tract. Hatchling and small juvenile Box Turtles appear to be more carnivorous than adults, gradually adding more plant foods to their diet as they grow.

Skunks, raccoons, and foxes seek out Box Turtle eggs, and the smaller juveniles are prey to these mammals as well as to shrews, birds, and snakes. Shrews are a particularly serious threat, since they move through leaf litter and along rotting logs where very young Box Turtles often hide. Hatchlings and small juveniles do not have functional plastral hinges, but they can produce a musky-smelling secretion that may deter some predators. Adult turtles can use the plastral hinge to completely close up their shells and are usually safe from most predators. Many specimens are found with shell injuries or scarring from past predatory attempts or ground fires. While most Box Turtles quickly retire into their shells when threatened, some individual turtles are reluctant (or sometimes too fat!) to fully withdraw and are more vulnerable to attack. In many places automobiles probably kill more Box Turtles than all natural hazards combined.

**Reproduction and Growth:** Eastern Box Turtles may mate at any time during the active season, but breeding activity is most frequent in spring and fall. Males sometimes fight each other, but territorial defense and hierarchy formation has not been demonstrated in the wild. (In captive groups of Box Turtles kept outdoors, it is often noted that one or two males will often be more active and do most of the mating.) During courtship, the male typically circles the female while biting the edges of her shell and shoving her with his front feet. The female usually withdraws into her shell, and the male soon climbs on top of her carapace and continues biting at her head. Eventually he slips back until his hind claws can grip under the edge of her carapace; the female may then close her plastron on his hind feet, holding him securely. Copulation can occur only when the female opens her rear plastral lobe and the male assumes a vertical position, allowing the vents on their short tails to come into contact. During intromission, he will fall backward until his carapace is resting on the ground. After mating is complete, the male is usually left upside down and must right himself quickly or face possible death by overheating or suffocation.

Most nesting occurs on warm evenings in June or early July. The female seeks a sunny, often elevated spot, preferably with moist sandy soil and sparse vegetation, and digs a nest cavity with alternating movements of her hind feet. From three to eleven eggs are laid, then covered and left to their fate. The eggs are oval, flexible-shelled, and from 3 to 4 cm (1.2 to 1.6 in) in length. Some female Eastern Box Turtles may produce more than one clutch per year, though a single clutch is probably the norm in the Great Lakes region. Females can store sperm and produce fertile eggs up to four years after mating. Incubation requires from fifty to ninety days, with warmer nest temperatures resulting in earlier hatching. Hatchlings typically emerge in September or October, but those from later nests may overwinter in the nest. Sex in this species is determined by nest temperatures about midway through embryonic development. Under laboratory conditions, mostly males were produced at 27°C (80.6°F) or lower, while only females developed at 30°C (86°F) or higher.

For the first few years of life Eastern Box Turtles can grow about 1 to 2 cm (0.4 to 0.8 in) per year, but growth slows after maturity. Sexual maturity may occasionally be reached in 5 or 6 years but often requires 10 years or more, especially in northern parts of the range. In most populations a majority of breeding adults will be greater than 15 years of age. Counting the annuli on a shell scute may give a reasonable estimate of age in a juvenile specimen, but annuli counts will tend to underestimate the age of adult turtles. This species is known for its longevity. Box Turtles routinely live to an age of 40 to 50 years, and a few individuals will surpass the century mark. The known longevity record is 138 years.

**Conservation:** Eastern Box Turtles are harmless to human interests. They occasionally wander into gardens and sample the produce, but this minor problem can be solved by installing a low fence or simply moving the offender a short distance away. Box Turtles may aid horticultural efforts by consuming slugs and insect pests. As noted above, these turtles act as seed dispersers and fill numerous other ecological roles in the woodland/woods edge community.

The rapid conversion of woodlands and wetlands to agricultural land over the last century has eliminated Box Turtles from much of their former range in the region, and the present spread of suburban development continues to fragment habitat and isolate the remaining populations. Due to their sedentary habits and longevity, these turtles often survive in small pockets of habitat such as farm woodlots, abandoned cropland, and parks. Unfortunately, these remnant populations may not be viable over the long term. Road mortality, illegal collecting, and forest and brush fires (sometimes including poorly planned prescribed burning) continuously whittle down local populations. An emergent disease caused by a ranavirus, formerly thought to largely affect amphibians, has caused mortality in both captive and wild Box Turtles. Though recent reports are mainly south of the Great Lakes basin, the spread of this disease could have serious consequences for turtle populations. Demand for Box Turtles in the commercial pet trade has encouraged poaching and caused an additional drain on their numbers. Box Turtles are afforded legal protection by states and provinces in the region and are listed in appendix II of the CITES treaty, curtailing international trade, but these laws fail to protect them from other serious threats, particularly bulldozers, automobiles, and fire.

Like related species, Box Turtle have a life history strategy that tends to balance very high egg and hatchling mortality and delayed sexual maturity with very high expected adult survivorship and potential longevity. Any factor that continuously removes juvenile and adult animals from an area faster than they can be replaced will result in an inevitable steady decline and eventual local extinction of the population.

## Blanding's Turtle (*Emydoidea blandingii*)

**Description:** The moderately high, domed carapace of an adult Blanding's Turtle is elongate and quite smooth, without keels or sculpturing. It is black, gray, or brown, often marked with a highly variable pattern of tan or yellowish spots or streaks. The plastron is yellowish, with a dark blotch at the outer rear edge of each scute, and usually has well-defined annuli and a shallow V-shaped notch at the tail. Rarely, dark color may cover most or all of the plastron. Most adult specimens have a hinge between the pectoral and abdominal scutes, but hinge flexibility varies greatly between individuals. The head is rather flat, with a short, rounded snout; the upper jaw is notched at the front, giving this turtle a permanent "smile." The top and sides of the head may be black, brown, or olive, with yellowish or brownish spots or mottling, while the chin, throat, and lower surface of the very long neck are bright yellow. Adult carapace length: 15.2 to 27.4 cm (6 to 10.8 in).

A male Blanding's Turtle's plastron is moderately concave, and the vent is beyond the rear edge of the carapace when the tail is fully extended. Females have a flatter plastron and a narrower tail, with the vent at or beneath the rear edge of the carapace when the tail is extended. The hatchling has a gray, brown, or black carapace, 3 to 3.5 cm (1.2 to 1.4 in) long, with a low keel and sometimes a light spot in the center of each scute. The plastron usually has a black central blotch rimmed with yellow or cream color; the hinge is not functional. The tail is proportionally longer and thinner than that of the adult. Immature Blanding's Turtles are often more brightly marked than the adults, and their carapace scutes often show distinct growth rings.

**Confusing Species:** Wood Turtles have a lower, broader, more sculptured carapace, an unhinged plastron, and an upper jaw with two sharp cusps in front. Spotted Turtles have larger, more rounded yellow spots on the head and carapace and also lack a plastral hinge. The Eastern Box Turtle has a hooked (not notched) upper beak and generally does not have a plain yellow throat and lower neck.

**Distribution and Status:** The primary range of the Blanding's Turtle extends from extreme southwestern Quebec and southern Ontario west to Minnesota and Nebraska and south to central Illinois. There are disjunct populations in parts of New England (southern Maine, southeastern New Hampshire, and eastern Massachusetts) and in eastern New York and southern Nova Scotia. This range fragmentation suggests that the species enjoyed a much wider distribution at some point since the end of the Pleistocene. In the Great Lakes basin Blanding's Turtles are found throughout southern Ontario (Point Pelee to Georgian Bay), along both shores of Lake Erie (though they may be nearly extirpated in Pennsylvania), in Michigan (Lower and central Upper Peninsula), northern Ohio, Indiana, eastern Illinois, and Wisconsin (Lake Michigan drainage). They are also reported from New York at sites near the St. Lawrence River (Jefferson County) and the Niagara River (Niagara County).

Destruction and degradation of wetlands and adjacent uplands, along with road mortality, has eliminated the Blanding's Turtle in many places, though they can remain fairly common where suitable habitat exists. Despite local declines, the Great Lakes area is presently a stronghold of this species, which is most vulnerable and often threatened at the periphery of its range. Blanding's Turtles are considered endangered in Illinois and Indiana, threatened in Ohio, New York, and Ontario, and a species of special concern in Michigan and Pennsylvania.

**Habitat and Ecology:** For most of the year Blanding's Turtles live in and around shallow, weedy waters such as ponds, marshes, fens, swamps, and lake inlets and coves. They are sometimes found in rivers but concentrate their activities in backwaters, embayments, and sloughs, and are only transient in portions of streams with more than a sluggish current. Terrestrial movement by adult males and females is common in spring and, to a lesser extent, in fall. Males may travel overland to increase their mating opportunities, while females are most likely concerned with finding suitable nesting sites.

On cool sunny days, Blanding's Turtles will emerge to bask on logs, grass clumps, sloping banks, or other high perches near water. In the heat of summer, they may restrict their activities to early morning and evening, or even adopt nocturnal habits. The drying of their shallow water habitats spurs some individuals to migrate overland to new bodies of water, while others will burrow under roots, mud, or plant debris and aestivate until conditions improve. They hibernate underwater (more rarely under debris close to water) from late October or early November until early April. They are quite cold tolerant, however, and are frequently seen moving sluggishly under the ice.

Crustaceans, particularly crayfish, are favored food items, with insects, worms, leeches, snails, small fish, tadpoles, frogs, and some plants rounding out the diet. Most feeding occurs underwater, though prey is sometimes seized onshore and carried to the water for swallowing. These turtles are capable of eating on land but appear to do so infrequently and with difficulty. They often forage by creeping along the bottom in shallow water, sweeping their lowered heads back and forth over the substrate. A Blanding's Turtle will stalk a crayfish or other prey by slowly creeping forward with its head partly retracted. When within range, the long neck darts out and the mouth and throat gape, causing water and prey to be sucked in. Small animals are swallowed whole, but larger prey are held in the jaws and torn into pieces with the front claws. In summer they often forage and feed after dark.

Raccoons, skunks, and foxes are the principal predators on Blanding's

Blanding's Turtle, adult

Blanding's Turtle, juvenile, plastron

Turtle eggs, and these mammals, along with fish, frogs, snakes, wading birds, crows, and other animals, will eat hatchling and juvenile turtles. Adult Blanding's Turtles have far fewer natural predators. When on land they depend on their shells for protection and rarely, if ever, bite defensively. As noted above, the plastral hinge varies in its utility. Many individuals can close up almost as tightly as a Box Turtle, while others have little or no hinge flexibility. Blanding's Turtles are often parasitized by leeches (*Placobdella* sp.). They are strong swimmers, and when surprised in or near water, these turtles usually dive in and either swim to deeper water or conceal themselves in bottom mud or vegetation.

**Reproduction and Growth:** Mating can occur from April to November but is most frequent in spring. A courting male typically approaches the female in shallow to fairly deep water and mounts her carapace in a quick rush. Clasping her carapace edges with his claws, he may bite at her head and forelimbs or extend his neck and press his chin on her snout, forcing her to remain withdrawn. He may also swing his head back and forth over the female's head or bob his head vertically and blow a stream of water or bubbles over her head. A copulating pair may sink to the bottom, float near the surface, or hang on to emergent branches or vegetation. Fewer than half the adult females in a population may reproduce in a given year.

Most nesting is in June. Gravid females may travel over a kilometer (0.6 mi) from the water to find suitable nest sites, which ideally are open, sunny spots with moist but well-drained sandy or loamy soil. Lawns, gardens, plowed fields, or even gravel road edges are used if better sites are lacking. The nest cavity is dug with alternating movements of the hind feet. Clutch size varies from six to twenty-two eggs, which are elliptical and average about 3.6 cm (1.4 in) in length. The eggshells may initially be quite rigid, but they absorb water and become more flexible as incubation progresses.

Eggs not destroyed by predators or other hazards will hatch in fifty-five to seventy-five days, with most hatchlings emerging in August or early September; overwintering in the nest is rare in this species. Blanding's Turtles have temperature-dependent sex determination; eggs experimentally incubated at 26.5°C (79.5°F) or lower produced nearly all males, while those incubated at 30 to 31°C (86 to 87.8°F) produced females. A Blanding's Turtle will grow to sexual maturity in fifteen to twenty-two years. Counting plastral scute annuli will usually give a reasonable age estimate in juvenile and young adult specimens; after maturity (when growth slows or ceases), annuli counts will tend to underestimate actual age. Adults are potentially long-lived; individuals sixty years and older are still reproductive, and may even produce larger egg clutches than younger animals. A Michigan female was known to be at least eighty-three years old, and it seems likely that a few individuals may reach the century mark.

**Conservation:** The lower Great Lakes basin is probably the present center of abundance for the Blanding's Turtle, but even here the loss and degradation of wetland habitats has greatly reduced or eliminated local populations. Efforts by government agencies and private citizens' groups to conserve the larger remaining wetlands will not ensure the future of these turtles unless attention is paid to protecting smaller ponds and marshes as well as adjacent upland corridors and nesting sites. Road mortality constitutes a major drain on turtle numbers, and the construction of a road between an aquatic habitat and the only available upland nesting sites may result in a long-term death sentence for a local Blanding's Turtle population. Blanding's Turtles rarely feed on game fish and are of no concern to fish management or other economic interests. They have, to date, attracted minimal attention from the pet trade, though they have been exploited in the recent past by biological supply companies and for human food in Ohio and Wisconsin and perhaps elsewhere. Blanding's Turtles receive some level of legal protection in states and provinces throughout their range.

The concept of "sustained harvest" cannot be applied to this or any other turtle species that displays a life history strategy that balances high nest mortality and delayed sexual maturity with high adult survivorship and longevity. An important long-term study of a Blanding's Turtle population in southern Michigan (Congdon, Dunham, and van Loben Sels 1993) revealed that to maintain population stability annual survivorship for adults had to exceed 93 percent, while at least 72 percent of juveniles (ages one through thirteen) had to survive each year. Any factor that increases losses beyond these normal very low levels will inevitably cause the population to decline.

## Northern Map Turtle (*Graptemys geographica*)

**Description:** The Northern Map Turtle is named for the network of dark-bordered, yellowish to orange lines on the otherwise olive or grayish-brown carapace, which, with some imagination, may resemble waterways or contour lines on a map. In older individuals this pattern may be obscured by dark pigment. The carapace is fairly broad, with a low to moderate keel along the midline and a flared hind margin that is serrated (due to the projecting rear edges of the marginal scutes). The broad, flat plastron is usually plain yellow, but juveniles and males may have dark markings along the scute borders. The head, neck, and limbs are dark olive, brown, or black, with numerous thin yellow, green, or orangish stripes. Most specimens will have a small oval or triangular light spot behind each eye. Adult female carapace length: 17 to 27.3 cm (6.7 to 10.7 in); adult male carapace length: 10 to 16 cm (3.9 to 6.3 in).

An adult male Northern Map Turtle is considerably smaller than the adult female and has a narrower, more oval carapace with a distinct vertebral keel. It also has a comparatively narrower head, longer front claws, and a longer, thicker tail, with the vent opening beyond the edge of the carapace when the tail is extended. Conversely, the adult female is larger than the male, with a broader carapace and a lower keel. Females have wider heads, shorter front claws, and short tails, with the vent beneath the edge of the carapace when the tail is extended.

A typical hatchling Northern Map Turtle has a rounded gray or grayish brown carapace about 2.8 cm (1.1 in) long, with light circular markings and a distinct central keel. The plastron is light yellow or off-white, with dark borders on the scutes. The striped pattern on the head and limbs is like that of the adult.

**Confusing Species:** The Wood Turtle lacks yellow striping on head, neck, and limbs and has a sculptured-looking carapace with prominent scute annuli. A Painted Turtle has a smooth, unserrated and unkeeled carapace with red markings under the marginal scutes and (in the Midland subspecies) red striping on the legs and neck. Red-eared Sliders have a broad reddish or orange stripe behind the eye and large black spots on the plastron (except for some old male Sliders, in which black pigment suffuses the shell and may obliterate skin striping). The False Map Turtle, which is probably not native to the Great Lakes basin (see "Marginal and Questionable Species" page 366), has a narrow head (in both sexes) marked with a yellow bar or crescent behind each eye, a more prominent vertebral keel, and usually retains dark markings on the plastron into adulthood.

Northern Map Turtle, female

Northern Map Turtle, male, plastron

Northern Map Turtle, hatchling

**Distribution and Status:** This species has been found from southern Quebec and northwestern Vermont (Lake Champlain) west to the Mississippi drainage of Minnesota and south to Arkansas and northern Alabama. Disjunct populations occur in eastern New York (Hudson River drainage), western New Jersey (Delaware River), and eastern Pennsylvania (Susquehanna River drainage). Its Great Lakes range includes Ontario from the St. Lawrence River west to Georgian Bay and south to Lake Erie, New York (south shore of Lake Ontario), all of northern Ohio and Indiana, the southern, central, and western Lower Peninsula of Michigan (and perhaps Dickinson County in the Upper Peninsula), northeastern Illinois, and central Wisconsin.

Northern Map Turtles have disappeared from the more heavily polluted urban rivers but remain locally common throughout much of the lower Great Lakes basin. They are a species of concern in Ontario.

**Habitat and Ecology:** These highly aquatic turtles inhabit larger lakes, rivers, reservoirs, oxbow sloughs, and open marshes, including some of the bays and inlets of the Great Lakes themselves. They are less common in smaller lakes and streams, though juveniles may reside in small ponds, then move into larger bodies of water prior to maturity. Acceptable bottom substrates range from soft mud to sand, gravel, or marl, and the habitat may be weedy or fairly open.

Northern Map Turtles are often seen basking in groups on emergent logs, brush, rocks, and sloping banks or sandbars; at the slightest disturbance they dive into the water and hide in mud or vegetation or head for deep water. They are mostly diurnal but may feed in the evening or after dark during the warm summer months. Northern Map Turtles cease feeding and are generally dormant from early November through early April, spending most of this time underwater, wedged beneath submerged logs, partially buried in shallow depressions in the bottom mud, or in muskrat burrows. However, they often change locations during the winter, at which time they may be seen moving slowly about under the ice.

Feeding always takes place in the water. Adult females, with their massive heads and powerful jaws with flat, bony crushing surfaces, are well equipped to process and consume the snails, clams, and crayfish that make up the bulk of their diet. The narrower-headed males depend more on aquatic insects and smaller crustaceans and snails. Both sexes also take carrion, such as dead fish, and small amounts of plant material.

The nests of Northern Map Turtles are frequently plundered by raccoons and other predatory mammals, and hatchlings and small juveniles are vulnerable to large fish, frogs, and herons. Older juveniles and adults probably have few natural predators, as they are powerful swimmers and extremely wary. Only nesting females are likely to be encountered away from water, and these tend to be shy, withdrawing into their shells at the slightest disturbance. Most specimens are reluctant to bite, but a large female that opportunistically seizes a predator's nose—or a human finger—with her oversized jaws can inflict a painful pinch.

**Reproduction and Growth:** Mating probably occurs in spring and fall, but has rarely been observed or described by biologists. The male may reportedly swim "nose to nose" in front of his intended mate and engage in vertical head bobbing. If the female is sufficiently interested, mounting and copulation presumably follow. Most mating probably takes place in deeper waters where observation by curious humans is less likely.

The nesting period lasts from late May through early July, with mid-June being the peak nesting time in the Great Lakes area. Females typically emerge from the water to seek a nest site in the early morning or evening. Warm rains, especially thundershowers on warm, humid days, may stimulate nesting even at midday. Unshaded sites with sandy or loamy soils are preferred, and a female may move distances of up to several hundred meters from the water to find suitable conditions. The flask-shaped nest cavity is dug with the hind feet. A clutch contains from six to twenty oval, flexible-shelled eggs, which range in length from 3.2 to 3.5 cm (1.2 to 1.4 in). After laying the last egg, the female fills the cavity and may then flatten the nest site with her plastron. Some females will lay two clutches of eggs during a season.

Hatching occurs fifty to seventy days after laying, with most hatchlings emerging in August or September. Hatchlings from late nests may overwinter in the nest and emerge from the ground in spring. This species has temperature-dependent sex determination. Eggs incubated in the laboratory at temperatures between 22.5° and 27°C (72.5° to 80.6°F) produced only males, while those kept at 30°C (86°F) resulted in females. The size difference between the sexes becomes apparent by the third year after hatching; females reportedly begin to grow faster than males after the second year of growth. Males reach sexual maturity in three to five years, while females may require ten to fourteen years to mature. A specimen captured as an adult lived in a zoo for eighteen years.

**Conservation:** Northern Map Turtles do not feed on game fish and do no harm to human interests. Their mollusk-eating habits may be beneficial; snails are the intermediate hosts for many species of trematode worms, which parasitize game and domestic animals and humans (including the blood fluke that causes "swimmer's itch"). Map Turtles are also reported to eat certain invasive mollusk species, such as the zebra mussel. These turtles were formerly trapped for the commercial food market in Iowa and elsewhere in the upper Mississippi River area. New regulations and perhaps a drop in demand have greatly reduced this exploitation. This species has rarely been targeted for the pet trade and has a well-deserved reputation for being difficult to maintain in captivity, perhaps due to its shyness and specialized diet.

Populations of the Northern Map Turtle have been reduced or eliminated in some areas, due largely or in part to pollution and destruction of suitable nesting sites. However, these turtles frequently persist in rivers running through suburban and agricultural areas, including those affected by modest levels of organic pollution. Map Turtles living in lakes are often injured or killed by boat propellers and are accidentally caught on fishhooks baited with live bait. The use of basking turtles as targets by vandals with firearms can be a serious drain on turtle numbers, and Northern Map Turtles are particularly vulnerable to this deplorable practice.

## Painted Turtle (*Chrysemys picta*)

**Description:** This well-named little turtle has a smooth, unkeeled black or olive carapace with red bars or blotches on the marginal scutes; some specimens have light borders on the larger carapace scutes, and there may be a thin red stripe down the midline. Rear marginals are unserrated. The flat, hingeless plastron is yellow, often tinged with red, pink, or orange, and usually has a dark central blotch or figure that varies according to subspecies (described below). Occasionally the entire shell is stained a dark reddish-brown from minerals absorbed from the water or substrate. The skin is black or olive. Both head and throat have yellow stripes, sometimes with a yellow spot, bar, or streak behind the eye; the eye itself is yellow with a dark horizontal bar through the pupil. The upper jaw has two toothlike cusps on either side of a terminal notch. The upper neck, legs, and tail are striped with red and/or yellow. Adult carapace length: 9 to 26.6 cm (3.5 to 10.4 in). Note that the western subspecies (*Chrysemys picta belli*, described below) reaches the largest sizes, while the midland race (*C. p. marginata*) is not known to exceed 19.5 cm (7.6 in) in shell length.

Male Painted Turtles are generally smaller and flatter than females and have greatly elongated front claws; with the tail extended, the male's vent is beyond the back edge of the carapace. Females have shorter front claws and shorter tails; with tail extended, the vent is at or beneath the rear edge of the carapace.

The hatchling has a rounded, slightly keeled carapace that averages about 2.5 cm (1 in) in length. Hatchling coloration is like the adult's but is brighter and more contrasting.

Note: Four distinct subspecies of this turtle are recognized here, two of which are found in the Great Lakes region. The Midland Painted Turtle (*Chrysemys picta marginata*) tends to have prominent red stripes on the forelegs and neck, and its plastron is usually yellow or orangish-yellow with an elongate dark central blotch that does not cover more than half the plastral width. The larger Western Painted Turtle (*Chrysemys picta belli*) typically has narrow yellow stripes on the forelegs and neck and a pattern of light lines on the carapace. Its plastron may be quite reddish or orangish, with a complex central pattern of dark and light lines that extends out along the scute seams and often covers more than half of the plastral width. These two subspecies overlap in the western Great Lakes area, with intergrade individuals displaying a variable blending of the above characteristics.

**Confusing Species:** Northern Map Turtles lack red markings and have a keeled carapace with a serrated (notched) rear margin. A Red-eared Slider has a single reddish band or stripe behind each eye, lacks red carapace markings, and has a yellow plastron, usually with a single black spot in each scute.

**Distribution and Status:** The range of the Painted Turtle encompasses most of the eastern, central, and northern United States and adjacent southern Canada, from Nova Scotia south along the Atlantic seaboard to southern Georgia and west to Louisiana and Arkansas, then north to the Great Lakes and west through the northern plains region from Kansas and Colorado to southern Saskatchewan and Alberta, and west to northern Oregon, Washington, and southern British Columbia. There are isolated populations in New Mexico and elsewhere in the Southwest. This species is found throughout the Great Lakes region, with the Midland Painted Turtle the dominant subspecies from the Lake Ontario drainage to Georgian Bay and west through lower Michigan, Ohio, and Indiana. The Western Painted Turtle occurs in the western Lake Superior basin and intergrades with the Midland race from the Upper Peninsula of Michigan south through Wisconsin to the Indiana Dunes. This is a common to abundant turtle throughout most of the region, though population densities tend to be lower in the far north.

Western Painted Turtle
Midland Painted Turtle
Eastern Painted Turtle
Painted Turtle Intergrade

**Habitat and Ecology:** Painted Turtles prefer quiet or slow-moving permanent waters with a soft bottom substrate, abundant aquatic plant life,
and basking sites such as emergent logs, rocks, or mats of floating vegetation. However, they will at least temporarily occupy vernal ponds, ster-
ile impoundments, ditches, and faster-moving streams and rivers and are
able to tolerate fairly high levels of organic pollution. These turtles do not
hesitate to move overland if necessary, and individuals of both sexes may
commute between several bodies of water. Deeper or spring-fed waters are
often favored during the fall and winter, followed by a spring movement to
shallower, more productive ponds, marshes, and lake edges. Hibernation
occurs underwater, with most Painted Turtles burrowing shallowly into the
bottom mud and remaining dormant from October or November until late
March or early April. These are cold-tolerant turtles, however, and it is not
uncommon to see one swimming under the ice on a sunny winter day or
attempting to bask in early spring when parts of the habitat are still ice covered. Active foraging and feeding begin when the water temperature reaches
about 20°C (68°F).

Basking is an important activity for this turtle, and numbers may congregate or even pile up at favored spots. During cooler weather, especially
in spring, they may bask intermittently throughout the day, but in summer
basking may be restricted to the morning or late afternoon. These turtles
are generally inactive at night but sometimes forage after dark during the
summer months. Painted Turtles are omnivorous, with aquatic insects,

Midland Painted
Turtle, adult female

Midland Painted
Turtle, plastron

Western Painted
Turtle, plastron

crustaceans, algae, duckweed, and rooted plants forming the bulk of their diet. Additional foods include snails, leeches, worms, tadpoles, small fish, and carrion. Foraging strategies include active searching and probing, quiet ambush, and surface skimming—the latter accomplished by opening the mouth at the surface and expanding the throat, causing floating plants and animals to flow into the throat cavity. These turtles are unable to swallow unless their heads are submerged. Hatchlings and juveniles are more carnivorous than adults. Painted Turtles living in nutrient-rich habitats with greater availability of animal foods have been found to grow faster and reach a greater size than those living in less enriched habitats and eating a higher percentage of plant foods.

Mammalian predators such as raccoons, skunks, and foxes destroy many Painted Turtle nests. Hatchlings and juveniles are eaten by frogs, snakes, herons, mink, and raccoons. Adults are wary and have few enemies in the water, but many are killed by predators or automobiles during terrestrial wandering. When handled, these turtles may retire into their shells or attempt to scratch and bite, although their weak jaws can cause little damage.

**Reproduction and Growth:** Courtship and mating can occur at any time during the active season but is most common in spring. A courting male will swim backward in front of his intended mate and vibrate his long foreclaws on the sides of her head and chin. If receptive, the female may touch his forelegs with her own claws. Eventually she will sink to the bottom, allowing the male to mount and clasp her shell from above. Copulation occurs when the male slips backward, bringing their vents into contact.

Painted Turtles nest between mid-May and mid-July, sometimes in the morning but more often in late afternoon or early evening. The females seek open, sunny sites with moist, workable sand or soil; they prefer to nest near the water but will travel distances of several hundred meters from water if necessary. In loose sand the female may dig a preliminary depression with her front feet, but the nest cavity itself is dug with alternating movements of the hind feet only. She frequently moistens the site with liquid from her cloacal bladders. A clutch contains from three to twenty-three elliptical, flexible-shelled eggs, which average about 3 cm (1.2 in) in length. The largest clutches are produced by female Western Painted Turtles and intergrades in the northern and western portions of the region; Midland females rarely lay more than ten eggs at one time. Some females produce two or more clutches per season, but they may not reproduce every year.

The incubation period depends on temperatures and humidity within the nest, but it generally ranges from fifty to eighty days. Many (probably most) hatchlings overwinter in the nest and postpone emergence until spring. The baby turtles are quite resistant to freezing, but prolonged cold temperatures with little insulating snow cover may result in high hatchling mortality. Painted Turtles have temperature-dependent sex determination. Eggs incubated at constant temperatures of 21.5° to 27°C (70° to 80.6°F) produced only males; females resulted if temperatures ranged between 29° and 32°C (84° to 90°F).

In good habitats, young Painted Turtles can grow rapidly; hatchlings may double their length during their first growing season. Fast growth is advantageous since survival chances improve as size increases. Growth rates slow once sexual maturity is attained, and older adults may not grow at all. Males reach maturity in three to seven years, females in six to ten. Potential life-span for this species is thought to be about thirty-five to forty years, and perhaps as high as sixty, though relatively few individuals will survive that long.

**Conservation:** Painted Turtles are harmless to human interests. Their consumption of aquatic insects, including mosquito larvae, may be useful, and they have considerable aesthetic value for many boaters and canoeists (though their attraction to live bait can be a minor annoyance to fishermen). These turtles are occasionally eaten by people, but they are too small to have commercial food value. In some places they have been exploited for laboratory use and the pet trade.

Painted Turtles remain common in many urban and suburban waters and have benefited from the construction of farm and ornamental ponds. On the other hand, great numbers are killed annually on roads, and human activities often lead to increased populations of nest predators, particularly raccoons. Basking Painted Turtles are sometimes shot by vandals with firearms, a deplorable and senseless practice. Local mass die-offs of Painted Turtles are occasionally reported, and it is important to determine whether the cause of such mortality is natural or human induced, since any pollutant that can kill these hardy reptiles could conceivably pose a threat to game species and people as well.

## Red-eared Slider (*Trachemys scripta elegans*)

**Description:** This medium-sized aquatic turtle has a relatively smooth brownish or olive carapace decorated with a variable pattern of yellow and black bands and stripes. The carapace may be unkeeled or have a low central keel, and the flaring rear edge is weakly serrated. The plastron is yellow, usually with a dark spot or smudge in the center of each scute. Head and legs are green, olive, or brown, with numerous narrow black and yellow stripes; a few broader yellow stripes slant downward from the snout, mouth, and lower corner of the eye. This turtle is named for the broad red or orange stripe that extends backward from each eye. In some individuals this band may be poorly developed or obscured. Large males (and very rarely females) can become quite dark (melanistic), with black pigment obscuring the normal color and pattern on the shell and skin. Adult carapace length: 12.5 to 28.9 cm (5 to 11.4 in).

The male Red-eared Slider is usually smaller than the female and has greatly elongated claws on the front feet and a comparatively longer tail. With tail extended, the male's vent is usually positioned beyond the carapace edge. Compared to the male, the female has shorter front claws, longer hind claws, and a shorter tail, with the vent beneath the rear edge of the carapace.

Hatchlings typically range from 2.8 to 3.3 cm (1.1 to 1.3 in) in length. The hatchling's carapace has a low keel, and both carapace and skin are bright green; yellow stripes and other markings may be less defined by dark pigment than those of older turtles, but the black spots on the plastral scutes are usually prominent.

**Confusing Species:** Painted Turtles have reddish markings on the marginal scutes and limbs and a centralized blotch or pattern on the plastron.

Red-eared Slider, adult male

Red-eared Slider, hatchling (left) and Red-eared Slider, juvenile plastron (right)

Northern Map Turtles lack the red stripe behind the eye and have a mostly unmarked plastron.

**Distribution and Status:** The Red-eared Slider is found from West Virginia west to northern Indiana and Illinois, south to the Gulf coastal states from western Georgia through Texas to northern Mexico and eastern New Mexico. Disjunct populations in California, Maryland, southern Ohio, southern Michigan, Wisconsin, southern Ontario, and elsewhere are usually attributed to human introduction. The natural range of this subspecies reaches the Great Lakes basin in Indiana at the southern end of Lake

Michigan. Whether any of the Michigan populations are natural remains problematic; shell fragments from archaeological sites (American Indian middens) in Michigan and Wisconsin indicate that the species once ranged farther north than at present, perhaps entering the Great Lakes area during a postglacial warm period. Thus it is possible that some Sliders in Michigan (and perhaps elsewhere) represent natural relict populations or perhaps a mix of relict and introduced animals; a recent genetic study (P. Terry 2015) may provide evidence for the latter hypothesis. Red-eared Sliders have been introduced into parts of Europe, Africa, and Asia (see the discussion under "Conservation" below). Two additional subspecies extend the range of *Trachemys scripta* to eastern Tennessee and the Atlantic coastal plain (southern Virginia to northern Florida). Introduced specimens of these subspecies, especially the Yellow-bellied Slider (*Trachemys scripta scripta*), occasionally are found in the Great Lakes region.

Though generally common throughout most of its range, the Red-eared Slider is restricted to small, widely scattered, and very localized populations in the Great Lakes region.

**Habitat and Ecology:** Sliders inhabit ponds, lakes, reservoirs, ditches, sloughs, swamps, and the backwaters and slower sections of streams and rivers—almost any permanent body of water with ample aquatic vegetation and suitable basking sites. They will travel overland in search of new habitats or to nest but are rarely far from water. Adult Sliders seem to prefer somewhat deeper water than do Painted Turtles in the same habitats, although juveniles of both species tend to remain in weedy shallows. Sliders spend much time basking on logs and other emergent debris or floating in mats of vegetation. The common name Slider refers to their habit of quickly sliding from basking sites into the water upon the slightest disturbance. They are inactive at night, generally forage underwater in the early morning and late afternoon, and often bask for much of the midday period if the weather is not too hot.

These turtles are inactive at water temperatures below 10°C (50°F) and are usually dormant from mid-October to early April in the northern part of their range. Most Sliders hibernate underwater, digging into the bottom substrate, under overhanging banks, or in muskrat tunnels. Red-eared Sliders are omnivorous, eating a variety of small aquatic animals and vegetation. The former include insects, snails, crayfish, and other crustaceans and occasionally small vertebrates (tadpoles, fish) and carrion. Plant foods include algae, duckweed, rooted plants, and seeds. Juvenile Sliders take a higher percentage of animal foods than adults do, perhaps due to their higher requirements for protein and calcium and/or the greater availability of small animal prey in the shallow waters frequented by the younger turtles.

Red-eared Slider eggs and hatchlings are readily consumed by raccoons, skunks, and other predators; typical mortality rates for eggs and new hatchlings range from about 70 to nearly 100 percent in any one year or place. Juveniles have fewer enemies as they grow, and the wary adults are fairly safe from most natural predators while in the water. Sliders are most vulnerable to predators when they leave the water seeking nest sites or new aquatic habitat.

Human-induced mortality is discussed under "Conservation" below. When handled, some feisty individuals will bite, but most retire into their shells or flail their legs in an attempt to escape. Hatchling Sliders may be distasteful to some predatory fish; Largemouth Bass have been found to reject hatchlings as prey, perhaps because the little turtles scratch and bite when ingested.

**Reproduction and Growth:** Most courtship and mating occur in spring and fall. Courtship behavior is similar to that of the Painted Turtle. The male swims backward in front of the female and, with "palms" turned outward, vibrates his long foreclaws on her head and chin. If receptive, the female eventually sinks to the bottom and allows the male to clasp her carapace from above. The male then curls his tail beneath that of the female to bring their vents into contact and usually assumes a nearly vertical position during copulation.

Sliders nest from late May through early July. The female leaves the water in the early morning or late afternoon and seeks a sunny, elevated location with moist soil or sand; the site is often moistened with water from the turtle's cloacal bladders. The globular nest cavity is dug entirely with the hind feet. After the eggs are laid, the nest opening is refilled with the premoistened soil and tamped with the hind feet and plastron, leaving a mud plug that can initially be fairly conspicuous. In the north most female Sliders probably lay one clutch per year, but some may produce a second clutch about two to four weeks after the first. A clutch can contain from two to thirty whitish, oval, flexible-shelled eggs ranging from 3.1 to 4.3 cm (1.2 to 1.7 in) in length; larger females generally produce more eggs—though not necessarily larger ones—than smaller females.

Incubation requires from sixty to eighty days under normal conditions. Hatchlings can either emerge and enter the water in late summer or fall, or overwinter in the nest and emerge in spring. Hatchling Sliders may be less freeze tolerant than Painted Turtles, and mortality in overwintering nests may be high when cold winter temperatures are severe or prolonged. Nest temperatures about midway through incubation determine the sex of the hatchlings; eggs incubated at constant temperatures between 22.5° and 27°C (72.5° and 80.6°F) produced only males, while eggs kept at 30°C (86°F) produced females.

Growth rate in Red-eared Sliders varies according to the availability and quality of food and the environmental temperatures. Males may reach sexual maturity in two to five years, at a minimum carapace length of about 12.5 cm (5 in). Females mature in six to eight years at carapace lengths of about 18 to 20 cm (7 to 7.8 in). Captive Sliders have lived at least forty-nine years, but very few wild individuals would survive that long.

**Conservation:** Red-eared Sliders do not normally eat game fish, and in their natural habitat and range they pose no threat to human interests. Their former, and in some places present, abundance suggests that these adaptable turtles play an important role in aquatic ecosystems. However, this species has long suffered from staggering levels of human exploitation and destruction. Great numbers of these turtles are killed annually by automobiles, and the mistaken belief that they compete with humans for fish results in direct persecution by fishermen. Basking turtles are often used as targets by vandals with firearms. Adult Sliders are trapped for the biological supply trade and human consumption. They are marketed domestically and shipped overseas as well. Unfortunately the larger female turtles bear the brunt of this demand. Slider eggs have been dug up and sold as fish bait; sometimes the collectors have killed gravid female turtles to obtain eggs rather than waiting for the turtles to nest.

Many thousands of hatchling and juvenile Sliders were once captured each year for the domestic and international pet trade, though few survived the often inadequate care offered them in captivity. Commercial turtle farms now produce several million baby Red-eared Sliders annually, although these farms may take large numbers of mature turtles from the wild to augment their breeding stock. Ironically, the hatchling turtles are mostly marketed overseas, since the sale of pet turtles under four inches (10.16 cm) in carapace length is presently prohibited in the United States. (Captive turtles raised or shipped under unsanitary conditions can become carriers of infectious bacteria, primarily *Salmonella* species. The "four-inch rule" is presumably an attempt to discourage people from buying the turtles as pets for small children.)

The international Slider trade has led to a further irony—while some native Slider populations are declining or even disappearing due to continued exploitation and habitat loss, these turtles are establishing themselves in many places outside their natural range due to the release of unwanted pets. Red-eared Sliders are reportedly established in California, France, South Africa, Bahrain, Japan, South Korea, Guam, Thailand, Brazil, and probably elsewhere. There is concern that introduced Sliders could detrimentally compete with native species, but there is presently no evidence that the small, possibly introduced populations in the Great Lakes region have caused any ecological problems.

# Softshell Turtles

## FAMILY TRIONYCHIDAE

Twenty-two species of Softshell Turtles are found in North America, Africa, and temperate and tropical parts of Asia. They have broad, rubbery shells with the underlying bony elements greatly reduced, and a complete lack of overlying scutes. These medium-sized to very large turtles are well adapted for an aquatic existence, with strongly webbed feet and piglike, elongated noses that function as built-in snorkels in some species. One species occurs in the Great Lakes region.

## Eastern Spiny Softshell (*Apalone spinifera spinifera*)

**Description:** This turtle is unmistakable, with its smooth, flat, oval or round carapace and long, piglike snout. Both carapace and plastron lack scutes and are soft and rubbery, with flexible edges. The tan, brown, or olive carapace is decorated with black spots, flecks, and circles in juveniles and males, while adult females darken and become blotched or mottled with gray or brown. The name "spiny" refers to the short, often inconspicuous spines at the front of the carapace. Plastron coloration is white or pale yellow, with the underlying bones visible as gray patches. The head, very long neck, and legs are tan or olive above, speckled or mottled with black. All four feet are fully webbed and often streaked or mottled with yellow and black. There are usually two black-bordered yellowish stripes on each side of the head, behind the eye and jaw. Adult female carapace length: 24 to 48 cm (9.4 to 18.9 in). Adult male carapace length: 12.7 to 24 cm (5 to 9.4 in).

Besides being smaller than the female and retaining the juvenile color pattern, the male Spiny Softshell has a slightly granular (rougher) carapace surface and a longer, thicker tail, which may project well beyond the rear carapace margin. Females have smoother carapaces and shorter tails, which barely project beyond the rear edge of the carapace.

The hatchling is 3 to 4 cm (1.2 to 1.6 in) long and has a circular tan or olive-brown carapace with a pattern of dark spots or circles and a light border. The new hatchling has a curled shell and a turned-up nose, but these unfold within a day or two after emergence from the confinement of the eggshell.

**Confusing Species:** No other Great Lakes turtle has a flat, scuteless carapace and tubular nose. The Smooth Softshell (*Apalone mutica*) is known from the Ohio and Mississippi river systems in Ohio, Indiana, Illinois, and Wisconsin but is not known to occur within the Great Lakes basin. As its name implies, the Smooth Softshell lacks the short spines on the front of the carapace that are found on the Spiny Softshell.

**Distribution and Status:** This subspecies is found from western New York and southern Ontario west to Minnesota and south to Oklahoma, Tennessee, western Mississippi, and northern Alabama. There are disjunct populations in Vermont (Lake Champlain area), adjacent southern Quebec (Ottawa River), eastern New York, and southern New Jersey. It intergrades with other subspecies that occur in the southwest (Arizona to Texas) and the lower Mississippi Valley and Gulf states. Spiny Softshells range across the lower Great Lakes region from the southern and western shores of Lake Ontario through southern Ontario and much of Michigan's Lower Peninsula, adjacent Ohio, and Indiana to the western Lake Michigan basin (north to Green Bay).

This turtle remains locally common in the western part of its Great Lakes range but is uncommon to rare and local in the east. Spiny Softshells have declined in some places due to pollution, exploitation, and elimination of nesting sites. It has been nearly extirpated from the western end of Lake Ontario, where it was once common, and is considered threatened in Ontario and a species of concern in New York.

**Habitat and Ecology:** Spiny Softshells inhabit rivers and the larger streams, inland lakes, reservoirs, and even protected bays and river mouth areas in the Great Lakes themselves. They tolerate a fairly swift current but prefer a sand or mud bottom and usually avoid streams with sharp-edged rocks or coarse gravel. Open habitats with little aquatic vegetation are favored over those with dense plant growth. Basking spots in the form of sloping banks or logs and open, preferably sandy nesting areas close to the water are also important habitat components.

These highly aquatic turtles are fast and powerful swimmers and rarely leave the immediate vicinity of water. They spend much of their time basking in late spring and summer, usually on a sloping bank or sandbar or on a low-floating log; they often sit at the shoreline facing the water, ready to dash in at any disturbance. Larger Spiny Softshells sometimes float at the surface in deeper water, especially on warm summer days. When not basking or actively foraging, these turtles spend much of their time buried in soft sand or silt. When in shallow water, they can use their long necks and snorkel-like noses to breathe with little effort. However, this species can remain submerged for long periods in well-oxygenated water, obtaining oxygen by cutaneous (through the skin) respiration; vascularized areas in the cloaca, and perhaps the pharyngeal membranes in the throat, may also function in underwater respiration.

Spiny Softshells are inactive and largely dormant from early October to April or even May in the north, spending this time shallowly buried in the bottom substrate. They often enter dormancy earlier in fall and resume activity later in spring than do most other turtle species sharing their habitats. Spiny Softshells are mostly carnivorous, with a preference for crayfish, aquatic insects, and other invertebrates. Small fish and tadpoles are also taken when available. Plants and seeds are occasionally consumed; at least some of the vegetable matter found in Spiny Softshell stomachs was probably ingested accidently. These turtles will actively seek food by probing along the bottom, beneath objects, or in clumps of vegetation, or they may conceal themselves in the mud or sand and ambush passing prey animals with quick thrusts of their long necks.

Many (probably most) Spiny Softshell nests are destroyed by raccoons,

Eastern Spiny
Softshell, juvenile
male

Eastern Spiny
Softshell, adult female

Eastern Spiny
Softshell, hatchling

skunks, foxes, and other mammalian predators. Hatchlings and juveniles are particularly vulnerable to raccoons, herons, and large fish. Adult Spiny Softshells have few predators other than humans. They are extremely wary when basking and can swim faster than most fish. Nesting females on land are rarely far from water; they will usually abandon a nest site if disturbed prior to egg laying and can run with surprising speed. If attacked or restrained, a Spiny Softshell can bite, and its sharp-edged jaws are capable of causing severe lacerations, while the long neck gives it a wide striking range. A large, slippery softshell is difficult to hold. A firm grip on the rear portion of the carapace or hind legs is necessary, using care to avoid the flailing claws.

**Reproduction and Growth:** Eastern Spiny Softshells mate in April or May. Courtship and copulation behavior are poorly known, perhaps because most mating activities occur in deep offshore waters. The male will swim alongside the female while nosing her head and shell, perhaps to determine her willingness to mate. During copulation, the male reportedly rests on or swims just *above* the female's carapace, rather than clinging tightly with the claws as in most other turtle species. Most females lay their eggs in June or early July, often nesting on a warm, sunny morning. Some will produce a second clutch a few weeks after the first. Nesting is frequently a hurried process, with the female choosing a nest site, completing the nest cavity, laying her clutch, and covering the eggs within an hour or less. Preferred nest sites are in open, elevated sand or gravel banks or sandbars as close to the water as possible. The nest cavity, which is dug with the hind feet, ranges from 9 to 25 cm (3.5 to 10 in) in depth and from 7.6 to 12.8 cm (3 to 5 in) in diameter. The eggs number from nine to thirty-nine and are spherical (round), with a hard, calcareous shell. Larger females tend to lay larger clutches. Eggs range from 2.4 to 3.8 cm (0.9 to 1.5 in) in diameter.

Incubation requires sixty-five to eighty-five days, with most hatchlings emerging in late August or September, although overwintering in the nest has been reported. The sex of Spiny Softshells is unaffected by nest temperature, and most clutches produce both males and females in roughly equal numbers.

Hatchling Spiny Softshells may double their length in their first year, but the growth rate gradually slows as they get older. Once they reach maturity, growth rate decreases significantly but remains greater for females than for males. Males may reach sexual maturity at an age of four to five years, while most females require eight to ten years to mature. An Eastern Spiny Softshell captured as an adult lived over twenty-five years in a zoo. It has been estimated that a female Spiny Softshell with a carapace length of 38 cm (15 in) would be about thirty years old, while a 43 cm (17 in) female could be over fifty years old. The maximum longevity is unknown.

**Conservation:** Eastern Spiny Softshells rarely eat game fish, and, while they may compete with fish for food, it is unlikely that they significantly impact fish populations in the region. Due in part to their use of aquatic (cutaneous and cloacal) respiration, they are sensitive to pollutants that kill fish, particularly fish species requiring high dissolved oxygen levels. When fisheries biologists use the chemical rotenone to survey fish populations or remove unwanted fish species, Softshells are often sickened or killed during these operations. (Rotenone kills fish by interfering with oxygen absorption by the gills.) Spiny Softshell Turtles have disappeared from the more polluted sections of many rivers and lakes in the region. Other threats to this species include shoreline development (particularly the reduction or elimination of critical nesting sites), direct destruction by vandals with firearms, and injuries from boat propellers.

These turtles are often captured, and occasionally marketed, for human consumption. They are taken with traps and set hooks, by probing in sand or mud with poles or by hand, and with bow and arrow. A Spiny Softshell typically weighs less (and offers much less usable meat) than a Snapping Turtle of the same length. For example, a Softshell 33 cm (13 in) long would weigh about 3.2 kg (7 lbs), while a snapper of the same carapace length would be likely to weigh at least 7.7 kg (17 lbs). Since few male Softshells reach a size worthy of harvest, mature females inevitably bear the brunt of human exploitation. Most states and provinces now regulate the harvest of this turtle with closed seasons, bag limits, and other controls.

# Lizards (Order Squamata, Suborder Lacertilia)

Lizards are a very successful group of reptiles, with over six thousand species distributed throughout the temperate and tropical parts of the world; one species even occurs above the Arctic Circle in northern Europe. Lizards are much more diverse in the tropics and subtropics and become progressively less so as one moves away from the equator. Snakes are taxonomically a group of highly specialized lizards but are traditionally placed in a separate suborder, the Serpentes.

Only four lizard species occur in the Great Lakes basin, and only one of these is widely distributed and reasonably common. It is thus not surprising that people living in the region are generally unfamiliar with lizards and often mistakenly apply the name to the superficially similar and more common salamanders. Salamanders are, of course, amphibians with typically smooth, moist skins and clawless toes. Lizards are reptiles, with dry, scaly skins and clawed toes on their feet (if they have feet).

The majority of lizards have four limbs, but in some species (in at least seven families) the limbs are reduced in size or even absent altogether. One Great Lakes species, the Western Slender Glass Lizard, is legless. Although legless lizards are sometimes confused with snakes, their external ear openings and movable eyelids are features absent in snakes. All lizards have tails, which are often as long or longer than their bodies. The tail frequently serves as a part of a lizard's defensive strategy. If seized by a predator, many species can detach their tails at weak points, or "fracture planes," in the vertebrae. The separated tail continues to wriggle for some time, possibly attracting the predator's interest and allowing the lizard to escape and later grow a new tail. Partly because many lizard specimens will have lost portions of their tails, herpetologists often note a lizard's body length (as measured from the tip of the snout to the vent) as well as the total length (from snout to tail tip).

Most lizards are predators. Small and moderate-sized species feed mostly on insects and other small invertebrates, while larger species also eat other vertebrates or their eggs. A few lizards are mostly herbivorous, though none of these inhabits our area. Lizards may locate food visually or by scent or they may use their tongues to pick up chemical clues from the environment, as do snakes. These molecules are transferred to paired nerve-lined pits in the roof of the mouth called the vomeronasal (or Jacobson's) organ, which send information directly to the brain.

Lizards communicate with each other using body movements, color patterns, and odors (from glandular secretions). These can include specific head and body movements, tail waving, the display of crests or skin flaps, and seasonal color changes. Males (and less commonly females) of many species advertise and defend territories to assure access to mates or feeding areas and may engage in direct combat when display and intimidation fail. Mating is often preceded by a series of behaviors by the male that aids in mate recognition and determining or inducing the female's receptivity. Fertilization is internal; during copulation the male inserts one of two copulatory organs called hemipenes into the female's cloaca, frequently while grasping the female's neck or body in his jaws.

The vast majority of lizards reproduce by laying eggs, which are usually oval in shape with leathery, flexible shells. There may be some embryonic development prior to egg laying, and a few species (generally in cooler climates) retain the eggs throughout development and give birth to fully developed young. Egg-laying lizards typically excavate a nest cavity in moist soil, sand, rotting wood, or leaf litter or beneath a rock, log, or other shelter. After depositing their eggs, most abandon their nests, but females of a few species (including Five-lined Skinks and Western Slender Glass Lizards in our area) will often stay with their eggs until they hatch. The temperature of the eggs during incubation can determine the sex of the hatchlings in some lizard species; males are usually produced at warmer temperatures, while females result from cooler temperatures—the opposite of the situation with most turtles.

Young lizards typically grow quickly and often mature and breed in their first or second year. Compared to turtles, lizards typically have shorter lives and faster "turnover" in their populations. Few lizards (other than some of the large tropical species) live longer than ten years.

Selected general references: Pianka and Vitt 2003; Powell, Conant, and Collins 2016; Smith 1946; and Sprackland 2010.

# Skinks

## FAMILY SCINCIDAE

This is the largest lizard family, with 1,582 species recognized to date. It occurs throughout the warm-temperate and tropical parts of the world. Skinks are mostly small to medium-sized lizards with elongated bodies and short legs (some species are nearly or completely legless). Their shiny, overlapping scales are underlain by bony plates (osteoderms). North American skinks tend to prefer somewhat moister habitats than do members of most other lizard families.

## Five-lined Skink (*Plestiodon fasciatus*)

**Description:** This is a shiny-scaled lizard named for the five yellowish or cream-colored stripes running from the snout down the back, sides, and tail. These stripes may darken and eventually disappear in older males. The background color is black in juveniles and young adult females but fades to brown, gray, or olive in older adults. Hatchlings and juveniles have bright metallic blue tails. Adult females often retain some bluish tail color, while the tails of males become gray. Adult total length: 12.7 to 21.6 cm (5 to 8.5 in). Maximum body (snout to vent) length: 8.6 cm (3.4 in).

In addition to losing the striped juvenile pattern and fading to a uniform color, adult males develop a widened head and reddish-orange coloration on the snout and jaws. These features intensify in the spring breeding season. Females normally retain at least a hint of the striped pattern and bluish tail.

Young Five-lined Skinks, about 5 to 6.4 cm (2 to 2.5 in) long at hatching, have well-defined white or yellow stripes on a black background and brilliant blue tails.

**Confusing Species:** Coal Skinks are brownish, have a wide dark stripe on each side bordered by narrow light stripes, and have no stripes on the top of the head. (The Five-lined Skink has two converging stripes on the head.) Northern Prairie Skinks have wide tan or brownish stripes separated by narrow black stripes on the back and wide dark stripes on the sides. Race-runners have six or seven dorsal stripes, and dull, granular (nonoverlapping) scales on the back and sides; their tails are encircled by rings of rough scales.

**Distribution and Status:** The Five-lined Skink ranges from eastern New York south to northern Florida and west to Wisconsin, Missouri, and eastern portions of Kansas, Oklahoma, and Texas. There are disjunct populations in west-central Minnesota and northeastern Iowa and adjacent parts of southern Minnesota and Wisconsin. Within the Great Lakes basin this lizard occurs in southern Ontario (from the Lake Ontario region west to Georgian Bay and south to Point Pelee), Ohio, Indiana, Michigan's Lower Peninsula, the western Lake Michigan basin (Indiana Dunes area north to Green Bay), and the central Upper Peninsula of Michigan (Menominee and Delta counties north to Marquette County).

This species is locally common in some parts of its Great Lakes range, but its distribution is quite spotty and colonial in nature, particularly in the north. It is considered endangered in the Great Lakes portion of Ontario.

**Habitat and Ecology:** Five-lined Skinks typically inhabit wooded or partially wooded areas with ample cover and basking sites in the form of stumps, logs, rocky outcrops, wood and brush piles, sawdust piles, and slabs of loose or fallen bark. They are more abundant in ecotone areas (woodland openings or edges, cleared areas, partial burns, etc.) than in unbroken forest. Skinks can be common in accumulations of driftwood along sandy Great Lakes beaches. Moist, but not wet, habitats are preferred over very dry ones. While less arboreal than some skink species, Five-lined Skinks will climb onto tree trunks and up the sides of buildings to bask in the sun or forage for food. Most individual skinks remain within small home ranges of about 9 to 30 m (30 to 100 ft) in diameter for much of their lives.

These lizards bask to raise their body temperature to preferred levels of about 28° to 34°C (82° to 93°F). They will forage and breed at temperatures somewhat lower but not much higher than these levels. If air temperatures are too cool or hot, they remain inactive and under cover. In the Great Lakes area these skinks are usually dormant between early October and late April or early May. Overwintering sites include mammal burrows, rotting stumps or logs, crevices in rock formations or building foundations, and piles of vegetation or sawdust.

Most of the diet is made up of invertebrates such as spiders, millipedes, termites, crickets, grasshoppers, beetles and beetle larvae, caterpillars, and snails. Larger skinks occasionally eat very small vertebrates such as newborn mice, frogs, and even smaller lizards. The blue tail color of juveniles may deter attacks by adult males. Captive skinks have reportedly eaten berries, and it is possible that wild ones will opportunistically do so as well.

Five-lined Skinks are eaten by various snakes, crows, hawks, shrews, moles, opossums, skunks, raccoons, and domestic cats. When warm these lizards are alert and fast moving and difficult to approach. If seized by a predator, a skink will disconnect a part or all of its tail, which continues to wriggle for several minutes, perhaps distracting the predator long enough to allow the lizard to escape. A new tail is later grown, although it tends to be shorter and duller in color than the original. Skinks will also bite defensively, though only the largest males are able to inflict more than a firm pinch.

**Reproduction and Growth:** During the spring breeding season, males will aggressively defend their territories against intrusion by other males while tolerating the presence of juveniles and females. It is likely that potential mates and rivals are recognized in at least two ways—by chemical clues picked up by the flicking tongue and transferred to the vomeronasal organ and by the presence or absence of bluish tail color (in females) and reddish jaw color (in males). A courting male will approach a receptive female from the side and grasp her neck with his jaws. He then wraps his tail around hers to align their cloacal openings, allowing insertion of one of the two hemipenes and effecting copulation, which lasts about four to eight minutes.

Five-lined Skink,
adult female

Five-lined Skink,
juvenile

Five-lined Skink,
adult male (Photo: Bill
Leonard)

Egg laying occurs at least a month after mating, usually between mid-May and mid-July. The female seeks a secluded nest site in an old rodent burrow, a rotted log or stump, or beneath loose bark, a rock, or a board. There she clears a small cavity and lays from four to twenty thin-shelled eggs, which vary in shape from nearly spherical to oval. Freshly laid eggs average about 1.3 cm (0.5 in) in length, but they absorb water and swell during incubation. Female skinks usually brood their eggs and defend them against small predators. They also maintain proper humidity by urinating in the nest and frequently turn the eggs, perhaps to discourage mold growth. Any spoiled eggs are eaten, and a displaced egg is retrieved by rolling it with the snout or body. By basking and then returning to the nest, the female may increase the nest temperature. Incubation requires twenty-four to fifty-five days, and parental care ends when the hatchlings disperse from the nest, usually within a day or two of hatching.

Young Five-lined Skinks reach maturity in their second or third year of life and may live at least six years based on captive longevity of related species.

**Conservation:** This species is harmless to human interests and where abundant may help in controlling insect pests. Five-lined Skinks may benefit from selective logging operations that open the forest canopy and leave behind stumps, bark slabs, and sawdust piles. On the other hand, the clearing of woodlands for development or the removal of fallen logs, stumps, or woody beach debris is detrimental to these lizards. Since Five-lined Skinks in the Great Lakes area tend to exist in small, often isolated populations, even small-scale habitat disruptions can lead (and have led) to local extirpation of the species.

## Northern Coal Skink (*Plestiodon anthracinus anthracinus*)

**Description:** This glossy-scaled skink has a brownish or greenish-brown back and a wide black or dark brown stripe on each side extending from the head onto the tail and bordered above and below by narrow white or yellow stripes. A very faint light brown middorsal stripe may be visible in some specimens, but there are no light stripes on top of the head. The belly is gray to bluish gray. Juveniles have blue to violet-blue tails; hints of the bluish tail color may persist into adulthood. Adult total length: 12.7 to 17.8 cm (5 to 7 in). Maximum body (snout to vent) length: 7 cm (2.8 in).

Fig. 9. Skink chin scales. In the Coal Skink (left) there is a single postmental scale (shaded). In the Five-lined Skink (right) and Prairie Skink, the postmental scale is divided. (Drawing by G. van Frankenhuyzen)

Males may develop orange or reddish-orange coloration on the sides of the head and jaws during the spring breeding season.

Very young Northern Coal Skinks are colored much like the adults but have brighter blue or violet tails. Total length at hatching is 4.8 to 5.6 cm (1.9 to 2.2 in).

**Confusing Species:** Five-lined Skinks usually have five light dorsal stripes and two converging stripes on top of the head. In older in-hand specimens lacking stripes, find the second broad scale behind the point of the chin (the postmental scale); it is usually a single scale in the Coal Skink but split in two in the Five-lined Skink (fig. 9).

**Distribution and Status:** The Northern Coal Skink has a highly fragmented range that extends from western New York to South Carolina and eastern Kentucky. Isolated colonies exist in Ohio and central Kentucky. This subspecies intergrades with the Southern Coal Skink (*Plestiodon anthracinus pluvialis*) in the western Carolinas, northern Georgia, and Alabama. Northern Coal Skinks occur in the Great Lakes basin in the area south of Rochester, New York.

These lizards are generally uncommon and local throughout their range and are rare and very localized in the Great Lakes area.

**Habitat and Ecology:** Coal Skinks typically inhabit damp forested areas, often near water, with ample cover in the form of leaf litter, logs, boards, loose bark, flat rocks, or crayfish chimneys. They may also occur on dry rocky hillsides, shale banks, and standing dead trees. These lizards are difficult to approach during their frequent basking sessions and are most often found while turning cover objects. They are inactive in fall and winter and probably hibernate in burrows or crevices below the frost zone.

Small insects and spiders are the primary prey of the Coal Skink. In turn, these lizards fall prey to various snakes, birds, and mammalian predators. Coal Skinks are secretive and wary and dart quickly beneath cover or even dive into a nearby stream if pursued. As with other skinks, they can detach a portion of the tail if seized, with the twitching shed appendage perhaps distracting the enemy long enough to allow the lizard to escape. The regrown tail is shorter and duller in color than the original.

**Reproduction and Growth:** Most mating occurs in May, with the male grasping the female in the neck region during copulation, as with the Five-lined Skink. Usually in June, the females deposit from four to thirteen thin-shelled eggs in a cavity under a rock or log or other shelter. The newly laid eggs vary in length from 0.6 to 1.7 cm (0.24 to 0.67 in). Females attend and presumably protect their eggs during incubation, which requires four or five weeks. Coal Skinks reach maturity in about two years; their potential lifespan is unknown.

Northern Coal Skink, adult male with regenerated tail (Photo: Richard D. Bartlett)

Northern Coal Skink, gravid female (Photo: by Richard D. Bartlett)

**Conservation:** Removal of critical cover components in the Northern Coal Skink's habitat would pose a serious threat to their survival. Due to the limited distribution of this lizard in the Great Lakes area, it can be assumed that it is vulnerable to local extirpation should its habitat be disturbed or degraded by human activities. The effects of specific pesticides on these small insectivorous animals should be evaluated and considered prior to implementing forest pest control programs.

# Racerunners and Whiptails

## FAMILY TEIIDAE

The Teiids include about 150 species restricted to the Western Hemisphere that reach their peak of diversity in Central and northern South America. Most have small, granular body scales, rows of large rectangular scales on the belly, and broad platelike scales on the head. The majority of species are small to medium-sized and very active and fast moving, but a few are heavier bodied and larger; the South American Tegus (*Tupinambis* sp.) and the Caiman Lizards (*Dracaena* sp.) can exceed 1 m (3.3 ft) in length. One genus, *Aspidoscelis,* inhabits the United States and is particularly interesting in that several species exist only as unisexual (all-female) populations and reproduce by means of the development of unfertilized eggs. The single Great Lakes area species, *Aspidoscelis sexlineata,* is a "normal" bisexual species, however.

## Prairie Racerunner (*Aspidoscelis sexlineata viridis*)

**Description:** This is a slim-bodied lizard with a very long tail and a pointed snout. There are usually six yellowish-green or whitish stripes running down the upper back and sides and often a seventh indistinct brownish stripe down the middle of the back. The dorsal color between the stripes can be black, gray, brown, or olive; in adults (especially males) the neck and forward part of the body may be suffused with green or bluish-green. The body scales are dull and granular (like tiny bumps), the head scales are large and platelike, and the belly scales are flat, rectangular, and arranged in straight rows. The tail is encircled by rings of rough scales. Adult total length: 15.2 to 26.7 cm (6 to 10.5 in). Maximum body (snout to vent) length: 8.6 cm (3.4 in).

The male typically has a more robust head and wider vent than does the female; in older males the stripes tend to be less distinct. During the breeding season, the male's chin and belly are tinged with blue, while the underparts of the female usually remain white or grayish. As noted above, the male's upper body is often suffused with green.

Juvenile Racerunners have distinct light stripes on a dark ground color and bluish or bluish-green tails. Body length (snout to vent) measures about 3 cm (1.2 in) at hatching.

Note: There are three recognized subspecies of *Aspidoscelis sexlineata*: the Six-lined Racerunner (*Aspidoscelis s. sexlineata*) of the east (ranges are detailed below) has six clear light stripes down the back but typically lacks a medial back stripe and greenish color on the sides, while the Prairie Racerunner (*Aspidoscelis s. viridis*) of the west usually has a seventh (medial) back stripe and (particularly in males) bright green color on the forward part of the body. The Prairie Racerunner appears to be the subspecies present in the Great Lakes region, but some herpetologists consider the question unresolved in the absence of studies comparing the genetic affinities of the various regional and nearby populations. A third subspecies occurs in southern Texas.

**Confusing Species:** All other lizard species in our area have smooth, shiny, overlapping scales (skinks) or are legless (Western Slender Glass Lizard).

**Distribution and Status:** The Prairie Racerunner ranges from the Mississippi River west to eastern New Mexico and Colorado and north to southern South Dakota and Missouri; it follows the Mississippi and Illinois River drainages to southeastern Minnesota, western Wisconsin, and western Indiana. The Six-lined Racerunner occurs from southern Indiana and western Kentucky to Virginia and southern Maryland and south to Florida and the Gulf Coast. Racerunners enter the Great Lakes basin in northeastern Illinois and northwestern Indiana, including the coastal Indiana Dunes area (Lake, Porter, and LaPorte counties in Indiana).

A disjunct colony of Racerunners exists in east-central Michigan (Tuscola County); these display characteristics of the Prairie subspecies. Although it seems likely that they were introduced, it is also conceivable that the Michigan lizards represent a natural relict population. Racerunners could have entered Michigan during the warmer, drier postglacial time known as the xerothermic period, when a prairie environment spread into southern portions of the state. Michigan lists the species as threatened. These lizards are at the edge of their range in the Great Lakes region, but they can be locally common in isolated colonies.

**Habitat and Ecology:** Racerunners prefer sunny, well-drained habitats with areas of bare sand or loose sandy soil between clumps of low vegetation. They occur in both natural and human-modified habitats such as prairies, dune edges, oak savannas, riverbanks, abandoned fields, vacant lots, and roadcuts. Shady forests are avoided, but they will inhabit drier, open woodlands, including those thinned by fire or logging. Most Racerunners spend their lives within a small home range, often an area of less than 800 square meters (0.2 acres) and in some places no more than about 160 square meters (0.04 acre), but they do not appear to defend territories. These lizards prefer warmer air temperatures than most temperate zone reptiles do and are normally active only on warm days when the sun is shining. At night and on cloudy or cool days they remain in burrows that they dig themselves, burrows abandoned by other animals, or under surface cover (e.g., woody debris, leaf litter, rocks, or boards). Racerunners have a relatively short activity season and are rarely observed (and presumably dormant) between mid-August and late May, though juveniles may feed until late September and emerge slightly earlier in spring than do adults. Racerunners actively pursue a variety of invertebrate prey, including spiders, snails, beetles, flies, plant hoppers, crickets, grasshoppers, and moths. Young Racerunners may preferentially seek out larger food items more frequently than adults do, perhaps to maximize energy intake as a proportion of the energy expended to obtain the food. As these lizards forage, they continuously "lick" the ground with their tongues, suggesting an important role for the vomeronasal organ in finding prey.

Predators of these lizards and their eggs include snakes (particularly Racers and Milk Snakes), birds, and small mammals. Racerunners, as their common name implies, are extremely fast runners and escape their ene-

Prairie Racerunner,
adult

Prairie Racerunner,
adult with
regenerating tail

mies by dashing to their burrows or nearby cover, often in a confusing stop-and-go manner. If seized, a Racerunner may drop all or a portion of its tail; later a new, shorter tail is grown. However, this species does not appear to lose its tail as readily as do the skinks.

**Reproduction and Growth:** Courtship and mating occur after emergence from hibernation in May or early June. A breeding male may display his blu-ish throat and chest and chase away potential rivals. The receptive female is straddled and nipped about the neck; eventually the male obtains a firm grip on her neck or back with his jaws and twists his tail beneath hers until their vents are aligned. He can then insert one of his hemipenes into the female's cloaca to effect copulation, which lasts only a few minutes.

In June, the female deposits from two to eight eggs in an underground burrow from 8 to 30 cm (3 to 12 in) deep; the eggs are oval, with thin, flexible shells, and on average are about 1.7 cm (0.7 in) long. Older females may lay a second clutch later in summer. Racerunners do not appear to brood or protect their eggs. Incubation requires about two months, with most hatchlings emerging in August or September.

Young Racerunners attain sexual maturity in their first or second year after hatching. Some females produce their first clutch late in their first full summer after hatching, when they are barely one year old. Natural longevity is unknown, but probably few Racerunners survive longer than four or five years.

**Conservation:** Racerunner populations in the Great Lakes area are localized and often isolated and thus subject to rapid decline or extirpation if their open, sparsely vegetated habitats are modified or degraded. Natural vegetational succession that results in increased shade and ground cover could ultimately pose as serious a threat as habitat loss caused by human development activities. Controlled use of fire resulting in maintenance of open habitat could benefit this species, particularly if the burning occurred at a time of year when the lizards were inactive. Pesticide-spraying operations that reduce insect prey numbers predictably would be harmful to Racerunners.

# Glass Lizards and Alligator Lizards

## FAMILY ANGUIDAE

This family includes seventy-five species in ten genera distributed through-out the Americas, Europe, northwestern Africa, and Asia. Anguids are typically elongate and short-legged; many species are legless and snakelike. Their scales are reinforced with bony plates called osteoderms, making their bodies rather stiff and limiting their flexibility. A fold along each side of the body partly compensates for this stiffness by allowing expansion for respiration, feeding, or egg development. One legless species, and subspecies, reaches the Great Lakes area.

## Western Slender Glass Lizard
*(Ophisaurus attenuatus attenuatus)*

**Description:** This lizard is sometimes called a "glass snake," and its legless, cylindrical body and very long tapering tail do give it a snakelike appearance. The tail, if complete and unregenerated, can make up about two-thirds of the animal's total length. The head is narrow (though relatively wider in males), with a pointed snout, movable eyelids, and visible ear openings. A deep skin groove or fold runs along each lower side, from the forward part of the body to the vent. Although Slender Glass Lizards can move quickly and gracefully, they lack the flexibility of snakes due to their stiff body scales. The general coloration is brown, greenish-brown, tan, or bronze. Young specimens usually have a dark brown stripe running down the middle of the back, another stripe above each lateral groove, and two or more thinner stripes below each groove. Striping extends onto the tail but fades about halfway to the tip. In mature adults the brown stripes often fade and break into spots or dashes and sometimes take the form of irregular crossbands. The belly is light yellow to white. Adult total length: 56 to 106.7 cm (22 to 42 in). Maximum body (snout to vent) length: 28.9 cm (11.4 in).

The sexes are similar and may be difficult to distinguish. Males are slightly longer on average and have wider heads than females do and often develop white flecking mixed with black spotting on the upper sides, giving them a "salt and pepper" appearance.

Juvenile Slender Glass Lizards are similar to adults but have more vivid brown dorsal striping. They range from about 11.4 to 18.5 cm (4.5 to 7.3 in) in total length at hatching.

**Confusing Species:** This species is likely to be confused only with snakes, which lack the lizard's movable eyelids and external ear openings. Snakes have thin, overlapping scales and very flexible bodies. A Glass Lizard's scales are underlain by hard bony plates (osteoderms), making its body less flexible. In addition, a snake has a single row of wide scales covering its belly, while a Glass Lizard has many small belly scales arranged in straight rows. When a Glass Lizard is grabbed by a predator (or a human hand), its tail easily breaks off, sometimes into several pieces. A snake does not easily lose its tail, and then only if it is subjected to severe trauma.

**Distribution and Status:** Western Slender Glass Lizards are found from north-western Indiana west through Illinois and Missouri to eastern Kansas and south to coastal eastern Texas and western Louisiana. A disjunct population occurs in west-central Wisconsin, a portion of which enters the Lake Michigan basin. This lizard also reaches the Great Lakes region in the extreme southern Lake Michigan basin, from Cook County, Illinois (where it is prob-ably extirpated) to Lake and Porter Counties, in Indiana, where it still occurs

Western Slender Glass
Lizard (Photo: Richard
D. Bartlett)

Western Slender Glass
Lizard (Photo: Richard
D. Bartlett)

in the Indiana Dunes area. Another subspecies, the Eastern Slender Glass
Lizard (*Ophisaurus a. longicaudus*), ranges throughout much of the southeastern United States. This lizard can be locally common but is generally
uncommon throughout much of its range; it is rare and local within its limited Great Lakes range. Wisconsin lists the species as endangered.

**Habitat and Ecology:** Habitats used by Western Slender Glass Lizards include
tallgrass and sand prairies, old fields, dunes, oak savannas, pine barrens,
other open woodlands, and woodland/field ecotones. Dry, sandy soils are
favored, but they can also be found where soils are fairly moist and loamy,
though shaded sites are avoided. They will bask or actively forage through-

out the day in spring and fall, but during the heat of summer they are most active in early morning or late afternoon or after rain. They are sometimes active at dusk or even after dark. This lizard is active over a wider range of air temperatures than many other native lizard species. By basking they can raise their body temperatures several degrees above that of the air; preferred body temperature appears to range between 26° and 31°C (78° to 88°F) . During very cool or hot weather they take shelter in abandoned mammal burrows or other underground retreats and hibernate in these places from October until April or May. Individual Slender Glass Lizards tend to remain within small home ranges of about 0.4 hectares (1 acre) or less.

Slender Glass Lizards mostly eat invertebrates such as insects (especially grasshoppers, crickets, and beetle larvae), spiders, and snails. Larger ones will also eat small vertebrates, including frogs, snakes, other lizards, and occasionally young mice and bird's eggs.

Snakes such as the Racer are known to eat Slender Glass Lizards; other probable predators include hawks, raccoons, foxes, skunks, moles, and larger Glass Lizards. When active on the surface these lizards are wary and agile and difficult to capture. They often dash for cover in tall vegetation, under surface debris, or in mammal burrows. As their common name suggests, the ability to disconnect the tail when attacked is well developed in this species. Since much of the Glass Lizard's length is tail, a predator that seizes one is likely to find itself in possession of one or more writhing sections of tail while the lizard itself escapes. Sometimes a startled lizard will break off its tail without having been physically contacted by the enemy. A new (but shorter) tail is eventually grown. Slender Glass Lizards may bite if grabbed, but only the largest can inflict more than a hard pinch to a human hand.

**Reproduction and Growth:** Mating takes place mostly in May. During courtship, the male holds the female's head or neck with his jaws while attempting to bring their vents into contact.

In June or early July, the breeding female lays a clutch four to seventeen eggs in a small underground cavity or under a log, rock, or other shelter. The oval eggs have thin, flexible shells and vary from 1.6 to 2.2 cm (0.63 to 0.87 in) in length, though they absorb moisture and expand considerably during incubation. Females usually curl around their eggs and remain with them until they hatch, though it is not known whether they actively defend the nest against predators. Most hatchlings appear in August, after an incubation period of fifty to sixty days.

The young grow relatively quickly; growth slows considerably after maturity but continues throughout life. The females attain sexual maturity in three to four years, and potential longevity in the wild is at least nine years.

**Conservation:** Populations of this harmless lizard are threatened by human activities, such as agricultural, residential, and industrial development, and by natural succession, which may result in open, grassy habitats being taken over by shady woodland. Although natural or human-caused fires can help preserve open habitats, this lizard appears to be quite vulnerable to fire. Many instances of mass mortality of Glass Lizards have been reported following grass and brush fires, perhaps due to their habit of taking shelter beneath surface debris when frightened. Compared to other native lizard species, Western Slender Glass Lizards are slower growing and take longer to reach sexual maturity; thus their populations would predictably take longer to recover from natural or human-caused disasters.

# Snakes (Order Squamata, Suborder Serpentes)

Snakes are a highly specialized group of squamate reptiles represented by more than 3,400 species distributed nearly worldwide, excepting Antarctica, other cold regions, and certain oceanic islands. With their unique body form, snakes have adapted to a variety of habitat types (e.g., forests, prairies, deserts, streams, lakes, and oceans) and a wide variety of lifestyles (tree climbers, burrowers, swimmers, etc.). Although they are outnumbered by their squamate relatives, the lizards, in a count of species, snakes are notably better represented in temperate North America. At least 22 snake species inhabit, or recently inhabited, the Great Lakes basin, compared to only 4 confirmed native lizards.

The fragile nature of the snake skeleton has resulted in a rather poor fossil record for the group, but the available evidence indicates that they evolved from a lizard ancestor in the mid-Mesozoic era, during the reign of the dinosaurs. Although some of the more primitive living snake families retain vestigial hip and hind leg bones (e.g., boas, pythons, and worm snakes), all snakes show a number of unique adaptations to a legless way of life. Their elongated bodies contain from 150 to more than 400 vertebrae, which interconnect to offer extreme horizontal flexibility combined with vertical rigidity. Their internal organs are arranged to fit the available space; most snakes have only one functional lung (the right one being greatly elongated, while the left is vestigial or absent), and the kidneys are in line rather than side by side.

Most snakes have a single row of wide belly scales (scutes) from head to vent, which are important in locomotion. The scutes are attached internally to muscles, allowing them to be tilted outward and then pulled inward. If the snake wants to crawl forward, it extends and contracts its belly scutes in sequence along its body; the scutes grip the ground and then push against it, propelling the snake forward. This type of movement, called rectilinear motion, is usually used when the snake is not in a hurry. To move faster, a snake may throw its body into a series of curves, pushing against the ground with the back of each curve. This movement, called lateral undulation, is also used when a snake is swimming. Although snakes appear to move very fast, this is largely an illusion—the North American Racer, probably the fastest Great Lakes area species, has a top speed of only about 6.5 kilometers (about 4 miles) per hour.

Most nonburrowing species of snakes appear to have reasonably good vision, at least for the detection of nearby motion, but their ability to see detail and detect nonmoving objects may be limited. Snakes lack movable eyelids, but their eyes are protected by a transparent cap of skin called the brille.

All snakes periodically shed the keratinous outer skin layer (epidermis), including the eye cap, to accommodate growth and wear. Skin shedding (ecdysis) occurs from two to four or more times per year, depending on the snake's growth rate and condition. Prior to shedding, a special secretion loosens the outer skin layer, including the eye coverings. A snake in this pre-shed phase is dull colored, has opaque bluish eyes, and will be particularly nervous and secretive due to its impaired vision. The skin is usually shed in one piece; starting at the snout or mouth, the snake catches the loosening skin on a rough object and literally crawls out of it, turning the shed skin inside out while moving slowly forward. A snake that has recently shed may look and feel glossy or velvety, and its coloration and markings will be at their greatest intensity.

Snakes do not have external ear openings but are able to sense low-frequency sounds and vibrations transmitted through their jawbones, and perhaps through the belly scutes and lungs as well. An important source of environmental information for snakes comes from the vomeronasal (Jacobson's) organ. This organ consists of two small adjacent structures in the roof of the snake's mouth; these contain sensory cells that are connected by nerves to the olfactory lobe of the brain. The constantly flicking forked tongue picks up chemicals from the ground or air and brings them into the mouth; there they are brought into contact with the vomeronasal organ, which sends the chemical information to the brain for analysis.

This process might be compared to a combined sense of taste and smell and is used by the snake to detect potential food, mates, or enemies. The tongue of a snake is thus a harmless sensing organ, never a weapon. A unique sense possessed by rattlesnakes, other pit vipers, and many boas and pythons is the ability to detect heat (as infrared radiation). This is helpful in determining the position and distance of warm-blooded prey or predators. Nerve-lined openings ("pits") between the eye and nostril (in rattlesnakes) or along the jawline (in boas and pythons) are the externally visible parts of this system. All snakes are predators and, lacking claws or chewing teeth, must swallow prey animals whole. Their teeth are curved backward to hold prey securely, and their jawbones and certain other skull bones are loosely connected and movable; thus a snake can swallow a prey item that is bigger around than its head or body. Many species have special adaptations to help in procuring food. Some species kill their prey before swallowing it. A constricting snake, such as a Gray Rat Snake or Milk Snake, will seize a prey animal and quickly wrap coils of its body around it, continuously tightening and thus compressing its heart and lungs. A warm-blooded prey animal usually dies quickly from lack of blood circulation or suffocation. A rattlesnake injects venom (a specially modified and complex form of saliva) into its prey through hollow fangs. It then trails the animal and waits until it dies and can be swallowed without fear of reprisal. On the other hand, most of the smaller snakes (such as Brown Snakes and garter snakes) simply seize their prey and swallow it alive; they are thus restricted to eating non-threatening prey such as worms or amphibians.

Male snakes possess paired copulatory organs, the hemipenes, another trait shared with their lizard kin. Mating usually occurs in spring, soon after emergence from hibernation, but a few species also mate in fall. Females of most snake species are oviparous, laying thin-shelled eggs in a burrow or other protected place. However, many species in several families retain the developing embryos in their bodies and give birth to living young; at birth they often emerge from the female's cloaca in a thin membrane from which they soon wriggle free. Some highly advanced snakes, including our native water and garter snakes (e.g., genera *Nerodia, Regina, and Thamnophis*), are truly viviparous; the developing embryos receive nourishment from the female's body through a placentalike connection similar to that found in mammals. Live-bearing snakes are particularly successful in cool-temperate climates and outnumber egg-laying species in the Great Lakes region.

Several scale characters are useful in identifying snake specimens that can be examined closely or safely held in-hand and may allow identification of a shed skin. (These are illustrated in fig. 10 and are included in the species descriptions.) First, look at the upper (dorsal) scales about midbody. Are they smooth and shiny, or does each scale have a keel, or ridge, down the middle? (Rat snakes have weakly keeled midbody scales that may appear smooth in juveniles.) Now count and record the number of dorsal scale rows at midbody, beginning with the row just above the wide belly scales on one side and continuing to the belly scales on the opposite side. Next find the scale that covers the vent opening, called the anal plate. Is it single or divided into two parts? (The vent marks the beginning of the tail.) Note that, unlike the belly scales, the scales under the tail, called subcaudals, are

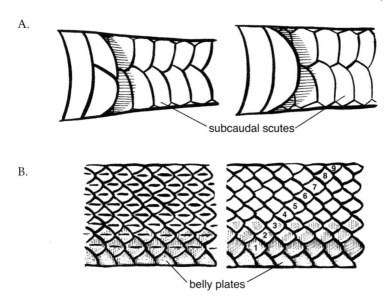

Fig. 10. Snake scale characteristics. A. Base of tail in snake with divided anal plate (left) and single anal plate (right). B. Dorsal scales in snake with keeled scales (left) and smooth scales (right), showing method of counting scale rows. (Drawing by G. van Frankenhuyzen)

in two rows in all our native nonvenomous snakes; the rattlesnakes have one row of subcaudals, except for a few near the tip. Finally, a count of the large labial ("lip") scales just above the mouth on one side will sometimes help confirm an identification.

Selected general references: Bartlett and Bartlett 2003; Ernst and Ernst 2003; Powell, Conant, and Collins 2016; Rowell 2012; Seigel and Collins 1993; and Wright and Wright 1957.

# Typical Snakes

## FAMILY COLUBRIDAE

The family Colubridae contains over 1,800 species or about 65 percent of all snake species. Members of this group are often called "harmless" snakes since the vast majority of species are indeed harmless to humans. However, some colubrids have enlarged teeth in the back of their mouths, and many have modified salivary glands (Duvernay's glands) that produce toxic substances useful in subduing prey and defense. A few tropical rear-fanged species, such as the African Boomslang (*Dispholidus typus*), produce venom sufficiently toxic to be deadly to humans.

Many attempts have been made to divide this large family into a number of smaller groups, most often by studying similarities and differences in the structure of the vertebrae, the hemipenes, and the teeth. Ongoing and future biochemical and genetic studies on snakes will surely result in changes to classification systems presently available. Following the text by Pough et al. (2016) we place Great Lakes region colubrids in the following three subfamilies.

Subfamily Natricinae: Many members of this group are either small, terrestrial, mollusk or worm-eating snakes or larger semiaquatic snakes that eat mostly ectothermic vertebrates (e.g., fish and amphibians). Included are the water snakes (*Nerodia*), Kirtland's Snake (*Clonophis kirtlandii*), crayfish and Queen Snakes (*Regina*), garter and ribbon snakes (*Thamnophis*), and Brown and Red-bellied Snakes (*Storeria*). All American natricines are viviparous (live-bearing).

Subfamily Colubrinae: This is a group of active terrestrial, largely oviparous (egg-laying) snakes. It includes the Smooth Green Snake (*Opheodrys vernalis*), *North American* Racer (*Coluber constrictor*), rat snakes (*Pantherophis*), and milk and king snakes (*Lampropeltis*).

Subfamily Dipsadinae: Many of these have enlarged teeth in the rear of the upper jaw and/or mildly toxic salivary secretions, but Great Lakes area representatives are harmless to humans. Our native Ring-necked Snake (*Diadophis punctatus*) and Eastern Hog-nosed Snake (*Heterodon platirhinos*) are usually assigned to this group, but most dipsadines are found in Central and South America.

## Common Water Snake (*Nerodia sipedon*)

**Description:** This is a moderately large, dark-colored snake usually seen in or near water. The tan, brown, or gray background color is typically overlaid by a variable pattern of black, dark brown, or reddish-brown crossbands and blotches on the back and sides. Complete crossbands usually predominate on the forward third of the body and break up into smaller, often alternating "saddles" and side blotches toward the tail. The blotched pattern may become obscured by dark pigment over time, and older adult Common Water Snakes can appear solid brown or black, particularly when their skin is dry; at least a hint of the blotched pattern is often visible when they are wet. (The Lake Erie subspecies, described below, can be solid gray or olive.) The white, yellowish, or orangish belly is usually marked with a pattern of reddish-brown half-moon-shaped spots, sometimes interspersed with, or grading into, grayish or brownish speckling. There are twenty-one to twenty-five scale rows at midbody; the scales are keeled, and the anal plate is divided. Total adult length: 61 to 140.5 cm (24 to 55.3 in).

Males are, on average, smaller than females and have proportionally longer tails. In males the subcaudal (undertail) scutes number from sixty-six to eighty-four, with the tail length representing 23 to 29 percent of the total length; females have from forty-two to seventy-seven subcaudal scutes, and their tails make up 20 to 25 percent of their total length.

Newborn Common Water Snakes range in length from 19 to 27 cm (7.5 to 10.6 in). They are more distinctly patterned than are adults, with black or reddish-brown bands and blotches on a grayish or tan background.

Note: This description applies to the wide-ranging subspecies *Nerodia sipedon sipedon*, the Northern Water Snake. *Nerodia sipedon* inhabiting islands in western Lake Erie (the Put-in-Bay Archipelago) are usually recognized as a separate subspecies, the Lake Erie Water Snake (*Nerodia sipedon insularum*). Typical specimens of this subspecies are pale gray, grayish-olive, or grayish-brown in dorsal coloration and lack the dark-blotched pattern of a typical Northern Water Snake. The belly is white to yellowish. The average size is slightly larger than *N. s. sipedon* (maximum total length for a female is 144 cm or 56.7 in). Populations of water snakes on the various islands often contain a fairly high percentage of intergrade specimens (having varying degrees of pattern development), along with smaller percentages of the "pure" patternless form and still smaller numbers of the "typical" dark, banded form. The existence of this subspecies may represent a classic example of natural selection, since it appears to more closely match the rocky (limestone) shoreline habitats in these islands (and may thus be less visible to predators such as gulls) than does the darker mainland form. However, the apparent ability of water snakes to move from the mainland to and between the islands and the high proportion of intergrade and "normal" patterned specimens on the islands have led some herpetologists to question the recognition of this subspecies.

**Confusing Species:** The Copper-bellied Water Snake has a plain red or orange belly, sometimes invaded by dark brown or black color along the edges of the ventral scales. Kirtland's Snake has a pink or red belly with a row of black spots down each side. Garter and ribbon snakes have lengthwise dorsal stripes and a single (undivided) anal plate. The Eastern Milk Snake has a black-on-white "checkerboard" belly pattern, smooth body scales, and a single anal plate.

**Distribution and Status:** The Northern Water Snake ranges from eastern Maine west through Nebraska and portions of eastern Colorado, south to Oklahoma and Arkansas, and east to Virginia and the Carolinas. It occurs throughout the

Northern Water
Snake, adult

Northern Water
Snake, newborn

Great Lakes region, except for the northern and western portions of the Lake Superior drainage basin. The Lake Erie Water Snake is found on certain islands in western Lake Erie in Ontario and Ohio, from Pelee Island and East Sister Island south through the Bass Islands to Kelleys Island. They also occur sparingly on the Catawba-Marblehead Peninsula in Ottawa County, Ohio. Additional subspecies extend the species' range from southern Indiana and Illinois to the Carolinas, eastern Louisiana, and the Florida panhandle.

Common Water Snakes can be common to abundant in some places, though many local populations have been reduced or eliminated by persecution or pollution. The Lake Erie Water Snake, once locally abundant in its limited range, has experienced drastic reductions in numbers on many Lake Erie islands in recent years. It is listed as threatened in Ohio and endangered in Ontario.

**Habitat and Ecology:** This snake will live in or near most permanent bodies of water, including rivers, streams, sloughs, lakes, ponds, bogs, marshes, swamps, and impoundments. Fairly open, sunny locations with ample cover and basking sites are preferred (e.g., low overhanging shrubbery, clumps of cattails or other vegetation, beaver and muskrat lodges, exposed root systems, logs, or piles of rocks, driftwood, or human-generated debris). They often frequent waterside structures such as wooden docks, boathouses, piers, bridge supports, earthen or rock dams, rock rip-rap, and causeways, spillways, and flowing culverts.

Common Water Snakes occasionally move overland (most often juveniles dispersing to new habitats) but are usually found in, or immediately adjacent to, water. These snakes are mostly active during daylight hours in spring and fall but may adopt nocturnal habits in summer. When not basking or foraging they tend to remain hidden beneath logs, flat rocks, boards, or other cover. Older juveniles and adults are often seen basking on shoreline debris but dive into the water at the slightest disturbance. A frightened snake will usually hide itself near the bottom for a few minutes, then resurface and swim parallel to the shoreline. If repeatedly threatened, however, most will eventually retreat to deeper water and may remain submerged for over an hour if necessary. Over most of their Great Lakes range these snakes hibernate from October to April, with the actual period of dormancy dependent on local climatic conditions. The colder months are passed (often with numbers of their own and other snake species) in mammal or crayfish burrows, rock crevices, overbank root systems, or other sheltered sites near their summer habitat.

Common Water Snakes eat mostly "cold-blooded" prey; small fish make up the largest part of the diet, followed in frequency by frogs, tadpoles, aquatic salamanders, and crayfish. Insects and earthworms are occasionally consumed, particularly by young snakes, while small mammals (mice, shrews) are rarely taken. Food is located by sight (particularly moving objects) and odor. They seek prey underwater by actively probing into clumps of vegetation or under rocks or other submerged objects and may charge open-mouthed into schools of small fish. On the other hand, they sometimes capture frogs or fish after a slow, deliberate stalk. These snakes will eat carrion, including partially decomposed fish. The Lake Erie Water

Snake seems to feed mostly on dead and dying fish that wash into its rocky shoreline habitat.

Natural enemies of the Common Water Snake include larger predatory fish, Bullfrogs, Snapping Turtles, other snakes (Racers, larger water snakes), hawks, gulls, herons (and other wading birds), raccoons, skunks, mink, and otters. Humans are the most serious enemy of these snakes in many places. A Common Water Snake will try to escape from a potential predator whenever possible but can aggressively defend itself when necessary. If cornered or seized, it may flatten its head and body and strike out repeatedly at the perceived enemy. While not venomous, this snake's tiny recurved teeth can cause pinpoint wounds or scratches that bleed freely and are, at least briefly, quite painful. In addition, this snake can release surprising quantities of a noxious, musky-smelling substance from its cloaca, which may discourage a predator (or human captor) not already deterred by its biting defense.

**Reproduction and Growth:** Courtship and mating occur in spring, typically mid-April to mid-June, and may take place on land or in water. A courting male will crawl over the female, matching her body position and movements, and rub his chin along her back, sometimes with occasional spasmodic jerks of his head or body. He must twine his tail around the female's and bring their cloacal openings into contact to effect copulation. It is not uncommon for two or more males to simultaneously court the same female; competing males may try to shove each other out of position but apparently do not bite or otherwise injure each other. Most females give birth to their young in August or September.

Reported litter size for the species ranges from four to ninety-nine (most often fifteen to forty), with larger females generally producing proportionally larger litters than smaller ones do. There is no parental care, though newborns may linger near the mother for several hours to a day or so. Growth is rapid in the young snakes, some of which may nearly double their length in their first growing season (though the average increase is closer to about 50 percent per year). Growth rate slows considerably at sexual maturity, which is attained in two to three years. A Northern Water Snake lived twenty-one years in captivity, and a wild Lake Erie Water Snake was thought to be twelve years old; the average life-span in the wild is unknown but undoubtedly is much less than these exceptional records.

**Conservation:** This is surely one of the most persecuted snake species in the Great Lakes region. People often kill Common Water Snakes out of fear, ignorance, or the belief that they reduce the number of game fish. Although these snakes will bite if cornered or seized, they are harmless if left alone. They are sometimes called "water moccasins" and erroneously assumed to be venomous. (The true "water moccasin," or Cottonmouth, *Agkistrodon piscivorus,* does not occur in the Great Lakes basin.) Common Water Snakes have little or no impact on sport fishing in natural bodies of water. They tend to eat smaller, slower-moving or injured fish, mostly species less desired by humans, and may actually improve fishing in some places by feeding on fish stunted by overpopulation and by consuming dead or diseased fish. Being opportunistic feeders, Common Water Snakes can occasionally be a problem in fish hatcheries and on fish farms, where reducing their numbers may be justified.

Unwarranted persecution, combined with shoreline development, has led to local extirpation of Common Water Snakes in some areas. Lake Erie Water Snakes have proven particularly vulnerable to these problems, and they now are absent, or present only in low numbers, on many of the islands where they were once common. They are considered endangered in Ontario. Public education programs, combined with legal protection, would greatly benefit remaining populations of this unique race.

## Copper-bellied Water Snake (*Nerodia erythrogaster neglecta*)

**Description:** This large water snake is typically a uniform black, gray, or dark brown when mature, though some individuals may retain a hint of the blotched juvenile pattern. The labial scales are orangish or reddish with dark edges, and the throat and chin may be whitish to orange. The plain, unmarked belly ranges in color from pale orange to red or coppery red, though the ventral scales are often tinged with the dark dorsal color along the edges; this effect tends to be more pronounced toward the rear of the snake. There are nineteen to twenty-three scale rows at midbody; the scales are keeled, and the anal plate is usually divided (single in about 10 percent of specimens). Total adult length: 67 to 141.5 cm (26.4 to 56 in).

Males are generally smaller than females and have proportionally longer tails. In males the number of subcaudal scutes ranges from seventy-one to eighty-one, and the tail comprises 23 to 30 percent of the total length. Females have sixty-two to seventy-one subcaudals, with tails making up 19 to 22 percent of their total length.

At birth Copper-bellied Water Snakes range in length from 21 to 27 cm (8.3 to 10.6 in). Newborn and juvenile specimens have a pattern of dark blotches on a reddish-brown or grayish-brown background color; the larger blotches on the back tend to alternate with smaller ones along the sides, though these markings may fuse into crossbands near the head. Juvenile belly color is often paler than that of the adult, varying from light yellow or orange to pinkish-red.

**Confusing Species:** Common (Northern) Water Snakes have rows of dark spots (often half-moon-shaped) on the belly and usually retain at least a hint of a blotched pattern on the back and sides. Kirtland's Snakes and Queen Snakes also have conspicuous belly markings (rows of spots or stripes, respectively). The little Northern Red-bellied Snake rarely exceeds a length of 30 cm (12 in), and has only fifteen midbody scale rows.

**Distribution and Status:** Until recently, the range of the Copper-bellied Water Snake was thought to be centered near the confluence of the Ohio and Wabash rivers in western Kentucky and adjacent southeastern Illinois and southwestern Indiana. Isolated (relict) populations occur, or have recently occurred, in west-central Ohio, southern and eastern Indiana, northern Kentucky, northwestern Tennessee, and (within the Great Lakes basin) south-central Michigan, northern Indiana, and northwestern Ohio. The northernmost confirmed records are in Eaton and Oakland counties, Michigan, where they are apparently extirpated; old unverified reports placed them as far north as Roscommon County, Michigan.

Three additional subspecies of *Nerodia erythrogaster* have been described, ranging from the Atlantic coast (Delaware and southern Virginia to Georgia) across the deep South to Texas and northern Mexico and north to Kansas, Missouri, and the Mississippi Valley as far as western Illinois and southern Iowa. Thus this is essentially a southern species that reaches its northern limit in the lower Great Lakes basin.

Note: We acknowledge a recent study using mitochondrial DNA that questioned the traditionally recognized subspecies of *N. erythrogaster* (Makowsky et al. 2010) but note that Great Lakes populations are morphologically distinctive and allopatric and choose to continue recognition of *N. erythrogaster neglecta* as a unique population unit worthy of concern.

The Copper-bellied Water Snake is in decline throughout much of its limited range. Within the Great Lakes region (where it is presently recognized as endangered in Michigan, Ohio, and Indiana) it is very rare and restricted to a few isolated colonies. Many populations have been recently extirpated, and those that remain face continued threats from human activities. This snake's future existence in the region is precarious at best.

**Habitat and Ecology:** Copper-bellied Water Snakes typically occur in or near shrub swamps, ponds, lakes, oxbow sloughs, fens, and slow-moving streams, usually associated with either mature or second-growth woodlands but occasionally in more open situations. In spring these snakes often inhabit the open edges of shallow ponds and buttonbush (*Cephalanthus occidentalis*) swamps and frequently bask on shoreline vegetation, muskrat lodges, or woody debris. When temperatures rise and these seasonal waters begin to dry up in early summer, the snakes migrate to permanent waters (lake and stream edges), often using fairly dry wooded or grassy upland corridors. They may become largely nocturnal during hot weather. Unlike the Northern Water Snake, this species may spend considerable periods of time in relatively dry habitats away from water, apparently by choice as well as necessity. They sometimes aestivate underground or beneath logs or debris piles during hot weather or drought. An individual Copper-bellied Water Snake may occupy a home range of 20 hectares (50 acres) or more, but the vast majority of its time will likely be spent in a few small areas within this range.

Declining temperatures in fall, especially several consecutive days with low temperatures below freezing, appear to trigger migration to hibernation sites. These snakes are typically dormant from late October or November until sometime in April, usually seeking shelter in burrows or debris piles that are higher than the nearby wetlands. Occasional individuals will overwinter in crayfish burrows or other lowland sites but risk death by flooding if water levels rise during dormancy.

Copper-bellied Water
Snake (Photo: Wayne
VanDevender)

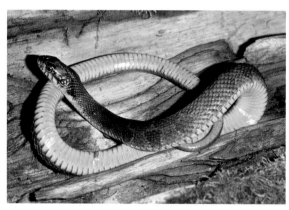

Copper-bellied Water
Snake, juvenile

Most reports on the food of Copper-bellied Water Snakes in the Great
Lakes area indicate a preference for amphibians (frogs, salamanders, and
their larvae) and crayfish, which may reflect this snake's habit of frequent-
ing shallow ponds and swamps where fish are scarce or absent. Fish are
readily eaten when available.

Natural predators of Copper-bellied Water Snakes (particularly juveniles) include large fish, Snapping Turtles, herons, hawks, opossums, raccoons, foxes, otters, mink, and skunks. They are also killed by humans and
domestic animals (cats, dogs, pigs). This species may be especially vulner-

able to attack by hawks and terrestrial mammals when moving through upland habitats; many individuals are found with injured tails, indicating unsuccessful predatory attempts. These are alert and agile snakes—they move quickly on land, and when frightened near water they can dive to the bottom and hide amid aquatic debris and vegetation. They can remain submerged for an hour or more. If cornered or seized, a "copperbelly" may flatten its head and body and strike repeatedly while discharging copious amounts of feces and an odorous musk from its vent.

**Reproduction and Growth:** Most mating takes place between postwinter emergence in April and early June, with a peak of activity in May. At this time the adult snakes are still concentrated at basking sites along the edges of ponds and swamps. Courtship behavior has not been described in detail but appears to be similar to that of the Northern Water Snake. Copper-bellied Water Snakes have a relatively long gestation period compared to most other viviparous snake species in the region. Females give birth to litters of five to thirty-seven young (most often eight to twenty) from mid-September through mid-October. Growth and longevity data on this subspecies are lacking, but captive specimens of other subspecies have survived to known ages of eight to nearly fifteen years.

**Conservation:** The Copper-bellied Water Snake is at the northern periphery of its range in the Great Lakes region, which it may have entered during the postglacial "climatic optimum," when the climate was warmer and probably wetter than at present. It possibly was fairly common and widespread in swampy forested bottomlands during presettlement times, but the cutting of these forests and conversion of wetlands to agricultural uses over the last century have left the few remaining populations of this snake isolated in pockets of ever-shrinking habitat. Human persecution and road mortality are additional threats to already diminished populations. Any attempt to create refuges for the Copper-bellied Water Snake must take into account its tendency to make seasonal migrations between shallow wetlands and permanent waters along upland corridors. Thus, preserving a fairly large and diverse block of habitat is desirable. These snakes may tolerate certain human activities in parts of their habitat, such as fishing, hiking, selective logging, livestock grazing (other than hogs), and harvest of forage crops, as long as the use of vehicles and heavy equipment is restricted to times of the year when the snakes are inactive and the snakes themselves are left alone. Where road mortality is a problem, the seasonal closing or even rerouting of roads should be considered. Public education, along with legal protection, can minimize the persecution of these snakes by people.

## Queen Snake (*Regina septemvittata*)

**Description:** The Queen Snake is a small-headed, slender, brown, olive, or gray snake with a light yellowish or white stripe along each side on the second and upper half of the first scale row. These side stripes continue onto the labial scales and meet on the lower part of the rostral (nose) scale. Three dark dorsal stripes may be visible in young and some adult Queen Snakes. Striping often fades in old individuals, which may become practically unicolored. The chin and throat are yellowish-white, and the belly is also yellowish, with four brownish lengthwise stripes that may merge or become obscured toward the tail. (Note that the two outer dark belly stripes occur on the lower half of the first scale row and the adjacent edges of the ventral scutes and are flanked above by the yellowish side stripes.) There are nineteen scale rows at midbody; these scales are heavily keeled, and the anal plate is divided. Total adult length: 34 to 92.1 cm (13.4 to 36.3 in).

The sexes are often difficult to distinguish based on external characters. Male Queen Snakes are smaller and have relatively longer tails than do females. Males have from sixty-five to eighty-nine subcaudal scutes (average is seventy-six), with the tail comprising from 23 to 34 percent of the snake's total length. Females have fifty-four to eighty-seven subcaudals (average is sixty-nine), with the tail comprising 19 to 27 percent of total length.

Young Queen Snakes range from 17.5 to 23 cm (6.9 to 9 in) in length and are colored much like the adults, although their markings (especially the belly stripes) are more distinct.

**Confusing Species:** Garter and ribbon snakes have an unstriped belly, a light stripe down the middle of the back, and a single (undivided) anal plate. In Graham's Crayfish Snake, the light side stripe is broader (on scale rows 1, 2, and 3), and the yellowish belly is either unmarked or with a single row of dark spots (or a faint dark line) down the center.

**Distribution and Status:** Queen Snakes range from the southern Great Lakes area south to the Gulf Coast (western Florida panhandle and adjacent Alabama) and eastward through the western Carolinas and central Virginia to southeastern Pennsylvania. There are small disjunct populations in north-central Arkansas. Within the Great Lakes basin, this snake is known from the southeastern corner of Wisconsin and northeastern Illinois through northern Indiana, Ohio, and the southern and western portions of Michigan's Lower Peninsula (isolated populations occur in the northeastern

Lower Peninsula and on Bois Blanc Island in western Lake Huron). The original range continued south from Lake Erie to western New York and in Ontario from Lake St. Clair and western Lake Erie north to Georgian Bay and possibly as far east as Toronto, though the species is now restricted to a few scattered colonies in the province.

Queen Snake numbers have declined in many places due largely to habitat degradation, although they can be locally common where ideal habitat remains. This is generally an uncommon and local species throughout most of its Great Lakes range; it is considered to be endangered in Wisconsin, New York, and Ontario and a species of special concern in Michigan and Ohio.

**Habitat and Ecology:** Queen Snakes are most often found in or near warm, shallow, rocky-bottomed streams with an abundance of crayfish; they also inhabit the edges of ponds, lakes, marshes, ditches, and canals. The edges of inhabited bodies of water may be largely open or partially to mostly forested, but totally shaded sites are avoided. These snakes often bask on debris at the water's edge or in overhanging shrubbery or tree branches; if disturbed, they dive into the water and either hide near the bottom or swim along the shore for a short distance before emerging. When not basking or foraging, Queen Snakes often remain concealed beneath flat rocks or woody debris on the shoreline. They are usually inactive at night.

Queen Snakes in the Great Lakes area tend to be active from late April

Queen Snake, adult

Queen Snake, belly
pattern

or early May until sometime in October or early November, depending on local climatic conditions. They reportedly hibernate near the water in mammal or crayfish burrows or other underground shelter.

The Queen Snake's primary food source is crayfish. Since large crayfish are protected by a hard exoskeleton and will defend themselves with their claws, the snakes prefer to eat those that have recently molted and are still "soft-shelled." Prey is sought by probing under rocks and other submerged objects, with the sense of smell (or, more precisely, the large tongue and vomeronasal organ) playing a major role in its detection. Occasionally (and opportunistically) a small fish or tadpole might be taken, but the Queen Snake is a crayfish specialist. Herons and raccoons are known to eat Queen Snakes; other likely predators include large fish and frogs, other snakes, hawks, otters, and mink. Ironically, crayfish are a potential danger to young Queen Snakes, since a small snake can drown if grasped in a crayfish's strong claws. Queen Snakes are not aggressive and prefer to avoid confrontation with potential predators, but some individuals will bite if cornered or seized, and nearly all will smear an attacker with malodorous feces and anal musk.

**Reproduction and Growth:** Queen Snakes typically mate in spring, probably most often in May, but fall mating has been reported. A courting male will approach a female with much flicking of his tongue, probably seeking chemical cues to her identity and readiness to mate. He then crawls over the female, aligns his body with hers, and may (according to one observer) "bounce" the forward part of his body, in a rapid vertical oscillation, on that of the female. To copulate, the male must align his vent with that of the female. In late summer or early autumn (late July to September) the female gives birth to five to thirty-one (usually about ten to twelve) young. The little snakes grow quickly, increasing in length by 50 to 80 percent in their first year and perhaps nearly as much in the second year, after which time growth slows considerably. Both sexes may reach sexual maturity when two years old, but females probably do not actually breed until their third year. Longevity in the wild is unknown, but a zoo captive lived for more than nineteen years.

**Conservation:** This very specialized snake is vulnerable to various forms of pollution and habitat alteration and is now scarce or absent in many Great Lakes area streams that once harbored healthy populations. Siltation from urban or agricultural runoff may reduce or eliminate the crayfish on which Queen Snakes depend. The introduced Round Goby (*Neogobius melanostomus*) fish feeds on small crayfish and may be a Queen Snake competitor. The invasive Rusty Crayfish (*Orconectes rusticus*), recently introduced throughout much of the Great Lakes region, is known to displace the native crayfish that are preferred prey for Queen Snakes. A preference for narrow streamside habitats makes these snakes particularly vulnerable to direct human persecution, and they are often killed by fishermen who erroneously believe that they consume game fish.

## Kirtland's Snake (*Clonophis kirtlandii*)

**Description:** This small snake has four rows of alternating dark, rounded blotches running down the back and sides; these blotches are often faded and indistinct in very young and old adult individuals. The background color is reddish-brown to grayish-brown. A faint stripe is sometimes visible along the middle of the back. The small, narrow head (scarcely wider than the neck) is black or dark brown above, occasionally with some light mottling, while the labial scales and the chin and throat are a contrasting white, cream, or yellow. The belly is pink, red, or orange, with a row of black spots along each side, and there may be some irregular dark spotting between these lateral rows as well. There are seventeen to nineteen scale rows at midbody; the scales are keeled, and the anal plate is divided. Total adult length: 36 to 62.2 cm (14 to 24.5 in).

Adult males tend to be smaller (shorter and thinner bodied) than females, and have on average proportionally longer tails (22 to 28 percent of total length, with fifty-six to sixty-nine subcaudal scutes). The stouter females have tails 19 to 24 percent of total length and forty-four to sixty-one subcaudals. Newborn Kirtland's Snakes range in total length from 11 to 16.8 cm (4.3 to 6.6 in). They are darker above than are the adults, with an indistinct (or nonexistent) blotch pattern, and have a deeper red color on the belly.

**Confusing Species:** Garter snakes have lengthwise dorsal striping, pale unspotted bellies, and a single anal plate. The smaller Red-bellied Snake lacks both dorsal blotching and rows of spots on the sides of the belly. Copper-bellied Water Snakes are larger and also lack the two rows of belly spots.

**Distribution and Status:** This species occurs in scattered populations across west and central Ohio, parts of Indiana, southern Michigan, north-central Kentucky, and northeastern and central Illinois; they have also been recorded in western Pennsylvania and extreme southeastern Wisconsin. Much of its known range is within the postglacial "prairie peninsula." Most recent Great Lakes area records for Kirtland's Snake are clustered near the southern end of Lake Michigan (Cook County, Illinois; northwestern Indiana; and southwestern Michigan) and in Lucas County, Ohio (Toledo area).

This snake must be considered a rare and declining species throughout its range, despite its occasional occurrence in fairly dense local populations. It is presently recognized as endangered in Michigan, Indiana, and Pennsylvania and threatened in Ohio and Illinois, and its future as part of the Great Lakes herpetofauna is precarious.

**Habitat and Ecology:** Kirtland's Snakes are usually found in damp habitats, often in the vicinity of streams, ditches, marshes, or ponds, but they are not aquatic. Open grassy habitats such as wet prairies, wet meadows, fens, swales, and pastures are preferred; they also occur in swampy woodlands, particularly in the unglaciated (southern edge) of its range. This species can be particularly abundant in undeveloped parcels of land in certain large metropolitan areas, but it is unclear whether these urban sites are preferred over more "natural" habitats or whether the snakes are simply more accessible and easily found in these places (since they often hide under boards and other human-generated debris).

    This is an extremely secretive species, which spends much of its time below ground in burrows constructed by other animals, under leaf litter, or beneath logs, rocks, or other surface objects. Burrows of the chimney crayfish are a preferred retreat. Movement through subterranean habitats may be enhanced by this snake's ability to flatten its body to almost ribbon-like proportions. Kirtland's Snakes are active from late March or early April through late October or early November. The same burrows used as shelter during the active season undoubtedly serve as hibernation sites in winter. Most sightings of Kirtland's Snakes are in early spring or fall; they appear to be largely nocturnal, particularly in summer.

Kirtland's Snake,
adult, flattening
defensively

Kirtland's Snake,
adult, showing belly
pattern

Earthworms are the preferred food for this species, although slugs and perhaps terrestrial leeches are also eaten. Captives reportedly have consumed these food items, as well as small fish, but refused to eat small frogs, toads, and salamanders.

Natural predation on Kirtland's Snake has not been reported in the Great Lakes region. Since they spend little time exposed on the surface, they are probably most vulnerable to burrowing predators such as Eastern Milk Snakes, shrews, and weasels. During their brief aboveground forays, they are vulnerable to hawks and owls, larger mammalian predators (foxes, raccoons, skunks, cats), and (inevitably) automobiles and unappreciative humans.

When threatened (especially when suddenly exposed), a Kirtland's Snake can flatten its body to a remarkable degree and remain stiff and immobile. Upon further disturbance or if touched, it may violently writhe its body and attempt to hide its head or suddenly dart into cover. Some individuals will strike and bite if cornered or grasped, but these little snakes are harmless to humans.

**Reproduction and Growth**: Mating has been observed in May under natural conditions. Females give birth to their young in late summer or early autumn (usually in August or September); litter size ranges from four to fifteen. At birth the young snakes are usually enclosed in a thin (chorionic) membrane from which they soon escape.

Baby Kirtland's Snakes grow rapidly, sometimes nearly doubling their lengths in the first full year. They probably reach sexual maturity within two years, with at least some females mating during their second spring after birth.

**Conservation**: The Kirtland's Snake certainly lost the vast majority of its original habitat as the wet grasslands of the "prairie peninsula" were converted to agricultural use beginning early in the nineteenth century. This species is now largely restricted to isolated colonies, often surrounded by intensively farmed or developed lands that offer little or no opportunity for dispersal or genetic interchange.

As noted, this snake has been able to thrive in vacant grassy habitats in and near some large cities; however, these places are extremely vulnerable to development, and many urban sites for *Clonophis* have completely disappeared in recent years. An additional problem is that these attractive and harmless little snakes are sometimes coveted by reptile hobbyists, and surviving urban populations are often discovered and exploited by illicit collectors. This practice is particularly tragic since Kirtland's Snake is considered a "difficult" captive by most herpetologists and zoo professionals; few specimens survive more than a year in captivity.

Conserving this species will require identifying and protecting critical habitats in both urban and rural areas. Legal protection by all states within its range would curtail pet trade exploitation, but a public education campaign would be more effective in reducing incidental collecting and gratuitous killing.

## Common Garter Snake (*Thamnophis sirtalis*)

**Description:** This extremely variable snake typically has three light stripes on a background of black, brown, gray, or olive. The stripes may be yellow, greenish-yellow, brown, bluish, or white. One stripe runs down the midline of the back, and another extends along each lower side, covering scale rows 2 and 3. Occasionally the stripes are inconspicuous or even absent. Many individuals have two alternating rows of dark spots between the stripes, giving them a "checkered" appearance. The head is wider than the neck and is dark above, while the labial scales are yellowish, often edged in black, and the tongue is red with a black tip. The chin, throat, and belly range in color from yellow, greenish-yellow, or tan to white or pale blue; there may be one or two small black spots visible along the edges of some of the ventral scutes. There are nineteen scale rows at midbody; the scales are keeled, and the anal plate is single (undivided). Total adult length: 46 to 137 cm (18 to 54 in).

Males are generally smaller and thinner bodied than are females and have proportionally longer tails. Tail length in males ranges from 21 to 30 percent of total length, while tail length in females ranges from 17 to 22 percent of total length.

Newborn Common Garter Snakes range in length from 12.5 to 23 cm (5 to 9 in) and are colored much like the adults.

Note: The Eastern Garter Snake, *Thamnophis sirtalis sirtalis,* is the subspecies of the Common Garter Snake found throughout most of the Great Lakes basin. Another subspecies, the Chicago Garter Snake, *Thamnophis sirtalis semifasciatus,* occurs at the southwestern end of Lake Michigan, from southeastern Wisconsin through northeastern Illinois to the Indiana Dunes area (Porter County, Indiana). It is distinguished by having the light side stripes on the anterior part of the body interrupted by vertical dark bars; the dorsal stripe may also be broken by dark markings. The validity of this subspecies has been frequently questioned, in part because snakes with this color pattern often turn up elsewhere in the region and in part because it intergrades broadly with the Eastern Garter Snake. Another color variant common in the Great Lakes area in *T. sirtalis* is the presence of reddish or orange color on the snake's neck and sides. A consistently red-sided subspecies, the Red-sided Garter Snake (*T. s. parietalis*), occurs in the prairies of the central and western United States and Canada, but no pure populations of this race are presently recognized in the Great Lakes basin.

Entirely black (melanistic) Eastern Garter Snakes are fairly common along portions of the Lake Erie coastline, particularly the Ohio coastal marshes between Toledo and Sandusky Bay, and at Point Pelee and Long Point, Ontario. Melanistic Eastern Garter Snakes also occur on some Great Lakes islands (e.g., Pelee Island, Ontario, and Isle Royale, Michigan) and, much more rarely, on the mainland. Melanistic individuals are entirely black except for some white on the chin and throat. This color phase is probably inherited as a simple Mendelian recessive trait.

**Confusing Species:** Ribbon Snakes and Plains Garter Snakes have the side stripes on scale rows 3 and 4 (counting up from the belly scutes). Both Butler's and Short-headed Garter Snakes have small heads, barely or no wider than the neck. In Butler's Garter the side stripe on the neck usually extends onto scale row 4. The neck stripe on the Short-headed Garter may or may not touch the fourth scale row, but this species has only seventeen scale rows (nineteen in the Eastern Garter). To distinguish melanistic Common Garter Snakes from other black snakes, note that only the Garter Snakes have both heavily keeled scales and a single (undivided) anal plate.

**Distribution and Status:** The Common Garter Snake ranges from northern Ontario (extending well north of the Great Lakes) south to eastern Texas and the Gulf of Mexico and east to the Atlantic seaboard from New England to Florida. (For notes on variation and subspecies in the Great Lakes area, see "Description" above.)

Eastern Garter Snake,
adult

Chicago Garter Snake
(Photo: Richard D.
Bartlett)

As the name suggests, Common Garter Snakes are generally common and are certainly the most familiar and frequently encountered snakes in the Great Lakes region. Unfortunately, even this tolerant species is reportedly less numerous in many places than it was just a few decades ago. The melanistic form is considered of special concern in Ohio.

**Habitat and Ecology:** This snake has been found in nearly every natural habitat (and some fairly unnatural ones) in the region. The largest populations tend to occur in moist grassy places, particularly near the edges of ponds, lakes, ditches, and streams, and in vacant urban and suburban lands with abundant cover in the form of scattered boards, metal sheeting, and piles of rocks or construction debris.

Common Garter Snakes are active in a wider range of temperatures than are most other Great Lakes species. They generally hibernate from late October or early November until late March or early April but may emerge to bask during warm spells in late fall or winter. Natural hibernation sites include rodent and crayfish burrows, stream banks, anthills, stumps, and tree roots. Human-made sites include road embankments, dams and cisterns, causeways, rock piles, postholes, and house or barn foundations. These snakes sometimes spend the winter in situations in which they are partially or completely submerged in water. Fairly long migrations between summer feeding areas and suitable hibernation sites may occur in some populations, but yearly movements are more restricted in many others. Home range size for this species can vary from about 0.8 to 14 hectares (2 to 35 acres), presumably dependent on the productivity of the habitat.

Earthworms often constitute a large part of this snake's diet, especially in urban habitats, though amphibians, particularly newly metamorphosed frogs and toads, are avidly eaten when available. Common Garter Snakes will eat adult toads, apparently without suffering harm from the amphibians' toxic skin secretions. Other food items noted for this species include leeches, slugs, insects, crayfish, small fish, other snakes, and (rarely) nestling birds and rodents. Prey is located by means of sight and/or use of the tongue and vomeronasal organ and is simply grabbed and swallowed whole.

A great many predators will eat Common Garter Snakes; a partial list would include large fish, Bullfrogs, Snapping Turtles, various snakes (e.g., Milk Snakes, Racers, and Massasaugas), birds (including crows, turkeys, hawks, and herons), and many mammals, from shrews and rodents to foxes, raccoons, and bears. Domestic animals, such as dogs, cats, hogs, and chickens, can take a heavy toll in farming and suburban areas. Accidental and intentional killing by humans is also a significant cause of mortality.

A Common Garter Snake's first line of defense is escape—its striped pattern makes it difficult to follow through grass or leaf litter. When seized, this snake invariably smears the attacker (or restraining human hand) with a foul-smelling anal musk. Some individuals will flatten their heads and bodies and attempt to bite, but most specimens tame quickly after brief handling. Garter snake saliva (in particular, secretions of the Duvernoy's glands) is slightly toxic to some small animals and may help to quiet struggling prey. Allergiclike reactions to bites from this and related *Thamnophis* species have been reported in humans, but such instances are rare, and the garter snake's long-standing reputation as a "harmless" snake is certainly deserved. Probably hundreds of people, including many children, are bitten by mishandled garter snakes each year with no medical effects beyond brief minor pain, bleeding, and embarrassment.

Common Garter Snakes are often found with portions of their tails missing. While many instances of "stub" tails are probably due to unsuccessful attacks by predators, these snakes are sometimes the victims of a parasitic nematode worm that resides in their tails. Damage to the host snake's tail reportedly occurs when the nematode larvae escape to the outside, causing a secondary infection. Intermediate hosts for this parasite are copepods and frog or salamander larvae; the parasitic cycle is thus perpetuated when the latter are eaten by the snakes.

**Reproduction and Growth:** Mating usually takes place in early spring before the snakes have dispersed from hibernation sites. Fall matings have been reported as well. Receptive females secrete chemical substances (pheromones) that attract the males. The courting male will move over the female's body, pressing his chin against her back and sides and rapidly flicking his tongue. Eventually he will lie over or adjacent to her and attempt to align his cloacal opening with hers; often at this point convulsive rippling movements will pass forward along his body. When ready, the female will lift her tail and expose her cloaca, allowing the male to insert a hemipenis. Copulation usually lasts from ten to fifteen minutes, and afterward the male may leave a plug of mucuslike material in the female's cloaca, which may prevent other males from mating with her for several days. It is not uncommon for many males to court a female simultaneously, sometimes forming a writhing mass or "ball" of avid suitors around her. Some males can secrete femalelike odors, perhaps to divert or confuse their rivals while they successfully mate with a real female.

Great Lakes area females give birth from late July to early October, with the majority of births in August and September. The young are usually born enclosed in a thin membrane, from which they soon wriggle. Litter size ranges from 3 to 101 young (most often from 10 to 40) and is directly related to the size of the female. The newborn snakes may remain near their mother for several hours or even days, but there appears to be no intentional parental care or protection.

Young Common Garter Snakes grow quickly, and most will reach breeding size in their second or third year, at about 55 cm (22 in) in length for females and 46 cm (18 in) for males. Growth slows considerably after sexual maturity but probably continues throughout life. A captive individual was thought to have been about twenty-years-old at death, but few (if any) wild ones would approach such a life-span.

**Conservation:** Common Garter Snakes are undoubtedly the most conspicuous and well known of our native snakes, due largely to their ability to survive in urban and suburban settings. Although widely recognized as harmless, this species is nevertheless often persecuted by homeowners and park visitors. Domestic animals (especially dogs, cats, and pigs) also kill them in great numbers, and many others are killed by lawnmowers and automobiles. The use of persistent chlorinated-hydrocarbon pesticides during the mid-twentieth century is known to have reduced many local garter snake populations; newer pesticides used around homes and farms are less persistent in the environment, but more information is needed about their effects on reptiles. Although Common Garter Snakes are adaptable and relatively prolific, they are not immune to the effects of human activities. The above factors, combined with the destruction of wetland and meadow habitats for urban development, has led to local or even regional population declines. It is essential to monitor the well-being of so-called common species, as they are important indicators of environmental health.

## Butler's Garter Snake (*Thamnophis butleri*)

**Description:** This is a rather small, stout-bodied garter snake with three distinct lengthwise yellow, orange, or cream-colored stripes on a background color of black, brown, or olive-brown. Some individuals have two rows of black spots running down the back, between the dorsal and lateral (side) stripes. On the forward part of the body the lateral stripes are on scale row 3 and adjacent halves of rows 2 and 4. The black or olive head is small (barely wider than the neck), and there are often two tiny yellow spots on the large (parietal) scales at the back of the head. The labial scales are yellow, sometimes shaded or speckled with brown. The belly is pale green or greenish-yellow, edged with brown, and there are often dark spots along the edges of the ventral scutes. There are nineteen (occasionally twenty or twenty-one) scale rows at midbody, and seven (rarely six) upper labial (lip) scales; the body scales are keeled, and the anal plate is single. Total adult length: 38 to 73.7 cm (15 to 29 in). Male Butler's Garter Snakes tend to be slightly smaller and more narrow bodied than females and have relatively longer tails. The subcaudal scale count in males ranges between fifty-seven and seventy-two and in females between forty-nine and sixty-four.

At birth the young of this snake range in length from 12.5 to 18.5 cm (5 to 7.3 in); they are colored like the adults but have proportionally larger heads.

**Confusing Species:** Other garter and ribbon snakes have relatively larger, longer heads (except for the Short-headed). In the Common Garter Snake, the side stripes are restricted to scale rows 2 and 3, while in the Eastern Plains Garter and both ribbon snakes they are on rows 3 and 4. The Short-headed Garter Snake usually has only 17 mid-body scale rows and 6 upper labial scales.

**Distribution and Status:** This snake's range is centered in the lower Great Lakes region, extending from north-central Indiana and western Ohio through the eastern portion of Michigan's Lower Peninsula and adjacent southern Ontario. There is an isolated population in southeastern Wisconsin, centered in and near the Milwaukee area, and possible hybridization between this species and the Plains Garter Snake (*Thamnophis radix*) has been reported from this area. Another isolated population occurs in Ontario, in the Luther Marsh Conservation Area south of Georgian Bay (Wellington and Dufferin counties). Some individuals in this latter site have reduced scale counts, which suggests possible intergradation with the Short-headed Garter Snake, *Thamnophis brachystoma*; however, morphological and genetic research to date has failed to support this hypothesis.

Note: Butler's Garter Snake is a close relative of the Short-headed Garter Snake, and both of these are, in turn, closely related to the Plains Garter Snake. It has been suggested, based on available morphological and fossil evidence, that one or more disjunct eastern populations of the Plains Garter Snake gave rise to the other two species, perhaps during the mid- to late Pleistocene or possibly earlier. However, recent genetic studies have clouded rather than clarified the ancestral/descendent relationships of these snakes (see de Queiroz, Lawson, and Lemos-Espinal 2002; and the discussion in Rowell 2012).

Within its known range Butler's Garter Snake has a somewhat erratic distribution, perhaps due in part to the concurrent creation and destruction of its preferred habitat by humans. In most places this species is outnumbered by the Common Garter Snake, although dense local populations can occur, where it may outnumber or even replace its larger relative. It is presently listed as an endangered species in Indiana and Ontario.

**Habitat and Ecology:** This is a snake of wet meadows and prairies, marshy pond and lake borders, and other moist grassy places. Large colonies can occur along railroad embankments and in vacant lots in urban and suburban areas.

Butler's Garter Snakes have a relatively long annual activity period, generally from late March or early April into October or November. They hibernate below ground in winter, taking advantage of rodent or crayfish burrows or the loose soil of ant mounds. They are most often seen in early spring and fall; they become highly secretive, perhaps even nocturnal, during the summer months. Much of their activity takes place underground or beneath sheltering objects or vegetation.

Earthworms are the most common prey of this little snake, though they will also eat leeches, salamanders, and small frogs. Captive Butler's Garter Snakes will eat small fish.

This snake is surely preyed on by most predators within its range; a list of known and likely enemies would include other snakes (such as Racers and Milk Snakes), various birds (such as crows, turkeys, hawks, and owls), and mammals (including raccoons, skunks, weasels, shrews, foxes, and domestic cats and dogs). When discovered, Butler's Garter Snakes will attempt to escape into thick vegetation or under rocks or debris; when seized they expel a musky fluid from the cloaca but rarely attempt to bite. If surprised or uncovered in the open, these snakes have the odd habit of frantically throwing their bodies into side-to-side loops while making little forward progress. This thrashing behavior may possibly serve to confuse some predators, though from a human perspective it would appear to expose the snake to added risk.

Butler's Garter Snake

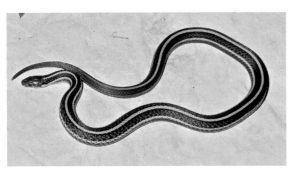

Butler's Garter Snake

**Reproduction and Growth:** Mating occurs soon after emergence from winter dormancy. The basic behavioral patterns by means of which males locate, court, and copulate with females are very similar to those described for the Common Garter Snake. As in the latter species, the male leaves a mucus plug in the cloaca of the female after copulation; this reportedly prevents or discourages other males from also trying to mate with her.

From about half to three-quarters of the mature females will breed in any given year. Females that have bred in spring will give birth in mid- to late summer, most often in late July or August. Litter size ranges from four to twenty, with larger females generally producing greater numbers of young. The young snakes grow rapidly, at least until they attain sexual maturity, which can occur during their second spring after birth. Potential longevity is unknown; a wild-caught adult survived in captivity for two years.

**Conservation:** Some of the largest populations of Butler's Garter Snake have been found in grassy, litter-strewn vacant lots in urban areas, and it is likely that the species has benefited from the conversion of forests into open grassy habitats in both urban and rural areas. However, it takes only a few minutes for a bulldozer to totally destroy a thriving colony, and the rapid development of urban and suburban lands has undoubtedly eliminated this little snake from many sites of former abundance. Numbers of these snakes are killed while crossing roads, particularly in the fall.

## Short-headed Garter Snake (*Thamnophis brachystoma*)

**Description:** A very short head, no wider or barely wider than the neck, should separate this snake from the other striped snakes in its restricted range. Background color above varies from brown to olive-gray or black, while the dorsal and side stripes may be light brown, tan, or yellow. On the neck and forward part of the body the side stripes are on scale rows 2 and 3, sometimes extending onto row 4. There are usually no obvious large dark spots between the stripes, although the stripes may be bordered with black lines. The chin, throat, and labial scales are yellowish, buff, or gray; the

Short-headed Garter Snake (Photo: Richard D. Bartlett)

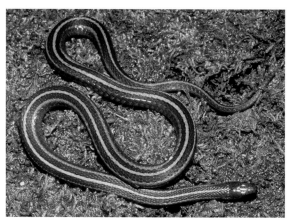

Short-headed Garter Snake

upper labials may have dark edges. The belly can be greenish, grayish, or tan. There are usually seventeen scale rows; the scales are keeled, and the anal plate is single. Total adult length: 36 to 56 cm (14 to 22 in).

External sex characters are not obvious. Male Short-headed Garter Snakes have slightly longer tails than females do; subcaudal scale counts range from fifty-seven to seventy-five for males, and fifty-one to sixty-four in females. Females tend to be thicker bodied, especially when gravid (pregnant) in summer.

Newborn Short-headed Garter Snakes range from 11.8 to 16 cm (4.6

to 6.3 in) in length. They are patterned similarly to the adults but have a darker background color and brighter striping.

**Confusing Species:** Common Garter Snakes and Northern Ribbon Snakes have necks distinctly narrower than the head. In the former the side stripes are entirely on scale rows 2 and 3 and on rows 3 and 4 in the latter. Butler's Garter Snake often has large dark spots between the stripes, a head slightly wider than the neck, and (usually) nineteen scale rows at the forward or middle part of the body.

Note: Snakes that appear intermediate in one or more characters between the Short-headed and Butler's Garter Snakes are sometimes found. It is probably best to identify questionable specimens by geographic location, since the two species are presently not thought to overlap in range. (A problematic population in the Luther Marsh area of southern Ontario is considered to be Butler's Garter Snake but contains a rather high percentage of individuals that appear intermediate in some scale characters; see "Butler's Garter Snake," above.)

**Distribution and Status:** The Short-headed Garter Snake is found in southwestern New York and northwestern Pennsylvania, with its range centered on the unglaciated Allegheny Plateau. It enters the Great Lakes basin in Erie County, Pennsylvania, where it may have been introduced, and perhaps in adjacent New York. Populations also reportedly occur (perhaps introduced) in the Pittsburgh area; Youngstown, Ohio; and south-central New York. This snake is locally common within its limited range but is vulnerable to local extirpation from human activities.

**Habitat and Ecology:** This species is usually found in grassy habitats such as meadows, old fields, pastures, and marsh edges and on hillsides and embankments, but it rarely occurs in shady woodlands. They are most often discovered by turning natural objects (logs, bark, rocks) or human-generated debris (boards, roofing metal, tar paper, cardboard, etc.). Large colonies can occur on undeveloped or fallow land in urban and agricultural areas.

Short-headed Garter Snakes feed largely, if not entirely, on earthworms. In places where this snake is abundant, other worm-eating species (such as Northern Brown Snakes and Common Garter Snakes) may be uncommon or even absent; this may be partly due to food competition, but climatic and habitat factors are also likely to be involved. Like other small snakes, this species undoubtedly falls prey to a variety of predatory reptiles, mammals, and birds. Its primary defense is to escape into thick grass or other cover.

It rarely, if ever, bites when first handled, but it will smear musk on the offending hand and make vigorous attempts to escape; a predator would probably elicit a similar reaction.

**Reproduction and Growth:** Short-headed Garter Snakes mate in early spring while they are still concentrated around winter hibernation sites. Courtship and copulatory behaviors differ in only minor details from those described for the Common Garter Snake. At times several courting males will pursue and coil about one or more females, forming a "mating ball" of snakes.

Females give birth to their litters from late July through early September. Litter size ranges from four to fifteen, with the largest females producing the greatest number of young. The newborn snakes grow quickly, perhaps doubling their length during the first full growth year, and most probably reach sexual maturity in their second year. Growth continues, but much more slowly, after this point.

**Conservation:** Though locally common at present, the Short-headed Garter Snake has a small natural range and could become vulnerable in the future. This species may benefit from human activities that create or maintain open grassy habitats at the expense of woodlands, but urban development or agricultural land use changes can quickly remove this habitat and the snake colonies that depend on it.

## Plains Garter Snake (*Thamnophis radix*)

**Description:** In this moderate-sized garter snake, the side stripes usually cover scale rows 3 and 4. The background color above varies from black or gray to dark brown or olive. The middorsal stripe is yellow, orange, or orangish yellow, while the lateral stripes may be the same color or paler. There are usually two rows of dark spots above the lateral stripes and another row of dark spots below them. The head is intermediate in size between the Eastern and Butler's Garter Snakes, being rather short but distinctly wider than the neck; the top of the head is dark (with two tiny light spots on the large parietal scales), while the upper labial scales are yellow to cream with prominent dark lines along the scale edges. The belly is yellowish to greenish, often with black spots at the outer edges of the ventral scutes. There are nineteen to twenty-one scales rows at midbody; the scales are keeled, and the anal plate is single. Total adult length: 38 to 84.5 cm (15 to 33.3 in).

Males are considerably smaller, on average, than females and have relatively longer tails (23 to 25 percent of total length in males, 19 to 23 percent in females).

Juvenile Prairie Garter Snakes have a darker background color than do adults, with less distinct spotting. At birth they range in length from 16 to 19 cm (6.3 to 7.5 in).

**Confusing Species:** The side stripe involves at least part of scale row 2 in the Common and Butler's Garter Snakes. Both the Northern and Western Ribbon Snakes have whitish or pale yellow labial scales without dark edges, and their tails (if undamaged) are usually 25 percent or more of their total length.

**Distribution and Status:** The Plains Garter Snake ranges from southern Alberta to northeastern New Mexico and east through Iowa, southern Minnesota, and southern Wisconsin to northern Illinois and northwestern Indiana. There are isolated populations in north-central Ohio (Wyandot and Marion counties), southwestern Illinois, and central Missouri. This snake enters the Great Lakes region along the southern shore of Lake Michigan (from southwestern Wisconsin and the Chicago area to Porter County, Indiana); the relict Ohio population is on the extreme southern edge of the drainage basin.

This is a common snake in suitable habitat throughout much of its

Eastern Plains Garter
Snake, adult (Photo:
Richard D. Bartlett)

Eastern Plains
Garter Snake, adult

range, but it is rare and local in the Great Lakes region. It is considered an endangered species in Ohio.

**Habitat and Ecology:** As its name implies, this is mostly a snake of prairies and other open grassy habitats. It is often found in meadows near ponds, streams, ditches, and marsh edges, but it can also occur in drier sites; vacant lots in cities and suburbs may support large populations. This species appears to prefer habitats on moist, black prairie soils (e.g., silt loams and clay loams) and is less common where the soil is sandy and well drained.

Plains Garter Snakes are active during daylight hours, though they spend much of their time hidden beneath rocks, logs, boards, and other natural or human-generated debris. Most individuals maintain a rather small home range, at least during the active season (usually early April to November). Winter hibernation sites include cracks in rocky outcrops, mammal or crayfish burrows, and anthills, as well as openings in house and barn foundations, postholes, wells, and rock piles.

Plains Garter Snakes subsist largely on earthworms, though they will also eat leeches, snails, frogs, toads, and salamanders, and captives will eat fish. They are, in turn, eaten by birds (herons, bitterns, hawks), mammals (raccoons, skunks, foxes, domestic cats), and probably snake-eating snakes such as Milk Snakes and Racers.

This snake is less likely to defend itself by biting than is the Eastern Garter Snake, but temperament varies, and some individuals are rather aggressive. Like most garter snakes, they will release feces and musky secretions from the cloaca if grabbed by a predator or a curious human.

**Reproduction and Growth:** Males locate females by following their scent trails; courtship and mating behaviors are very similar to those described for the Common Garter Snake. It is likely that most mating takes place in early spring, soon after emergence from hibernation, though fall matings have also been noted.

Females give birth to litters of five to sixty young (there is one record of ninety-two) between late July and mid-September. The young snakes grow quickly during their first two years, although females may grow faster than males. Both sexes probably reach maturity by their second spring, with growth then slowing. A captive Plains Garter Snake survived for over eight years.

**Conservation:** Although Plains Garter Snakes are still common in or near some cities and suburbs, many urban populations have been eliminated by land development. They have also largely disappeared from areas converted to intensive agricultural use. These snakes are frequent victims of cars or mowing equipment, especially while moving between overwintering sites and summer habitats in spring and fall. Large numbers of these inoffensive creatures are killed by fearful or ignorant people as well.

## Northern Ribbon Snake (*Thamnophis sauritus septentrionalis*)

**Description:** This is a slim-bodied, striped snake with a very long tail that comprises at least a quarter, and sometimes nearly a third, of the snake's total length. The three yellow, greenish-yellow, or white stripes contrast sharply with a background coloration of dark brown or black. (The dorsal stripe is sometimes brownish or tan.) Each side stripe is on scale rows 3 and 4; below this stripe (on scale rows 1 and 2 and the adjoining edges of the ventral scutes) there is a brown stripe. The head is distinctly wider than the neck, and the large eyes are bordered in front by a light bar; the seven (occasionally eight) upper labial scales are bright white or pale yellow, without dark edges. There may be two faint light spots on the large parietal scales on the back of the head. The belly is an unmarked pale green, yellow, or white. There are nineteen scale rows at midbody; the scales are keeled, and the anal plate is single. Total adult length: 46 to 86.2 cm (18 to 34 in).

The sexes are often difficult to distinguish based on external characters, but females are, on average, slightly larger and thicker bodied than males (especially noticeable when they are gravid in summer).

Newborn Northern Ribbon Snakes range in length from 16 to 24 cm (6.3 to 9.4 in) and are colored like their parents but with proportionally larger heads.

**Confusing Species:** The thin body, long tail, and unmarked labial scales will distinguish the ribbon snakes from all garter snakes in the region. The Northern Ribbon Snake overlaps with the Orange-striped Ribbon Snake (*Thamnophis p. proximus*) in the Indiana Dunes area and, potentially, in southern Wisconsin. The latter species usually has eight upper labial scales and prominent (often fused) parietal spots, and its dorsal stripe is often a bright orange or orangish-yellow.

**Distribution and Status:** The Northern Ribbon Snake ranges from southern Nova Scotia and Maine west through New York, southern Ontario, northern Ohio, northern and central Indiana, and all of Michigan's Lower Peninsula. Isolated (relict) populations occur in eastern and southern Wisconsin. Other subspecies of *Thamnophis sauritus* occur from New England south to Florida and the Gulf states and northward east of the Mississippi River to Kentucky and southern Illinois and Indiana. This snake is largely absent from the more mountainous parts of the eastern United States.

Northern Ribbon Snakes can be quite common in the appropriate habitat, but they tend to be uncommon to rare and local at the periphery of the range. They are considered to be endangered in Wisconsin, threatened in Illinois, and a species of special concern in Ontario.

**Habitat and Ecology:** Look for Northern Ribbon Snakes along the edges of lakes, ponds, bogs, streams, and marshes, especially where there are clumps of grasses or sedges and scattered low shrubbery. Sunny sites are preferred over shaded ones, but they sometimes occur in the more open portions of swamps or near woodland ponds. In the Indiana Dunes area and southern Wisconsin, where this species overlaps with the Western (Orange-striped) Ribbon Snake, it seems to prefer bog edge habitat, while the latter is more common in open marshland.

These are active, rather nervous snakes that are usually seen moving through vegetation near or at the water's edge, though they sometimes move into nearby upland meadows in late spring and summer, perhaps in pursuit of dispersing amphibian prey. Northern Ribbon Snakes often climb into low shrubs to bask. They are active from April into October in most years and spend the colder months hibernating in the burrows of other animals (e.g., crayfish, voles, or muskrats) or in anthills, either close to the water or in higher, better-drained sites.

Frogs and salamanders and their larvae make up the bulk of this snake's diet; small fish are also taken. Unlike other eastern *Thamnophis,* Northern

Northern Ribbon
Snake, adult

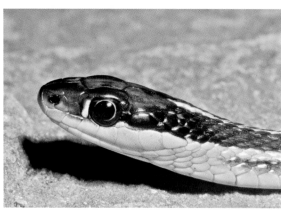

Northern Ribbon
Snake, head detail

Ribbon Snakes rarely, if ever, eat earthworms. Prey is either stalked slowly or actively pursued and is simply seized in the jaws and swallowed alive.

Northern Ribbon Snakes are eaten by many predators of wetland edges, particularly herons, hawks, mink, and raccoons. Juveniles are vulnerable to large fish and frogs. These snakes can dart through the dense vegetation with great agility and do not hesitate to swim to escape an enemy. They prefer to glide along the surface parallel to the shoreline, but if closely pursued they may dive to the bottom and hide in vegetation or debris. Many specimens are found with portions of the tail missing, perhaps attesting to close encounters with predators; lost tails are not regrown. If cornered or seized, a Northern Ribbon Snake may flatten its head and bite (although many do not) and will almost invariably thrash about, smearing musky anal secretions on its tormentor.

**Reproduction and Growth:** Most courtship and mating take place in early spring, often soon after emergence from winter dormancy, but fall mating may also occur. Gravid females may move short distances away from water before giving birth since they and newborn young are sometimes observed in nearby upland habitats. Most young are born in late July or August in the Great Lakes region; litters range in size from three to twenty-six for the species, though ten to twelve is more typical.

The young snakes grow quickly at first, with many maturing by their second year and the rest the following (third) year. Growth slows for both sexes after maturity, though females seem to continue growing at a faster rate than males. Average longevity in the wild is probably less than the ten years attained by one Northern Ribbon Snake in captivity.

**Conservation:** The fate of this species is certainly tied to the availability and health of wetland and littoral habitats and to the numbers of amphibian prey that these habitats support. Populations invariably decline where frequent human activity results in degradation of shoreline vegetation and thus loss of cover and food. Direct persecution and road mortality are further threats.

## Orange-striped Ribbon Snake (*Thamnophis proximus proximus*)

**Description:** This slender striped snake has a very long tail, which, when undamaged, equals at least a quarter to nearly a third of the animal's total length. Of the three lengthwise stripes, the dorsal stripe is usually bright orange or yellow, while the side stripes (on scale rows 3 and 4) are a paler yellow or greenish-white. The background color is black or dark brown, including the narrow dark stripe that usually covers scale rows 1 and 2 and the edges of the ventral scutes. The remainder of the belly is an unmarked pale yellow or greenish-white. There are typically eight unmarked white or cream-colored upper labial scales. The eyes are large, and there are usually two bright yellow parietal spots (often fused together) on the back of the otherwise dark head. There are nineteen scale rows at midbody; the scales are keeled, and the anal plate is single. Total adult length: 51 to 107.5 cm (20 to 42.3 in).

Males are, on average, smaller and slimmer than females and have slightly longer tails, but sex is often difficult to determine based on external characters.

Newborn Orange-striped Ribbon Snakes are 19 to 29 cm (7.5 to 11.4 in) long and are colored like the adults.

**Confusing Species:** Garter snakes have shorter tails (less than a quarter of total length) and usually have some dark markings on the labial scales. The Northern Ribbon Snake is similar but typically has seven upper labial scales and paler, unfused parietal spots. (In the Great Lakes region the two species of ribbon snakes overlap only in the Indiana Dunes area and possibly in southern Wisconsin.)

**Distribution and status:** The range of the Orange-striped Ribbon Snake, our local subspecies of the Western Ribbon Snake, extends from southwestern Wisconsin and western Illinois south to Louisiana and Texas and west to eastern Nebraska, Kansas, and Oklahoma. Populations in or near the Great Lakes basin (in southeastern Wisconsin, northeastern Illinois, and northwestern Indiana) may represent an eastern disjunct population, or perhaps a series of isolated relict populations, possibly the result of postglacial dispersal via the "prairie peninsula." Other subspecies occur in portions of Texas, Louisiana, New Mexico, and northern Mexico.

This snake is locally common in suitable habitat throughout its primary range and in the Indiana Dunes area (although Indiana considers it a species of special concern); it is very rare and local in the Chicago area and Wisconsin (where it is considered an endangered species).

**Habitat and Ecology:** The Orange-striped Ribbon Snake is usually seen in vegetation adjacent to ponds, lakes, marshes, sloughs, or streams. It seems to prefer more open, drier sandy sites (though close to water) in Wisconsin and northern Indiana compared to the moister bog-edge habitats used by Northern Ribbon Snakes in the same area.

The annual period of activity generally runs from mid-April to sometime in October but varies with local climatic conditions. Orange-striped Ribbon Snakes hibernate in rodent burrows, anthills, decaying stumps and logs, drainpipes, and other shelters and may share hibernation sites with other snake species.

Frogs, toads, salamanders, and small fish make up most of the diet.

Orange-striped Ribbon Snakes may depend, at least locally, on the annual "crop" of tadpoles and newly metamorphosed frogs, and a failure in amphibian breeding success (as in a drought year) may be detrimental to their survival. These snakes have been seen swimming with open mouths, clamping down whenever small fish were contacted.

The natural enemies of this snake include herons and bitterns, hawks, mink, weasels, raccoons, and other wetland birds and mammals. Reptiles such as Snapping Turtles, Racers, and Milk Snakes probably eat them on occasion, and large frogs and fish would pose a danger to juveniles. Orange-striped Ribbon Snakes are alert, quick-moving creatures and often elude capture by dashing (or swimming) into thick shoreline or emergent vegetation. Most individuals do not bite when handled (though occasional ones will bite aggressively), but they often smear malodorous anal secretions on the handler.

**Reproduction and Growth:** Mating takes place soon after emergence in early spring. In late summer (July through September) the females give birth to litters of four to twenty-seven (usually around twelve) young. The young snakes grow rapidly and may increase in length by 50 percent or more prior to their first winter. Most will reach sexual maturity in two years or less, with males maturing earlier than females. Some females may not breed until their third year.

Orange-striped Ribbon Snake (Photo: Richard D. Bartlett)

Orange-striped Ribbon Snake, adult

**Conservation:** Orange-striped Ribbon Snakes presumably extended their range into the western Great Lakes area postglacially by following the "prairie peninsula" eastward, and their present scarcity in the region may reflect the loss of prairie wetlands to natural succession and agricultural development. Other threats include continued wetland drainage and degradation of existing habitats by groundwater pollution (e.g., pesticides or livestock waste) and recreational activities.

# Dekay's Brown Snake (*Storeria dekayi*)

**Description:** This is a very small brown, grayish-brown, or tan snake with two parallel rows of dark spots down the back. The spots may be connected across the back by dark crossbars, forming a ladderlike pattern; occasionally the spots are faint or entirely lacking (see below on subspecies differences). The area between the dorsal spots is usually lighter in color than the sides, giving the impression of a single wide dorsal stripe. Some individuals have scattered dark spots along the sides. The head is small and dark above; there is often a vertical dark bar at the back of the jawline, a dark spot (sometimes two) beneath the eye, and a dark blotch on each side of the neck. The belly varies in color from cream to buff or light pink, and there may be small dark dots at the edges of the ventral scutes. There are usually seventeen scale rows at midbody; the scales are keeled, and the anal plate is divided. Total adult length: 23 to 52 .7 cm (9 to 20.7 in); very few Dekay's Brown Snakes exceed a length of 38 cm (15 in). Males are slightly smaller, on average, than females and have relatively longer tails; the male's tail is usually 23 to 26 percent of total length (subcaudal scutes number forty-six to seventy-three), and the female's tail is 17 to 23 percent of total length (with thirty-six to sixty-six subcaudals).

The newborn young measure 7 to 11.7 cm (2.7 to 4.6 in) in length. They are darker than their parents, and have a light band or "collar" around the neck.

**Confusing Species:** Northern Red-bellied Snakes usually have red or pink bellies and fifteen scale rows at midbody. Garter snakes have light stripes along the sides and a single anal plate. Northern Ring-necked Snakes lack spots or stripes on the back and have yellow or orange bellies and smooth scales.

**Distribution and Status:** This species ranges from southern Maine, Quebec, and Ontario to Florida and the Gulf Coast and west to Minnesota, eastern Nebraska, Kansas, Oklahoma, and eastern Texas southward into Mexico and Honduras. It occurs throughout the Great Lakes region except for the area north of Georgian Bay and Lake Superior; it is rare and sparsely distributed in northern Wisconsin and Michigan's Upper Peninsula. It does occur on some of the Lake Erie islands and on the Manitou islands in Lake Michigan.

Dekay's Brown Snakes are locally common in the region but become considerably less common toward the northern periphery of their range.

**Habitat and Ecology:** Dekay's Brown Snakes occur in a great variety of habitats, from dense woods and shrublands to open prairies, meadows, and marshes. Moist soils are preferred, but they are sometimes found on dry hillsides, on railroad embankments, and in pine woods. This species is tolerant of human-modified habitats and can be common in agricultural, urban, and suburban areas, particularly in weedy fields and dump sites strewn with sheltering debris such as boards, bricks, tar paper, sheet metal, carpeting, or cardboard.

These secretive little snakes spend much of their active season below ground or under leaf litter or surface debris, although a heavy rain will sometimes induce them to move about in the open. They are largely nocturnal, especially in summer. Most surface activity occurs in fall (October and November) and in early spring (late March and April), when they are moving to or away from hibernation sites. They overwinter in animal burrows and abandoned anthills, beneath stumps and logs, and in crevices in rock ledges and house and barn foundations. Individual Brown Snakes typically return to the same hibernacula used the previous winter, sites often shared with other small snake species such as various garter, Red-bellied, and Smooth Green Snakes.

Earthworms and slugs form the greatest part of the diet, although snails, pill bugs, soft-bodied insects, and small amphibians are also eaten on occasion. Brown Snakes have specializations of the jaws and teeth that assist them in pulling snails from their shells. Since most prey is taken underground and/or at night, it is likely that food is located largely by use of the tongue and vomeronasal organ.

Dekay's Brown Snakes are readily eaten by a host of predators, including large frogs and toads, larger snakes, crows, hawks, shrews, weasels, and domestic cats and dogs. Ground-feeding birds that sift through leaf litter, such as jays, thrushes, and thrashers, probably take many of these snakes. This is a docile species that rarely attempts to bite; in any case the tiny teeth would be an ineffective defense against most enemies. When cornered or seized a Brown Snake may flatten its body and assume a threatening posture and often releases a musky fluid from the cloaca.

**Reproduction and Growth:** Courtship and mating occur in early spring, with the males undoubtedly taking advantage of the presence of females prior to dispersal away from group hibernacula. The male locates a potential mate by following a pheromone (odor) trail left by the female. The female is approached and identified by means of numerous tongue flicks; the male then moves over or alongside the female, aligning his body with hers. The male attempts to keep his chin on the female's neck and align his cloacal region with that of the female; at this point a succession of ripplelike movements may travel up the male's body, from tail to head. Eventually the male inserts a hemipenis into the female's cloaca to effect fertilization. Sometimes two or more males may court the same female; they may engage in mild shoving to gain the best position, but there is no actual fighting among the rivals.

Most females give birth to their litters in late July or August (the range is late June through September). Litter size ranges from three to forty-one, but ten to fourteen young is most typical. There is no parental care, but newborn Dekay's Brown Snakes often remain in close association for some time after birth. Growth can be rapid, and some young Brown Snakes will nearly double in length by the end of their second summer, when they are probably sexually mature. A captive specimen lived more than seven years in captivity.

**Conservation:** Despite their local abundance in many less intensively developed city parks and residential areas, these secretive snakes often remain undetected (or unappreciated) by their human neighbors. When seen, many people assume they are "baby garter snakes." Dekay's Brown Snake colonies in urban and agricultural settings are in constant danger of rapid extirpation by development activities or exposure to toxic chemicals. They are harmless to human interests and may help control slug damage in gardens.

DeKay's Brown Snake, adult

DeKay's Brown Snake, newborn

These interesting little snakes are worthy of consideration in urban and suburban park and open-space conservation planning efforts.

## Northern Red-bellied Snake (*Storeria occipitomaculata occipitomaculata*)

**Description:** This is a very small, brown, reddish-brown, or gray snake with a narrow neck and small head. (In a given population the brown and gray phases may be equally common, or one phase may predominate.) The upper surface may be unmarked or have two or four thin dark stripes running down the back and/or sides; there is sometimes a suggestion of a light mid-dorsal stripe. The top of the head is usually dark brown or reddish-brown, while the chin and throat are white. There often is a light spot behind and below the eye (on the fifth upper labial scale), and three light tan or yellow spots on the neck—one at the nape and another on each side of the neck; these spots may fuse to form a light collar or they may be absent. As the common name implies, the belly is usually bright red, though it can also be pink, orange, light yellow, or (rarely) gray or black. There are fifteen scale rows at midbody; the scales are keeled, and the anal plate is divided. Total adult length: 20.3 to 40.6 cm (8 to 16 in). The sexes are similar and often difficult to distinguish based on external characters, except when females are gravid and thus heavier bodied than males. Males have proportionally slightly longer tails (21 to 25 percent of total length) than do females (17 to 22 percent of total length).

Newborn Red-bellied Snakes are 7 to 11 cm (2.8 to 4.3 in) in total length at birth. They tend to be darker above and paler below than their parents and have a prominent light spot or collar on the neck.

**Confusing Species:** Dekay's Brown Snakes have paler (cream or buff colored) bellies and seventeen scale rows at midbody. Kirtland's Snakes have a blotchy dorsal pattern and two rows of black spots down each side of the belly. Garter and ribbon snakes have paler bellies and undivided (single) anal plates. Northern Ring-necked Snakes have smooth, unkeeled scales

Northern Red-bellied
Snake, subadult

Northern Red-bellied
Snake, adult in hand

and yellow bellies.

**Distribution and Status:** Northern Red-bellied Snakes range from Nova Scotia south to northern Georgia and Tennessee, west to eastern Oklahoma and Kansas, and north to southeastern Saskatchewan, Minnesota, and southern Ontario; they are rare or absent in large portions of the former "prairie peninsula." They occur throughout most of the Great Lakes region but are absent from the northern Lake Superior basin and are known from only a few scattered localities between the western end of Lake Erie and the southeastern end of Lake Michigan (northwestern Ohio, northern Indiana, and extreme southern Michigan). A southern subspecies, the Florida Red-bellied

Snake (*Storeria occipitomaculata obscura*), extends the range into the Gulf coastal region, from north Florida to eastern Texas. A relict population in the Black Hills of South Dakota and adjacent Wyoming has been designated a third subspecies, *Storeria o. pahasapae*. Red-bellied Snakes in Iowa, Minnesota, the Dakotas, and adjacent Canada may show genetic influence from this race, in which the light spots on the neck and fifth upper labial scale are faint or lacking.

The Northern Red-bellied Snake is locally common throughout most of the Great Lakes region.

**Habitat and Ecology:** This snake inhabits deciduous or mixed woodlands, as well as adjacent fields, pastures, road embankments, marshes, and sphagnum bogs. A moist substrate is preferred, but they do turn up in drier sites. This species is often found hiding under boards and other trash in urban or suburban parks and vacant lots, along with Dekay's Brown Snakes and various garter snakes. Even in more natural situations much of their time is spent hiding under bark, logs, or rocks or in leaf litter. They occasionally bask in the open, particularly in spring, sometimes climbing into low shrubs, vines, and grass clumps. They may become nocturnal during hot weather. Surface activity in summer and fall is often associated with heavy rainfall. Their abundance in northern parts of the Great Lakes basin suggests that they are quite cold tolerant.

The yearly activity period extends from April or May into October or November, depending on local conditions. Mass migrations toward and away from hibernation sites may occur in fall and spring, respectively. These snakes often hibernate in groups of their own and other small snake species, taking refuge in anthills, abandoned animal burrows, old building foundations, and other shelters.

Northern Red-bellied Snakes feed mostly on slugs and earthworms, with snails, pill bugs, soft-bodied insect larvae, and perhaps small salamanders rounding out the diet. Like the Brown Snake, this species has jaw and tooth adaptations that assist in the extraction of snails from their shells. These little snakes are undoubtedly eaten by a variety of predators; a partial list would include other snakes (Milk Snakes, Racers), birds (hawks, crows, turkeys), shrews, weasels, skunks, raccoons, and domestic animals (dogs, cats, chickens). They rarely, if ever, bite in self-defense, and their tiny jaws and teeth would be ineffective against all but the tiniest predators. When threatened they sometimes flatten their bodies and curl their upper "lips" outward in a gesture that might be interpreted as a warning, however futile it might be. As with most native snakes, they can excrete a musky-smelling substance from the cloaca. A few "red-bellies" will, when handled, suddenly stiffen their bodies and roll onto their backs—a behavior that could be interpreted as "playing dead" (but might also be a type of seizure brought on by stress); this does serve to expose the red belly, possibly startling the potential predator.

**Reproduction and Growth:** Mating occurs most often in spring but sometimes in late summer or fall. In our region most females give birth between late July and early September. From one to twenty-one (usually about seven or eight) young are produced per litter.

The young snakes may double their length in the first year of growth, and most become sexually mature in their second year. A captive Red-bellied Snake survived over four years, but the average and potential life-spans in the wild are unknown.

**Conservation:** Northern Red-bellied Snakes are often most easily found by turning boards, tar paper, sheet metal, and other debris at the edges of trash dumps or near abandoned buildings; they can sometimes be quite abundant in these situations. It is unclear whether the availability of such artificial cover leads to higher populations or simply makes the snakes easier to find. Human activities that create open edges in and around woodlands probably benefit this species. However, when roads separate wintering sites and summer feeding areas, large numbers may be killed during spring and fall migrations. These harmless and inoffensive little snakes should be welcomed around yards and vegetable gardens due to their slug-eating habits.

## Smooth Green Snake (*Opheodrys vernalis*)

**Description:** This is the only Great Lakes area snake that is entirely bright green on its upper surfaces. The head, only slightly wider than the neck, is green above, with yellowish or white on the labial (lip) scales, chin, and throat. The belly is white, ivory, or pale yellow. Occasional specimens are light brown, tan, or bronze instead of green; this variant is most common in Wisconsin, Illinois, and northern Michigan. Snakes that are close to ecdysis (skin shedding) may appear dull olive green, then revert to normal bright green after shedding. There are fifteen scale rows at midbody; the scales are smooth, and the anal plate is divided. Total adult length: 30 to 66 cm (11.8 to 26 in).

Males are smaller, on average, than females but have relatively longer tails. Subcaudal scute counts range from seventy-four to ninety-six for males and sixty to eighty-four for females.

Newly hatched Smooth Green Snakes range in length from 8.3 to 16.5 cm (3.25 to 6.5 in). Hatchlings and small juveniles tend to be duller in color than the adults; most are olive green, but a few may be brownish or bluish-gray.

**Confusing Species:** This is the only bright green snake in the region. The green color fades to pale blue or bluish-gray after death, leading to possible confusion of dead or preserved specimens with the Blue Racer; however, a Racer the size of the largest Smooth Green Snake would retain at least a hint of its spotted juvenile pattern. Brown-phase Green Snakes can be recognized by their smooth (unkeeled) scales and lack of stripes, spots, or other markings on the head and back.

**Distribution and Status:** This snake is found from Nova Scotia west to southeastern Saskatchewan and south to Illinois, Ohio, and northwestern Virginia. This range includes most of the Great Lakes basin, except for the area north of Lake Superior and northeastern Indiana, and northwestern Ohio. There are scattered disjunct (relict) populations from Iowa, Nebraska, and Missouri to Utah, Wyoming, and Colorado and south into New Mexico, Texas, and Chihuahua, Mexico.

Smooth Green Snakes remain locally common in portions of the Great

Smooth Green Snake

Smooth Green Snake

Lakes region, but their numbers have declined drastically in many areas. They appear to be increasingly rare or locally extirpated over much of the southern Lower Peninsula of Michigan and northwestern Indiana; the species is considered endangered in Indiana and Ohio.

**Habitat and Ecology:** This is largely a snake of moist grassy places such as prairie remnants and savannas, meadows, old fields, pastures, roadsides, and marsh and lake edges. They also occur in open deciduous or pine woodlands and along woodland borders. Most activity is on or near the ground, though on occasion they will forage in stumps or low shrubbery, and they often bask or hide beneath logs, bark, flat rocks, or human-generated debris such as boards, concrete, or tar paper.

Smooth Green Snakes are generally active from mid-April to late October (probably May through September in the northern Great Lakes basin). In winter they may hibernate communally with other small snake species, taking refuge in underground shelters such as anthills and abandoned rodent burrows. They are active during daylight hours, though they appear to confine their activities to morning and early evening during hot weather.

This is the only Great Lakes area snake that is predominantly an insect eater. They have a preference for crickets, grasshoppers, and hairless caterpillars but also take beetles (and their larvae), spiders, centipedes, millipedes, snails, slugs, and (rarely) small amphibians. Green Snakes may feed reluctantly or not at all in captivity and are generally a poor choice for laboratory study, educational exhibits, or hobbyists. Though well camouflaged in their grassy habitats, Smooth Green Snakes are undoubtedly eaten on occasion by hawks and other birds, various mammals, and reptile-eating snakes. They depend on their cryptic coloration and rapid escape for defense and very rarely strike or bite when seized or handled; in any case they are too small to do any harm to humans or most predators. They will smear musky-smelling cloacal fluids on a restraining hand.

**Reproduction and Growth:** Smooth Green Snakes have been observed mating in spring and (perhaps more often) in mid- to late summer. Females produce from three to thirteen cylindrical, thin-shelled white eggs, which range in length from 1.9 to 3.4 cm (0.75 to 1.3 in). The eggs are laid in shallow burrows, rotting wood, or plant material or under logs, rocks, boards, or similar shelters. Several females may deposit their eggs in the same nest site. The egg-laying period extends from late June into September, with the later dates usually occurring toward the northern parts of the region.

Most Smooth Green Snake eggs hatch in August or September. This species has a relatively short incubation period ranging from thirty to only four days, and at least one anecdotal account suggests that the young may occasionally be born alive. The ability of this snake to retain its eggs for long periods during embryonic development (and, presumably, to hasten development by basking) may be an adaptation to the cool-temperate climate, and relatively short growing season, that prevails over much of its contiguous range.

The young snakes probably mature in their second year. Average and potential life-spans are unknown, but one individual survived for six years in captivity.

**Conservation:** Decreasing numbers and local extirpation of the Smooth Green Snake, particularly in the southern Great Lakes basin, have been blamed on the conversion of its habitat to intensive agricultural use and on the widespread application of pesticides. The insectivorous diet of this species would presumably increase its vulnerability to direct and indirect effects of certain pesticides. This distinctively colored little snake is often recognized and tolerated by persons who generally fear or persecute other equally harmless and potentially beneficial snake species.

## North American Racer (*Coluber constrictor*)

**Identification:** Racers are large, active snakes with smooth, shiny scales and (in mature individuals) a uniform black, blue, gray, olive, or brownish dorsal coloration. The head is relatively narrow, though wider than the neck, and the large eyes are bordered above by distinct brow ridges. The upper labial (lip) scales, chin, and throat are whitish or yellowish, grading to a belly color that varies from black or dark gray to light blue, white, cream, or light yellow. There are seventeen scale rows at midbody and fifteen rows near the tail; the scales are smooth, and the anal plate is divided. Total adult length: 90 to 190 cm (35 to 75 in).

Males have slightly longer tails (on average) than do females; the base of the male's tail is nearly as wide as the body at the vent or may even bulge slightly (due to the presence of the hemipenes). In contrast, the female's tail usually tapers more abruptly from the body.

At hatching Racers range in length from 19 to 35.5 cm (7.5 to 14 in). They are colored very differently than the adults, having a pattern of black-bordered gray, brown, or maroon dorsal blotches on a grayish or brownish background. There are also numerous dark spots on the head, sides, and belly. This pattern gradually fades as the snake grows, with the belly spots often persisting the longest. Most young Racers have lost all traces of the juvenile pattern by the time they reach a length of 70 to 90 cm (27.5 to 35 in), in their second or third summer.

Note: Two subspecies of the Racer are recognized in the Great Lakes region. The Northern Black Racer (*Coluber constrictor constrictor*) occurs in the eastern portion of the basin to the south of Lake Ontario and eastern Lake Erie (New York, Pennsylvania, and eastern Ohio). Mature specimens of this subspecies are black above and dark gray on the belly; the chin and throat are white, sometimes speckled with dark spots.

The Blue Racer (*Coluber constrictor foxii*) ranges from the western end of Lake Erie across northern and western Ohio, northern Indiana, and the southern and western portions of Michigan's Lower Peninsula to eastern Iowa and central Wisconsin; an isolated population reportedly occurs in southern Menominee County in Michigan's Upper Peninsula. It is extremely rare (perhaps extirpated) in southern Ontario, though a population on Pelee Island persists. Mature Blue Racers can be blue, gray or bluish-gray, turquoise, olive, or (rarely) brownish above; the head may be darker than the body, and most have a black "mask" behind the eye. The belly is usually bluish, white, or cream but may be yellowish, especially in Illinois and Wisconsin, where the range of this subspecies approaches that of the Eastern Yellow-bellied Racer (*Coluber c. flaviventris*), a subspecies found largely west of the Mississippi River. Areas of intergradation may be expected wherever the ranges of two subspecies meet (e.g., northeastern Ohio or western Wisconsin).

**Confusing Species:** The Racer's smooth scales and rounded body shape (in cross section) will distinguish it from Gray Rat Snakes and both Fox Snakes, which have weakly keeled dorsal scales and a more rectangular cross-sectional body shape. Young Gray Rat Snakes have a black stripe angling from the eye to the rear edge of the jawline. Entirely black (melanistic) Common Garter Snakes have heavily keeled scales and a single anal plate.

**Distribution and Status:** This wide-ranging species is found from southern Maine and the southern Great Lakes basin south to Florida, the Gulf Coast states, eastern Mexico, and northern Guatemala and west through the central and southern plains states to southern British Columbia, Oregon, and

Blue Racer, adult

Northern Black Racer, adult (left) (Photo: Richard D. Bartlett), Blue Racer, hatchling (right)

Blue Racer, head detail

California. They are largely absent (or restricted to isolated colonies) in the northern coniferous forest zone, the arid Southwest, and higher altitudes in the Rocky Mountain region. At least eleven subspecies are presently recognized, two of which occur in the Great Lakes region and are described above. However, ongoing and future genetic studies will almost certainly result in proposals to change the classification of this species.

Racers can be locally common in the southern Great Lakes region, but their numbers have declined in many places, notably in southern Michigan and northern Indiana. The Blue Racer is considered an endangered species in Ontario.

**Habitat and Ecology:** Racers generally prefer dry, sunny habitats with access to cover, including old fields, hedgerows and shrubby fence lines, thickets, open woodlands, and woods edges; however, damper sites, such as grassy lake borders, fens, and marshes, are also used. These alert animals forage with head and neck raised and often bask in the open, stretched out or loosely coiled on clumps of vegetation or in the branches of low shrubs. When inactive, they seek shelter in mammal burrows or under flat rocks, logs, fallen bark, boards, and other objects. This species is diurnal and tolerates warmer temperatures than most other snakes of this region; body temperatures of active Racers can range from 22° to 38°C (72° to 100°F).

Racers occupy summer home ranges that vary in size from about 1 hectare (2.5 acres) to 10 hectares (25 acres) or larger, depending on the diversity and productivity of the habitat. They often seem to know their home area quite well and have favorite foraging routes and places of refuge. This may explain at least some of the alleged instances of these snakes "chasing" people, for a startled Racer will frequently head directly for a preferred shelter, even if this route takes it directly toward its presumed attacker.

The active period for this species in the southern Great Lakes region generally lasts from early to mid-April until sometime in October. Hibernation takes place in mammal or crayfish burrows, rock crevices, rotted stumps, old building foundations, and other sites that provide refuge from subfreezing temperatures. Very cold winters, especially those with little snow cover, can result in the deaths of many hibernating Racers. When necessary, Racers may make lengthy migrations between summer ranges and overwintering sites and often share hibernacula with numbers of their own and other snake species.

Racers have the most diverse diet of any Great Lakes snake. Included on the menu are insects (especially crickets, grasshoppers, large moths, and their larvae), spiders, frogs, salamanders, small turtles, lizards, snakes (including smaller Racers and venomous species), birds and bird eggs, and mice and other small mammals. Juvenile Racers probably depend more on insects, small frogs, and other young snakes, while adults favor larger prey, especially rodents. Food is probably detected mostly by sight, although chemical cues (using the tongue and vomeronasal organ) play a part as well. Most prey animals are simply chased down, seized, and swallowed; these snakes are attracted to movement, and a potential victim that remains still may avoid detection. Racers do not constrict their prey (contrary to the implication of their scientific name), but larger or more active animals may be held down by a coil of the body and "chewed" into submission.

Racers, particularly the juveniles, are potentially eaten by many predators, including larger Racers and other snake-eating snakes, hawks, turkeys, crows, and mammals such as skunks, raccoons, foxes, and domestic dogs and cats. Racer eggs are vulnerable to some of these same enemies. Shrews and mice may threaten these snakes during winter dormancy or other periods of inactivity.

A Racer's first line of defense is its speed and agility, and the vast majority will attempt to escape a potential predator (or approaching human) if given an opportunity to do so, darting into a burrow, thick vegetation, or rock crevice or climbing into a tree or shrub. They are relatively fast-moving animals, though human observers tend to overestimate the Racer's actual speed, which probably does not exceed about 6.5 km (4 mi) per hour—or about the rate of a fast walk for a human. If cornered, a typical Racer will coil and strike, while vibrating its tail nervously. The Racer is nonvenomous, but the slashing bite and sharp recurved teeth can leave scratches on human skin that may bleed freely for several minutes. They will also release a foul-smelling anal musk, particularly after being seized or injured. Racers rarely become tame or accept confinement and are poor candidates for pets or captive study.

**Reproduction and Growth:** Mating takes place in spring, from late April into early June. During this season the males may appear quite nervous and excitable, and perhaps become somewhat territorial, although there is little evidence that they actually defend areas or females against other males. Occasional reports of Racers "holding their ground" or even acting aggressively toward people may be based in part on encounters with feisty territorial males.

Males probably locate prospective mates by following their pheromone (chemical scent) trails, and two or more males may end up courting the same female. During courtship the male attempts to move over or alongside the female; rippling movements may travel down his body at this time. The pair often entwine their bodies, or at least their tails, as the male tries to align his vent with that of the female; a receptive female will raise her tail to assist copulation.

In June or early July the female Racer will lay from three to thirty-two (usually eight to twenty) eggs in a hidden nest site such as in an old mammal burrow, in a rotted stump or log, under a rock or board, or in a new cavity in sand, sawdust, or leaf litter. Two or more females sometimes share a nest site. The oval, white eggs range in length from 2.5 to 3.9 cm (1 to 1.5 in) and, when freshly laid, have leathery, flexible shells with a rough granular texture (appearing as though they were sprinkled with salt). As incubation progresses, the eggs swell and become firmer and may nearly double in size by the time they hatch, which usually occurs in August or early September. The hatchling Racers grow quickly, with some individuals increasing in length by 50 percent or more prior to their first winter. Males become sexually mature in one to two years, females in two to three, after which growth continues at a slower rate. Racers are comparatively long-lived snakes, sometimes exceeding an age of ten years in the wild.

**Conservation:** These large, active snakes require relatively large areas of habitat, and their populations quickly decline in the face of intensive agriculture or suburban/urban development. Pesticide residues pose a danger, particularly to the insectivorous young Racers. Additional problems include road mortality and direct killing of snakes by people. The tendency of Racers to converge in numbers on a few favored winter dens makes them vulnerable to mass destruction by intolerant humans. These snakes undoubtedly have economic value as destroyers of rodent and insect pests. Despite their occasional displays of bravado, Racers are harmless to people willing to leave them alone.

## Gray (Central) Rat Snake (*Pantherophis spiloides*)

**Description:** This is the largest snake in the Great Lakes region. Adult Gray Rat Snakes are mostly black or dark gray and/or dark brown above, with white on the labial scales, chin, and throat. An indication of the blotched juvenile color pattern may persist well into adulthood (or throughout life in some individuals and populations); most older specimens show at least a trace of white, yellow, or orange flecking, especially on the skin between the body scales. The head is distinct from the neck, rather elongated and flattened, and widest behind the eyes. The belly may be whitish or yellowish, marked with a dark checkerboard pattern on the forward part of the body but becoming clouded by gray or brown toward the midbody and tail. The body is rather rectangular in cross section, with fairly straight sides and a flat belly. There are twenty-three to twenty-seven scale rows at midbody; the upper midbody scales are weakly keeled (often unkeeled elsewhere), and the anal plate is divided. Total adult length: 100 to 256.5 cm (40 to 101 in).

The sexes are difficult to distinguish based on external characters. Males have slightly longer tails relative to total length; the female's tail tends to taper quite rapidly from the body (particularly noticeable in gravid females), while the male's tail tapers more gradually from the body. Newly hatched young Gray Rat Snakes are strongly patterned, with a dorsal row of dark gray or brown saddles alternating with smaller side blotches on a pale gray background. There is a black band just in front of (and connecting) the eyes and a black stripe slanting from behind the eye to the rear edge of the jawline. Hatchlings range in length from 27 to 37 cm (10.6 to 14.5 in).

**Confusing Species:** Racers have smooth scales and a rounded body in cross section; juvenile Racers lack the stripe from the eye to the rear edge of the mouth seen in Rat Snakes. Western and Eastern Fox Snakes generally display a lighter brown background color and retain a prominently blotched pattern throughout life; they have 213 or fewer ventral scutes (there are 221 or more ventral scutes in Gray Rat Snakes).

**Distribution and Status:** Gray Rat Snakes are found from western New York east to Wisconsin and extreme southeastern Minnesota south through Kentucky and Tennessee to the Gulf Coast from Alabama to eastern Louisiana. In the Great Lakes region they occur south of Lake Ontario and west through the Lake Erie basin and southern lower Michigan to the southern end of Lake Michigan. A disjunct population occurs near the eastern end of Lake Ontario (in the Frontenac Axis of Ontario and adjacent New York).

Note: Prior to 2001, the Gray Rat Snake was known as the Black Rat Snake (*Elaphe obsoleta obsoleta*) in our area, which was one of several subspecies of *Elaphe obsoleta* that ranged to the East (Atlantic) Coast south to Florida and west to the southern and central Great Plains. A genetic and morphological analysis by Burbrink (2001) resulted in the discarding of these subspecies and the naming of three separate species; a year later the genus *Elaphe* was split into several new genera by Utiger et al. (2002). The Gray Rat Snake (now *Pantherophis spiloides*) occupies the central portion of the original range, including the Great Lakes region, hence the alternative common names "central" or "midland" rat snake. To add to the potential confusion, the rat snakes in eastern Ontario may be hybrids between this species and the Eastern Rat Snake, *Pantherophis alleghaniensis* (Gibbs et al. 2006).

The Gray Rat Snake is uncommon to rare and local over most of the Great Lakes region. Many populations have been greatly reduced or extirpated in recent decades, particularly in the western and northern Lake Erie watershed in Ontario and southern Michigan. It is a species of special concern in Michigan and is considered endangered in Ontario.

**Habitat and Ecology:** Gray Rat Snakes typically occur in or near woodlands but also use adjacent open habitats such as shrubby fields, pastures, hedgerows, and marsh and bog edges. They often forage or seek shelter in or around barns, outbuildings, old foundations, trash dumps, and abandoned cars or farm machinery. They are quite arboreal, sometimes climbing as high as 9 to 12 m (30 to 40 ft) and are capable of scaling vertical surfaces such as tree trunks, fence posts, and the sides of buildings. These snakes are usually active from late April through October. They are largely diurnal in spring and fall but may forage in the early evening or even at night during hot summer weather. In fall they move to den sites that offer refuge from freezing temperatures, such as mammal burrows, tree root systems, or deep rock crevices. Rat Snakes may hibernate communally with other large snakes such as Racers and Timber Rattlesnakes, and they often return to

Gray Rat Snake,
young adult

Gray Rat Snake,
hatchling

Gray Rat Snake,
constricting prey

previously used hibernacula. (This species was often called the "pilot black snake" in past years due to the erroneous belief that it leads Timber Rattlesnakes and Copperheads to winter dens.)

Gray Rat Snakes may occupy specific home ranges for much of their lives; an average home range would be about 600 m (2,000 ft) in diameter, based on studies outside the Great Lakes area. There is no evidence that these snakes actually defend territories against others of their kind, but males will engage in ritualized combat behavior, probably to establish social dominance related to reproduction. During combat episodes, a male attempts to pin his rival down using his head and body. The efforts of each male to "top" the other results in considerable twining, jerking, and occasional biting; eventually one combatant will tire and try to escape the confrontation.

Small mammals make up the largest part of this snake's diet, followed by birds and bird eggs. Mice, rats, chipmunks, squirrels, shrews, moles, rabbits, opossums, and other larger prey animals are killed by constriction prior to being swallowed. Most birds are taken as nestlings, which, along with eggs and other small, nonthreatening prey, may be simply seized and swallowed. Juvenile Gray Rat Snakes (and occasionally the adults) will also eat small frogs, reptiles, and reptile eggs. Adult Gray Rat Snakes appear to have relatively few enemies other than people. Large hawks and owls are probably the most important natural predators, though the snakes could also be attacked by mammals such as raccoons, coyotes, dogs, and swine. The list of enemies for juvenile Rat Snakes would be longer and could include shrews, weasels, and other snakes. The defensive attitude of this snake varies considerably between individuals. They are a relatively slow-moving species compared to most other large snakes, and many adults will "freeze" when confronted with danger, perhaps to reduce the chances of being detected. Some individuals (especially older adults) refuse to defend themselves even when handled. However, most juveniles and some adults will coil, vibrate their tails, and strike if cornered or seized. They can also release a foul-smelling musk from the cloaca.

**Reproduction:** Mating occurs in spring, mostly in May and early June. Gray Rat Snake courtship is similar in many respects to that of the Racer but is comparatively a more slow-motion affair, in keeping with this species' more placid demeanor. The male presses his chin on a receptive female's back and moves forward, aligning his body with hers; waves of rippling muscular contractions often move forward along the male's lower body, and he may also grasp the female's neck or body with his jaws. Cloacal contact is accomplished after much tail twitching and twining, with copulation lasting about twenty minutes on average.

Females lay their eggs in summer, between late June and early August. Typical nest sites include burrows in loose soil or leaf mold, rotted stumps or logs, manure or sawdust piles, and cavities under rocks or boards. At times, two or more females will share a nest site. The eggs number from five to forty-four (usually about a dozen) per clutch; have flexible, granular shells; and may stick to each another in a clump. They are oval to almost spherical in shape and range in length from 3.5 to 5.5 cm (1.4 to 2.1 in).

Incubation takes from sixty to seventy-five days, with most hatchlings emerging in late August or September. The young snakes grow relatively quickly at first, but then growth slows, and they probably do not reach sexual maturity until their fourth or fifth year; in some northern populations ten or more years may be required. This is a potentially long-lived snake, with a known life-span (in a captive) of nearly twenty-three years.

**Conservation:** Gray Rat Snakes are harmless to humans and are economically useful in the destruction of rodent pests around farms and gardens. The fact that they also eat birds may be objectionable to some people, but their impact on bird numbers would be insignificant compared to that of more abundant bird predators.

This species requires a comparatively large living area and certainly has suffered from the loss of forest and forest-edge habitats to intensive agriculture and urbanization. However, the species can benefit when logging and low-intensity agriculture or livestock grazing create a mosaic of wooded and open land. There are many areas in the lower Great Lakes region that could (and, in many cases, once did) support healthy Gray Rat Snake populations, and the species' scarcity or absence in such places suggests that additional problems exist. These conspicuous and slow-moving snakes are frequent victims of human persecution and destruction on roads; these losses may pose a serious threat to a slow-growing species already stressed by habitat degradation.

## Western Fox Snake (*Pantherophis vulpinus*)

**Description:** This fairly large, stout-bodied snake has a row of dark brown or black blotches running down the back and onto the tail, alternating with smaller dark blotches on the sides. The background color is usually dull yellow to yellowish-brown, grayish-brown, or tan, sometimes grading to orangish on the tail. The head is distinct from the neck and widest behind the eyes, and the snout is bluntly rounded. The head varies in color from a yellowish or reddish brown to coppery orange; many (especially younger) individuals have a dark band between the eyes that continues behind the eye to the end of the jawline (a vestige of the darker juvenile pattern). The belly is yellowish to cream with scattered squarish dark spots. The tail is stout, tapering to a spinelike tip. There are twenty-three to twenty-five scale rows at midbody; the scales are keeled on the upper back, becoming smooth on the sides, and the anal plate is divided. Total adult length: 90 to 155 cm (35.4 to 61 in).

Male Western Fox Snakes attain a slightly larger body size than do females and have comparatively longer tails. Males have fifty-two to seventy-one subcaudal scutes, while females have forty-five to sixty.

Young Western Fox Snakes range in length from 23 to 31 cm (9 to 12.2 in) at hatching. They have gray or brown, black-bordered blotches on a light gray background; the head markings are distinct, with a dark band in front of the eyes and a stripe slanting from the back of each eye to the end of the jawline.

**Confusing Species:** Eastern Milk Snakes have smooth scales and single anal plates. Juvenile Racers have smooth scales and lack the stripe from the eye to the mouth. Bullsnakes have more heavily keeled scales, single anal plates, and rather pointed snouts (bluntly rounded in the Western Fox

Western Fox Snake,
adult

Western Fox Snake,
head detail

Snake). Juvenile Gray Rat Snakes are similar but have more than 220 ventral scutes (there are 216 or fewer in both Fox Snakes). The range of the Eastern Fox Snake does not overlap that of the Western Fox Snake, but captives of unknown origin could be confusing. Easterns have fewer but larger dorsal blotches on the body (from twenty-eight to forty-three, averaging thirty-four) and tail, while Westerns have a greater number of smaller dorsal body blotches (from thirty-two to fifty-two, averaging forty-one); those with blotch numbers within the range of overlap may not be identifiable.

**Distribution and Status:** This species ranges from the central Upper Peninsula of Michigan south through most of Wisconsin to northern Illinois, and the northwestern corner of Indiana. Its Great Lakes range extends from upper Michigan through the western Lake Michigan basin in eastern Wisconsin and Illinois to the Indiana Dunes area. Recent records for this snake on South Fox Island and North Manitou Island in northern Lake Michigan may indicate that occasional over-water dispersal is possible in this species.

Note: This species and the Eastern Fox Snake (discussed below) are considered subspecies of *Pantherophis vulpinus* by some herpetologists; we tentatively recognize them as full species due to the complete separation of populations (allopatry) and consistent, though overlapping, differences in color pattern and habitat preferences, which suggest diverging evolutionary trajectories. We also note that the North American herpetological checklist published by the Society for the Study of Amphibians and Reptiles (Crother 2012) recognizes a separate fox snake species, *Pantherophis ramspotti*, west of the Mississippi River (see Crother et al. 2011 and Row et al. 2011, for further discussion on fox snake taxonomy).

Western Fox Snakes are locally common in their Great Lakes range.

**Habitat and Ecology:** This is a snake of prairie, pasture, and farmland in the southern and western parts of its range, but it inhabits open woodland and forest-edge habitats farther north. In northern Michigan and Wisconsin they occur in pine and oak woodlands and adjacent farm fields and stumpy, brush-covered clear-cuts (people in upper Michigan and Wisconsin often call this species "pine snake"). They occur in dry habitats as well as moister sites near streams or ponds.

Western Fox Snakes are less arboreal than the Gray Rat Snake but occasionally climb into low shrubs, stumps, and abandoned buildings. Although most active during the day, much of their foraging occurs out of sight in rodent burrows or under rock or trash piles. They sometimes move about on warm rainy nights. They hibernate, often communally, from late October until mid-April in dens that offer refuge from freezing temperatures, such as mammal burrows, rock crevices, and old wells and barn foundations. In some den sites the snakes successfully overwinter while submerged in water.

Small mammals such as mice, voles, chipmunks, ground squirrels, gophers, and baby rabbits are this snake's favored prey, but bird eggs and nestlings are also eaten when available. Juveniles will also eat insects, earthworms, frogs, and small reptiles. Prey animals are killed by constriction prior to swallowing The natural enemies of adult Western Fox Snakes undoubtedly include the larger birds of prey and predatory mammals, while their eggs and young would be vulnerable to snake-eating snakes, shrews, weasels, and many other small predators. These snakes are relatively sluggish in their movements, but most will attempt to escape into the closest cover when threatened. If cornered they will coil and raise their heads, vibrate their tails, and sometimes strike; younger individuals seem more willing to bite than older ones. The musky anal secretion that this species produces when disturbed or handled has been described as smelling "foxlike," however the common (and scientific) name may not be directly related to this odor but more likely honors Reverend Charles Fox, who collected a specimen used in the original formal species description published in 1853.

**Reproduction and Growth:** Male Western Fox Snakes will engage in ritualized combat similar to that described for the Gray Rat Snake. During these "wrestling matches," each combatant attempts to "top" and "pin" his rival by twining around him and pushing down on his head and body. The winners of these bouts appear to maintain a temporary dominance over the losers and to have better success at mating with nearby females. Mating can take place in late April or May while the snakes are still near the winter dens but also occurs later (June or July) after dispersal to summer feeding areas. A courting male will vigorously pursue his intended mate for some time until she finally accepts him. The male then attempts to align his body with the female's, at which time both snakes may begin jerking their heads and bodies in a forward movement that may continue throughout mating. The pair eventually twine their tails together, bringing the anal openings together and allowing the male to insert a hemipenis into the female's cloaca. The male may grasp the female's neck with his jaws during copulation.

In late June or July the female seeks a nest site in loose soil, in a decaying log or stump, or under a rock, board, or other surface litter. She produces a clutch of from seven to twenty-seven elliptical, flexible-shelled eggs, which average about 4.5 cm (1.7 in) in length. The eggs often stick to each other and may tear if forcibly pulled apart. Incubation requires from thirty-five to seventy-five days, with most hatchlings emerging between mid-August and early September. Natural growth patterns for this species are in need of study. If Western Fox Snakes have growth rates similar to those reported for related North American *Pantherophis* species, they would attain sexual maturity in about four years. Potential longevity is unknown; a captive specimen survived for seventeen years.

**Conservation:** Populations of this snake can persist in areas largely devoted to agriculture, and this species undoubtedly benefits when densely forested tracts are opened up by timber harvest or creation of pastures and croplands. However, agricultural trends that favor intensive "shoulder to shoulder" cultivation at the expense of hedgerows, shrubby fence lines, and fallow fields can lead to declines and local extirpation. Its rodent-eating habits make this a beneficial species to the farmer and gardener.

Western Fox Snakes are frequent highway victims, and many others are needlessly killed by fearful people. Due to its often reddish-colored head and habit of vibrating its tail when frightened, this harmless snake is sometimes mistaken for a rattlesnake or a Copperhead (*Agkistrodon contortrix*), a venomous snake not native to the Great Lakes region.

## Eastern Fox Snake (*Pantherophis gloydi*)

**Description:** This is a robust yellowish or light brown snake with a row of large black or dark brown mid-dorsal blotches alternating with smaller dark blotches on the sides. The head varies in color from light brown to a coppery reddish-brown, and there is usually an indistinct dark band between the eyes, another band extending downward from the eye to the mouth, and another slanting back from the eye to the corner of the mouth; these markings may fade completely in old adults. The belly has irregular rows of dark squarish spots on a yellowish background. The tail is rather short and has a spinelike tip. There are usually twenty-three to twenty-five scale rows at midbody; the upper-body scales are weakly keeled, and the anal plate is divided. Total adult length: 90 to 179 cm (35.4 to 70.5 in).

External sex differences are not obvious. Males have proportionally longer tails than females do; adult females, particularly when gravid in summer, are noticeably thicker bodied than are males, with more abruptly tapering tails (males have a gradual body-to-tail taper). Juvenile Eastern Fox Snakes are paler in background color than adults, with more distinct head markings and gray or brown dorsal blotches edged in black. They range from 26 to 31 cm (10.2 to 12.2 in) in total length at hatching.

**Confusing Species:** Eastern Milk Snakes have smooth scales and single (undivided) anal plates. Racers also have smooth scales and no slanting line from eye to corner of mouth. Gray Rat Snakes, with similar juvenile coloration, have 221 or more ventral scutes (there are 216 or fewer in Eastern Fox Snakes). Differences between Eastern and Western Fox Snakes (which do not overlap in range but are considered subspecies of *Pantherophis vulpinus* by some biologists), along with further comments on classification, are noted under the latter's species account.

**Distribution and Status:** This snake's range is entirely within the Great Lakes basin. It inhabits coastal marshes and other near-shore habitats along Lake Huron from Saginaw Bay (Michigan) and Georgian Bay (Ontario) south to Lake St. Clair and the Detroit River, then east along the northern Lake Erie shore to Long Point Bay (Norfolk County, Ontario) and along the southern Lake Erie shore to Erie County, Ohio. They also occur on Pelee and Kellys islands, as well as on some of the smaller Lake Erie islands. Isolated reports of this snake in the Buffalo, New York, area and at the western end of Lake Ontario (in Ontario) are in need of verification.

The Eastern Fox Snake is now uncommon or rare in many areas where it was once abundant, but it can be locally common where ample habitat remains. This snake is considered threatened in Michigan, endangered in Ontario, and of special concern in Ohio.

**Habitat and Ecology:** This is a snake of the Great Lakes shoreline marshes and vegetated dunes and beaches, although it sometimes wanders into nearby farm fields, pastures, and woodlots. Rocky shorelines and open woodlands are occupied on the Lake Erie islands and around Georgian Bay. This snake will bask or forage on raised dikes, rock riprap, muskrat houses, and road embankments and are mostly terrestrial but occasionally climb into shrubbery or even tall trees. Although not strictly aquatic, they are strong swimmers capable of moving considerable distances over open offshore waters and between islands.

In a typical year Eastern Fox Snakes are active from mid-April until late October but are most often seen abroad from May through July. Whether they are truly inactive during late summer or perhaps become more nocturnal in response to warmer temperatures is unclear. They hibernate during the winter months in abandoned mammal burrows, rock crevices, or other frost-free shelters.

Small mammals, particularly meadow voles (*Microtus*) and deer mice (*Peromyscus*), make up the largest part of this snake's diet. They will also eat bird eggs and nestlings. Smaller prey items and eggs are simply seized and swallowed, but larger prey are killed by constriction. Young Eastern Fox Snakes may possibly eat "cold-blooded" animals such as earthworms and frogs.

Potential predators of Eastern Fox Snakes include egrets, herons, hawks, raccoons, foxes, and mink; the juvenile snakes would be vulnerable to a longer list of predators that could include large fish and frogs, turtles, shrews, weasels, and even rodents. When threatened, this harmless snake will vibrate its tail, which can sound quite "rattlerlike" if it is in contact with dry leaves. Some individuals, especially younger ones, will strike defensively, but older snakes are often reluctant to bite even when handled, though they will spray a musky-smelling (arguably foxlike) anal secretion on the offender.

**Reproduction and Growth:** The mating habits of this snake are similar to those of the Western Fox Snake and other rat snakes (*Pantherophis*). Court-ship and mating have been reported largely in May and June, with males sometimes engaging in "wrestling matches," perhaps to establish domi-nance and access to mates. Females lay their eggs during late June and July, depositing clutches of seven to twenty-nine eggs in rotted stumps or shal-low burrows or under logs, boards, or mats of decaying vegetation. At times several females will lay their eggs in one nest site. The white, leathery-shelled eggs are elongated and range from 2.9 to 5.8 cm (1.2 to 2.3 in) in length. They often adhere together in one or more clumps.

Incubation requires from fifty to sixty-five days, with most hatching occurring in late August or September. The young snakes probably reach maturity in three or four years. An Eastern Fox Snake obtained as an adult lived for over seven years and five months in a zoo.

Eastern Fox snake,
adult (Photo: David A.
Mifsud)

Eastern Fox snake,
head detail

**Conservation:** The Eastern Fox Snake is harmless to humans, and its rodent-eating habits make it an economically useful species in agricultural areas. Unfortunately this snake's reddish head color and tail-buzzing habits can lead uninformed persons to mistake it for a venomous species, and many are killed out of needless fear.

Over most of its limited range, the fate of the Eastern Fox Snake is tied to the fate of the coastal marshlands. Considerable portions of this habitat has been ditched and drained for agriculture and residential and industrial development, and remaining marshland often suffers from pollution and other forms of degradation. Even where the marsh is protected (and on the offshore islands) local snake populations are vulnerable to depletion by the aforementioned persecution, road mortality, and possibly collecting for the commercial pet trade. The Eastern Fox Snake presently has legal protection in Michigan, Ohio, and Ontario.

## Eastern Milk Snake (*Lampropeltis triangulum triangulum*)

**Description:** Eastern Milk Snakes are slender, medium-sized snakes with a dorsal row of brown or reddish brown blotches on a gray or tan (occasionally pinkish) background. The saddlelike blotches are edged in black and alternate with one or two rows of smaller dark blotches along each side. The head is rather small but slightly wider than the neck; there is usually a light marking on the back of the head roughly shaped like a *Y* or *V*. The iris of the eye is often reddish, and a dark band is often present from the eye to the back of the mouth. The belly is white, cream, or pale yellow with an irregular checkerboard pattern of rectangular black spots; much of the belly pattern may be obscured by dark pigment in some older individuals. There are usually twenty-one (nineteen to twenty-three) scale rows at midbody; the scales are smooth, and the anal plate is single. Total adult length: 61 to 132 cm (24 to 52 in).

Males on average are slightly longer than females and have relatively longer tails, but there are no generally reliable external characteristics that separate the sexes. Gravid females in summer will have thicker bodies posteriorly, which quickly taper at the start of the tail (anal plate), while males have no abrupt narrowing where the body meets the tail.

Very young Eastern Milk Snakes are more brightly colored than adults, with black-bordered red or maroon blotches on a pale gray background. At hatching they range in length from 16.8 to 28.0 cm (6.6 to 11 in).

**Confusing Species:** Water snakes have distinctly keeled scales and divided anal plates. Juvenile Racers, Gray Rat Snakes, and Eastern and Western Fox Snakes also have divided anal plates.

**Distribution and Status:** The Eastern Milk Snake ranges from southern Maine and Quebec west to Minnesota and south to the uplands of Tennessee and South Carolina. It occurs throughout much of the Great Lakes region but appears to be absent from the northern and western Lake Superior watershed and is rare and local in Michigan's Upper Peninsula, where it is confirmed only for Mackinac and Marquette counties. Additional subspecies of *Lampropeltis triangulum* extend the species' range west to Montana and Utah, south to Florida and Texas, and into Mexico and Central America to Ecuador.

This snake seems to be locally common throughout much of its Great Lakes range, but it is secretive and difficult to survey. It is considered a species of special concern in Ontario.

**Habitat and Ecology:** This snake is found in a wide variety of habitats, from open woodlands, bogs, swamps, and woods edges to marshes, lakeshores, old fields, pastures, farmyards, and suburban parks and gardens. In some areas they make seasonal migrations between higher, drier winter hibernation sites and moister summer habitats. They often occur in or near farm outbuildings, barns, and sheds and are attracted to piles of rocks, logs, firewood, or building materials—virtually any place that offers shelter to the snakes and their rodent food.

This snake's habit of foraging around barns probably earned it the name "milk snake," since it became associated with an absurd (and today rarely believed) myth that these snakes can steal milk from cows. Some people call this snake the "house snake," which is more reasonable than another vernacular name, "spotted adder," since this is a nonvenomous species.

Eastern Milk Snakes are secretive and remain underground or under cover much of the time. They appear to be largely nocturnal, particularly during the warm summer months. Adults are most often seen on the surface in late spring, while new hatchlings and small juveniles are frequently observed in September and October. (Late summer often brings a flurry of calls to zoos, nature centers, and college biology departments from people wondering if the "little red-spotted snakes" in their yards and garages are dangerous!)

Milk Snakes typically hibernate, often communally, from late October or November until mid-April. Suitable hibernacula include rodent burrows, rock or soil crevices, cavities under rotted stumps, rock-filled road embankments, old wells and root cellars, and house foundations and crawl spaces. (Additional worried telephone calls to the above-mentioned institutions are often generated by Milk Snakes that fall into poorly sealed basements while seeking winter den sites.) Small mammals (mice, voles, young rats, and shrews) make up about 70 percent of the Eastern Milk Snake's food, with snakes, lizards, birds, and reptile and bird eggs rounding out the diet. Very young Milk Snakes may feed largely on smaller snakes, switching to rodents as they grow. Larger prey animals are killed by constriction, while helpless prey (e.g., baby mice) and eggs are simply seized and swallowed.

Eastern Milk Snakes are undoubtedly eaten on occasion by various predatory birds and mammals, but their secretive habits may make them less vulnerable than snake species that spend more time exposed on the surface. Underground hunters such as weasels and shrews would pose a danger to young or dormant Milk Snakes and eggs. Milk Snakes are known to feed on smaller individuals of their own species.

This species prefers escape to confrontation; when closely chased or cornered an Eastern Milk Snake may vibrate its tail, hiss, and strike or coil tightly into a ball and attempt to hide its head under its body. Although most individuals seem to tame down quickly when handled, they often remain nervous and unpredictable and may turn and bite a restraining hand without warning. This habit, along with a reluctance to feed when confined, makes this snake a poor choice for captive study or display.

**Reproduction and Growth:** Mating may take place in early spring, prior to dispersal from winter den areas, or later in May and June; males can locate females by following their scent trails. The courting male will press his chin on the female's back and twine around her body and tail, attempting to bring their cloacas into contact. During copulation the male may grasp the female's neck in his jaws.

Females produce from five to twenty-four eggs in late June or early July. Typical nest sites include rotted stumps or logs; piles of vegetation, manure, or compost; shallow burrows in soil or sand; and cavities under rocks, bark, boards, or other surface litter. The eggs are white, cylindrical or oval in

Eastern Milk Snake, juvenile

Eastern Milk Snake, curled into defensive ball

shape, and range in length from 2.5 to 4.2 cm (1 to 1.7 in). They often adhere to each other, forming one or more clusters. Most eggs hatch in late August or September, after an incubation period of six to nine weeks. The young snakes reportedly reach maturity in their third or fourth year. A zoo specimen captured as an adult lived for more than twenty-one years, but seven to ten years might be a more normal longevity in the wild.

**Conservation:** The Eastern Milk Snake's tendency to remain out of sight and to forage mainly after dark are useful adaptations for living near humans. While intense agricultural or urban development has surely eliminated some local populations, Milk Snakes remain common in many farming and suburban areas. Unfortunately, many people are still needlessly frightened by their startling color pattern and tail-buzzing habit and kill them on sight. However, increasing numbers of farmers and homeowners now recognize the value of having these harmless rodent-eating snakes as neighbors. Milk Snakes are often fatally attracted to the lingering warmth of black-topped roads at night.

## Northern Ring-necked Snake (*Diadophis punctatus edwardsii*)

**Description:** This is a small, dark, shiny-scaled snake with a bright orange or yellow ring around its neck. Coloration on the back and sides is a solid bluish-black, gray, or brownish-gray. The head may be darker than the body and is slightly flattened and wider than the neck. The belly is bright yellow or yellowish-orange, bordered with dark spots that produce a jagged pattern where the ventral scutes meet the dorsal scales. There may be a few small black dots scattered along the midline of the belly. There are usually fifteen scale rows at midbody; the scales are smooth, and the anal plate is divided. Total adult length: 25.4 to 70.6 cm (10 to 27.7 in); very few exceed 50 cm (19.7 in) total length. Mature males have ridges on the scales in the anal area, are slimmer bodied, and have slightly longer tails (as a percentage of total length) than females.

Hatchlings typically range from 9 to 14 cm (3.5 to 5.5 in) in length and are similar in color to their parents, though somewhat darker on the back and paler on the belly.

**Confusing Species:** Very young Brown Snakes and Northern Red-bellied Snakes are also dark colored with a light neck blotch or collar, but the former has at least a hint of dorsal spotting and a pale whitish or beige belly, while the latter usually has a pink or red belly. Both have keeled scales.

**Distribution and Status:** Northern Ring-necked Snakes are found from Nova Scotia west to northeastern Minnesota and south through New England and the Appalachian highlands to northern Georgia and west to southern Illinois. They occur throughout the Great Lakes region excepting the northern Lake Superior watershed (in Ontario); they also appear to be scarce or absent in the former prairie and "prairie peninsula" portions of northern Illinois, Indiana, and Ohio. Several other subspecies of *Diadophis punctatus* extend the species' range south to Florida and west to Mexico and the Pacific Coast of the United States.

Its secretive habits make this a difficult species to survey. In some places Ring-necked Snakes may be locally common but overlooked, while elsewhere they may be presumed to be common (based on old records) when in actuality the local populations have declined or even disappeared. Northern Ring-necked Snakes tend to exist in small localized colonies throughout much of the central and western Great Lakes basin; within these colonies they can be numerous. The species remains notably common on several of the larger islands in northern Lake Michigan (including Washington Island in Wisconsin and Beaver Island, North and South Fox islands, and North and South Manitou islands in Michigan).

**Habitat and Ecology:** The Northern Ring-necked Snake is usually characterized as a woodland inhabitant and indeed is one of the few snake species that regularly occurs in moist, shady woodlands, although flood-prone bottomlands are avoided. They also use more open habitats close to the woods, such as clear-cuts, old fields, grassy (stabilized) dunes and beaches, and trash dumps. They are rarely seen on the surface but instead remain under leaf litter or cover objects such as flat rocks, logs, pieces of bark, or boards or within the tunnels of small mammals, earthworms, or insects. This snake is largely nocturnal, but heavy rains may stimulate daylight activity on the surface.

The annual activity period depends on local climatic conditions, but probably extends from early April to late October in the southern parts of the region and late April or early May to mid- or late September in the north. Ring-necked Snakes hibernate underground, in burrows made by other animals, in deep rock crevices, or in anthills. They often move to higher ground when seeking winter den sites, which are frequently shared with numbers of their own and other snake species.

Northern Ring-necked Snakes feed on a variety of small animals, including smaller snakes, lizards, frogs, salamanders, earthworms, slugs, and insect larvae. However, local populations may specialize in certain types of prey; in the northern Great Lakes region Red-backed Salamanders seem to make up a large portion of this snake's diet, followed in frequency by small snakes and earthworms. Most food items are simply seized and swallowed, but larger prey may be held tightly until they stop moving. This species has a pair of slightly enlarged teeth at the back of the upper jaw, and its saliva may be mildly toxic to the small animals on which it preys. By any measure, however, Northern Ring-necked Snakes are harmless to humans.

The tendency of Northern Ring-necked Snakes to remain underground or under cover reduces their vulnerability to many predators. During their occasional surface forays, they risk being eaten by owls, hawks, foxes, domestic cats, and other surface hunters. Predators willing to enter burrows or dig, such as Eastern Milk Snakes, Racers, shrews, weasels, and skunks, are a more constant threat. A Northern Ring-necked Snake rarely attempts to bite, even when seized by a predator or held in the hand, but instead will usually writhe vigorously and release a foul-smelling musky substance from its cloaca.

**Reproduction and Growth:** Mating may occur in spring, late summer, or fall. Females that mate late in the year can store active sperm in their oviducts over the winter and fertilize their eggs in spring. Females deposit from one to ten (usually three or four) eggs in late June or July. Nests may be in rodent burrows, beneath flat rocks or boards, or within rotted logs or stumps; several females will often share a particularly favored spot, which may be used for several consecutive seasons. The eggs are thin shelled and elongate, sometimes tapered or even slightly curved in shape, and measure from 2.2 to 3.6 cm (0.9 to 1.4 in) in length. Incubation time varies from four to nine weeks, with most hatching occurring between mid-August and early September.

Growth is rapid during a young Ring-necked Snake's first summer and gradually tapers off as it approaches sexual maturity during its third or fourth year. Males tend to mature slightly earlier than females. This seems

Northern Ring-necked
Snake, adult

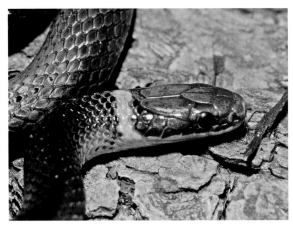

Northern Ring-necked
Snake, head, showing
smooth scales

to be a fairly long-lived snake considering its small size; average life-span
may approach ten years in some populations, with occasional individuals
reaching twenty years or more.

**Conservation:** Northern Ring-necked Snakes require moist woodland and
woodland edge habitats; large-scale clear-cutting or even selective logging
could be detrimental to its survival. The colonial nature of this snake's distribution would make it particularly vulnerable to rapid local extirpation
when its habitats are disturbed. The apparent decline of Ring-necked Snake

populations in many areas (e.g., southern Michigan) may be due largely to habitat loss, but the widespread use of persistent pesticides during the mid-twentieth century may have played a role as well. Ring-necked Snakes are occasionally killed while crossing roads at night.

## Eastern Hog-nosed Snake (*Heterodon platirhinos*)

**Description:** This moderate-sized snake is thick bodied with a short tail and a flattened, upturned snout. Its unique defensive behavior (described below) is also a good identifying characteristic. Coloration is extremely variable; some individuals have a distinct pattern of irregular dark blotches down the back, alternating with dark spots on the sides, on a mottled background of gray, brown, tan, olive, orange, yellow, or even pinkish. Others lack the dorsal blotching and are a plain gray, brown, or olive; occasional ones are melanistic (entirely black). Many specimens are intermediate in pattern, with indistinct, faded blotches, and there appears to be a tendency for the distinct blotches of young individuals to fade or even disappear with age. Elongated dark neck blotches are present in all but the darkest individuals. The head is wide, triangular in shape, and slightly distinct from the neck (unless the neck is flattened during defensive display); there is a ridge of scales over each eye. The rostral (nose) scale is slightly upturned and keeled above. Well-patterned individuals usually have a dark band between the eyes and another extending from each eye to the back of the mouth. The belly can be yellowish, cream, gray, or pinkish, often mottled with darker color; the chin, throat, and subcaudal (undertail) scales are usually lighter than the rest of the underside. There are usually twenty-five (ranging from twenty-three to twenty-seven) scale rows at midbody; the scales are keeled, and the anal plate is divided. Total adult length: 50 to 115.6 cm (20 to 45.5 in).

Males are somewhat smaller and less robust, on average, than females and have relatively longer tails. A male's tail is typically 17 to 22 percent of its total length, while a female's is usually 12 to 17 percent of total length.

Very young Eastern Hog-nosed Snakes have distinct dark dorsal blotches and lateral spots on a light gray or brown, or occasionally pinkish, background; as noted above, this pattern tends to become less distinct with age. The belly of the hatchling is dark gray or black, though the throat and undersurface of the tail are white or yellowish. Total length at hatching ranges from 12.5 to 25.4 cm (5 to 10 in).

**Confusing Species:** This snake is likely to be confused only with the Eastern Massasauga or the Timber Rattlesnake, both of which have buttonlike rattles on the tail tip, elliptical eye pupils, and facial pits (visible as an opening between eye and nostril). In addition, rattlesnakes lack the Hog-nosed Snake's upturned snout and neck-spreading ability.

**Distribution and Status:** The Eastern Hog-nosed snake is found from southern New England south through Florida, west to central Texas, north to southeastern South Dakota, southern Iowa, and eastern Minnesota, and east through southern and eastern Ontario. Its Great Lakes range includes much of Wisconsin (except for the north-central counties), Michigan's Lower Peninsula and Menominee and Dickinson counties in the Upper Peninsula, northern Indiana, northern Ohio (east to Erie County), and southern Ontario (north to the Algonquin Park area). It appears to be absent from the Lake Superior basin and much of the area south of Lake Ontario and eastern Lake Erie. An isolated population has been reported near the Lake Erie shore in northwestern Pennsylvania.

This species can be locally common in suitable habitat, particularly where human activity is minimal, but this has become an uncommon to rare snake in many parts of the region where it was reasonably common only few decades previously. It is considered a species of special concern in Ohio and New York and a threatened species in Ontario.

**Habitat and Ecology:** Eastern Hog-nosed Snakes inhabit many types of terrestrial habitats, from open pine or deciduous woodlands to old fields, meadows, and pastures. Although they are occasionally found along wetland edges, they have a decided preference for habitats with sandy, well-drained soils. These snakes are largely diurnal but tend to be most active in the morning and early evening during the warm summer months. When not foraging or basking in the open, Eastern Hog-nosed Snakes remain underground or (less commonly) beneath logs or other surface debris. They are excellent burrowers; the broad, sloping "forehead" and upturned snout are used to push downward, with a side-to-side motion, into the soil or sand. While capable of making their own burrows, they also use or enlarge burrows made by other animals. The colder months (typically late October to early April) are spent hibernating in a deep burrow or under a rotted stump or similar shelter.

Food items recorded for the Eastern Hog-nosed Snake include toads, frogs, salamanders, small reptiles, reptile eggs, small mammals, birds, and insects; however, toads are by far the most frequent food taken. This snake has a number of adaptations for finding and consuming toads—its digging abilities facilitate the search for burrowing amphibians, and its wide gape, flexible jaws, and recurved teeth aid in holding and swallowing chunky-bodied toads (which often inflate themselves with air when seized). Hog-nosed Snakes have a pair of enlarged teeth at the back of the mouth. It has often been suggested that these teeth are used to puncture the lungs of inflated toads, but this function has been refuted on anatomical grounds. This snake's large adrenal glands secrete hormones that may help to counteract toxic toad skin secretions.

Hog-nosed Snakes have specialized salivary glands (Duvernoy's glands) that produce a substance toxic to some amphibians, but its effects are so mild and slow acting that it would seem to be of little use in subduing struggling prey. One person accidentally bitten on the arm while handling an Eastern Hog-nosed Snake suffered subsequent pain and discoloration near the wound, leading to speculation that this snake's saliva could be toxic to humans. On the other hand, one of us (J.H.) was firmly bitten and chewed on the thumb while handling a large female Hog-nosed Snake (which was undoubtedly responding to the smell of a previously handled toad) and suffered only minor pinprick wounds (and considerable humiliation). Some people might be hypersensitive to this snake's saliva, but its traditional designation as a harmless species appears to be fully justified. This snake rarely bites defensively, even when handled.

Hawks, turkeys, and snake-eating snakes will kill and eat Eastern Hog-nosed Snakes, but reports of natural predation on these slow-moving and conspicuous snakes are surprisingly rare. This snake is well known for its exaggerated defensive display, which probably discourages many would-be

Eastern Hog-nosed
Snake, neck-flattened
defensively

Eastern Hog-nosed
Snake, death feigning

natural predators, but, as noted below, it may be less successful in confrontations with humans. An alarmed Hog-nosed Snake will typically raise its head and neck, slowly flick its oversized tongue in and out, and inhale deeply while flattening its head and neck into a cobralike "hood." The dark neck blotches suddenly become quite conspicuous, perhaps resembling large eyes to a predator. The snake then exhales slowly, producing a series of loud hisses, and may strike at the presumed enemy—though most often with the mouth closed. The tail may be repeatedly coiled and uncoiled, and odorous anal secretions and feces are often smeared over the snake's body.

If the snake continues to be harassed, or is physically attacked, it may then go into convulsions and show signs of extreme distress—writhing violently, dragging its everted cloaca and open mouth in the dirt, and sometimes vomiting its last meal. Eventually its writhing movements slow, and it turns upside down, lying limp with mouth open, covered in dirt and musk and feces, looking (and smelling) thoroughly disgusting and quite dead. If at this point the snake is turned right side up, however, it belies its supposed demise by promptly twisting onto its back again. Once the enemy leaves (or the curious human observer withdraws to a hidden position) the snake eventually raises its head, flicks its tongue, and (if all seems quiet) flips over and goes on its way. It should be noted that there is much individual variation in defensive behavior; some individual snakes will skip all or portions of the "typical" display, while others go right into writhing and death feigning at first threat. Captive Hog-nosed Snakes soon cease this "bluff and death" display and become tame, but a preference for a toad diet makes this species a poor choice for captive display or study.

**Reproduction and Growth:** Most mating probably occurs in April or May but has also been reported in August and September. In June or July the female deposits a clutch of from 4 to 61 eggs in a shallow burrow in sand or soil, or under a log or rock. The thin-shelled eggs are broadly oval, sometimes nearly spherical, and range in length from 2.1 to 3.9 cm (0.8 to 1.5 in), though they expand considerably in size during incubation. Hatching typically occurs in late August or September, after an incubation of about 50 to 65 days. The newly hatched young will hiss, expand their necks, and "play dead," even before they are totally free of their eggshells. Growth is rapid at first, then slows as the young snake approaches sexual maturity in its second or third year. A captive Eastern Hog-nosed Snake lived for eleven years, but average longevity in the wild is unknown.

**Conservation:** Eastern Hog-nosed Snakes are harmless to humans, but their defensive bluffing behavior gives them the appearance of being dangerous. Adding to the potential confusion is the fact that some "spotted phase" Hog-nosed Snakes have a color pattern that is remarkably similar to that of the Eastern Massasauga Rattlesnake. Many local names have been applied to this snake, most of which imply that it is a venomous species (e.g., puff adder, hissing adder, sand adder, spreading viper, blowing viper, blow snake, spreadhead, Michigan cobra, etc.). It is an unfortunately safe assumption that many (perhaps most) confrontations between humans and Hog-nosed Snakes end up being fatal to the snakes. When we add in the numerous snakes killed on roads and by farm and recreational equipment, it is not surprising that their populations are declining throughout much of their Great Lakes range, even where their preferred sandy woodland habitats are still available. Reported local declines in toad populations in parts of the region would, if sustained over time, present an additional challenge to Hog-nosed Snake survival.

# Pit Vipers and Vipers

## FAMILY VIPERIDAE

Snakes in this family of about 328 species have a pair of hollow fangs at the front of the very short upper mouth (maxilla) bones, connected to venom glands on either side of the head. When the snake strikes, the gaping of the mouth causes the fangs to rotate forward (from a normally folded position) to stab into the target animal; powerful muscles then squeeze the venom glands, injecting venom (a greatly modified saliva) into the wound. Most viperids strike their prey and then wait until the animal dies before attempting to swallow it.

The so-called true vipers (subfamily Viperinae) are found in Europe, Asia, and Africa. All North and South American viperids are "pit vipers" (subfamily Crotalinae, also represented in Eurasia), so named because they possess heat-sensitive organs called pits; these pits are visible as an opening on each side of the head, between (and slightly lower than) the eye and nostril. Each pit contains a membrane lined with nerve cells, which are extremely sensitive to infrared radiation (i.e., heat). Using these pits, the snake can detect the heat given off by a nearby endothermic ("warm-blooded") animal that may be a potential predator or prey and determine its exact location.

Species in two genera of American pit vipers (*Sistrurus* and *Crotalus*) are called rattlesnakes, with one representative of each genus recorded in the Great Lakes region. The rattle is a series of loosely connected, hollow, buttonlike segments on the tail tip formed from thick scale material; when the tail is vibrated, a buzzing sound is produced that can warn away possible enemies. A new segment is added each time the snake sheds its skin, replacing older ones that break off the end. (Thus, the number of segments does not indicate the age of the snake, despite a popular belief.) All rattlesnakes are stout-bodied snakes with vertically elliptical eye pupils in daylight. *Sistrurus* (which includes the Massasauga and the Pygmy Rattlesnakes) is considered by some herpetologists to be the more primitive rattlesnake genus, in part because its members have nine large scales on the crown of the head as in most nonvenomous snakes. It was possibly ancestral to *Crotalus* (which includes all other rattlesnakes), in which the head is largely covered by numerous small, irregular scales (fig. 11).

# Eastern Massasauga (*Sistrurus catenatus catenatus*)
## VENOMOUS

**Description:** This is a medium-sized, thick-bodied snake with a segmented rattle on the tail tip, an opening ("pit") between eye and nostril, and elliptical ("catlike") eye pupils. A row of twenty-one to forty large, dark brown, black-edged blotches runs down the back; these are sometimes outlined with thin white or yellowish margins. Two or three additional rows of dark spots alternate along the sides, the lowest of these contacting the ventral (belly) scutes, and there are alternating dark and light bands around the tail. The background color is gray, brown, grayish-brown, or (rarely) yellowish- or reddish-brown. The head is widened toward the back and distinct from the neck. A dark stripe extends back from the eye, bordered below by a white stripe, and there are two dark stripes on the back of the head extending onto the neck. The belly is usually black with gray, yellowish, or white mottling. Occasional individuals are entirely black (melanistic) except for light markings on the chin, throat, and "lip." The subcaudal (undertail) scutes are undivided except for a few near the rattle. There are usually twenty-five (range: nineteen to twenty-seven) scale rows at midbody; the scales are keeled, and the anal plate is single. Total adult length: 47 to 100.3 cm (18.5 to 39.5 in).

Males have relatively longer tails than do females. Tail length is usually equal to or greater than 10 percent of the total length in males but less than 10 percent of total length in females. Newborn Eastern Massasaugas range

Fig. 11. Rattlesnake heads. The Massasauga (left) has nine enlarged scales on top of the head. The Timber Rattlesnake (right) has many small scales on top of the head. (Drawing by Trish Brockman)

in length from 18 to 25.6 cm (7 to 10 in). They are similar to adults but with a lighter background color; the tail is yellowish below, and the rattle is represented by a single "button." The spotted pattern is present even in young Massasaugas that will be melanistic as adults. Fangs and venom glands (and the ability to use them) are present at birth.

**Confusing Species:** All nonvenomous snakes in the region have round (not elliptical) eye pupils in daylight, and do not have a "pit" between eye and nostril or rattles on the tail—though many species will vibrate the tail tip when alarmed. Timber Rattlesnakes have many small scales on the head between the eyes, and the tail is usually entirely black; Massasaugas have nine enlarged head scales and banded tails.

**Distribution and Status:** The Eastern Massasauga ranges from western New York, western Pennsylvania, and southern Ontario west to Wisconsin, eastern Iowa and eastern Missouri. If recognized, western subspecies would extend the species' range from western Missouri and southeastern Nebraska south to the Texas Gulf Coast and west to Arizona, with isolated colonies in east-central Colorado and northern Mexico. Many biologists now consider the Eastern Massasauga a full species, separate from the western massasaugas (Kubatko, Gibbs, and Bloomquist, 2011).

Eastern Massasaugas were once common across much of the lower Great Lakes basin but are now restricted to scattered and often isolated

Eastern Massasauga, adult (Photo: Jon Schechter)

Eastern Massasauga, head detail and rattle

colonies. Only two populations are known to remain in the Lake Ontario drainage of New York. They are locally common in southern Ontario (e.g., on some Georgian Bay islands, the Bruce Peninsula, and a few scattered shoreline sites along Lake Erie and Lake St. Clair) and uncommon and local, though widely distributed, across Michigan's Lower Peninsula; they are not found on the Upper Peninsula mainland but are present on Bois Blanc Island (which is part of Mackinac County in the Upper Peninsula). They occur very locally across northern Ohio and northern Indiana, including the Indiana Dunes area, but are nearly (if not completely) extirpated in the Lake Michigan drainage of Illinois and Wisconsin. At this writing the Eastern Massasauga is considered endangered throughout its Great Lakes range, except in Michigan, where it is protected as a "special concern" species. It is listed as "threatened" by the U.S. Fish and Wildlife Service under the U.S. Endangered Species Act.

**Habitat and Ecology:** Eastern Massasaugas are usually associated with damp lowlands, including river bottom woodlands, conifer and shrub swamps, bogs and fens, marsh borders, sedge meadows, and moist prairie. The preferred habitat is reflected in the name *massasauga*, which means "great river mouth" in the Ojibwa language. Such lowland habitats are occupied from early fall into late spring (typically from late September or October into June). In early summer many Massasaugas move into adjacent well-drained uplands to spend the warmer months foraging in shrubby fields and grasslands, including pastures and hay fields. Farmers often report seeing these snakes (and occasionally baling them up!) while harvesting forage crops in summer.

These snakes usually overwinter individually in crayfish or mammal burrows, often close to, or even partly submerged in, the groundwater, and emerge in April as water levels rise. Although they swim well when necessary, they spend much time in spring basking on whatever high ground is available, such as sedge and grass clumps, muskrat and beaver lodges, or the edges of dikes and other embankments. At this time, and in fall, Massasaugas are most active during daylight hours. Later in the heat of summer their periods of activity shift to the early morning, evening, or after dark. The total area utilized by a Massasauga during a year can be quite small, frequently encompassing less than 1 or 2 hectares (2.5 to 5 acres), though in some areas they may range over 50 hectares (124 acres); the extent of an individual snake's home range is probably dependent on the availability of prey, places to hibernate, or other habitat resources.

Small mammals make up the bulk of this snake's diet, with voles being a favorite prey, followed in frequency by deer mice, jumping mice, shrews, and chipmunks. Nonmammalian prey taken on occasion includes other snakes, frogs, fish, small birds and bird eggs. Young Massasaugas are particularly inclined to eat smaller snakes and may lure prey animals (especially frogs) within range by twitching their yellowish tail tips. Massasaugas may actively forage on occasion but more often ambush prey from concealment. They typically strike and release adult rodents and shrews, then wait for the venom to immobilize the animal before swallowing it; nonthreatening prey (e.g., frogs, baby mice) may be simply seized and swallowed without envenomation.

Large snakes such as Racers are known to eat Massasaugas, and it is likely that some birds (herons, hawks, turkeys) and mammals (raccoons, foxes, coyotes) are able to kill them at times. Deer are said to trample these (and other) snakes, and domestic hogs, well known for their tendency to kill snakes, have been used by people to eliminate rattlesnakes from certain areas. (According to local legend, Belle Isle, now a park in the Detroit River in Southeast Michigan, was cleared of a once abundant rattlesnake fauna in the eighteenth century using this method.) There is little doubt that humans are this snake's most important enemy.

The Massasauga's first line of defense is to avoid being seen, and its earth-toned color pattern offers excellent camouflage. Most will "freeze" when approached and frequently remain undetected by people passing close by. Should a potential enemy come too close or even touch a Massasauga, it may try to flee into thick vegetation or choose to stand its ground—at which time it may vibrate its rattle as a warning (which in this species usually sounds like a high-pitched hiss or an insect-like buzz, with little carrying power). Many Massasaugas seem hesitant to strike unless actually seized or stepped on, but some individuals are more nervous and strike out immediately at any threatening object, at times without rattling in advance.

Accidental bites to humans are rare and sometimes result from efforts to kill or handle the snakes. Human fatalities are known, but the vast majority occurred prior to the early twentieth century and the advent of antivenin treatment and modern supportive medical care. Massasaugas have a potent venom that contains components that destroy muscle tissue, blood vessels, and blood cells, and it also has neurotoxic (nerve-destroying) elements. Fortunately, compared to larger rattlesnake species, Massasaugas deliver only small amounts of venom at a time through relatively short fangs, which often fail to penetrate loose clothing and leather footwear. Curious dogs are far more frequently bitten than people, and most survive the experience with prompt veterinary care. Symptoms of envenomation can include intense pain, swelling, and discoloration (due to ruptured blood vessels) at the bite site, as well as possible systemic reactions (nausea, sweating, fainting, shock). Massasauga bites should always receive immediate professional medical treatment; with such care, serious long-term complications are rare and fatalities rarer still.

**Reproduction and Growth:** Male Eastern Massasaugas will engage in "pushing and shoving" combat to establish dominance and thus access to mates. Mating can happen from spring into fall. A courting male will align his body with that of the female while rubbing his chin on her head and body; he may also twitch or jerk his body and head. At the same time he attempts to loop his tail around the female's tail and thus bring their cloacas into contact, allowing copulation to occur.

The females give birth to litters of five to twenty young in August and early September, usually while they are still in their drier summer habitats. The young are born enclosed in a thin membrane from which they soon emerge. They may remain near their mother for several days before dispersing. Many females reproduce only every other year.

The young snakes reach sexual maturity in their third or fourth year. Captive Massasaugas have lived more than twenty years, and longevity in the wild may potentially be as long.

**Conservation:** Populations of the little "swamp rattler" have declined rapidly over the last few decades as its habitats have been converted to human uses, while incessant persecution has reduced their numbers even in the small pockets of remaining habitat. This snake prefers shrubby or marshy lowlands that are immediately adjacent to open uplands. Thus, conservation efforts that focus on preserving wetlands while ignoring contiguous upland will fail to preserve this species.

This rattlesnake is a potential hazard to humans and their pets, yet it is, in general, a shy and unaggressive animal and offers little danger to reasonably cautious people willing to leave them alone. The gratuitous killing of Massasaugas encountered in their natural habitat is needless and regrettable, although their removal from the vicinity of human dwellings is justified. Ironically, Massasaugas found in residential areas are often simply seeking traditional habitats that have been lost to recent development.

## Timber Rattlesnake (*Crotalus horridus*) VENOMOUS

**Description:** This large, thick-bodied snake has a prominent segmented rattle on the tail tip, an opening ("pit") between eye and nostril, and elliptical eye pupils. Two color phases of this snake, yellow and black, are often recognized in the region, though the background color of the head, back, and sides may be yellow, tan, brown, olive-brown, gray, or black. The tail is almost always black with a yellowish or tan rattle. A dorsal series of irregular black or brown crossbands runs from neck to tail; these are often broken into saddlelike blotches and spots on the forward third of the body. These bands and blotches may have yellow or white borders one scale wide. The banded pattern is less prominent in individuals with a darker background color; melanistic (all-black) specimens are occasionally found. A brownish stripe running down the center of the back, from head to tail, may be apparent in some individuals. The head is broadly triangular and distinct from the neck, with numerous small scales between the eyes. The belly may be yellowish, tan, white, or gray, often with dark gray or black speckles, which become heavier toward the tail. The subcaudal (undertail) scales are undivided except for a few near the rattle. There are usually twenty-three (out of a range of nineteen to twenty-six) scale rows at midbody; the scales are prominently keeled, and the anal plate is single. Total adult length: 90 to 189.2 cm (35.4 to 74.5 in); few specimens exceed 140 cm (55 in).

The sexes are difficult to distinguish based on external characters; males are, on average, longer than females, although gravid females will appear proportionally bulkier and more robust. Males tend to have longer tails relative to body length, but there is considerable overlap in numbers of subcaudal scutes (eighteen to thirty in males, thirteen to twenty-six in females).

At birth Timber Rattlesnakes range in length from 20 to 41 cm (7.9 to 16 in); they are colored much like their parents, except that the banded pattern may be more distinct against a lighter background, and the tail is often banded instead of solid black. The rattle is represented by a single button. Some juveniles have a reddish-brown stripe down the back. Young rattlesnakes can strike and inject venom from birth.

**Confusing Species:** All nonvenomous snakes in the region have round eye pupils and lack facial pits and rattles. The Eastern Massasauga has nine enlarged scales on the crown of the head and a banded tail, while the Timber Rattlesnake has mostly small scales on the head and a black tail.

**Distribution and Status:** The Timber Rattlesnake ranged historically from southern Maine and New England west through southern New York, Pennsylvania, and the Ohio River valley to eastern Minnesota, Iowa, and Nebraska, south to Texas, the Gulf states, and northern Florida, and north along the Atlantic seaboard to Virginia. Within the Great Lakes basin it has been found in New York State (southern Lake Ontario drainage), southern Ontario (confirmed for Pelee Island, the area in and around the Niagara Gorge, and the western end of Lake Ontario near Hamilton), and northern Ohio (several of the Lake Erie islands and the Catawba and Marblehead Peninsulas, Ottawa County). Old records for Kalamazoo and Ottawa counties in Michigan are almost certainly erroneous and in any case unverifiable. Populations of the Timber Rattlesnake are in steep decline nearly rangewide; it is listed as endangered in Indiana and Ohio, threatened in New York, and of special concern in Pennsylvania. This snake has been eliminated from

Ontario (latest likely reports in the late 1950s) and northern Ohio (not confirmed since the late 1950s) and is rare and local in western New York State, with a few recent records for Wyoming, Livingston, and Ontario Counties.

**Habitat and Ecology:** Timber Rattlesnakes are found in and near forested upland habitats, particularly those associated with rock outcrops, ledges, and talus slopes. Most local populations are centered around communal winter den sites, which are usually situated on rocky south-facing hillsides. The den itself is typically in a deep rock fissure, but mammal burrows, root systems, and other underground retreats are also used and often shared with other snake species. Formerly hundreds of rattlesnakes could return to ancestral dens that may have been used continuously for hundreds, perhaps thousands, of years, but persecution and habitat destruction have destroyed most of these large congregations.

The snakes move to their den sites in September and October, though they spend much time basking, at least on warmer, sunnier days. They retreat underground for the winter and emerge again in late April or early May. They may remain near the den area, basking but apparently not actively feeding, for several days or weeks before dispersing (usually by mid-May) into nearby woodlands for the summer. Timber Rattlesnakes are diurnal for much of the year, but hot summer weather may restrict their activities to the evening or night. When conditions are not conducive to foraging or surface basking, they remain under cover, beneath rocks, logs, or other

Timber Rattlesnake,
yellow phase

Timber Rattlesnake,
black phase

debris, or underground in rock crevices or mammal burrows. Although they are usually seen on the ground in fairly dry habitats, these snakes occasionally climb into shrubs or trees and also swim well when the need arises.

Male Timber Rattlesnakes tend to disperse farther from den sites (usually up to 1.6 km [1 mi], but occasionally 3.2 km [2 mi] or more) and to occupy more densely wooded terrain than do females. Gravid females, in particular, seem to prefer more open, sunny locations and often remain closer to their den sites during the summer. Males sometimes engage in "wrestling matches" in which they twine the forward parts of their bodies and attempt to throw and pin their opponents against the ground. The winner is determined when one combatant tires and retreats from the scene. The purpose of these aggressive encounters is unclear, but they probably serve to establish social dominance, perhaps increasing reproductive or feeding opportunities for dominant individuals.

Small to moderate-sized mammals are the preferred food of the Timber Rattlesnake, although birds, eggs, and (rarely) amphibians and other reptiles are also eaten. Common prey animals include shrews, mice, squirrels, chipmunks, and rabbits, but many others are taken opportunistically, including young woodchucks and skunks, weasels, mink, bats, quail, grouse, and songbirds. Timber Rattlesnakes sometimes actively forage for prey but more often conceal themselves in a likely spot (e.g., next to a fallen log or other natural prey corridor) and wait for prey to come to them. They can strike and then relocate prey animals at night by using their heat-sensitive facial pits and vomeronasal organ.

Fully grown Timber Rattlesnakes appear to have few enemies other than humans, but their young are undoubtedly eaten by various thick-feathered and furred predators (e.g., crows, hawks, owls, turkeys, raccoons, and foxes), as well as other snakes (Racers, Milk Snakes, Rat Snakes). It is probable that even the adults are vulnerable when slowed or immobilized by cold temperatures. Deer and hogs are known to kill rattlesnakes, and the latter have been used by people to eliminate snakes from settled areas.

Though individual temperament is variable, this species is generally shy and unaggressive. When approached by a potential enemy, a typical Timber Rattlesnake will either "freeze" and attempt to go unnoticed or move toward the nearest cover, often rattling a warning as it goes. If cornered, it will likely coil and continuously buzz its rattle and perhaps hide its head under its body. However, they do not hesitate to strike if closely harassed or attacked.

This is a large and potentially dangerous snake, with the ability to deliver a potent venom through fangs that are long enough to penetrate clothing and standard footwear. Symptoms of envenomation can include localized pain, swelling, bleeding, and discoloration (from the breakdown of blood vessels and cells), as well as nausea, fainting, paralysis, and respiratory and circulatory difficulties. Perhaps up to a quarter of bites are "dry," with no venom being injected. Human fatalities are very rare, but prompt medical attention, including use of antivenin therapy when appropriate, is indicated for any bite from this species. The best way to avoid being bitten is to use reasonable caution when hiking in known habitat and to maintain a respectful distance from any rattlesnake that is encountered.

**Reproduction and Growth:** Courtship behavior is similar to that described for the Eastern Massasauga. Mating probably can occur at any time during the active season but is observed most often from mid-July through September, when the snakes are concentrating near their den sites. Sperm is stored in the oviducts over the winter and fertilizes the eggs in spring. Female Timber Rattlesnakes may produce young only every third or fourth year in the northern parts of their range. Gravid females seek sunnier habitats where basking can raise body temperature and tend to stay close to the overwintering dens; feeding often ceases completely during pregnancy. Litters of three to nineteen (most often six to nine) young are born between late August and early October. Although there is no demonstrated period of intentional parental care, a mother snake may remain near her young for several days; the newborn snakes are able to follow the scent trails of older snakes and presumably use this ability to locate communal overwintering sites.

Young female Timber Rattlesnakes reach sexual maturity at six to fourteen years of age, depending on individual growth rates; males mature somewhat earlier, at ages four to seven. These are potentially long-lived snakes; a captive lived for more than thirty-six years, and many individuals survive for twenty years or more in the wild.

**Conservation:** Despite the loss of much former habitat to agricultural and urban development, viable populations of Timber Rattlesnakes can (and in a very few places still do) persist even in close proximity to humans by occupying wooded rocky bluffs and ridges that are poorly suited to farming or housing. Incessant killing and exploitation of this snake has led to its decline and extirpation over much of its former range. Not surprisingly, the few remaining areas that support larger numbers of Timber Rattlesnakes are fairly distant from human activity centers. Unfortunately, persistent (and often systematic) persecution and commercial collecting are threats to even the most remote populations.

Until fairly recently, bounties were paid in several states (including Minnesota and Wisconsin) to encourage the extermination of rattlesnakes. Such control efforts were ill advised from a wildlife management standpoint and wasteful of taxpayer dollars. In any case, people have rarely needed a monetary incentive to destroy rattlesnakes. Demands for Timber Rattlesnakes by hobbyists, zoos, venom researchers, and the leather trade have provided reptile collectors with financial incentives to exploit this species; as the snakes are protected or regulated in many of the states where they occur, most recent collecting activity is illegal. The tendency of Timber Rattlesnakes to gather in large numbers at a few winter den sites makes them particularly vulnerable to organized efforts to destroy or exploit them. In addition, this snake has several biological traits (such as slow maturation rates, low reproductive output, low juvenile survival, and slow population replacement rates) that reduce its ability to recover from large-scale losses of adult animals in a population. In this regard its reproductive strategy is perhaps less like that of many snake species and more like that of some turtle species. For this reason, persistent or large-scale killing or collecting of rattlesnakes, even when perpetrated by only small numbers of people, can drastically reduce or eliminate local populations.

Conserving a potentially deadly animal clearly presents a challenge to wildlife managers, biologists, and environmental educators. It can be emphasized that Timber Rattlesnakes prefer to avoid confrontation with humans and can utilize rugged habitats that humans often spurn, at least for wholesale development. Many people find them beautiful, a symbol of wilderness and "untamed nature," though one to be admired from a safe distance. Preserving remaining populations will require a combination of public education, careful land use planning, and the elimination of commercial exploitation and unwarranted persecution.

# Marginal and Questionable Species

A number of amphibian and reptile species have ranges that closely approach the Great Lakes drainage basin or are represented therein only by isolated specimens but are not presently known to have breeding populations within the basin. These species are described briefly below so that biologists and naturalists will recognize the possible significance of new discoveries. Extralimital (out-of-range) specimens of amphibians and reptiles may represent previously overlooked populations, recent natural dispersal, or intentional or accidental introductions by humans.

Eastern Hellbender (Photo: Richard D. Bartlett)

## Eastern Hellbender (*Cryptobranchus alleganiensis*)

This is a very large, blotchy brown, olive, or gray salamander with a broad, laterally flattened head and body, four short stocky legs, and wavy folds of skin along the sides. It is completely aquatic, though adults lack external gills. Maximum total length: 74 cm (29 in). Hellbenders inhabit fast-flowing, rocky-bedded rivers and streams and historically range from southern New York to northern Alabama and Missouri. They occur in the upper Allegheny River and its tributaries (in northern Pennsylvania and southwestern New York); old records for the Great Lakes (Lake Erie) drainage are probably erroneous. It is an uncommon and declining species over much of its range.

Long-tailed Salamander (Photo: Richard D. Bartlett)

## Long-tailed Salamander (*Eurycea longicauda*)

This is a slender, long-tailed, yellow or orange salamander with dark spots scattered over the upper surface, irregular dark bars on the sides of the tail, and thirteen or fourteen costal grooves. Maximum total length: 19.7 cm (7.75 in). Long-tailed Salamanders inhabit cool, shady woodlands near small streams, springs, or seepages and are usually found under flat rocks or logs. They range from southern New York south to the Gulf Coast and west to Missouri and Oklahoma. They may enter the Great Lakes basin in extreme northeastern Ohio, but their presence in the Lake Erie drainage is in need of verification.

Plains Leopard Frog

## Plains Leopard Frog (*Rana blairi*)

This species is similar to the Northern Leopard Frog but stockier and nearly always brown or tan, with a light spot on the tympanum and, usually, yellowish color on the groin. The dorsolateral folds are "broken" over the hind legs, with the posterior portions displaced toward the midback. Maximum body length: 11.1 cm (4.37 in). A prairie species that breeds in marshes, ponds, and small streams, this frog ranges from western Indiana west to eastern Colorado, eastern New Mexico, and central Texas; it approaches the Great Lakes area in northeastern Illinois (southern Cook and Will counties) and northwestern Indiana (south of the Kankakee River). It is considered endangered in Indiana.

Eastern Mud Turtle

## Eastern Mud Turtle (*Kinosternon subrubrum*)

This turtle is similar to the Eastern Musk Turtle but has a relatively larger plastron with two flexible transverse hinges; there is no skin between the plastral scutes. The smooth, oval carapace is brown, olive, or black, and the robust head is usually mottled or streaked with light color. Maximum carapace length: 12.4 cm (4.87 in). It is a semiaquatic turtle of shallow ponds, marshes, and ditches, ranging from Long Island, New York, south to Florida and west to the Mississippi River drainage in southern Illinois, Kentucky, and Indiana. An isolated (and probably extirpated) population occurred south of the Kankakee River in northwestern Indiana, the species' closest approach to the Great Lakes region. Indiana considers this turtle an endangered species.

Yellow Mud Turtle

## Yellow Mud Turtle (*Kinosternon flavescens*)

This turtle is similar to the Eastern Musk Turtle but with a relatively larger plastron with two transverse hinges. It lacks distinct yellow head stripes. The smooth, oval carapace is dark brown to olive-brown with a maximum length of 14.5 cm (5.7 in). The ninth marginal scute on each side (counting from the front of the carapace) is distinctly higher than previous marginals; this is not true in the Eastern Mud Turtle. This turtle feeds in shallow, often temporary, waters and often wanders or burrows on land. It ranges from Nebraska south into northern Mexico. A disjunct population occurs in northwestern Illinois and adjacent Iowa and Missouri. One specimen is known from the Illinois Dunes area (Lake County, Illinois), but there is presently no evidence of a breeding population in the Great Lakes region.

Ornate Box Turtle

## Ornate Box Turtle (*Terrapene ornata*)

This is a small land turtle with a domed carapace and hinged plastron. It is similar to the Eastern Box Turtle but differs in having a slightly flattened, unkeeled carapace that is dark brown or black with narrow, radiating yellow lines on each scute. The large plastron is also conspicuously marked with light lines and streaks. Maximum carapace length: 15.4 cm (6.1 in). This turtle typically inhabits sandy grasslands and open savannas. It approaches the Great Lakes region in relict prairie in northwestern Indiana but apparently does not occur north of the Kankakee River; it is considered endangered in Indiana, where its numbers have greatly declined in recent years, due mostly to land use changes resulting from agricultural development.

False Map Turtle

## False Map Turtle (*Graptemys pseudogeographica*)

This medium-sized turtle is similar to the Northern Map Turtle but has a more distinct, pointed or knobby vertebral keel on the midline of its brown or olive carapace, leading to the vernacular name "sawback." The dark legs, head, and neck have numerous yellow stripes; two upper head stripes usually angle downward to form a bar, crescent, or blotch behind each eye. Maximum carapace length: 27.7 cm (10.9 in); females grow much larger than males. This turtle inhabits larger rivers and adjacent sloughs and is often seen basking but is wary and difficult to approach. It ranges from the Dakotas, eastern Minnesota, and central Wisconsin south to the Gulf Coast. There is a disjunct population in southern Ohio, and scattered extralimital specimens have been found in eastern Wisconsin (Green Bay, Oconto County), northern Indiana (Kankakee River, St. Joseph County), southern Michigan (Grand River, Ingham County), and elsewhere. Hatchling False Map Turtles were once collected and sold in the pet trade, along with greater numbers of the Red-eared Slider; thus, escaped pets may account for many out-of-range sightings.

Northern Prairie Skink (Photo: Kristen Genet)

## Northern Prairie Skink (*Plestiodon septentrionalis*)

This is a smooth-scaled, olive-brown or tan lizard with six or eight dark stripes running down the back and sides. The two dark stripes nearest the midline of the back are very narrow (occasionally broken or missing), and there are one or two broad dark stripes on each side, extending onto the tail. Juveniles have metallic blue-black tails; adult males in the breeding season have reddish-orange coloration on the sides of the head. Maximum total length: 22.4 cm (8.8 in). A burrowing lizard of open, sandy grasslands, savannas, and pine barrens, it is often found along stream banks, riverbanks, or road embankments. This skink ranges from northern Minnesota south to central Kansas, with a disjunct population in southern Manitoba. Recent surveys suggest that this lizard may have extant populations in the Lake Superior drainage basin in northwestern Wisconsin and northeastern Minnesota.

Graham's Crayfish Snake (Photo: Richard D. Bartlett)

## Graham's Crayfish Snake (*Regina grahamii*)

This olive or brown snake is very similar to the Queen Snake, but the yellow stripe on each side is on scale rows 1, 2, and 3, and its yellowish belly is either unmarked or has a single medial dark stripe or series of dots (most evident on the posterior part of the belly). The body scales are keeled, and the anal plate is divided. Maximum total length is 119.4 (47 in), though it rarely exceeds 71 cm (28 in). A largely aquatic snake of marshes, ponds, sloughs, and slow-moving streams and rivers, it ranges from central Illinois and Iowa south through Kansas and Oklahoma to the Texas and Louisiana coast and northward along the Mississippi drainage to southern Missouri. At some point this snake apparently followed the Illinois River system eastward and established a presence in the Chicago area. Local, isolated populations occur in Cook and Will counties (Illinois); at least one specimen is also known from Lake County.

Bullsnake

## Bullsnake (*Pituophis catenifer sayi*)

This is a large, yellow or light brown snake with a strong dorsal pattern of dark squarish blotches and spots, which are often black near the head and tail and brownish at midbody. The snout is rather pointed, the labial scales are marked with black bars, and there is a black band in front of the eyes and another slanting from each eye to the back of the mouth. The body scales are keeled, and the anal plate is single. Maximum total length: 259 cm (102 in). Bullsnakes occur in sandy prairie, grassland, savannas, and pastures and are considered beneficial to agriculture due to their rodent-eating habits. This subspecies ranges from western Illinois, Wisconsin, and southern Minnesota west through the Great Plains from southern Alberta to northern Mexico. Like the Ornate Box Turtle, this snake has an isolated population in the remnant prairie of northeastern Illinois and northwestern Indiana; recent specimens from Lake and Porter counties (Indiana) suggest that the Bullsnake has recently extended its range (or was introduced) north of the Kankakee River and into the Great Lakes basin.

# RESOURCES

## Bibliography and Information Sources

Adler, K. 1968. Turtles from archeological sites in the Great Lakes region. *Michigan Archaeologist* 14 (3–4): 147–63.

Adler, K. 1970. The influence of prehistoric man on the distribution of the box turtle. *Annals of the Carnegie Mus.* 41:263–80.

Altig, R., and R. W. McDiarmid. 2015. *Handbook of Larval Amphibians of the United States and Canada.* Ithaca, N.Y.: Cornell Univ. Press.

Altig, R., R. W. McDiarmid, K .A. Nichols, and P. C. Ustach. 2015. Tadpoles of the United States and Canada: A Tutorial and Key. USGS. http://www.pwrc.usgs.gov/tadpole/

Bartlett, R. D., and P. Bartlett. 2003. *Guide and Reference to the Snakes of Eastern and Central North America (North of Mexico).* Gainesville: Univ. Press of Florida.

Bartlett, R. D., and P. Bartlett. 2006. *Guide and Reference to the Amphibians of Eastern and Central North America (North of Mexico).* Gainesville: Univ. Press of Florida.

Bishop, C. A., and K. E. Pettit, eds. 1992. *Declines in Canadian Amphibian Populations: Designing a National Monitoring Strategy.* Occ. Pap. No. 76. Ottawa: Canadian Wildlife Service.

Bishop, S. C. 1941. The salamanders of New York. New York State Mus. Bull. No. 324. Albany.

Bishop, S. C. 1943. *Handbook of Salamanders.* Ithaca, N.Y.: Cornell Univ. Press.

Bogart, J. P., K. Bi, J. Fu, D. Noble, and J. Niedzwieck. 2007. Unisexual salamanders (genus *Ambystoma*) present a new reproductive mode for eukaryotes. *Genome* 50:119–36.

Boundy, J. 1995. Maximum lengths of North American snakes. *Bulletin of the Chicago Herpet. Soc.* 30 (6): 109–22.

Breckinridge, W.J. 1944. *Reptiles and Amphibians of Minnesota.* Minneapolis: Univ. Minnesota Press.

Breden, F. 1988. Natural history and ecology of Fowler's Toad, *Bufo woodhousei fowleri* (Amphibia, Bufonidae), in the Indiana Dunes National Lakeshore. *Fieldiana (Zoology)* 49:1–1 6.

Brooks, R. J., D. A. Galbraith, E. G. Nancekivell, and C. A. Bishop. 1988. Developing management guidelines for snapping turtles. In Management of amphibians, reptiles, and small mammals in North America, edited by R. C. Szaro, K. E. Severson, and D. R. Patton, 174–79. USDA Forest Service, Gen. Tech. Rep. RM-166.

Brown, W. S. 1993. Biology, status, and management of the Timber Rattlesnake (*Cro-*

*talus horridus*): A guide for conservation. Herpet. Circular No. 22. Soc. Study Amph. and Rept.

Burbrink, F. T. 2001. Systematics of the Eastern Ratsnake complex (*Elaphe obsoleta*). *Herpetol. Monographs* 15:1–53.

Burton, T. M., and G. E. Likens. 1975. Salamander populations and biomass in the Hubbard Brook Experimental Forest, New Hampshire. *Copeia* 1975:541–46.

Bury, R. B. 1979. Review of the ecology and conservation of the Bog Turtle, *Clemmys muhlenbergii*. U.S. Dept. of the Interior, Fish and Wildlife Service. Special Sci. Report-Wildlife No. 219.

Carr, A. F. 1952. *Handbook of Turtles*. Ithaca, N.Y.: Cornell Univ. Press.

Casper, G. S. 1996. *Geographic Distributions of the Amphibians and Reptiles of Wisconsin.* Milwaukee: Milwaukee Public Museum.

Casper, G. S., R. D. Rutherford, and T. G. Anton. 2015. Baseline distribution records for amphibians and reptiles in the Upper Peninsula of Michigan. *Herpetol. Review* 46 (3): 391–406.

Cleland, C. E. 1966. The prehistoric animal ecology and ethnozoology of the upper Great Lakes region. Univ. Michigan, Museum of Anthropology. Anthro. Pap. No. 29.

Collins, J. T. 1991. Viewpoint: A new taxonomic arrangement for some North American amphibians and reptiles. *Herpetol. Review* 22 (2): 42–43.

Collins, J. T. 1993. *Amphibians and Reptiles in Kansas.* 3d ed. Lawrence: Univ. Kansas Mus. Nat. Hist.

Conant, R. 1938. *The Reptiles of Ohio.* Notre Dame, Ind.: Univ. Notre Dame Press. Reprint *Amer. Midl. Nat.* 20 (1): 1–200.

Conant, R. 1951. *The Reptiles of Ohio: Revisionary Addenda.* Notre Dame, Ind.: Univ. Notre Dame Press. Reprint. *Amer. Midl. Nat.* 20 (1): 200–284.

Congdon, J. D., A. E. Dunham, and R. C. van Loben Sels. 1993. Delayed sexual maturity and demographics of Blanding's Turtles (*Emydoidea blandingii*): Implications for conservation and management of long-lived organisms. *Conserv. Biol.* 7 (4): 826–33.

Congdon, J. D., A. E. Dunham, and R. C. van Loben Sels. 1994. Demographics of Common Snapping Turtles: Implications for conservation and management of long-lived organisms. *Amer. Zool.* 34:397–408.

Cook, F. R. 1984. *Introduction to Canadian Amphibians and Reptiles.* Ottawa: National Mus. Nat. Sciences.

Crother, B., ed. 2012. Scientific and standard English names of amphibians and reptiles of North America north of Mexico, with comments regarding confidence in our understanding. *SSAR Herpetological Circular* 39:1–92.

Crother, B., M. White, J. Savage, M. Eckstutt, M. Graham, and D. Gardner. 2011. A reevaluation of the status of the Fox Snakes *Pantherophis gloydi* Conant and *P. vulpinus* Baird and Girard (Lepidosauria). *ISRN Zoology* 2007:1–15.

Curtiss, J. T. 1959. *The Vegetation of Wisconsin.* Madison: Univ. Wisconsin Press.

Daniel, G., and J. Sullivan. 1981. *A Sierra Club Naturalist's Guide: The North Woods of Michigan, Wisconsin, Minnesota, and Southern Ontario.* San Francisco: Sierra Club Books.

De Queiroz, A., R. Lawson, and J. Lemos-Espinal. 2002. Phylogenetic relationships of North American garter snakes (*Thamnophis*) based on four mitochondrial genes: How much DNA sequence is enough? *Molecular Phylogenet. and Evol.* 22 (2): 315–29.

Denny, G. L. 1990a. *Ohio's Amphibians.* Ohio Dept. Nat. Res. Columbus.

Denny, G. L. 1990b. *Ohio's Reptiles.* Ohio Dept. Nat. Res. Columbus.

Dickinson, W. E. 1949. *Lizards and Snakes of Wisconsin.* Pop. Sci. Handbook Ser. No. 2. Milwaukee: Milwaukee Public Mus.

Dodd, C. K., Jr. 2001. *North American Box Turtles: A Natural History.* Norman: Univ. Oklahoma Press.

Dodd, C. K., Jr. 2013. *Frogs of the United States and Canada.* Baltimore: Johns Hopkins Univ. Press.

Duellman, W. E., and L. Trueb. 1986. *Biology of Amphibians.* New York: McGraw-Hill.

Ernst, C. H., and E. M. Ernst. 2003. *Snakes of the United States and Canada.* Washington, D.C.: Smithsonian Books.

Ernst, C. H., and J. E. Lovich. 2009. *Turtles of the United States and Canada.* 2d ed. Baltimore: Johns Hopkins Univ. Press.

Evers, D. C., ed. 1994. *Endangered and Threatened Wildlife of Michigan.* Ann Arbor: Univ. Michigan Press.

Ewert, M. A., D. R. Jackson, and C. E. Nelson. 1994. Patterns of temperature dependent sex determination in turtles. *Exper. Zool.* 270:3–15.

Feder, M. E., and W. W. Burggren. 1992. *Environmental Physiology of the Amphibians.* Chicago: Univ. Chicago Press.

Fisher, C., A. Joynt, and R. J. Brooks. 2007. *Reptiles and Amphibians of Canada.* Edmonton: Lone Pine Publ.

Frost, D., T. Grant, J. Falvovich, R. Bain, A. Haas, R. de Sá, A. Channing, M. Wilkinson, S. Donnellan, C. Raxworthy, J. Campbell, B. Blotto, P. Moler, R. Drewes, R. Nussbaum, J. Lynch, D. Green, and W. Wheeler. 2006. The amphibian tree of life. *Bull. American Mus. Natural History* 297:1–370.

Gibbons, J. W., ed. 1990. *Life History and Ecology of the Slider Turtle.* Washington, D.C.: Smithsonian Inst. Press.

Gibbs, H. L., S. J. Corey, G. Blouin-Demers, K. A. Prior, and P. J. Weatherhead. 2006. Hybridization between mtDNA-defined phylogeographic lineages of Black Ratsnakes (*Pantherophis* sp.). *Molecular Ecology* 15:3755–67.

Green, D. M., L. A. Weir, G. S. Casper, and M. J. Lanoo. 2013. *North American Amphibians: Distribution and Diversity.* Berkeley: Univ. California Press.

Green, N. B., and T. K. Pauley. 1987. *Amphibians and Reptiles in West Virginia.* Pittsburgh: Univ. Pittsburgh Press.

Harding, J. H., and J. A. Holman. 2014. *Michigan Turtles and Lizards: A Field Guide and Pocket Reference.* Publ. E-2234. East Lansing: Michigan State Univ. Coop. Extension Serv.

Harding, J. H., and J. A. Holman. 2015. *Michigan Frogs, Toads, and Salamanders: A Field Guide and Pocket Reference.* Publ. E-2350. East Lansing: Michigan State Univ. Coop. Extension Serv.

Harless, M., and H. Morlock. 1979. *Turtles: Perspectives and Research.* New York: John Wiley and Sons.

Heyer, W. R., M. A. Donnelly, R. W. McDiarmid, L. C. Hayek, and M. S. Foster, eds. 1994. *Measuring and Monitoring Biological Diversity: Standard Methods for Amphibians.* Washington, D.C.: Smithsonian Inst. Press.

Hillis, D. M. 2007. Constraints in naming parts of the tree of life. *Molecular Phylogeny and Evolution* 42:331–38.

Holman, J. A. 1995a. *Ancient Life of the Great Lakes Basin.* Ann Arbor: Univ. Michigan Press.

Holman, J. A. 1995b. *Pleistocene Amphibians and Reptiles in North America.* New York: Oxford Univ. Press.

Holman, J. A. 2012. *The Amphibians and Reptiles of Michigan.* Detroit: Wayne State Univ. Press.

Holman, J. A., and J. H. Harding. 2006. *Michigan Snakes: A Field Guide and Pocket Reference.* Publ. E-2000. East Lansing: Michigan State Univ. Coop. Extension Serv.

Hoverman, J. T., Z. Olson, S. LaGrange, J. Grant, and R. Williams. 2015. A guide to larval amphibian identification in the field and laboratory. Purdue Univ. Coop. Extension Serv., West Lafayette, Ind. FNR-496-W.

Hunter, M. L., J. Albright, and J. Arbuckle, eds. 1992. *The Amphibians and Reptiles of Maine.* Orono: Maine Agricul. Exp. Station. Bull. 838.

Johnson, B. 1989. *Familiar Amphibians and Reptiles of Ontario.* Toronto: Natural Heritage/Natural History.

Johnson, B. K., and J. L. Christiansen. 1976. The food and food habits of Blanchard's Cricket Frog, *Acris crepitans blanchardi,* in Iowa. *J. Herpet.* 10 (2): 63–74.

Karns, D. R. 1986. *Field Herpetology: Methods for the Study of Amphibians and Reptiles in Minnesota.* Occ. Pap. No. 18. Minneapolis: J. F. Bell Mus. Nat. Hist., Univ. Minnesota.

Kaufmann, J. H. 1992. The social behavior of wood turtles, *Clemmys insculpta,* in central Pennsylvania. *Herpetol. Monographs* 6:1–25.

Klemens, M. W. 1993. *Amphibians and Reptiles of Connecticut and Adjacent Regions.* Bull. 112. Hartford: State Geol. and Nat. Hist. Survey of Connecticut.

Klemens, M. W., ed. 2000. *Turtle Conservation.* Washington, D.C.: Smithsonian Inst. Press.

Kraus, F., and G. W. Schuett. 1982. A herpetofaunal survey of the coastal zone of northwest Ohio. Cleveland Mus. Nat. Hist., Kirtlandia 36.

Kubatko, L., H. Gibbs, and E. Bloomquist. 2011. Inferring species-level phylogenies and taxonomic distinctiveness using multilocus data in Sistrurus rattlesnakes. Systematic Biol. 60: 1-17.

Kurta, A. 1995. *Mammals of the Great Lakes Region.* Ann Arbor: Univ. Michigan Press.

Lannoo, M. J., ed. 2005. *Amphibian Declines: The Conservation Status of United States Species.* Berkeley: Univ. California Press.

Lehtinen, R.M., A. F. Steratore, M. M. Eyre, E. S. Cassagnol, M. L. Stern, and H. A. Edgington. 2016. Identification of widespread hybridization between two terrestrial salamanders using morphology, coloration, and molecular markers. Copeia 104 (1): 132-139.

Litzgus, J. D. 2006. Sex differences in longevity in the Spotted Turtle (*Clemmys guttata*). *Copeia* 2006:281–88.

Logier, E. B. S. 1952. *The Frogs, Toads, and Salamanders of Eastern Canada.* Toronto: Clark, Irwin.

Logier, E. B. S. 1958. *The Snakes of Ontario.* Toronto: Univ. Toronto Press.

MacCulloch, R. D. 2002. *The ROM Field Guide to Amphibians and Reptiles of Ontario.* Toronto: Royal Ontario Museum.

Makowsy, R., J. C. Marshall Jr., J. McVay, P. T. Chippindale, and L. J. Rissler. 2010. Phylogenetic analysis and environmental niche modeling of the Plain-bellied Watersnake (*Nerodia erythrogaster*) reveals low levels of genetic and ecological differentiation. *Mol. Phylogenet. Evol.* 55 (2010): 985–95.

Martin, P. S., and R. G. Klein, eds. 1984. *Quaternary Extinctions: A Prehistoric Revolution.* Tucson: Univ. Arizona Press.

McCoy, C. J. 1982. *Amphibians and Reptiles in Pennsylvania: Checklist, Bibliography, and Atlas of Distribution.* Spec. Publ. No. 6. Pittsburgh: Carnegie Mus. Nat. Hist.

Meylan, P. A. 1987. The phylogenetic relationships of soft-shelled turtles (Family Trionychidae). *Bull. Amer. Mus. Nat. Hist.* 186:1–101.

Mifsud, D. A. 2014. Michigan amphibian and reptile best management practices. Herpetological Resource and Management Technical Publ. 2014.

Minton, S. A., Jr. 2001. *Amphibians and Reptiles of Indiana.* 2d ed. Indianapolis: Indiana Academy of Science.

Moll, D., and E. O. Moll. 2004. *The Ecology, Exploitation, and Conservation of River Turtles.* New York: Oxford University Press.

Moriarty, J. J. 1987. *Distribution Maps for Reptiles and Amphibians of Minnesota.* Minneapolis: Minnesota Herpet. Soc.

Moriarty, J. J., and D. G. Jones. 1988. *An Annotated Bibliography of Minnesota Herpetology, 1900–1985.* Minneapolis: J. F. Bell Mus. Nat. Hist., Univ. Minn.

Moriarty Lemmon, E., A. R. Lemmon, J. T. Collins, J. A. Lee-Yaw, and D. C. Cannatella. 2007. Phylogeny-based delimitation of species boundaries and contact zones in the trilling chorus frogs (Pseudacris). *Mol. Phylog. Evol.* 44:1068–82.

Morris, M. A., R. S. Funk, and P. W. Smith. 1983. An annotated bibliography of the Illinois herpetological literature, 1960–1980, and an updated checklist of species of the state. *Illinois Nat. Hist. Survey Bull.* (Champaign) 33, art. 2: 123–37.

Murphy, J. B., K. Adler, and J. T. Collins. 1994. Captive management and conservation of amphibians and reptiles. Soc. Study Amph. Rept.

Oldfield, B., and J. J. Moriarty. 1994. *Amphibians and Reptiles Native to Minnesota.* Minneapolis: Univ. Minnesota Press.

Pauly, G. B., D. M. Hillis, and D. C. Cannatella. 2009. Taxonomic freedom and the role of official lists of species names. *Herpetologica* 65 (2): 115–28.

Parker, H. W., and A. G. C. Grandison. 1977. *Snakes: A Natural History.* Ithaca, N.Y.: Cornell Univ. Press; London: British Mus. Nat. Hist.

Pentecost, E. D., and R. C. Vogt. 1976. *Environmental Status of the Lake Michigan Basin.* Vol. 16: *Amphibians and Reptiles of the Lake Michigan Drainage Basin.* Argonne, Ill.: Argonne Nat. Lab.

Petranka, J. W. 1998. *Salamanders of the United States and Canada.* Washington, D.C.: Smithsonian Inst. Press.

Pfingsten, R. A., and F. L. Downs, eds. 1989. Salamanders of Ohio. *Bull. Ohio Biol. Survey* 7 (2): xx+315 pp.

Pianka, E. R., and L. J. Vitt. 2003. *Lizards: Windows to the Evolution of Diversity.* Berkeley: Univ. California Press.

Pope, C. H. 1947. *Amphibians and Reptiles of the Chicago Area.* Chicago: Chicago Nat. Hist. Mus. Press.

Pough, F. H., R. M. Andrews, M. L. Crump, A. H. Savitsky, K. D. Wells, and M. C. Brandley. 2016. *Herpetology.* 4th ed. Sunderland, Mass.: Sinauer Assoc.

Powell, R., R. Conant, and J. T. Collins. 2016. *A Field Guide to Reptiles and Amphibians of Eastern and Central North America.* 4th ed. New York: Houghton Mifflin Harcourt.

Rossman, D. A., N. B. Ford, and R. A. Seigel. 1996. *The Garter Snakes: Evolution and Ecology.* Norman: Univ. Oklahoma Press.

Row, J., R. Brooks, C. Mackinnan, A. Lawson, B. Crother, M. White, and S. C. Lougheed. 2011. Approximate Bayesian computation reveals the factors that influence genetic diversity and population structure of foxsnakes. *Journ. Evol. Biol.* 24 (2011): 2364–77.

Rowell, J. C. 2012. *The Snakes of Ontario: Natural History, Distribution, and Status.* Winnipeg: Art Bookbindery. Privately printed.

Ruthven, A. G., C. Thompson, and H. T. Gaige. 1928. *The Herpetology of Michigan.* Handbook Ser. No. 3. Ann Arbor: Museums, Univ. Michigan.

Schmidt, K. P. 1938. Herpetological evidence for the postglacial eastward extension of the steppe in North America. *Ecology* 19 (3): 396–407.

Seigel, R. A., and J. T. Collins, eds. 1993. *Snakes: Ecology and Behavior.* New York: McGraw-Hill.

Shaffer, L. L. 1991. *Pennsylvania Amphibians and Reptiles.* Harrisburg: Pa. Fish Comm.

Smith, H. M. 1946. *Handbook of Lizards: Lizards of the United States and Canada.* Ithaca, N.Y.: Cornell Univ. Press.

Smith, H. M., and D. Chiszar. 2006. Dilemma of name recognition: Why and when to use new combinations of scientific names. *Herpetol. Conserv. and Biol.* 1:6–8.

Smith, P. W. 1957. An analysis of post-Wisconsin biogeography of the prairie peninsula region based on distributional phenomena among terrestrial vertebrate populations. *Ecology* 38 (2): 205–18.

Smith, P. W. 1961. The amphibians and reptiles of Illinois. *Illinois Nat. Hist. Survey Bull.* (Urbana) 28, art. 1. 298 pp.

Snider, A. T., and K. Bowler. 1992. Longevity of reptiles and amphibians in North American collections. 2d ed. Herpet. Circular No. 21. Soc. Study Amph. and Rept.

Sprackland, R. 2010. *Guide to Lizards.* Neptune City, N.J.: TFH Publ.

Stearns, F., and N. Kobriger. 1975. *Environmental Status of the Lake Michigan Region.* Vol. 10: *Vegetation of the Lake Michigan Drainage Basin.* Argonne, Ill.: Argonne Nat. Lab.

Stebbins, R. C., and N. W. Cohen. 1995. *A Natural History of Amphibians.* Princeton: Princeton Univ. Press.

Sullivan, B. K., K. B. Malmos, and M. F. Given. 1996. Systematics of the *Bufo woodhousii* complex (Anura: Bufonidae): Advertisement call variation. *Copeia* 1996 (2): 274–80.

Terry, P. J. 2015. Elucidating the conservation status of Michigan's Red-eared Slider (*Trachemys scripta elegans*): A phylogenetic approach. M.S. thesis, Eastern Michigan University.

Thomas, T. M., M. C. Granatosky, J. R. Bourque, K. L. Krysko, P. M. Molar, T. Gamble, E. Suarez, E. Leone, K. M. Enge, and J. Roman. 2014. Taxonomic assessment of the Alligator Snapping Turtles (Chelydridae: *Macrochelys*), with the description of two new species from the southeastern United States. *Zootaxa* 3786 (2): 141–65.

Tyning, T. F. 1990. *Stokes Nature Guides: A Guide to Amphibians and Reptiles.* Boston: Little, Brown.

U.S. Department of Agriculture, Forest Service. 1988. *Management of Amphibians, Reptiles, and Small Mammals in North America: Proceedings of the Symposium.* Gen. Tech. Rep. RM-166. Fort Collins, Colo.: U.S. Forest Service.

Utiger, U., N. Helfenberger, B. Schatti, C. Schmidt, M. Ruf, and V. Ziswiler. 2002. *Molecular systematics and phylogeny of Old and New World ratsnakes, Elaphe* AUCT., and related genera (Reptilia, Squamata, Colubridae). *Russian Journ. of Herpetol.* 9 (2): 105–24.

Vogt, R. C. 1981. *Natural History of Amphibians and Reptiles of Wisconsin.* Milwaukee: Milwaukee Public Mus.

Watermolen, D. J. 1995. *A Key to the Eggs of Wisconsin's Amphibians.* Research Rep. 165. Madison: Wisconsin Dept. Nat. Res.

Watermolen, D. J., and H. Gilbertson. 1996. *Key for the Identification of Wisconsin's Larval Amphibians.* Wisconsin Endangered Resources Rep. 109. Madison: Wisconsin Dept. Nat. Res.

Williams, K. L. 1988. *Systematics and Natural History of the American Milksnake, Lampropeltis triangulum.* 2d ed. Milwaukee: Milwaukee Public Mus.

Wilsmann, L. A., and M. A. Sellers. 1988. *Clonophis kirtlandii* rangewide survey. Final report (unpubl.) to U.S. Fish and Wildlife Service, Region 3. Office of Endangered Species. Twin Cities, Minnesota.

Wright, A. H., and A. A. Wright. 1949. *Handbook of Frogs and Toads of the United States and Canada.* Ithaca, N.Y.: Comstock Publ.

Wright, A. H., and A. A. Wright. 1957. *Handbook of Snakes of the United States and Canada.* 2 vols. Ithaca, N.Y.: Cornell Univ. Press.

Wright, H. E., Jr., ed. 1983. *Late-Quaternary Environments of the United States.* Vol. 2: *The Holocene.* Minneapolis: Univ. Minnesota Press.

Wright, H. E., Jr., and S. C. Porter, eds. 1983. *Late-Quaternary Environments of the United States.* Vol. 1: *The Late Pleistocene.* Minneapolis: Univ. Minnesota Press.

# Herpetological Organizations

*National/International*

Addresses for membership or correspondence for these organizations change frequently but can be obtained by consulting their recent publications or websites or by contacting the information desks in most public and college libraries.

HERPETOLOGIST'S LEAGUE

Publications: *Herpetologica; Herpetological Monographs*

SOCIETY FOR THE STUDY OF AMPHIBIANS AND REPTILES

Publications: *Journal of Herpetology, Herpetological Review, Catalogue of American Amphibians and Reptiles, Contributions to Herpetology, Facsimile Reprints in Herpetology, Herpetological Circulars, Herpetological Conservation*

AMERICAN SOCIETY OF ICHTHYOLOGISTS AND HERPETOLOGISTS
Publication: *Copeia*

*Regional*

There are a number of smaller, regional herpetological societies in the Great Lakes area. Traditionally, these local societies have largely focused on captive husbandry and breeding of amphibians and reptiles, but some groups place considerable emphasis on field studies and surveys and conservation issues. Information on contacting or joining these local groups can often be obtained through zoological parks, nature centers, or libraries. The organization noted below has a larger, more broadly based membership and a particularly noteworthy publication.

CHICAGO HERPETOLOGICAL SOCIETY

Publication: *Bulletin of the Chicago Herpetological Society*
Correspondence: 2430 North Cannon Drive
Chicago, Ill. 60614 U.S.A.

# GLOSSARY

The definitions given here are based on usage in this book and may not include all possible meanings of these words or terms.

*Aberrant:* Deviating from the normal form or coloration of a species.

*Aestivation:* A state of dormancy or inactivity during hot or dry weather. Sometimes spelled *estivation.*

*Algae:* Primitive, mostly aquatic, one-celled or colonial plants that lack true stems, roots, and leaves.

*Allopatric:* Referring to a population of animals that is disjunct and separated geographically from other populations of the same or related species.

*Amnion:* A membrane-enclosed, fluid-filled sac surrounding the embryo in reptiles, birds, and mammals. These three vertebrate groups thus form a larger natural group, the *amniotes.*

*Amplexus:* A reproductive behavior in frogs and toads in which the male grasps the female's body from above with his forelegs. From this position the male can fertilize the female's eggs externally as they are laid.

*Anal plate:* The enlarged scale that precedes and partly covers the vent (anal or cloacal opening) in snakes; depending on the species, it can be single (entire) or divided into two parts.

*Annuli:* The concentric ridges ("growth rings") on the scutes of certain turtles that are formed during periods of growth and separated by indentations indicating periods of little or no growth. In some Great Lakes species, the annuli (singular = *annulus*) may be used to estimate the age, or at least a minimum age, of a specimen.

*Anterior:* Toward the front (head) of an animal.

*Anuran:* A collective term for frogs and toads.

*Aquatic:* Living in water.

*Arboreal:* Living in or climbing trees.

*Arthropod:* A member of the phylum of invertebrate animals with jointed legs; includes the insects, spiders, crustaceans, and other groups.

*Band:* A marking or contrasting strip of color that extends across an animal's body from side to side.

*Bar:* A short, contrasting stripe or band.

*Barbel:* A fleshy, often pointed projection of skin on the chin, throat, or neck of some turtles.

*Blotch:* An irregular large spot or patch of color that contrasts with the background color.

***Calorie:*** A unit used to measure heat energy, especially the energy available in food after digestion.

***Carapace:*** The upper part of a turtle's shell.

***Carnivore:*** An animal that eats other animals.

***Carrion:*** The remains of a dead animal.

***Caruncle:*** A temporary horny, toothlike structure on the snout of a hatchling turtle, which may help the hatchling slice or break the eggshell during hatching.

***Caudal:*** Referring to the tail (e.g., *caudal scutes,* the scales under a snake's tail).

***Centimeter:*** A metric measure of length equal to 0.01 meter or about 0.39 inch. There are 2.54 centimeters per inch. Abbreviated as "cm."

***Chromosomes:*** Structures in each body cell composed of hereditary material (genes). Most sexually reproducing animals have two sets of chromosomes per cell (the diploid, or 2N, number), one derived from the father and the other from the mother.

***Cirri*** *(singular = cirrus):* Downward projections of the upper lip, extending from the nostrils, in some plethodontid salamanders. They serve to extend the nasolabial groove and are especially prominent in mature males of certain species.

***Cloaca:*** An internal chamber in amphibians, reptiles, and birds that receives and discharges both reproductive materials and body waste products. It opens to the outside at the vent, or anus.

***Clutch:*** A complement of eggs in a nest.

***Colony:*** A small, local population of an animal species, usually separated from other populations of the same species.

***Concave:*** Curved inward; bowl-like.

***Convex:*** Curved outward.

***Costal grooves:*** Vertical grooves or creases along the sides of some salamanders that correspond to the positions of ribs; numbers vary between species and are thus useful in identification.

***Cryptic:*** Tending to remain concealed; inconspicuous; camouflaged.

***Dermal:*** Growing on, or originating in, the skin.

***Disjunct:*** A population separated from the main range of a species.

***Diurnal:*** Active in the daytime.

***Dorsal:*** Referring to the upper surface or back.

***Dorsolateral fold*** *(= dorsolateral ridge):* A ridge of glandular skin extending backward from the eye along the lower back in some frogs (especially in the genus *Rana*).

***Ecdysis:*** The shedding of the outer layer of skin.

***Ecotone:*** An edge or transitional area between two habitat types.

***Ectotherm:*** An animal that obtains most of its body heat from the surrounding environment (e.g., amphibians and reptiles).

***Elliptical:*** Oval in shape.

***Endotherm:*** An animal that generates much of its body heat internally (e.g., birds and mammals).

***Extirpated:*** Extinct within a localized area or a portion of a species' range. Use of this term often implies a local extinction caused by human activities.

***Extralimital:*** Occurring outside a species' accepted or previously known range.

***Froglet:*** A recently metamorphosed young frog.

***Gelatinous:*** Jellylike.

***Globular:*** Rounded like a ball; spherical.

***Granular:*** Appearing like small bumps or grains.

**Gravid:** Carrying mature eggs or embryos in the body (i.e., pregnant).

**Habitat:** Where an animal lives. An animal's habitat is largely defined by the vegetation and physical characteristics of the area it inhabits.

**Hectare:** A metric measure of land area equal to 10,000 square meters or about 2.47 acres.

**Hemipenes:** The paired copulatory organs of male lizards and snakes.

**Herbivore:** An animal that feeds largely on plants and plant products.

**Herpetofauna:** The amphibians and reptiles occurring in a defined geographic area.

**Herpetology:** The scientific study of amphibians and reptiles.

**Hibernaculum:** The place where an animal hibernates in winter.

**Hibernation:** An extended period of dormancy or inactivity during the coldest part of the year. Some herpetologists use the word *brumation* for winter dormancy in amphibians and reptiles.

**Hinge:** A flexible connection between sections of a turtle's plastron, usually allowing partial or complete closure of the shell.

**Home range:** The area in which an animal spends most or all of its time.

**Hybrid:** Offspring resulting from the mating of two different species.

**Intergrade:** An animal that is genetically and/or morphologically intermediate between two or more races or subspecies.

**Invertebrate:** An animal that does not have an internal skeleton of true bone or cartilage (insects, spiders, mollusks, worms, etc.).

**Juvenile:** An immature animal, especially one that has grown beyond the newborn or hatchling stage (or, in amphibians, one that has metamorphosed but is not yet sexually mature).

**Keel:** A raised ridge. Examples include the keeled scales of some snakes and the central keel on the carapace of certain turtle species.

**Keratin:** A tough, fibrous protein material that makes up the horny (keratinous) outer covering of reptilian scales and claws, as well as mammalian hair and bird feathers.

**Labial:** Referring to the lips, such as the *labial scales* around the mouths of lizards and snakes.

**Larva** (plural = *larvae*): The immature aquatic (usually gilled) form of an amphibian after hatching and prior to metamorphosis to the adult form. The larvae of frogs and toads are called *tadpoles.*

**Lateral:** Referring to the side or sides of an animal.

**Littoral:** Pertaining to a shoreline of a lake, river, or other water body.

**Medial:** Occurring at the middle or midline.

**Melanistic:** Refers to an animal that is darker in color than normal for its species (sometimes entirely black) due to an abundance of the pigment melanin.

**Mental gland:** A glandular area under the chin of some male salamanders, sometimes visible as a conspicuous bump.

**Metamorphosis:** The physical changes that occur when a larval amphibian (e.g., a tadpole) transforms into the adult form. (Note that most newly transformed amphibians are not yet sexually mature.)

**Meter:** A metric measure of length equal to 100 centimeters, or about 39.37 inches (3.28 feet).

**Mollusk:** A phylum of invertebrate animals that includes the snails, slugs, clams, and squids.

**Morphological:** Referring to the form, structure, or appearance of an animal.

*Mortality:* A measurement of deaths in a population; death rate.

*Mottled:* Covered with irregular spots or streaks of different colors or shades of colors.

*Nasolabial groove:* A groove or slit running from the nostril to the upper lip in metamorphosed plethodontid (lungless) salamanders.

*Neotenic:* Attaining sexual maturity and breeding while retaining larval characteristics (a condition seen in certain salamander species).

*Niche:* An animal's function and role in an ecosystem, often largely defined by what and how it eats.

*Nocturnal:* Active at night.

*Omnivore:* An animal that eats both plants and other animals.

*Organism:* A living thing, such as an animal or plant.

*Oviparous:* Egg-laying.

*Parotoid glands:* The large wartlike glandular lumps located behind the eyes in toads and some salamanders.

*pH:* In chemistry, a measurement of acidity and alkalinity, with a range from 0 to 14. A pH of 7.0 is neutral; above this point is increasingly alkaline, below is increasingly acid.

*Pheromone:* A chemical substance given off by an animal that can influence the behavior or physical condition of another individual of its own species.

*Plankton:* The community of very tiny (usually microscopic) plants and animals that moves or floats through the water column in a pond, lake, or other body of water.

*Plastron* (plural = *plastra*): The bottom part of a turtle's shell.

*Pleistocene:* A geological time period, beginning about 1.8 million years ago and ending 10,000 years ago, during which continental glaciers intermittently advanced and retreated over portions of North America and Eurasia.

*Polyploid:* An individual animal with more than the normal two sets of chromosomes in the nucleus of each body cell (*normal* is one chromosome set from the mother and one from the father—the *diploid* condition).

*Population:* All individuals of a species living in a certain (defined) area at a certain point in time.

*Posterior:* Toward the back (tail end) of an animal.

*Predator:* An animal that kills and eats other animals.

*Prey:* An animal that is hunted or eaten by a predator; also used as verb meaning "to attack, kill, and eat" (another animal).

*Recruitment:* The addition of new individuals to an animal population by means of natural reproduction or immigration.

*Relict population:* A surviving population of animals that is isolated from the main portion of the species' range after all adjacent populations of the same species have disappeared.

*Reticulate:* A netlike pattern of crisscrossing lines or streaks.

*Savanna:* A habitat type intermediate between forest and prairie; a grassland with a few scattered trees or isolated small woodlands.

*Scute:* A large scale (e.g., the scutes on a turtle's shell). Sometimes these scutes are called *plates* or *laminae.*

*Sedimentary rock:* Rocks that formed from the settling or consolidation of sediments such as soil, sand, mud, organic matter, or salts.

*Serrated:* Having pointed projections or indentations along the edge.

*Spermatophore:* A cylindrical or cone-shaped gelatinous mass capped with sperm, discharged from the cloaca of the male of some salamander species during or after courtship.

*Spherical:* Rounded in shape, like a ball or globe.

*Spiracle:* In a tadpole, the funnel-like opening that connects the opercular (gill) chamber to the outside.

*Squamate:* A reptile group that includes lizards and snakes.

*Stripe:* A narrow strip of color that usually occurs in the long dimension of part of an animal's body (e.g., head to tail or hip to knee).

*Tadpole:* The aquatic larval stage of a frog or toad (from Middle English *taddepol,* meaning "toad head"); occasionally called "polliwog" (also from Middle English, *polwygle,* meaning a "wiggling head").

*Terminal:* On the end; the tip.

*Terrestrial:* Living primarily on land.

*Territory:* An area that is defended by an animal against others of its own species (often part of, but not necessarily equivalent to, the animal's home range).

*Tetraploid:* An individual (or species) having four sets of chromosomes in each body cell (4N) or twice the number of chromosomes possessed by its parents (or its ancestral species). See *chromosome.*

*Tetrapod:* A four-footed animal or an animal directly descended from four-footed animals (i.e., amphibians, reptiles, birds, and mammals).

*Tibia:* the portion of the leg between the knee and the ankle; also one of two bones in the lower leg of most tetrapods.

*Toadlet:* A tiny, recently metamorphosed young toad.

*Tortoise:* Any member of the family Testudinidae, a family of turtles adapted for a terrestrial lifestyle. This is North American usage; in the United Kingdom and Australia this word is sometimes used to refer to freshwater turtles.

*Trill:* A type of anuran call in which a series of notes is repeated very rapidly in succession.

*Triploid:* An animal with three sets of chromosomes in each body cell (3N). See *chromosome.*

*Tympanum:* The rounded eardrum visible behind the eye in most anurans and turtles.

*Unisexual:* A population of animals consisting of only one sex. As used here, it refers to a population of salamanders in the genus *Ambystoma* consisting largely, if not entirely, of female individuals.

*Vent:* The external opening of the cloaca; the anal opening.

*Ventral:* Referring to the lower surface, or belly, of an animal.

*Viviparous:* Retaining developing embryos in the female's body until birth; bearing the young "alive." In true viviparity, the embryo usually obtains some direct nourishment from the mother's bloodstream.

*Vomeronasal organ:* a sense-organ opening in the roof of the mouth (in squamates) that is used to detect heavier (nonvolatile) odor molecules; also called "Jacobson's Organ."

# INDEX

This section combines a general index to selected topics discussed in the Introduction with an index to common and scientific names of amphibians and reptiles found throughout the book. Use common names when seeking complete text references to particular species or subspecies. Go to the general category (i.e., "salamanders," "turtles," etc.) and find the species/subspecies in question below. Species accounts and illustrations are in **bold** type (photos of Great Lakes species occur within each account).